IN THE LINE OF DUTY
A Soldier Remembers

IN THE LINE OF DUTY
A Soldier Remembers

Lt Gen (Retd) Harbakhsh Singh VrC
Padma Bhushan, Padma Vibhushan

LANCER PUBLISHERS & DISTRIBUTORS
New Delhi

www.bharat-rakshak.com

First published in India by
Lancer Publishers & Distributors
56 Gautam Nagar, New Delhi-110 049
lancer1@vsnl.com

All rights reserved
© Mrs Sanam Harbakhsh Singh, 2000

Printed at Sona Printers, New Delhi.

ISBN 81 7062 106 2

Dedication

This book is dedicated to the
memory of the brave Indian soldier
who has made endless sacrifices
for the protection of his country

"The first momentum of the armoured attack overran many of our forward defences and it looked as though the Pakistanis would achieve a major break-through. The Corps Commander's unnecessarily alarmist report put Chowdhury in a panic. He rushed from Delhi to Harbakhsh's HQ in Punjab and ordered him to abandon the Amritsar salient and pull back behind the Beas – just one *coup* that Pakistan must have hoped for; but Harbakhsh was admant and refused to comply. He told Chowdhury that he would not accept a verbal order on such a crucial issue. Instead he went to the threatened sector to see things for himself."

A written order from the Army Chief never came. In any case the crisis was overcome when "under Harbakhsh's leadership the outgunned Centurions and Shermans of 2nd Independent Armoured Brigade and the recoilless 106 mm guns of the 4 Mtn Div played havoc with Pakistani Patton tanks in one of the great tactical victories of the war."

Maj Gen DK Palit (Retd) VrC
Former Director Military Operations, on 1965 War

CONTENTS

	Preface	ix
1.	Introduction	1
2.	Parentage	7
3.	Education	19
4.	The Indian Military Academy	28
5.	Second Battalion: The Argyll and Sutherland Highlanders	41
6.	5th Battalion the Sikh Regiment, Aurangabad	51
7.	The Brevet Rank and Regimental Marriages	63
8.	North West Frontier Province – Razmak	74
9.	The Second World War	86
10.	Surrender to the Japanese	104
11.	Prisoner-of-war	108
12.	Destined for Rabal Island & the Death Railway; Passed on to the Japanese Air Force Instead	115
13.	Early Days as Prisoners-of-war at Kluang Camp	123
14.	Our Life as Prisoners-of-war Continues	130
15.	Fighting Illness and Disease with Lady Luck	141
16.	Hospital Facilities for Prisoners-of-war at Singapore	148
17.	The Japanese Soldier	161
18.	The Struggle to Stay Alive	166
19.	The End of the War	171

20. Of Leadership & Luck 177
21. Coming Home 182
22. Jammu and Kashmir 191
23. Commander, Sri Garrison 209
24. Dropped 1 Star – Took Over 1 Sikh 218
25. Gilgit 226
26. 1 Sikh Offensive – Winter of 1948 228
27. General Thimayya Takes Over Srinagar 252
28. Advance of 163 Infantry Battalion to Tithwal 255
29. The Capture of Tithwal 266
30. Recce–in Force by 3 Royal Garhwal Rifles 281
31. Deputy Commandant, IMA 289
32. Inter-Services Scientific Team for J&K Operations 292
33. Brigadier General Staff – Western Command 294
34. Commander 19 Infantry Brigade, Damana 299
35. The Imperial Defence College Course, London 303
36. Project Jyoti 305
37. Commander 4 Corps 308
38. Taking over Command of 33 Corps at Siliguri 314
39. Army Commander Western Command 325
40. The 1965 War with Pakistan 334
41. General Chowdhary, Intelligence Empires and Awards 364
42. Peace Talks & Visit to Lahore 368
43. Retirement 380
44. KCIOs and ICOs 383
45. Postscript 387

Appendices

A - The Victorious Will 391
B - Portraits of Courage 397
C - Reviewing Officer's Address at the IMA 402
D - Genesis of Yahya's Crack-down on Bangladesh 404
E - The Surrender of Dacca – Pakistan's Faulty Deployment of Forces 409
F - Manpower Versus Sophistication 414
G - Some Failings in the Present Day Game of Indian Hockey 423

Index 429

PREFACE

For many years my father resisted writing a book about his days in the Army, despite the fact that after his retirement he was under pressure from several publishers to do so.

He cited, primarily, two reasons for his reluctance. One, that an autobiography tended to exaggerate the role of the individual writing it and second, if he wrote he would write the truth and this would be a bitter pill for some people to swallow. Eventually, it was persuasion on the part of Lt Gen MS Bhullar, PVSM, VSM, Colonel of the Sikh Regiment, that worked. He was able to convince my father that his memoirs would serve as a valuable lesson for young recruits joining the services.

Lt Gen Bhullar was also kind enough to engage a stenographer from the Army for this purpose. However, once my father got going, he decided that it was best to do the job himself, and spent the last ten months of his life rooted to his desk, typing furiously on his doughty typewriter.

While he was able to finish the manuscript shortly before his death on 14th November 1999, he was unable to select, arrange or label his photographs. This unfinished task, as well as the editing of the manuscript, have been done by me and I do hope that had he been alive he would have approved of the final product.

Finally, I should like to say that this book should be read not only by those in the services but also by those with an interest in India's recent past, which continues to shape her present. My father lived through interesting times, and the first hand record he provides of these as well as of human nature in adversity are fascinating.

To sum up, this is a book about a soldier who had the courage of his convictions and was therefore not afraid, at several crucial times, to use his own judgement and face the consequences. He not only set a standard for himself to perform to the best of his ability in the defence of his motherland but also inspired others to do the same – all in the line of duty.

30 June 2000   Harmala Gupta

1

INTRODUCTION

I think it was Bismark who said: 'people like to learn from their own experiences; I like to learn from other peoples' experiences'. So the object of writing this book at the fag-end of my life, is to pass on my experiences to the younger generation of officers, who are now coming up to serve the country. I do not consider that I have had an ideal life, but I can say for certain that I was lucky to have had a wide range of experiences, particularly in the army, which do not come to the lot of most people. The main thing is that at the end of it all I have come out relatively unscathed, mentally and physically.

What I consider the greatest virtue in life is to always tell the truth. From an early age the dictum, 'Never state an untruth' was drilled into me by my religious-minded father.

I remember attending my first court martial in the army as an observer, when I was a 2nd lieutenant, having just joined the British battalion at Rawalpindi. For the first time I saw witnesses take oath with their religious books in hand and swear that they would; 'tell the truth and nothing but the truth'. And yet, while giving evidence, what they stated was anything but the truth! I was appalled, and made up my mind there and then to always stick to the truth throughout my military career, subject, of course, to the limitations of personal knowledge and belief. I have stuck to this resolve throughout my life.

I must admit that I am a great believer in my religion, though I do not have confidence in rituals of any kind, nor in the so-called human gurus that one meets or hears of, so often these days. Neither am I a frequent visitor to gurudwaras, as I have always believed that the gurudwara resides in your heart!

I have been nurtured in the Sikh Regiment and have spent most of my life with Sikh troops. I have adopted as my own the vow that Guru Gobind Singh took and made other Khalsas take, at the time of their baptism. It goes as follows:

> "De Shiva bar muh eh hai; shub karmana te kabhun na taron;
> Naa darun har son jab jaie larun; nishche kar apni jeet karon;
> Ar Sikh hon apne hi man ko; eh lalch hon gun teun uttron;
> Jab abb ki owdh nidhan bane; at his ran mein tab jhuj maron!"

Translated broadly in English it means:

> Oh Lord! Grant me this boon; that I may never falter from doing good;
> That when confronted by the enemy in battle I may have no fear of him;
> And that I may be sure of my victory.
> May my mind be so trained as to dwell upon Thy goodness,
> and when the last moment of my life should come;
> May I die fighting in the thick of battle!"

I call this the vow of the first nationalist leader of our country. When I was Colonel of the Sikh Regiment, I made it obligatory on the part of the newly attested recruits of the Regiment to take this vow, after the attestation parade, around the War Memorial of the Regiment. I also made it binding on all soldiers of the Sikh Regiment to memorise the vow and be ready to repeat it, when asked. In 1966, I had an opportunity to take the salute at the Passing-out Parade of Gentlemen Cadets at the Indian Military Academy, and since it coincided with the 300th Anniversary of Guru Gobind Singh's birth, I repeated this vow to the cadets on parade and enjoined them to make it their own, as I believe that this vow applies to soldiers all over the world.

A Soldier Remembers

I have tried to follow certain principles in my life.

I have always believed in looking at the lighter side of life, whatever the circumstances. I followed this principle during my prisoner-of-war days when I was held captive by the Japanese in Malaya during the Second World War, and because of it, I can claim to have come out of prison quite unaffected. In fact, when the Occupation Forces were being sent to Tokyo, I volunteered to go with them, but the medical authorities refused to accept my offer, for they felt that since I had been a prisoner-of-war, I undoubtedly nursed a grudge against the Japanese. I pleaded with them that this was not so, as, despite their notorious ill-treatment of prisoners-of-war, I held nothing against them. But they would just not believe me. You see, they did not know that I had already learnt the lesson that if you are kind and considerate to your worst enemy, you can eventually win him over!

This had been brought home to me in a dramatic fashion, at the end of the War, when a British War-Crimes Investigation Team arrived at our prisoners-of-war camp. All the Japanese officers in station were lined up in front of us and we were asked to point out those officers who had been cruel to us. Our camp commandant, Lt Col Gurbakhsh Singh, who also happened to be my elder brother, had already warned us of their arrival and had instructed us not to lay blame on any one. So, we remained silent. After the members of the team left, the seniormost Japanese officer, a Major General, drove up to our camp in his official car, with his flag flying and all that, and asked to speak to the commander of the camp. While we were wondering what calamity was to follow, Lt Col Gurbakhsh Singh appeared in his usual torn and scanty attire, wooden clogs on his feet, and to our surprise, the Japanese Station Commander, resplendent in his uniform, bowed down low in front of my brother and with tears flowing down his cheeks, declared, in broken English: "You bigger man than myself". He then clicked his heels, turned around and walked past his car leaving it on the road in front of the camp commandant. After going about fifty yards, while we stood where we were absolutely stunned, he turned to my brother again, and bowing low asked for permission to take his cigarette-box out of the car. My brother nodded his assent, and the Japanese General clicking his heels once again, turned back, took his cigarette-box (a 555) out of the dash board of the car and walked away. The next day, the General sent his junior officer and handed us a complete list of vehicles, arms and stores in their possession, as they were now our prisoners-of-war!

I also believe that to a large extent one controls one's own destiny. The following song meant for small children has always been my favourite:

"Nahne munne bache teri muthi mein kya hai?"
"Muthi mein hai takdir hamari; ham ne isko qabu kia hai!"
("Young child, what is that you hold in your fist?"
"It is my destiny; over which I have control!")

I never tire of repeating these lines at gatherings of young students. What I intend to convey to the youngsters is that they control their destiny to the extent that their good thoughts and actions will turn it in their favour. Every individual, I feel, should elevate his or her conduct to such an extent that even God is constrained to seek his or her permission before doing anything. This is best exemplified in the following Urdu verse:

"Khuda ko kar buland itna, keh har tajveez se pahle,
Khuda bende se yeh puche, bata teri raza kya hai."

It has been my practice, when in a position of command, to always give my subordinates due warning and another chance to mend their ways.

During the war with Pakistan in 1965, when I found Major General Niranjan Prasad in a disoriented state, I decided to give him another chance. With this in view, I sent for the commander of his reserve brigade, Brigadier Pathak, and gave him orders, in the presence of Major General Niranjan Prasad and his Corps Commander, Lt Gen Dhillon, to re-capture the ground lost by the leading brigade of the division, and made Major General Niranjan Prasad responsible to see that the orders were carried out. It was only after the latter failed to supervise the conduct of these orders that I agreed, on his Corps Commander's recommendation, to remove him from command of the division.

A similar case was that of Major General Bir Chopra, an engineer officer, promoted to command an Infantry Division (the 10th Infantry Division) at Akhnoor, in Jammu and Kashmir. He had recommended, and asked for permission from his Corps Commander, Lt Gen Kashmir Katoch, to withdraw his Brigade at Jaurian, which was close to the enemy, during the night of 3rd/4th September. I had to countermand his advice as impracticable, and decided that I would myself arrive at Akhnoor, with the Corps Commander, at 9 am on the morning of the 4th, and would give orders for the withdrawal of the Jaurian Brigade only after studying the situation for myself. Till then the brigade was ordered to stay where it was. I arrived at Akhnoor along with the Corps Commander, and learnt that so far all was well with the Jaurian Brigade. However, it appeared that the personnel of a field regiment, supporting the Jaurian Brigade, had deserted en-mass, leaving behind their guns, vehicles and stacked ammunition. I ordered the Divisional Commander, in the presence of his Corps Commander, to pass orders that afternoon for the withdrawal of the Jaurian Brigade that night, but only after all the guns, vehicles and ammunition left behind by the field regiment had been collected. Unfortunately he failed to do so, and it was on the recommendation of his Corps Commander that I had to order his removal. These were two cases of removal from command of senior officers. There were others of junior rank who were also found deficient in commanding their troops during the war and had to be removed from command, but only after due warning had been given.

If you ponder for a moment you will realise that life is so ephemeral and yet we have such a false sense of our own importance and act as if we are going to be here forever. It reminds me of a lesson I learnt from a story read out to me from the English classics, by my father, when I was quite young and full of myself. The story pertains to two tiny flies sitting on the axle of a racing chariot. One of them, flutters its puny wings and proudly proclaims to the other: "Look, what dust I raise". I have kept this lesson close to my heart, and have tried to always act on it. I also value the following English verse that reminds us to place our own problems in perspective:

"I was in the blues
For I had no shoes;
I went into the street
And saw a man without feet!"

I remember the pithy exchange of words, to which I was privy, between two of Delhi's richest men, Sardar Sobha Singh and Shri

Sohan Lal, at a luncheon party given by the latter at his palatial home at 16, Golf Links. This was one of Shri Sohan Lal's weekly luncheons which he always laid out in great style with a variety of delicious dishes and French champagne, and to which my wife and I were frequent invitees. Sardar Sobha Singh, sitting on a sofa, pointed to the lavishly laden table and remarked to his friend in Punjabi, "Sohan, tain ta apna sara paise isi tarhan zaia keeta hai" ("Sohan, you have squandered all your money in this manner."). To this Shri Sohan Lal replied, "Han thik hai tera kehna, par ki tun apna sara paisa apne naal lai jaega?" ("Yes, you are right, but will you be able to take all your money with you to the next world?") It is worth remembering that at the time of this exchange both men were in their eighties and did not have long to live!

Having been a very keen boy-scout in my younger days at school I have also tried to follow the ten tenets of life laid down for all boy-scouts. They read, in limerick form, as follows:

"Trusty; loyal and helpful;
Brotherly, courteous, kind;
Obedient, smiling, thrifty;
Pure in body and mind."

And last but not least, during my career as a soldier I have tried to live up to the motto of the Indian Military Academy, my alma mater, emblazoned in gold on the steps of Chetwode Hall:

"THE SAFETY, HONOUR AND WELFARE OF YOUR COUNTRY COME FIRST ALWAYS AND EVERY TIME.
THE HONOUR WELFARE AND COMFORT OF THE MEN YOU COMMAND COME NEXT.
YOUR OWN EASE COMFORT AND SAFETY COME LAST, ALWAYS AND EVERY TIME."

2
PARENTAGE

I come from a well-to-do peasant family from the village of Badrukhan, which is located two miles away from Sangrur - the capital of erstwhile Jind State. The village is only a mile and a half away from the famous gurudwara of Mastuana Sahib, which at one time served as the seat of a well-known Sikh Saint, Sant Attar Singh. After his death a new gurudwara, known as Angitha Sahib, was built at the site of his cremation. My father, a very religious man, was a great follower of Sant Attar Singh and he often invited the Sant to stay with us either in the village or in our house near the Military Hospital, of which my father was in-charge. Therefore, I can claim to have been greatly influenced by the Sant's presence in our house who always stressed that it was necessary to tell the truth; whatever be the circumstances.

I remember my eldest sister telling us, having heard it from our elders, that there used to be a Police Chowki in our village during mughul times, and that our ancestors used to serve as Siledars. This meant that they had to raise and lead a body of soldiers on horseback to fight for the mughals. They also had to keep a full complement of swords, lances and shields in readiness. This would explain the presence on the walls of the main bedroom in our village house - known as

Sant Attar Singh.

'Swaat' - of a number of swords, lances and shields. The last were made of animal-hide, with four shining stars of a copper like metal on them.

My father was the first person from his village to become a doctor. He stood first in his class, and was awarded a gold medal, which is still in the family. He, however, carried on the family's martial tradition by participating with the Jind Infantry in the Tirah Campaign of 1897-98. He was then a bachelor. I remember him regaling us with stories of the Kut Almarah fort where he had served as a medical officer during the campaign. He was witness to the unprecedented bravery and spirit of self sacrifice of 22 men of 4 Sikh Batallion in the Saraghi picket when they were assaulted and completely overwhelmed by 10,000 Pathans. On his return he was put in charge of a newly built military hospital and given a house to stay in within the compound. He soon decided that it was time to settle down and married a girl from a well-to-do family of Sherpur village, which was about 10 miles from the village of Badrukhan.

Besides being an intellectual my father was a very kind-hearted man always willing to help the poor and the needy. In those days the plague pestilence used to be a regular visitor to the village in the winter months and the entire population used to shift to temporary jhuggies (hutments) outside the village till such time as the village was cleared of rats. As medicine in those days was quite primitive, the toll on human life was high.

After one such bout of the plague, father came to know of two low caste boys who had lost both their parents and were living a desperate and forlorn existence. He sent for them – they were five and seven years of age at the time – and adopted them. While the elder boy's name was Bawa, the younger one was named Dharam by my father. Bawa was put in charge of my elder brother and I, aged four and two at the time, while Dharam was sent to study at a charitable school in the gurudwara of Mastuana. Dharam often visited us from school and stayed over as a member of the family. He finally became a full fledged 'Giani' and decided to stay in the gurudwara and devote his life to serving the public. Bawa continued to live with the family and looked after the well being of the two of us.

Father: Dr Harnam Singh.

Father was later to adopt one of my eldest brother's schoolmates. He was from a Bania family from the neighbouring township of Sunam, and was studying with my eldest brother in the final class. He used to visit the family at Sangrur quite often. When my father found out that the boy was an orphan, and had no relations to look after him, he adopted him as his fifth son, and he was accepted as such by the family. My father, who was very keen that one of his sons should follow in his foot-steps and become a doctor, encouraged this newly adopted son, whom he named Balwant Singh to study medicine. Balwant Singh was a very clever student and passed from the Medical College with flying colours, obtaining an MBBS degree and specialising as an eye surgeon. He later married and started his practice in Dehradun. Throughout his life, he maintained a filial relationship with our family. And so have his sons, who now have grown-up families of their own.

We were seven brothers and sisters in the family, born at an approximate interval of two years. The eldest was a girl, fourteen years older than I, then came two boys, another two girls and finally my elder brother and I who were two years apart. Being the youngest in the family I was mother's great favourite and she never tired of reminding me that even when I was four years old and attending school I would come back home, throw away my satchel and jump into her lap demanding to be breast fed! Perhaps this is the secret of my good health even at the age of eighty five! I am also credited with drinking a glass of kerosene oil at the age of three. As we did not have electricity in Sangrur a corner of the courtyard was reserved for the collection of petromaxes, oil-lamps and lanterns used to illumine the house. There was always a tin of kerosene oil nearby to refill the lamps and on this occasion it appears the glass used to pour out the kerosene was accidently left full of oil. I must have felt thirsty and taking it to be water, drank it. Fortunately, I was immediately rushed to the Military Hospital where my father gave me a stomach wash and consequently I have lived to tell the tale!

My father took part with the Jind Infantry in the First World War, both on the North Western Frontier of India and in East Africa. During his absence we continued to occupy the house that had been specially built for him as medical officer in charge of the Military Hospital at Sangrur. It was from here that all us seven brothers and sisters went to our respective schools.

The town of Sangrur, had been built over generations by the royal family of Jind and was a well planned little township. For reasons of security it had a moat around it and a rampart that had only four doors. These were named after the towns they faced: Dhuri, Nabha, Patiala and Sunami. Each gate had huge steel doors that were studded with spikes to prevent elephants of the enemy from pushing them open. There was a small gate for the passage of people. The gates were closed punctually at 10 pm and only those who had a pass could enter or leave through them.

As the rulers of Jind State were Sikh, the first floor of each gate had a room where a bhaiji sat and read from the Guru Granth Sahib (the religious book of the Sikhs). Outside each gate was a 'pucca' pond, made of bricks and 'chuna' (as cement was unknown in those days), in which humans swam and from which animals drank. Next to the pond was a Hindu temple which was looked after by a priest, while for the Muslim subjects, who were all Shias, there was a 'Id Gah' just outside the Dhuri gate.

In addition to the pond outside the Nabha gate there was also a cremation ground, enclosed by a high wall, which was meant only for members of the royal family. The cremation ground for the Hindus of the town was outside Sunami gate while the burial ground for the Muslims was outside Nabha gate. Four institutions were located outside Patiala gate: the Ranbir primary and high schools, the veterinary hospital, an orphanage and barracks for the Jind Infantry.

Outside the town there were mango, almond, guava and pomegranate orchards surrounded by a high wall and wooden gates. Through these orchards ran a road on either side of which were beds of roses looked after by the 'droga' (the head mali) appointed for this purpose by the state. Under his charge were also grape-vines planted around brick-arches in one of the orchards.

Within the town, roads crisscrossed from gate to gate. In the middle of the roads ran a channel of fresh water culminating in a fountain. The shops on either side of the roads were built with arches in the Indian architectural style. They had embedded in their walls hoops of steel intended as holders for earthen 'diyas' during the festival of Diwali. A practice that unfortunately was abandoned before my time, but which must have made a very pretty sight indeed.

At one end of the town was a 'Ghanta Ghar' (a clock tower), a museum and an ornamented Darbar Hall that had a special gallery around it meant for ladies in 'purdah'. This was where the Maharaja held his 'darbars' when in town. Banasar garden with a 'bara dari' (twelve doors) made of white marble set next to an artificial lake also graced this complex. The garden itself had well tended lawns and was full of roses and other seasonal flowers.

As already mentioned we lived within the compound of the Military Hospital. Our house had what was known as a 'bari' (a vegetable garden) behind it - a couple of acres of fertile land, enclosed by a fence of dried-thorny-bushes. There we grew vegetables for our daily use. Beyond the 'bari', across some local agriculture fields, was 'Dussehra Bagh', which was a patch of jungle, with a 'dera' (a few built-up houses) where a local Saint (Sant) lived with some of his followers and ran an open kitchen for the poor. In and around the jungle grew a great deal of hashish that was used by the residents of the 'dera' to prepare 'bhang'. In fact, for most of the time they were in a state of intoxication. For food, the resident followers of the 'Sant' took turns to visit households in the neighbourhood where they begged for 'chapaties'. They always announced their arrival by shouting aloud the name of God and we, the kids of the house, used to feel honoured to be able to place a few ready-made 'chapaties' into the 'jholas' of these so-called beggars. There was one particular beggar amongst them, whose voice we could recognise from a distance as he used to ring out the name of

God loud and clear while leaving the 'dera'. He had a white flowing beard and a serene face with half closed eyes (being completely intoxicated on 'bhang') and to us children his appearance came closest to what we imagined God must look like and so we called him 'Rabh' (God) and competed with one another to offer him alms.

Dussehra Bagh, being a jungle of tall trees, was famous for its 'thandi kuee' (a well), situated right in the middle of the jungle. My brothers and I used to walk across to this well on hot summer days for a cool bath. There were a couple of 'chabachas' around the well, made of mortar (chuna). These 'chabachas' used to be filled with cold water from the well and on a hot day we used to happily wallow in them. I remember that the 'jungle' of Dussehra Bagh was surrounded by wild thorny bushes of castor-oil. If you touched any one of them by mistake, you experienced a very nasty smell indeed!

As the youngest two, my brother and I were the ones who usually accompanied our mother, during harvest time, to the village of Badrukhan, which was not very far from Sangrur.

The village of Badrukhan, I recall, was divided into various 'bases' (divisions), which were named after the main gate of entry. Our house was in 'Bara-Bas', on its first street. In our street, there were only two double-storeyed 'pucca' houses - one belonged to us and the other to a Bania family. The portion between these two 'pucca' houses also belonged to us, where cows, buffaloes, bullocks, a camel and a horse were tied and fed. We were very friendly with the Bania family and used to walk over the roof of the cattle yard to their house. This family had three boys who were being brought up by their maternal aunt 'Masi' as their parents, we were told, had died when the boys were quite young. They were named Jhandu, Daulat and Chiranji. Jhandu was the eldest, and by virtue of being so, did not go to school but instead helped his 'Masi' look after his two younger brothers. He did however learn some 'Lande', which was the script used in villages for taking down accounts in a 'bahi' (a local accounts register). Jhandu also ran a provisions store at the corner of the street. To further augment their finances Jhandu kept a 'khadi' at home and wove colourful 'darees' and 'khes' (rough coverings used under bedding and as sheets) which he would sell. The younger two brothers were encouraged to go to school and while Daulat studied upto Matric and became a teacher, Charanji, who was the same age as my elder brother, studied homeopathy after middle school and used to practice in the village.

Although practically illiterate, mother used to look after all aspects of our land in the village. In this she was helped by Jhandu who became her trusted 'Muneem'. She was also a sturdy and athletic woman with great presence of mind. I remember an incident that illustrated this. My brother and I along with a nephew (our elder sister's son), all little kids at the time, were travelling with her in our 'thokar', the forepart of a 'rath' (a ceremonial carriage), which was being pulled by a pair of young, and beautifully adorned, bullocks. We were on our way to the town of Sangrur and Jhandu was handling the reins. We were going round the village and were near the grazing-ground of the bullocks. It was normal for the bullocks, when yoked to a 'thokar', which was very light, to travel at a canter. Suddenly, they broke into a gallop and made straight for the grazing-ground. Jhandu tried his best to rein them in, but lost control. Mother, realising the gravity of the situation, and no doubt, concerned for our safety, jumped down from the vehicle and running faster than the bullocks, ran to the front, and holding on to their nose-strings with both her hands brought them to a halt. From then on, she took the reins from Jhandu and controlled the bullocks herself till we reached home. Needless to say, she was able to do this as she was very athletic and fit.

She kept fit, she used to say, by grinding her own grain on the 'chakki' (stone-mill) and churning milk every morning, although she had all the help she could wish for. While living in the village, I remember listening to the whine of the 'chakki' and the melodious rhythm of the churning of milk in our house which was so conducive to sleep! The grinding of grain and the churning of milk were common tasks in almost all house-holds in the village, as there were no grinding mills in those days, which are so common now.

Being a well-to-do family, attached to our house was a cattle-yard that housed our bullocks, buffaloes, cows and camels. As a result, there was always a plentiful supply of milk and butter for us children in the house. 'Sarson ka sag', with loads of butter in it, was the most popular fare during the winter months as was 'Mathon ki dal', with 'chibbards' (a wild-growing miniature gourd) in it. We also munched on a variety of fresh vegetables - carrots, radishes and turnips, straight from the field - when ever we could.

I loved my years in the village as a child. They were such happy and carefree times. While I had my elder brother, who was two years older than I, to play with, there was Bawa always there to chaperone and look after us.

I still vividly remember the day when we were sitting with Bawa and he was supervising our play just outside the main gates of the village. The local cowherds ran in with their cattle raising a cloud of dust and shouting "The Sigri Gurs have come". In an instant, Bawa ran up to us, caught us by our sleeves and rushed us home. Later he sat us down and explained that these 'Sigri Gurs' kidnapped small children and took 'akhni' out of their heads by shaving their hair, making a big gash in their heads and hanging them upside down. He recited this story with such seriousness that even today when I think of it it makes my flesh crawl, though I now know that the 'Sigri Gurs' were just gypsies who had nothing more on their mind than the desire to sell implements such as scissors, knives, etc., to village households.

My mother's brother, Sardar Gajjan Singh, who often visited, also had his repertoire of horror stories to tell us. Each time he came he would bring with him news about the latest gruesome dacoities and murders, which were so common in the villages those days. The targets of most dacoities were usually the homes of rich 'sahukars'. One also heard of wayside murders and robberies. The Jind Infantry was usually asked by the State to hunt down these desperate men. My elder brother who joined the Jind Infantry as a Second Lieutenant shared with us his adventures as they pursued these desperadoes through the sand dunes between Sangrur and our village. Midway there used to be a well called 'adhi kuan' and this was the scene of many an encounter. We were also told to beware of beggars who came to the door asking for alms as they may be murderers in the guise of sadhus!

This was also the time of superstition and people believed in the power of various 'tunas' and 'mantras'. We would often come across a mesh of threads lying on the road with a dash of 'sindhoor' in the middle, intended to bring bad luck, a 'graha', onto some family. Although we did not believe in the genuineness of such occult practices we preferred to leave them alone. Our uncle, Gajjan Singh, however, was a great believer and I can recall him telling us in all seriousness about a 'handi' of burning coal which he professed he had seen travelling along the ground at great speed, driven by an unseen power. This was usually intended for an enemy and was guaranteed to decimate him on arrival.

Outside the village of Badrukhan were 'marhees', small mud structures white washed from the outside. These were considered the abode of the spirits and women usually left offerings of food outside to appease the spirits within so as to ward off epidemics of small-pox, dysentery and cholera. People also believed in ghosts and fairies that dwelt in 'peepul' trees and in dead bodies. As a child I remember passing under a 'peepul' tree at great speed, especially if it was dark. The greatest feat of bravery that could be performed by youngsters in the village was to visit the site of a burning body, known as 'chitha', and to drive a wooden peg into the ground next to it as a mark of having been there. It is said that one youngster while doing this almost died of fright for he accidently drove the peg through his shirt and thus while fleeing thought that the dead person's ghost had pinned him down!

We spent most of the time in the village while father was away at war. When we heard that he was returning, we came back to the house, next to the Military Hospital, where my elder brothers and sisters were already residing and going to their respective schools in Sangrur.

I remember, but only just, as I must have been 5 years old at the time, the return of my father's battalion from the War at the end of 1919. The battalion marched from the railway station, in a column, with a pipe-band leading the way and my father marched with them. I also remember my father's baggage arriving at the house. I particularly recall the two leather boxes, that unfastened at the top and out of which two copper-boxes emerged. The boxes contained the medals presented to my father by the King Emperor; at least that is what I believed! I still have these small boxes with me. They have an ornamental lid embossed with a likeness of the Queen's (Queen Victoria, I presume) head on them.

My father also brought back a tale or two from this campaign. Apparently the Jind Infantry had came across an animal which they had never seen before. It was described as unique, with armoured plates around it, so that you could kill it only if you fired between the plates, or at the head, from the side. The battalion managed to kill one and later had its head mounted on a wooden shield, and hung it up in their Quarter-Guard. The animal was a rhinoceros! There was quite a story that did the rounds in the battalion about how it was eventually killed, after firing hundreds of rifle shots at it!

I must mention here that at the time there was a great deal of segregation between high and low castes in the village. For example, the sweepers ('chamars' as they were called) who skinned dead animals and made shoes; the weaving castes, mostly Muslim; the carpenters; and iron smiths all lived in separate sections in the village. Of course, all this was an outcome of lack of education and prejudice.

Our household, the only educated one in the village, practiced no segregation and we were not at all conscious of untouchability. We were taught not to distinguish between caste and creed or between religion and class. My father's compounder, who prepared all his medicines and mixtures, was a Muslim by the name of Ibrahim who lived in a quarter especially built for him and his family in the compound of the Military Hospital. We used to live next door and as youngsters would go in and out of his house and were on familiar terms with all the members of his family. He had a young daughter who went to school with my sisters. Fortunately my father's liberal views extended to his daughters for he not only educated them but insisted that one of them become a doctor, which she did.

Our house was open to all. As a result whenever any one of us returned to the village we were visited by so called 'menials'. I remember, Gujjar, a shoe-maker, who always came to the house whenever any of us came back, and brought with him a 'do khalli jutie' (double crome Indian shoe) which he could bend all the way back as it was so delicate and thin. It cost only Rs 2/- and we brothers invariably bought a pair from him. My brothers always insisted that he sit in a chair and we had no hesitation in sharing our meals with him.

My mother, too, had her circle of friends in the village who would come to see her whenever she visited the village. I particularly remember Narain Singh and his wife, both 'shimbas' (cloth sewers), and again of low caste, who were always welcome in our house. Narain

Singh was so dedicated and selfless that he would put his shoulder to any task that my mother assigned him. Consequently we used to call him mother's ADC. His wife used to cook our meals. This was always a source of puzzlement to our other visitors, mostly Jats (land-owners), and some of them close relatives, who could not understand our non-observance of caste distinctions.

Our house also served as a refuge for the homeless. One day we were visited by a young Brahmin boy by the name of Bharmeen who was close to physical collapse. He claimed to be the sole survivor of a family that had perished in the last plague epidemic that had hit the village. He was hungry and unwashed and said he had no close relatives to live with. My mother immediately took him in as her personal retainer and thereafter he lived with us like a member of the family. He had a very loud voice, and was always talking. I remember my mother's nickname for him, 'bhaonka' - one who barks! He proved to be a very loyal member of the family, and became a handyman.

There was another admirable type of relationship that existed between individuals of the time that bears mention. It certainly affected my life.

When I was a child I did not know that my father and General Gurnam Singh were not real brothers. Gen Gurnam Singh was a big landlord from a village in Jind State, older than my father. Each family used to treat the other's home like their own. Besides, not only did my father and Gen Gurnam Singh bear an uncanny resemblance to each other, but we used to call him and his wife 'Taya Jee' and 'Tayee Jee' respectively. While my father had seven progeny, General Gurnam Singh had only one daughter who was approximately the same age as my eldest sister and became her playmate. At one stage, I believe,

'Pagh Bat' brothers: Dr Harnam Singh and Gen Gurnam Singh.

Gen Gurnam Singh and his wife, had expressed a desire to adopt one of us four brothers, but my mother, I was told, refused to part with any of us. Gen Gurnam Singh's daughter was later to marry the Maharaja of Patiala, Bhupindra Singh, as his first wife; and it was her son, Yadavindra Singh who became the Maharaja after the death of Maharaja Bhupindra Singh, in 1937.

It was only much later that I realised that Gen Gurnam Singh and my father were not real brothers, but, what they used to call 'Pagh-Bat' brothers in those days. One seldom hears this term, which denoted a special and close friendship, being used any more today. In the case of my father and Gen Gurnam Singh their friendship lasted a lifetime. In fact the last year of Gen Gurnam Singh's life was spent with my father at Dehradun where the latter had settled. After his death, it seemed that my father no longer wished to live and passed away within a year.

It is a matter of pride to me that, in early 1966, when I was General Officer Commanding, Western Command, at Simla, knowing about Gen Gurnam Singh's last will, which had been deposited with the erstwhile Jind State administration, I was able to locate it from the office of the then Deputy Commissioner (Mr Tejinder Singh, who recently retired as Lt Governor of Delhi). According to the will, which was read in the presence of his grandson, Yadavendra Singh, the then Maharaja of Patiala, Gen Gurnam Singh wished to start a public school on his property, on the Circular Road, in Sangrur, the erstwhile capital of Jind State. This has since become a reality.

3

EDUCATION

The Early Years - Schooling in Sangrur

In Sangrur, when my elder brother became five years old, he was put into the primary school, and I started accompanying him. I was about three years old at the time, and sat with him in the same class. At school, we were taught Urdu and arithmetic. With regard to the latter, the emphasis was on remembering tables, up to 20, by heart! In fact, the tables used to be repeated, by rote, every morning in the arithmetic class - with the result that even today I can remember them, when required, and I do not have to depend on a ready reckoner!

After attending five classes in the primary school, we were admitted into High School where Persian and English were taught. Geography and the Sciences, Physics, a bit of Chemistry and Hygiene, were introduced in the ninth and tenth classes. The stress in Hygiene was on learning the names of all the bones in the body - for which purpose a human-skeleton was hung up in the class-room - of which we were all terrified.

While in school, I joined the Boy Scouts movement and as already mentioned in the introduction, have since then striven to abide by their Ten Commandments in my dealings with others.

A Family Photograph
L to R Seated: Dalip Kaur, Mother, Father, Raj Kaur and Ranjit Kaur.
L to R Standing: Gurbakhsh Singh, Ranjit Singh, Dalip Singh and the Author.

Jind State had two Infantry battalions (the First and the Fourth) and two squadrons of Cavalry - all armed and supervised by the British, the colonial power then. On our way to school we used to pass through the Parade Ground and used to watch with interest the various activities being carried out. These included exercises in riding, military drills, field-works, etc. I particularly remember the annual graduation ceremony of the cavalry squadron where they had to display their expertise in the use of the lance and the sword. These were the weapons still used by the cavalry of the time. The cavalry squadrons would spend much time in preparing the riding arena, which was round, bedded with straw and enclosed by a dry and thorny fence. The entrance too used to be closed with a thorny bush. The cavalry-men on horses would enter this arena, one equipped with a sword (represented by a 'gatka') and the other with a 'malathi' (representing the lance) with both ends blunted by leather-balls. This was not the medieval period, but 1921; unbelievable, as it may seem!

The stem of the 'gatka' and the leather-balls at both ends of the 'malathi' would first be wetted with water and then immersed into powdery lime, so as to leave their mark on the jacket of the opponent, when a thrust or a cut was made by the two contestants. For their safety, each contestant wore a leather jacket and a leather helmet, with a stiff-wire visor. Both contestants were given the freedom of attacking each other with their respective 'weapons', and points were recorded for each 'jab' of the lance and 'cut' of the sword. Each 'Swar' (cavalry-man) was given the chance of fighting with the weapon of his choice, and points scored by each were recorded in a register. This provided the yardstick to measure each Swar's individual progress.

During this time, one of my older brothers, Gurbakhsh Singh, joined the First Infantry Battalion as a Second Lieutenant and so these military parades began to hold an added interest for us both, and perhaps inspired us to join the Army, despite the fact that my father, being a doctor, was very keen that we should all follow in his footsteps and become doctors!

Government College, Lahore

After my matriculation from Ranbir High School in Sangrur, I was keen to join Government College, Lahore, which was considered very prestigious. I was told the two things that mainly counted for admission to the College were a high academic grade, or one's capability in sports.

I had passed my Matric in the Second Division, which was not considered a high enough grade, but I had the advantage of being the captain of my school's hockey team and besides I was good at all sports. We, the new aspirants for admission, were interviewed by a College Board presided over by the Principal of the College, Mr HLO Garret. I was accepted for admission by the Board, subject to my being good at hockey. So a trial game of hockey was held in the evening at the College hockey ground, known as the 'Oval', set in very picturesque surroundings in front of the College building, which was impressive in the Gothic style. We just loved it and I thank God that I passed my hockey test and got admission.

We, the First Year students, were accommodated as boarders, four to a room, in the hostel, known as the Quadrangle. We were asked to decide amongst ourselves who our room mates would be. Besides myself,

Government College, Lahore.

Author as fourth year student at Government College, Lahore.

Dhian Chand - the hockey wizard.

our foursome comprised Bhagwan Singh Rosha (who was my classmate from Sangrur, the son of a police official in the employment of the State), Gulam Bheek (son of a Nawab from Karnal) and Rizvi. Gulam Bheek and I (as directed by my father) joined the Pre-medical course and took up physics, chemistry and biology (botony and zoology). We both sat on the same bench, doing our 'practicals' and developed a special liking for each other. Infact, the four of us got along famously and soon developed nicknames for each other based on each other's peculiarities as well as played well meant tricks on one another. For example, Gulam Bheek was called 'Tooty', for he always smoked his cigarette through a special, silver-tipped, cigarette-holder. He was also a habitual drinker of Scotch whisky; and kept a bottle of Scotch under his pillow, even as a fresher.

Bhagwan was a very sound sleeper, and always the last one to get up every morning; and even then we had to wake him! During the winter of 1929, on a Sunday, the three of us decided to pick up his bed as he lay asleep and dump it in the swimming pool, which was next door to the Quadrangle. Bhagwan was sound asleep in his bed, wrapped in a quilt on a thick mattress, when we pushed it to the middle of the pool, and waited for his startled reaction in the corridor nearby. It was only when the mattress was fully soaked and cold water touched his body, through the quilt, that he woke up with a start and realised what had happened. Besides providing us with a bit of fun we had hoped that by playing this trick on Bhagwan we would manage to get him up earlier. But this was not to be. Till the last day of college he continued to be a late sleeper.

Gulam Bheek and I parted company after our Pre-Medical Examination (Intermediate, as it used to be called), because he joined Medical College, while I got so involved in hockey (having won my College Colours in my Second Year), that I was easily persuaded by my hockey-friends to stay on in the College and enrol for a Bachelor of Arts degree. This I did, without telling my father; so irresponsible is one at that age! The real attraction for me in staying on in Government College was to sit for the military examination to get into the Army in a commissioned rank, as many of my friends had already done. Being in Government College was considered a plus point for the interview. The subjects I had been recommended for my BA (History, Economics and Political Science) were known as the 'Royal Road', as one never failed in them!

Despite being apart, Gulam Bheek and I kept in touch with one another. In fact, the relationship became closer when, in the second year, he got engaged to the daughter of a Major in the Jind State Forces, in Sangrur. I had known this girl as a little kid, for she used to come for the treatment of her eyes to my father. After giving our Intermediate Examination, and, before the results were announced, Gulam Bheek decided to marry. I accompanied the 'barat' and caught a glimpse of his wife-to-be who was then a very pretty girl of about 15 years of age. Little did I know that the next time I would see her would be in 1987, when I was able to take my wife to Lahore for a visit. After a very successful career as a famous gynaecologist in Pakistan, Gulam Bheek had retired as Civil Surgeon of Lahore and was now Emeritus Professor of the Medical College. It was a surprise to learn that he had given up whisky completely, and had, as a result, I suppose, lost a lot of weight. I must say that for the sake of our old friendship, he spent all the five days that I was in Lahore with me. I was extremely touched by this gesture and I have subsequently kept up correspondence with him.

My period of education in Government College was the most interesting one, politically. In December 1929, an Annual Meeting of the Congress was held on the banks of the river Ravi, which flows only a few miles from Lahore. We, although belonging to what was considered the most unpatriotic college, went to listen to Pandit Nehru, who had been elected President of the Congress and was to deliver an important speech. This was the first time that the Congress was to declare 'Purna Swaraj' (complete independence) as its primary aim. Till now it had been thought that the Congress might accept Dominion Status for India within the British Commonwealth. After this declaration, Pandit Nehru was mounted on a white steed and taken at the head of a huge procession, which was declared by the Indian National Congress as a momentous event! This event was followed by a period of very active agitation by the Congress against British rule in the country. We used to read reports of processions, police repression, lathi charge, etc, in the newspapers.

An agitation for Independence was started in Lahore, and apart from picketing educational institutions, a series of political processions were taken out through Anarkali bazar, the main street of Lahore. Some of them were lead by Lala Lajpat Rai, a well-known politician of Punjab, at the time. Whenever it was announced that he was going to lead a procession, we, the students of Government College, would go and watch from the side-lines, and thus were witness to the processionists' many encounters with the police who would lathi-charge them. It was in one such encounter with the police, that Lala Lajpat Rai sadly met his end. It also immortalised him and to this day he is known as the 'Hero of Punjab'. I still remember the stanza that was on the lips of every youngman then:

"Sar feroshi ki tammana ab hamare dil mein hai;
Dekhna hai zor kitna bazue qatil mein hai."

Government College was considered pro-British as it had mostly British staff. Our Principal at the time was a well-known educationist, Mr HLO Garret, while the Vice-Principal was Mr Duncliff. Mr Langhorn taught essay writing, Mr Wilkinson English poetry, and so on. Our college blazer, coloured red, carried the emblem of a burning torch, with a motto beneath it which read: 'Let Heaven's Light be my Guide'. So we were the butt of all political agitations. Even small children from the neighbouring school while passing by the green hedge which divided the 'Oval' hockey ground of the college from the main road, would peep through the hedge and shout: "Toady Bacha Hai! Hai!", "Lal Kurti Hai! Hai!". All we could do was bear it with a smile! These were also the days of boycott of foreign clothes, and I remember the incident when some little kids managed to enter the main gate of the college and made a bonfire of foreign clothes and hats right in front of the main-door of the college. I also remember the picketing of the main gates of the college, initially by the students of the neighbouring DAV College and later, by the two pretty Zutshi sisters who belonged to the college itself! The picketeers were generally arrested by the local police and taken away in police-vans and later, we were told, released some distance away from the college.

I must tell you the story of a friend of mine in the college, Mr Inder Kumar. He was a day-scholar and studied with me in the pre-medical class. On one of these picketing mornings, he came and sat with me on one of the pillars of the main gate of the college. Watching the two pretty Zutshi sisters picketing the gates, he got so worked up that he removed his coat and throwing it at me volunteered to picket the gate with them! He was soon removed by the police in one of their vans, and we never heard of him again. It was only in 1957, when I went to London to attend the Imperial Staff College that I met Inder there at an evening party. It was a meeting of friends long lost, and he told me what had transpired after the picketing episode. Apparently, his father, who was quite influential in official circles at the time, and knew the British Governor, had been presented by the latter with the choice of either visiting his son in jail, or sending him abroad for studies. And that was how Inder came to be a dentist with a roaring practice in London! He had married a local English girl and lived happily ever after. He is, regrettably, no more, having died a few years ago. I shall always treasure his friendship.

Those days, we also read in the newspapers about the activities of three patriotic young men: Bhagat Singh, Satguru and Sukhdev. Bhagat Singh, who was reputed to be a student in one of the local colleges, was said to have shot and killed a Police Warrant Officer, Saunders, and lobbed a bomb in the Assembly Hall. He, along with both his friends, was arrested and tried in the Jail Court. Local papers would carry their statements, made in Court, and these would agitate the young minds of even those like us studying in a so-called 'Toady' college. To be honest, however, for me and most of my friends getting an education was more important than anything else at this stage and though we talked about these things and felt agitated we did not think of taking any concrete action.

What was more important to me at that time was to try for a Commission in the Indian Army. So while I continued studying for my BA, I also prepared for the Army Entrance Examination. Agya Singh, a class-fellow of mine (who was also with me in the college hockey team), was keen for the same. As a preliminary requirement you had to be between the ages of 18 and 20, and for some one like me, who belonged to one of the so-called Native States, I had to get permission from the Governor of Punjab to sit for the examination. Once this was done, I proceeded to Delhi for the Entrance Examination. There I found that there were 10,000 of us from different parts of India vying for ten vacancies! The Selection Board decided to conduct a preliminary interview and selected only 500 candidates for the final examination. Fortunately I was one of them. We sat for the competitive examination in the main hall of Metcalfe House building in Old Delhi. There were five subjects for the test and each carried 100 marks. This was followed by an interview by the Board of Selectors, mostly British Army Officers, which also carried 500 marks. It was really on the strength of the interview that you were finally selected for the value of the academic examination was only nominal. The test took place in the month of June, and we were told that the results would be published in the dailies three months later. It is interesting to note that it was at the railway platform in Gwalior, while Agya and I were both travelling with the college hockey team, on its all-India tour, that I picked up a copy of the Tribune and read the results of the entrance examination. Lo and behold, both Agya and I had made it!

I must say something here about the hockey tour we were on. It was undertaken every year during the summer holidays by the Government College hockey team, known as (hockets). We travelled all over India playing hockey with the best teams. We were at the Gwalior railway station on our way to Manavadar, a local state that ran a Golden Cup Hockey Tournament in which all the well known teams in India participated. It was there that we encountered for the first time the 'Jhansi Heroes', a team captained by the the hockey wizard Dhian Chand who was playing in the centre-forward position for his team. His play was admired by everyone for he had such a wonderful control over the ball. I was later to meet him in the finals of the 'Indian Native Hockey Tournament' when he was playing as a Naik in the 1/14 Punjab Regimental Team and I was representing the team of 5/11 Sikhs (from Aurangabad). This was in 1937. Dhian Chand was to go on to become a famous hockey player and captained the All India Hockey Team at the Olympics held in Berlin in 1936.

On return from the tour, I continued my studies in the college, in the hope that I might be able to sit for my BA examination, but it was not to be, for the call for the Indian Military Academy (IMA) came earlier. So, I am only an under-graduate, as far as University education is concerned.

4
THE INDIAN MILITARY ACADEMY

I continued in college till I joined the Indian Military Academy (IMA) at Dehradun, in March 1933. On the morning of our arrival, by train, a funny thing happened to me which I must describe here. While Agya was coming from Lahore, where he lived, I was coming from Sangrur and had to change to a through-bogey at Ambala for Dehradun. This through-bogey was supposed to be attached to the direct train coming from Lahore, at the Bareilly Junction. Having shifted to the bogey going to Dehradun, when the Lahore train arrived at Ambala, I went to meet my friend Agya Singh. I sat in his compartment, chatting about college days, and when the train was about to start, Agya persuaded me to stay on, saying that, in any case, my bogey was bound to be attached to the train at Bareilly. I readily acquiesed, without bothering to find out if this was indeed the case. When we were a station short of Dehradun, I decided to shift into my bogey for I had to change into a suit before getting down at Dehradun. Imagine my consternation when I ran up and down the platform and could not find my bogey! In the end I had no choice but to go back to Agya's compartment before the train left me behind. Agya offered me his suit,

An aerial view of the Indian Military Academy (IMA), Dehradun.

but since I was a couple of inches taller than him it was too short for me. What was I to do? I felt utterly helpless and no less nervous. There was no way out. So I let down the folds at the bottom of Agya's trousers, and in the absence of an iron, straightened them by wetting them, and squeezed myself into Agya's coat. On the platform at Dehradun, I saw that people in uniform had come to receive us, but I dare not come out of the compartment and meet them! I let Agya do that; while I waited for him to come and tell me what arrangements had been made for getting us to the Academy. Once I knew that a bus was ready to take us I rushed out of the compartment and made straight for it avoiding the reception party. And this is how I sneaked into the IMA on our first day!

When the bus arrived at our destination, an English breakfast was laid out for us on a long table. I ate my breakfast hurriedly, and did not show myself to any of the Academy staff till my own baggage had arrived, nearly six hours later. What an experience for a newly joined cadet! After breakfast, we were asked to look at the notice board which had a list of our names with the room numbers alloted against each, as also the Company and Section. There were just two Companies at the time; A and B. I was detailed to A Company, commanded by Captain Savory. My Section Commander was Lance Corporal Mohammad Zaman. My room number was 64. Throughout my stay at the Academy, 64 remained my number, and it was stamped on all the items I possessed there. I was given an aluminium disc, with this number stamped on it, and told to draw a rifle of the same number from the Academy Magazine.

As part of our orientation we were taken around the premises of the Academy and learnt that it had been a Railway School that had later been handed over to the Academy. The old building, consisting of four blocks, housed the cadets. Each block was joined by a common ante-room and a billiards room. It was in the ante-room that cadets assembled before dinner every evening and sometimes the Company Commander (Captain Savory of the Sikh Regiment in the case of A Company) also joined in, in full mess kit, to play games with the cadets. Each of the residential blocks had centrally located laterines and bathrooms with hot and cold water laid on. There was enough accommodation for the first and second term cadets who numbered

A Soldier Remembers

about 60. We were each alloted a cubicle and assigned an ex-serviceman whose duty it was to polish our boots, clean our brass buttons with Brasso, etc. Another set of similar quarters were under construction nearby to accommodate the third, fourth and fifth terms. A little known fact is that our parents had to pay a sum of approximately Rs 8000 (I do not remember the exact figure) towards our training. Out of this we were given Rs 30 per month as pocket money which went towards hiring bicycles and paying for our meals when we visited the town.

In front of the main building, two World War I vintage guns (relics) were on display, as also a couple of Sea-Mines, bulky hulks of steel, with their gun-powder removed. They were meant, I suppose, to give the Indian Military Academy a martial look! The parade ground in front of the building was metal-paved. Beyond the main gate, opening on the parade ground, was the riding school for the cadets. Incidentally, we were going to be called 'Gentlemen Cadets' - GC for short. Each term, we were told, was to be of roughly 6 months' duration while the courses at the Academy would extend over five terms - a total period of two and a half years.

The first few days at the Academy were spent in the tailor's shop. We were to be measured and fitted for an extensive wardrobe. Two sets of uniform: a couple of shorts (khaki) with a drill jacket and a khaki tie (to be worn for ceremonials) and a forage cap, or muslin turban for Sikhs. For sports and physical training we were issued white drill shorts and vests. For visits to town the dress code was a grey and red striped (light and woollen) blazer, a blue-patrol suit with GRI buttons, or a grey-flannel suit to be worn with a forage cap or turban with a GRI copper badge pinned on it. Accessories included a pair of brown leather boots and a leather belt, with a GRI buckle, and a pair of Fox's putties. From fourth term onwards we were issued a Sambrown belt and a sword. For those wondering what GRI meant, it stood for Georgeous-Regorious-Imperatus, and was intended to remind us that we belonged to the Imperial Government!

The staff for the newly started Academy were the pick of the Indian Army, and included those who were sympathetic to the Indians, for there is no doubt that the British wanted to make this experiment of Indianisation, however small, a success. The Commandant, Brig Collins, was truly a fine gentleman for the job, and he was very popular with the Gentlemen Cadets, as were his wife and young daughter. The other officers too had been selected for similar attributes, except, perhaps, for the Deputy Commandant, Colonel Bird, of the Royal Engineers, who was very rough and gruff with the cadets, and was thus very unpopular. The Company Commanders: Captain Savory of A Company; Captain More of B Company; Major Le Fleming of C Company and Major Cowan of D Company were very kind and sympathetic, as were their families. They were expected to invite cadets of their Company to their homes for entertainment as this was a part of social training. The Adjutant was Captain McLaren, a Blackwatch Officer, very tall, trim and correct, but on the Drill Square, a bit of a 'fire-eater'!

After a year's stay at the Academy, we, Gentlemen Cadets, had become quite bold and familiar with our surroundings and the staff. After dinner on the 31st of March, a Saturday, we decided to play an 'April Fool's' joke on the IMA, in general, and on our officer-instructors, in particular. We were keen to get our own back on the Deputy Commandant, Colonel Bird who, as already mentioned, was for most of the time ill-tempered and stand-offish with the Gentlemen Cadets. Yet he was a very religious man in the sense that he and his family never missed going to church on a Sunday morning, and the 1st of April was to be a Sunday! At midnight, under the cover of darkness, all the cadets (at least most of them) were out of their beds and busy turning the whole of the Institution upside down out so that by the morning of 1st April the IMA was unrecognisable. The two draught-guns (of World War I vintage) decorating the front of Chetwode building as trophies, were pulled out of their permanent places and dragged by sheer weight of numbers along the metalled road and dumped in front of the Deputy Commandant's gateway and that of the Adjutant's. The sports store was flung open and sports-gear scattered all over the playing-fields. The high-hurdles were hauled up to the roof of the main building and were installed there on its sloping roof. All the photographs and paintings in Chetwode Hall were turned upside down. The arms of the main clock in the tower of the building were fixed at 12 o'clock. Fire fighting equipment was laid out in a ready position - hoses and all. Danger-signs displayed on electric-transformers were removed and stuck on the name-plates of the not-so-popular staff. In fact, by the morning of the 1st of April nothing in the IMA was as it should have been! We were lucky that no one had woken up that night for the rickety old guns had made a great deal of noise while being moved. Everyone it seemed was fast asleep and oblivious to what awaited them next morning.

The idea behind all this activity was to drive Colonel Bird into an absolute frenzy as he came out of his bungalow on Sunday morning to go to church with his family and found his way blocked by the old gun in front of his gate. And that's exactly what happened.

The fury of the Colonel knew no bounds as he assembled as many of his own and the neighbours' servants as he could to move the obstacle in his path, which, despite their best efforts, refused to budge. Eventually, he had no choice but to send for the Adjutant who found a similar obstacle barring his path! He was, however, able to by-pass it on foot. The Deputy Commandant (who, incidentally, was officiating for the Commandant that day, because the Commandant was away on some duty) directed the Adjutant to sound an alarm and assemble the cadets. We were waiting for such a call, assembled hastily and made double time to the Deputy Commandant's bungalow. We were told, in no uncertain terms, to put every thing back to where it belonged, within an hour, without fail! This done, we were asked to assemble in Chetwode Hall for the officiating Commandant's address. The officiating Commandant, Colonel Bird, harangued and derided us for having played an 'April Fool's' joke which according to him was essentially an English custom, and we being Indians, had no business to indulge in it. We were accused of having misbehaved and of having broken the discipline of the Academy; and as a punishment we were all confined to our barracks till further orders. At 2 o'clock, immediately after lunch, we would assemble for a Ceremonial Parade under the Adjutant.

Now, our Adjutant was Captain McLaren (A Blackwatch Highlander), nicknamed 'fire-eater' by us for he seemed to emit fire at the Drill Square. In normal times we would have been quite unhappy to have to parade under him but we were so happy with our escapade that we took it all in our stride this time.

Five minutes before time (as was the practice), we were to fall-in on the concrete Drill Square, dressed in our khaki-drill jackets, with ties, and shorts underneath (which was a great relief in the scorching heat of the sun and the metalled Drill Square). The Adjutant (the fire-eater!) came in his ceremonial dress, a khaki-drill jacket with a tie, tartan (warm) breeches and black leather top-boots, with spurs. An outfit which, compared to ours was much warmer, and likely to cause discomfiture, especially to a westerner! We gloated over this and forgot our own discomfort. As Captain McLaren threw his drill-orders at us, froth was visibly exuding from his mouth. But that day the more he shouted at us, the more we liked it. Colonel Bird was there, too, supervising the parade from the edge of the Drill Square and, to our delight, equally suffering from the heat of the mid-day sun!

The drill lasted for about an hour and, as cadets, I don't think, we had ever drilled better! Despite all this we still felt the thrill from having done something unique. The parade over, we returned to our quarters and began our daily routine. The next day was no different. On the third day, we learnt that our Commandant, Brig Collins, the great man whom we loved, had returned to the Academy, and we were ordered, once again, to assemble in Chetwode Hall - which was always ominous! We wondered how he would address us. Brig. Collins started with a greeting and said that he had learnt about all that had happened in his absence and that he was happy to know that we had celebrated 'April Fool's Day' with such vigour! He was proud that the cadets had shown such a display of initiative and spirit! He went on to say that 'April Fool's Day' did not belong to any single community and that all were free to celebrate it. He ended by saying that he was sorry that we had had to suffer for it and announced, "Your confinement to your barracks is off. As a compensation for having lost the Sunday, you have this afternoon off. Be ready to go to town today. The buses of the Academy will be ready to take you to town at 3 o'clock this afternoon. Enjoy yourselves". What a grand chap he was this Brig Collins! We simply loved him!

Equitation was part of our training, and I am glad to say that at the end of the first term, I was the only cadet in my term to be awarded his spurs, which was considered a distinction for it signified having acquired enough skill to ride a horse alone. The others in my term were awarded their spurs either at the end of the second term or the third. As a result of having been given my spurs, I was given the honour of leading my class in cross-country riding, and horse

As Under-officer C Company we win IMA Banner and all trophies.

jumping. I participated in almost all sports, including athletics at the IMA. In the latter, I held the Academy record in high-hurdles and the long jump, for many years. I was awarded Academy Colours in swimming, hockey and athletics and qualified for life-saving and first-aid in swimming in my final term. I was also in the water-polo team of the Academy. When I was Under Officer of C Company, we won trophies in almost all the sports and games, and in drill (including sword-drill). I was particularly proud to have won the Academy Colour (a Flag) - a prestigious award - for my Company, that is C Company, for this was awarded to the best of all the four Companies.

I would like to remind the readers that in each term we were just 30 Gentlemen Cadets. Ten of us came through open competition (like Agya and I), ten from the Army (as Y Cadets) and ten from the State Forces. Even in this small group there were some real characters. I particularly remember Makhan Singh who was a cadet in my term (from the Army).

We felt that he must have been a wrestler in his unit, for he was keen to build up his body. For breakfast, butter used to be laid out in small china plates for each cadet, on the tables, by Companies, in the dining hall. Makhan Singh would be the first to arrive for breakfast and would swipe the bits of butter from the first ten places on the table, and then sit down for breakfast at the 11th place. We used to say, that by doing, so he was only living upto his name! He was a strange character in more ways than one and there are a host of stories about his days at the Academy. I can vouch for the truth of two of them.

Once, when we, the cadets of the second term, were asked to tea by the Commandant's wife at her house, we all arrived, Makhan Singh included, in the drawing room of the Commandant's house punctually at 4 o'clock, and after some small talk with the Commandant's wife and their young daughter, we were asked to move into the dining room for tea. Here sweets were served to us by liveried bearers of the house, while the hostess served us tea. For this purpose, tea cups were laid out at one end of the table with a chair for the lady of the house, who was to fill the cups with tea and serve them to us. She asked us to get around that end of the table and started filling the cups from a rather large pot which admittedly she was finding hard to handle. Now,

Makhan Singh, seeing the lady's predicament, decided to help. He went upto her and, rather forcefully, tried to wrench the pot out of her hand, saying: "I can't let you do this, give it to me as it is too large for you to handle". She remonstrated with him that as a hostess she had a duty to perform and that there was no need for him to bother. But Makhan Singh was insistent and almost pulled the pot out of her hand, till we all intervened to say that he should leave the lady alone.

Another time I, among others, was invited to an officer's house for drinks in the evening and Makhan Singh happened to be present. There were some British guests also invited to this drinks party. After being introduced to others by our host, we were standing leisurely in the drawing room with Makhan Singh standing at one end. Presently, the lady of the house started going around and asking each guest what they would like to drink. She finally reached Makhan Singh and asked him what he would like. Makhan Singh, who was used to having a strong drink on the sly in his room, thought of playing safe in that gathering and declined to have anything to drink at all. In the end, the hostess turned to her husband who answered, "As usual, darling". On hearing this, Makhan Singh pricked up his ears for here was a new drink that he had not heard of before! Having asked every one else, and thinking that Makhan Singh was the odd man out who had not asked for a drink, the hostess addressed him again and said: "Are you sure, you won't change your mind and have something to drink?" Now Makhan Singh, having been taught that at social gatherings, when in doubt, it was best to follow your neighbour (and in this case his own Instructor!), promptly answered: "Thank you, Madam, I would like to have a 'as usual darling' also." And that, foxed the lady!

Now, this is a story about Makhan Singh that I cannot vouch for. It was related to me by his Company Under Officer who had been invited along with Makhan Singh to dinner at the house of their Company Commander.

They both arrived together at the Company Commander's house at the appointed hour. It being summer, a small dining table, set for four, was laid out in the open on the lawn. After a round of soft drinks for the cadets they sat down at the dining table, with the Company Commander and his wife sitting opposite each other while Makhan Singh and the Under Officer sat facing each other on the other two chairs. Dinner was served by a liveried bearer and the table made a pretty sight with its starched cover and serviettes, white as snow, and silver knives and forks gleaming in the moonlight. At one stage of the dinner, the Under Officer noticed that Makhan Singh appeared to be a little uneasy, as if he had lost something. While trying his best to keep his posture erect (having been taught not to slouch at the dining table) he seemed to be searching for something on the ground in front of him. The Under Officer surmised that he was trying to retrieve his serviette without being too obvious about it. Finally, he seemed to have succeeded, as the Under Officer could make out that he was spreading something on his knees, ofcourse all this without looking down. Makhan Singh looked happy once again. Very soon, however, the Company Commander's wife began to look ill at ease. Her husband, noticing it, asked if Jack (Jack being their cocker-spaniel dog) had slipped under the table. It was an occasion for every one to look under the table, and poor Makhan Singh discovered that while groping for his serviette he had picked up the lady's dress instead. Realising his mistake he quickly threw the dress down like a red-rag! I could go on and on with stories about Makhan Singh, but enough is enough!

The routine at the Academy was really tough. We got up promptly at 6 o'clock in the morning and were given a mug of tea in bed by the ex-servicemen batmen. We then dressed for physical training class and went off to the class running. The PT class was taken by a British Sargeant Major, from the Army Physical Training School in the UK. Under his instruction, besides ground work, we used the wooden horse and the parallel bars. This was followed by rope climbing and sometimes fist boxing also. Then came an hour's drill, with and without rifles. In the senior terms – the fourth and the fifth – we had sword drills as well. Then began three hours of academic routine. We studied subjects such as military history, mathematics, geometry and general knowledge. English phonetics were taught in the junior classes while the seniors were taught accounting. Lunch was at 1 o'clock in the Cadets' Mess and by 2 o'clock we were to report for games which included swimming, cricket, hockey, athletics, football, and, in the evenings, tennis and squash. At the end of the day we were expected to bathe and change into a white jacket, or blue jacket suit, depending on the prevailing season. We then assembled in the ante-room for the next day's orders,

At the IMA swimming pool.

or to play games. The most common were 'More Arty, where are you?' played under a blanket with a rolled up magazine to beat your opponent with and 'the toppling game' where you tried to topple your opponent with a tackle using the right leg. Often our British Company commanders joined in. Then it was off to dinner to the Cadets' Mess and soon it was time to sleep.

Because of this very busy schedule at the IMA a few of us had

Breaking the Academy record in the High Jump.

trouble concentrating in class. I remember an incident in our military history class, being taken by Captain Savory, an officer of high calibre whom I greatly admired. He was always upright and perfectly dressed, both in uniform and civil dress, and I must admit that it was due mainly to him that I put in for the 5th Battalion of the Sikh Regiment, as he belonged to the 1st Sikh. The incident I am about to relate illustrates his many qualities. When Captain Savory noticed that a few heads in the last two rows in the class were nodding away he quietly sent for the Gurkha bugler on duty and asked him to stand at the rear of the class and play the 'Reveille'! The poor cadets who were nodding off woke up with a start while the rest of us had a good laugh. What a way to teach them a lesson! But then Captain Savory was an exceptional man.

I remember yet another occasion when he was taking a class outdoors on military history and wished to teach the cadets the meaning and effect of 'covering fire'. He divided the class into two halves, with one representing the enemy and the other were 'our' troops. He asked them to occupy two opposite trenches at a stone's throw from each other and armed 'our' troops with brick-bats. He asked the 'enemy troops' to pop up from the trench and pretend to shoot at their opponents, while 'our' troops were instructed to pelt any head they saw with stones. The demonstration was very pragmatic and effective, though it was at the expense of a few battered heads.

The third term arrived and I was transferred to the newly formed C Company with Major Le Fleming as my new Company Commander. He was a fine officer and I learnt a great deal from him. He thought well of me and promoted me to a Lance Naik. I became a Naik in my fourth term and an Under Officer in my fifth and final term. I passed out second in the final examination in my last term at the Academy in July 1935.

In the last number of the Magazine of the Indian Military Academy, at the time of my passing out, I noticed an excerpt, put in, under the authorship of the Commandant, Brigadier Collins, under the heading 'The First Person Singular', which said that I was the only Gentleman Cadet who was passing out of the Indian Military Academy without the blemish of a punishment of any kind during my two and a half years' stay. I felt elated to read it.

5

SECOND BATTALION: THE ARGYLL AND SUTHERLAND HIGHLANDERS

For a year, I was posted to a British unit of my choice, the 2nd Battalion Argyll and Sutherland Highlanders, at that time posted in Rawalpindi. I arrived in the battalion, towards the end of July 1935 and was straightaway put on cadres to learn about the new weapons which were then available only with the British Army. I was given a platoon of JOCKS to command in B Company and soon the battalion departed for Hunza State in the North West Frontier to carry out what were known as Mohmand Operations against the tribals. It was a great experience for me. We marched from the Peshawar railway station to the scene of action, a place called Gallanai, which was the base camp for the operations.

I saw for the first time the institution of the 'Chaiwalah' at work. It was generally manned by Pathans, who marched with the British troops on the journey and at each stipulated halt plied them with ready-made tea.

The Platoon of Jocks the Author commanded.

Hockey team of the battalion - started at the Author's initiative.

Some Indian troops were also marching along the same route. While the British troops were allowed to reach their destination in stages, Indian troops were expected to march almost double the distance covered by their British counterparts each day.

On arrival at our destination - Gallanai - we were required to march-past in front of the Brigade Commander in-charge of the operations, Brigadier Auchinleck, who had just taken over from Brigadier Alexander (both officers rose to occupy very eminent positions during the Second World War).

We were at rest at the last stage of our march, getting ready to leave for the final march-past, when we heard a pipe-band playing in the distance - obviously an Indian battalion on the march was approaching us. It was customary in the Army to stand up and salute the passing-troops. So, we stood where we were and gave the battalion passing through a salute. About a mile further, we passed the same Indian battalion - 3rd Sikh – again as they had halted in order to spruce themselves up for the final march-past.

As we marched past the Commander of the Forces, we were asked by Brig Auchinleck (who incidentally belonged to the Indian Army) to line up behind the sangar wall of the camp and watch the 3rd Sikh, who were to march behind us. The idea was to show us the difference between Indian and British troops!

In Gallanai, we soon participated in operations against the tribals. I might mention that in this camp, initially there was a great shortage of water and we were rationed one canvas bucket of water per platoon for our morning ablutions. I used to wash my face first in this bucket, and then pass it on to the rest of the platoon. By the end, the bucket was nothing but a thick emulsion of mud! For drinking, we were allowed one bottle of water a day per person. This was the practice at the beginning of the campaign. But, fortunately for us, within a month, the Army engineers discovered that there was a subterranean stream flowing in the vicinity of the camp and they were able to bring up this perfectly clean water. In addition to having plenty of water for drinking and cooking, the camp now had a swimming pool, flush with freshwater!

In these operations, for the first time, night operations were undertaken against the Pathans. Tanks (Stuarts) were used against

Underground stream at Gallanai.

them during the hours of darkness. The practice was to have breakfast at 10 o'clock at night and then carry out a night-march to our pickets so that we would be in position when the Pathans would wake up and be ready for action after their morning prayers. In this way, we very often caught them 'napping'. The Mohmand Operations ended after a dramatic encounter, when the Guides Battalion - 12th Frontier Force Regiment - was caught on a knife-edge ridge by the Pathans, just awakened from their morning prayers. The battalion had inadvertently stopped a hill short during their night-operations mistaking it for their final destination. When they realised their mistake, they tried to rush to their objective across a knife-edge approach, without taking the necessary protective measures before embarking upon such a risky operation. They were, thus, caught by the Pathans at a disadvantage. The battalion suffered heavy casualties, with all officers either killed or wounded, and lost nearly 90 men. The command of the battalion, finally, fell on a Second Lieutenant, who was awarded a Victoria Cross for this action. I watched the whole drama of the Guides misadventure through my binoculars from the neighbouring picket where my Platoon of Highland troops was deployed. This misadventure occurred not because the operations were being conducted at night, as some people might think, but because of faulty map-reading on the part of the battalion. If they had arrived at the objective given to them, under cover of darkness as planned, they would have found the Pathans

Officers with Argyll & Sutherland Highlanders at Gallanai (Mohmand Operations).

Governor of the NWFP holds a 'Jirga' with the local Pathans.

sleeping in their lair, but luck was against them and having misread the map they stopped a hill short of their objective. Then, having discovered their mistake, without taking proper safety precautions, the battalion tried to rush to the hill, their objective, over a knife-edge ridge, and fell into a trap, so to say, and hence suffered heavy casualties.

After a month, the operations ended successfully with a 'Jirga' with the locals, presided over by the Governor of the North West Frontier Province, and peace was declared. Soon the troops dispersed and returned to their peace stations. We also returned to Rawalpindi. This had been my first experience of commanding a Platoon of JOCKS in active operations and it was the first time that I had come under fire, which, indeed, was an experience that stood me in good-stead for the rest of my service!

I was detailed to return to Rawalpindi with the advance party of the battalion. This advance party, consisting of representatives of all the Companies of the battalion, travelled from Gallanai to Peshawar railway station by Army vehicles and then took the train. It was September 1935. This was the first time that I came to know of the 'Muster Parade', which used to be held in the Barracks each morning, where everybody was expected to assemble and be accounted for. This lasted for about ten to fifteen days, till the rest of the battalion arrived at Rawalpindi by train from Peshawar. Soon, preparations were made to proceed to the hill-station earmarked for the battalion, known as Garial, a few miles beyond Murree. The battalion arrived there towards the end of October, marching on foot.

Before proceeding any further, I must also tell you about the post of the 'Senior Subaltern' in a British battalion. He was the senior-most Lieutenant in the battalion - in our case, Lieutenant F. Graham - who had nearly twenty years' service, and was responsible for the conduct of all young officers in the Officers' Mess and elsewhere. In our case, Mr Freddy Graham taught us newly joined officers a thing or two, such as never to address a senior by his first name until asked to do so by the person concerned; never to leave the Mess ante room after dinner (which was considered an official meal) before the senior dining-member; never to expect, as an attached officer (in our case, we were two Indian ICOs and a British officer) to be asked to join the Regimental guest-night in the Mess. In fact, throughout our one year's stay, we three attached-officers were never asked to a Regimental guest-night at the Mess. What went on there, in terms of mess traditions, etc., we only learnt from the Indian mess-staff. For example, we were told, that after drinking to the King's health, all the officers of the battalion used to, by tradition, break the glasses in which they drank the toast. I believe this had been instituted in memory of the Scottish Queen killed by the British. How true this is, I do not know. We were told, by our Senior Subaltern, never to visit the British NCOs' Mess, except with the rest of the officers on certain ceremonial occasions. We were also instructed not to fraternise with the British other ranks or their families; and certainly never to invite them to our living quarters. It was, generally, good advice, and it held us in good stead throughout our service. Therefore, while other officers, lieutenants and captains, had asked us during our stay with the battalion to address them by their first names; Lieutenant Graham, the Senior Subaltern, never did, and so we always addressed him as Mr Graham, which was the least that was due him considering his twenty years of service!

I decided to spend the first two months of leave that I got while with the British unit at Garial, in the Murree hills, trekking in the Kashmir Valley. My companions were Anant Singh, who was at the time a junior GC at the Academy (only one term behind me) and

Second Lieutenant Kashmir Katoch (who's father was in the Maharaja's employment), who I knew well as he had been my term mate at the Academy. Anant's elder brother, Harnam Singh, was at the time Conservator of Forests in Kashmir and this held us in good stead on our trek as we could stay in various forest rest houses along the way.

Our trek started from the source of the river Jhelum, which flows through the town of Srinagar. We took plenty of photographs which testify to the pleasant times we had en route: feeding the fish in a large pond and then bathing in it, sitting in big earthern jars, etc. We passed through Pehalgam and then Mattan where the 'pandas' in the local temple claimed that they could trace our ancestry all the way back to the beginning of time! We were not impressed! From Pehalgam we also did a trek to Sheshnag lake where we spent the night on its banks in our tents. It was extremely cold and we were convinced that we could turn the milk we had with us into ice cream. To our disappointment it did not work! We abandoned our plan to go to the famous temple at Badrinath in favour of staying on in Pehalgam which we found a lovely scenic place, full of interesting places to visit. On our return to Srinagar we did what all tourists do – visited all the beautiful gardens, Shalimar, Nagine and Nasim. Our trek not only familiarised us with the city of Srinagar, but with almost the entire valley: Kukarnag, Ganderbal among other places, as well as Bandipur and the valley of Sonamarg. Thanks to Anant's brother we also took a trip through Dachi Gam, the Maharaja's reserved forest where we saw 'bara singas' and bears. All in all it was a most memorable trip.

In a forest dak bungalow at Pehalgam.

Sitting in earthern jars at the ruins in Avantipura.

Relaxing at Sheshnag after a day's climb.

Sitting across the 'snow bridge' at Jazpal.

6

5TH BATTALION THE SIKH REGIMENT, AURANGABAD

After a year's attachment with the British unit, I joined the 5th Battalion of the Sikh Regiment at Aurangabad, in July 1936. The Indian officers already posted to the battalion, in their order of seniority, were: Captains Khanolkar and Allahabad and Lieutenants Baghel Singh, Ajaib Singh, Dewan Ranjit Rai and Mohmad Hussain. The latter two were from the first batch of the Indian Military Academy, Dehradun. Lieutenant Mohmad Hussain joined the battalion with me. Before joining, I had been advised to call at the Rankins Tailors, in Connaught Place, New Delhi, and order my battalion mess-kit. They were by appointment the regimental tailors of the Sikh Regiment. The mess-kit consisted of: a woollen red jacket with yellow facings, two white cotton waist-coats (in chequered material) and a woollen navy-blue over-all (of stretchable material), with red-piping on the sides. The latter was to be worn over calf-length black leather boots, fitted with a metal box in the rear of each heel to hold enamelled spurs. The over-all was held under the boots with a black leather-strap, fastened with a buckle. While taking my measurements for the kit, the Rankin's fitter asked me, which side I normally dressed from - right or left? I had never heard of this before, but thinking that he might be referring to my take-off foot, I, instinctively, replied: "left" and it seemed to satisfy him. I later learnt that for me the correct answer was "right"!

On arriving at the battalion, I was asked by the officiating Adjutant, Captain Allahabad to have a cup of tea with him that evening at his residence. I arrived there punctually at four and, over a cup of tea, the Adjutant addressed me thus: "In this battalion, we give you a rope; you either pull yourself up or hang yourself!" I believe that he gave this warning shot to every newly joined officer. The other bits of advice were straightforward and less menacing. For example:

— Be on parade at least five minutes before the time set;
— Never wear the same uniform/clothes twice over i.e. before they are washed, starched and ironed, for which purpose the battalion had any number of competent washermen;
— Never enter the Mess ante-room without a coat and a tie except after sports, when a muffler, instead of a tie, was permissible;
— Ladies alone, or accompanied by their husbands, are prohibited from entering the Mess, except once in the year, and that is on the 1st of January (New Year's day), if specially invited to the New Year's Banquet in the Mess;
— Never leave the Mess, after a meal, till the senior dining member has left, or without his permission;
— The morning physical training period, at the crack of dawn, is the Commanding Officer's Parade and attendance is compulsory for every one;
— Never carry or use an umbrella when in uniform; instead use a water-proof coat;
— Badminton, considered a 'sissy-game' in the Army, is never to be played in the Mess or the club;
— Look after your finances; avoid borrowing money and do not let your cheque 'bounce', as it is considered the lowest act of moral turpitude in the Army.

I was posted to C Company with Captain Field as my Company Commander, and I fell into the routine of the Company straight away. After the morning physical training parade, and breakfast in the

Officers' Mess, there was a drill period for the men, for about an hour, under the NCOs, while officers supervised, followed by an hour of Musketry, or Field Craft Training. The men then went off to their educational classes while the officers retired to their offices to perform various chores awaiting them. Shooting on the ranges, and field firing, across the country, every year, were a must for all men in the battalion, and junior officers were expected to shoot with the men. There were also pool-shoots for those who wished to participate. The unit ranges for this purpose were allotted to Companies by turn.

By mid-day, the officers (dining members) assembled in the Mess for a short-drink of their choice, followed by buffet lunch. By 2.30 pm officers retired to their quarters for the afternoon siesta. At 4 pm punctually, a whistle would be blown in the Barracks which was a signal for every one to be out, either for organised games, or for a cross-country run. The emphasis was on physical fitness. The dinner in the Mess, punctually at 8 pm was an official affair (but only for dining members), for which we had to dress in our mess kit. The diners were led into the dining room by the senior member present, and sat together at the table where they were served the meal, ceremonially, by the Mess Staff supervised by the Mess Havildar in his ceremonial dress, who stood at the head of the dining table. Sunday dinner, for which you had to dress in a dinner-jacket, was a casual affair and dinner was placed on the dining table and you could serve yourself.

Usually, at about 10 pm, we left the Mess, after the senior member had departed. Sometimes, the senior dining member, in this case, Major Conoly - a bachelor who liked his whisky after dinner - would stay on till late, after giving permission to leave to those who wished to do so. Once, since he was also my Company Commander, I decided to stay up with him, and while I was having my 'Nimbu Pani', as usual, he was drinking whisky and soda, which he continued to do till 2 am in the morning! I couldn't have got to bed much before 3 am; and was expected to report for the PT parade by 6 am that morning. I got up, later than usual, with a groggy head, had a quick wash up, dressed for PT and set off on my bicycle for the PT parade, a couple of minutes later than usual. Imagine my surprise when I see, my Company Commander, Major Conoly (from whom I had parted company at 2 o'clock in the morning) marching up-and-down the parade ground, with the Company fallen-in, ready for my inspection. I quickly looked at my watch and saw that it was already 6 am. I recalled the rule: "Always arrive five minutes before the set-time for a parade" and quickly ran upto Major Conoly and, standing to attention in front of him, said: "I am sorry, Sir, I am late". And he replied, "Yes, you are, but don't let this happen again". I was really ashamed! I rushed upto the senior JCO, took the parade-state from him, carried out a hurried inspection of the ranks and rushed back to the Company Commander, to report that the parade was ready. Major Conoly nodded his head and asked me to carry on. The parade over, he never uttered another word about my late arrival at parade either to me, or to any one else. Nevertheless, I had learnt a lesson of my life - never to be late again!

The first of January 1938, New Year's Day, was eagerly anticipated by us bachelors in the Mess, as this was the day when ladies were invited to the Mess for the annual banquet - the only evening in the year that they were allowed to attend in the Mess! This year, there was an added attraction, for our Commanding Officer had some house-guests - a couple from France, with a very attractive daughter of 18 years of age. We surmised that they were bound to be invited, as the Commandant's guests; and were looking forward to their coming. Invitations had been issued by the PMC to all the ladies. After some social games, dinner started. We the younger lot, including the young visitor, were sitting at one end of the table. After the meal, during an informal chat, the subject veered towards remembering names. The young lady claimed she never forgot a name. I promptly asked her to repeat mine. She scratched her head for a moment and then blurted out "hair-brush"! Obviously this was her way of remembering names, by association with a familiar object! Since then this name has stuck to me as a nick-name.

The organisation of the battalion in those days was quite different from present times. We had four rifle companies, organised into four platoons, each with four sections. Each section consisted of a Section Commander (a Naik) and 8 men. The Fifth Company was known as the Headquarters Company, again with four platoons: The Signal Platoon, the Quartermaster's Platoon, the Medium Machine Gun Platoon and the Medical Platoon (the Piped Band). We marched past in two lines, followed by marching columns of four, with arms sloped and bayonets fixed. There were drill movements known as 'form four' and 'form two deep'. The Commanding Officer, Second-in-Command, the Company Commanders and the Commander Signal Platoon were the only ones authorised chargers (horses) to ride, and could wear, if they so chose, breeches and leather-gaiters with ankle-boots on parade. The rest of us, including the men, wore drill shorts and cotton shirts.

On ceremonials, the officers wore drill-jackets, with shirt and tie, and brown leather boots with refined Fox's putties, while the men wore high-neck drill jackets with black ammunition-boots with normal (rather rough) putties. During winter, grey flannel shirts replaced the cotton ones. Warm jerseys were issued against extreme cold. For sentries, a limited number of great coats (warm) were also authorised. The putties were worn over warm hoses, both by men and officers.

In musketry, only three weapons had to be mastered: The .303 Lewis Gun (with a drum magazine), the .303 Rifle (Enfield), and the No 36 hand grenade (which could also be fired from a rifle, with a discharger-cup). The .303 Medium Machine (Wickers) Guns were handled by specially trained men of the Medium Machine Gun Platoon, and were carried on mules. Officers carried .45 revolvers, in a leather upholster. The men wore leather belts with pouches. 'Web-equipment' was issued to us, for the first time, in 1938, when we were bound for Razmak (in the North West Frontier Province). There were then no mortars in existence, nor the Vickers Berthier (VB), Light Machine Gun.

Outdoor sports, such as tiger-stalking, pig-sticking/hunting, black-buck stalking, duck and partridge-shooting and fishing, were encouraged among officers. Hockey and athletics were very popular in the Regiment, and a lot of stress was laid on them.

Route-marches were the order of the day. In the Sikh Regiment there used to be an Inter Battalion Route-march Competition. It involved covering 45 miles at a stretch, carrying a full-pack. Afterwards, the battalion was made to march-past in front of the reviewing officer, on local basis, and marks were awarded to each battalion. A winner was thus selected and given a rotating trophy. This practice was given up when the Second World War started; in fact, when vehicle transport was introduced into the Army.

At Aurangabad - Officers with 5/11 Sikh.

Lt Kushalpal Singh.

Lieutenant Kushalpal Singh joined 5/11th Sikh in Aurangabad, six months after I did. He came from Nabha and I from neighbouring Sangrur - about 20 miles apart. We knew each other and decided not to go home during our first two-months' leave from Aurangabad (which was so far away) but instead spend it in visiting temples and old monuments in the south of India. Now this was in early 1937, and for the purpose of our travel, we bought a car - a Chevrolet Coupe - for Rs 500 and replaced its four tyres and tubes for another Rs 100 and set off, with a servant in the dicky, for Sikanderabad as our first destination. 4/19th Hyderabad Battalion (another Indianised battalion) was stationed there, and we had written to Lieutenant Jilani, my term-mate at the IMA, recently posted to the battalion, that we were going to stay with them. Other Indian officers in the battalion were: Captains Thimayya, Srinagesh and Lieutenant Melvile D'Mello (who soon after left the Indian Army and joined All India Radio, attaining great success there). We stayed there for a short while and then continued our journey to the south of India, visiting all the old temples and monuments along the way. We arrived next at Madras where we had booked accommodation, before hand, in the newly constructed railway hotel called 'Connemara', if I recall rightly. We used to travel in khaki shirts and shorts, which were, generally, spotted with grease as were our hands, as on the journey we were often required to lie under the car to repair it. And that's how we arrived at the reception counter of the Connemara Hotel, which, incidentally, accommodated mostly European clientele. The man behind the counter, an Englishman, was hesitant to give us the number of our room, which had been reserved earlier, through a letter. To him, we did not seem to be what we were – a couple of lieutenents. Eventually he did give in, and after a hot bath we both appeared in the dining room of the hotel, in our dinner-jackets (to the satisfaction of the receptionist) and had a tasty meal.

We needed some money - those were not the days of travellers cheques, or credit cards - and were finding it difficult to cash our cheques. So, we decided to visit Fort St George, and ask for the Station Staff Officer's help. We eventually found his office, and who do I see but Captain Daroch, my ex-Adjutant from the British unit that I did my attachment with. He was probably as surprised to see me as I was to see him. I mentioned our problem to him, and he had no hesitation in cashing our cheques. It just shows the camaraderie in the service.

As we continued our journey on rather indifferent roads we were reminded that this was Congress territory by the rows and rows of bullock-carts we saw driven by villagers wearing Gandhi caps. It was so difficult to get them off the road to make way for the car, as they appeared to think that as the Congress was governing the state we should make way for them! We visited almost every temple in the vicinity of the road and were appalled to see that all the beautiful statues and figurines in the temples had been disfigured for their noses and ears had been knocked off - as if by a hammer. We were told that this damage had been inflicted on them by the mughals. The only temple that seemed to have escaped this fate was deep in the heart of the jungle that had recently been discovered and which we also visited.

Of this journey, I particularly remember our visit to Trichinapally. We had booked accommodation before-hand in a rest-house, looked after by an Indian chowkidar. When we arrived there in our soiled clothing, the chowkidar used to only European occupants, enquired as to when our sahibs were arriving? We had a hard time convincing him that we *were* the sahibs! This was to become an almost familiar routine.

Before going to Ceylon, we visited Pondicherry, then a French colony. There we saw, on a round-about, a big statue of the French

General, Dupleix, who had set up the colony. We arranged to spend the night at what looked like a private hotel. Our room had two posterbeds which seemed never to have been fumigated, or exposed to fresh air. And, although the sheets looked clean and starched, we could not sleep a wink, thanks to bed-bugs. So, at midnight, we paid for the room and left. At the international check-post, the customs showed a desire to examine all our baggage, including the under carriage of the car. We assured them that we were casual visitors and had nothing that was contraband, but they refused to listen. So we left our bag and baggage, along with the car, at their disposal, with our servant supervising the search, while Kushalpal and I went to sleep on the ground. Early in the morning our servant woke us up and said that we had been given the green signal, and so we proceeded on our journey.

We finally arrived at the port of Tuticurin and left our car there and boarded a coastal steamer for Ceylon, which was at the time part of India, so there was no need for visas, etc. We arrived at Colombo, and found it to be a very modern city. There we met a Sikh, selling precious stones, who in his spare time indulged in fortune-telling! From there, we travelled by train to Candy, where we had booked accommodation. Our hotel was next to a huge lake; and the scenery was truly beautiful. We hired a car and visited all the temples in the area, including the Tooth Temple, where we were told the tooth of the Buddha is still preserved. We saw the 'Reclining Buddha', which we were told was made of solid gold; quite honestly it looked like copper to us. We also travelled on narrow paths, leading to the North, which though treacherous were draped in colourful foliage. We also visited Nuwara Eliya – a scenic and salubrious hill-resort - in the 'toy-train'. It had match-box compartments, and you sat on opposite seats with your knees touching each other. Nuwara Eliya, we were told, also boasted of the highest golf-course in the world!

We spent about a week in Ceylon, and enjoyed our visit thoroughly. On our return to Tuticurin, we motored to Trivandrum. Here we visited the Aquarium, and the next day made for Kanyakumari, situated on the southernmost tip of India. We had booked ourselves at the resthouse and had a film-shooting party as our neighbours. It was at the time an untouched place - no buildings, no statues - and at night you could see steamers, beautifully lit, passing by the southern most tip of

India. There were an abundance of sea-shells to be collected on the beach, and the beauty of the place was truly breathtaking. We sojourned there for three days.

I must relate what transpired when we visited a temple at Trivandrum, considered the holiest of the holy. Unknown to us, no one could enter the precincts of this temple, which is located near a huge tank of water, unless one wore an unsewn piece of cloth on one's body, and came with a bare-head. When we arrived at the entrance to the temple, which was a mere door, we found our entry barred by a man with a stick in his hand. Thinking him mad, we pushed him aside and made a forcible entry. He sounded an alarm, but we did not care and went straight to the room of the diety, paid obeisance and proffered some money, and returned the way we had come. To our surprise, we found that an angry crowd had collected around our car and were shouting at the top of their voices in a language we could not follow. We signalled to a girl silently standing in the crowd who we hoped would help us make sense of what was happening. We were relieved to know that she spoke English and on being questioned she explained to us the sartorial tradition of the temple, and also added that the crowd had never seen people like us with turbans before. We could have been from another planet! We apologised to the girl for the breach of their tradition, and asked her to explain to the crowd that we were Indians, from the Punjab, and were thus ignorant of their traditions. Her explanation seemed to pacify the crowd which quickly dispersed. We requested her to be our guide during our visit to the town and she agreed. We learnt that many of the men and women in Trivandrum State were educated and understood English. Our guide took us to most of the arts and crafts workshops of the town where we made some purchases. But wherever we went, we were stared at and looked upon as strangers – not truly Indian.

After leaving Trivandrum, we decided to travel along the west coast of the Deccan. It was the month of April now, and pre-monsoon rains had started in the area. We found ourselves driving on indifferent roads through the jungle. What we missed most during this trip was the good old 'chapati'. So at one of the rest-houses, where we were to settle for the night, we asked the chowkidar in-charge if he would get us some wheat-flour and cook us 'chapaties'. I do not know from where he got the wheat-flour but there was so much grit in it that we could not even chew those 'chapaties', and satisfied our hunger by consuming dozens of small, yellow bananas, which abound in the area.

We found that language, for conversing with the locals, was our main problem; they understood a few words of English, but that was all. We were once stranded on a muddy road, during a sudden shower of rain, and there was no question of our being able to make our destination by nightfall. We tried our best to explain to a local that we were looking for a place nearby to spend the night. He mentioned the word 'swami', and pointed in a particular direction. This appeared promising so we asked him to stand on the foot-board of the car and show us the way. He took us along several by-lanes and it was not long before we arrived at the swami's place. The swami hailed us from a distance as long-lost friends. To our surprise, and relief, he was a Punjabi. Not only did he assure us that we would get all we wished to eat at his Ashram, but first of all he offered to quench our thirst with coconut water, which he poured out for us himself. From then on we were treated like honoured guests and the cook even cooked a Punjabi meal for us. He told us that there were a number of Punjabi swamis living in the area. However, we avoided them, as our objective was to meet people from the south.

On the way, we visited Marmagoa, a Portuguese colony, at the time. There we found that liquor, especially wine - both red and white - was very cheap (only one Indian rupee a bottle). We also saw the famous Garsopa Falls, which were a little disappointing as the water was quite sparse. We spent the night in a jungle rest-house that was completely wired-in by strong mesh. When we asked the Chowkidar the reason he explained that being in the middle of a jungle, there was a danger of wild animals visiting the bungalow at night. Although, according to the Chowkidar, there were lions in the forest we heard nothing and spent a restful night.

Finally we arrived at Bangalore and sojourned there in the Engineers' Mess. There we met Second Lieutenant Harkeerat Singh (who had not been promoted because of some differences with his British Commanding Officer), Lieutenant Kumar Kochar and some newly joined Engineer Officers from the Indian Military Academy. From Bangalore it was on to Mysore, a beautiful city, with a multi-coloured fountain at each crossroad. We had the pleasure of visiting the Krishnaraja Sagar Dam which had a colourfully-lit garden in its lee. From there, we travelled to Ootacumand (commonly known as 'Ooty'), a hill-station in the area. There, we paid a visit to Major Cariappa, who was a Brigade Major, newly married and had a child, a boy. We were told that the Maharaja of Nabha, Ripdaman Singh, had also been incarcerated in Ooty by the British. The rest of our journey was uneventful. We arrived back at Aurangabad, none the worse - towards the end of April - and at the end of our two-months' leave!

We were glad to have undertaken this trip to the South, as there was a lot to learn by way of history, customs, etc. Although we had problems communicating, neither had it been easy driving in the South as there were a lot of ferries to cross - there being no bridges on the highways - and each ferry meant a toll to be paid, we were glad for the opportunity that had added to our experiences.

Trip to South India & Ceylon

7

THE BREVET RANK AND REGIMENTAL MARRIAGES

I had hardly been a year with the battalion, when we learnt that our Commanding Officer was due for a change. Shortly, a young looking officer was posted to the battalion in the Brevet rank of a Lieutenant Colonel as Second-in-Command to our Commanding Officer. This was the first time we learnt of a Brevet rank in the Indian army. We also learnt that this newly posted Brevet Lieutenant Colonel had been a brilliant officer in his younger days and that is how he had earned this Brevet rank of a Lieutenant Colonel while still quite young. We also came to know, which we did not like, that in the Army List, by virtue of this Brevet rank, he was senior to our old Commanding Officer. Consequently, in the station, he took over from our Commanding Officer the duties of the Station Commander, as well as the Treasury. This was in early June and a rehearsal of a Ceremonial Parade, in celebration of the King's Birthday, was due in the Station the next day. There were two battalions in the Station, and on earlier occasions for such parades, our Commanding Officer used to take the salute as a Reviewing Officer. We took this as normal, and expected our Commanding Officer to take the salute at this rehearsal also.

But, to our surprise, we found that the Brevet Lieutenant Colonel stood at the Saluting Base, being senior to the other two Lieutenant Colonels in station. We dutifully marched past the saluting base, and saluted the new Brevet Lieutenant Colonel with swords, and so did our old Commanding Officer as the head of the battalion. After the rehearsal, the Reviewing Officer addressed the officers assembled behind the dais, as was the practice, with our old Commanding Officer amongst us. The Reviewing Officer harangued us thus: "I find that the sword drill of officers, generally, is very poor; they do not keep the sword upright, nor swing it smoothly while saluting. Would you kindly see that this aspect of the Parade is put right before tomorrow's rehearsal?"

After this we all dispersed to our offices, which, in our case, were not very far from the parade ground, and our old Commanding Officer was amongst us. He went straight to his office - the Orderly Room, as it was called - and after settling down comfortably, directed his office-orderly to request the Second-in-Command, the Brevet Lieutenant Colonel, to come and see him in his office. The officer came, stood to attention before his Commanding Officer and saluted. The old Commanding Officer took his time to respond, pretending to be busy with his files. Slowly he looked up and remarked to his Second-in-Command, "You no doubt remember what the Reviewing Officer had to say, at this morning's Rehearsal Parade, about the sword drill of our officers. It is shameful that it is not up to par. Therefore, would you kindly fall-in all the officers of the battalion this afternoon, at 3 o'clock, after lunch, and take them for sword drill, for we must ensure that all the defects pointed out by the Reviewing Officer are removed. I will come and supervise." The Brevet Lieutenant Colonel sprang to attention, saluted and marched out of the office, to carry out his Commanding Officer's orders!

The British, according to their 'divide and rule' policy, had added another (artificial) division to the Indian Army, that of Majha, Malwa, Doaba and Punjabi Musalman (PM). The term Majhas was used to denote those Sikhs of the Punjab who lived west of the river Beas; Doabas, were those who lived between the rivers Beas and Satluj, and the Malwas were those who lived east of the river Satluj. In the 5th Battalion of the Sikh Regiment, A Company comprised of Majhas, B of Punjabi Musalman, C of Malwas, D of Doabas, and Headquarters

Company had a mixed composition. The fact was that these communities, separated by rivers, which had no connecting bridges before the British came, had lived very isolated lives, and had thus developed their own distinctive characteristics, which the British exploited to their advantage.

The promotions in the battalion were carried out, upto Junior Commissioned Officers level, by classes. Thus the British had a complete stranglehold on the men as they pitted them against each other on the basis of this sub-division. Of course, this division existed among the other ranks and did not apply to the Commissioned Officers - either KCIOs or ICOs. For example: a Malwa officer could be put in command of a Majha or a Punjabi Musalman Company and vice-versa. Here again, officers were put in command, keeping in mind the policy of 'divide and rule'.

Towards the middle of 1938, there were two marriages in the battalion; Lieutenant Mohamad Hussain, the younger brother of the Nawab of Laharu, married a girl from Hyderabad, the daughter of a local Nawab. By then, four more ICOs had joined the battalion from the IMA, namely, Lieutenants Kushalpal Singh, Taj Mohammad Khanzada, Muzzafar Khan and Nausherwan Khan. We all attended this wedding at Hyderabad. There is an incident to be related in connection with this wedding.

In the evening, the first ceremony of the wedding was to be held at the Nawab Sahib's house. The bride and the bridegroom were to view each other's faces, using a mirror, from under a cover. This is meant to be entirely a ladies function, and the ladies of the household and guests had collected in the courtyard of the Nawab Sahib's house for the ceremony. Only the bridegroom was supposed to be allowed into the courtyard. However, we tutored Hussain not to go alone, but insist on taking all of us, his brother-officers, with him. Many calls came for Hussain from the ladies of the household but he refused to budge. There was an impasse. Nawab Sahib, who was a well-educated and cultured person, suggested that he would have the door opened by calling his Begum Sahiba, on the pretext of letting-in the bridegroom, and then it was upto us to rush in and see the result! And that's what we did, and there was panic in the courtyard as the ladies (all of them in purdah) scattered away in all directions like a flock of pigeons while we were left to ourselves. But this did not deter us in the least. The bride was already seated under a well-decorated canopy on a wooden takhat-posh (bed) and we helped Hussain to also get under the canopy and proceed with the ceremony. Hussain complained that it was very dark inside, and that he could not see anything in the mirror. So we handed him a torch, and he remarked; "Oh, what a beautiful face", although we knew that he had seen that face very closely many a time while he was courting her in Aurangabad, where the girl had come to stay with her elder sister, married to a local judge. And that's when they had decided to get married. By this time all the 'supposed to be' in purdah ladies had composed themselves and collected around the canopy and so the ceremony ended on a very pleasant note! The other marriage ceremonies were all public and we enjoyed them thoroughly.

While in Hyderabad, we also called on another newly married officer of the battalion, Lieutenant Pritam Singh Chowdhry, who had just returned from his honey-moon in London, and had been posted to a local RIASC Unit, having joined the Army Service Corps, for which no infantry officer would happily volunteer. He seemed to be reconciled to his fate. We lunched with the newly married couple the next day and it was a very interesting re-union.

Now the next wedding of note was that of our then Second-in-Command Major Conoly. He had met his bride-to-be, an Australian, while on long leave. The marriage was set to take place in a church in Bombay, and we all turned up for it in Ceremonial Dress, complete with swords, ready to make an arch-way of swords, for the newly wedded couple to pass under after the ceremony in the church. For this occasion, we had travelled to Bombay in Ajaib's newly acquired Chevrolet Coupe Car.

After attending the wedding, we decided to visit Juhu Beach that evening. We started walking up and down the carpet of wet sand, like so many visitors do. As was his habit, Ajaib was twirling his bunch of car-keys on his forefinger and in so doing apparently lost the key meant to open the door of the car. We realised this only when we returned to the car to get into it. So we had no choice but to retrace our steps on to the beach, with our eyes glued to the ground, looking for the key. We had almost given up hope of finding it when we met someone we knew on the beach and started chatting with him about our strange predicament. My eyes were still on the ground and the instant Ajaib lifted his left foot, leaving an impression of it on the wet-sand, I spied something that shone embedded in it. On scraping the spot we found the lost key! What a co-incidence!

By now - 1938 - we had a number of Indian officers in the Mess. All the posts in the Mess such as Mess Secretary, Mess Member (for ordering menus), Garden Member, etc. were all held by Indians. The sister battalion in the station - the Rajputs (not Indianised at the time) were about to leave and so we invited their officers for a farewell dinner to our Mess. It was a sedate affair, with the usual social games, before dinner, and a little rough-house in the Billiards Room after dinner. In return, the Rajputs also asked us over for a meal in their Mess. They had a mischievous intent. After dinner, being hard-drinkers, they decided to play rough-house with us and began to tear clothes (the mess kit, in our case), pull down curtains; and threw things at us. Most of us slipped away and managed to escape. Kushalpal, however, who was also fond of his drink, was caught by these officers and had his mess-kit torn off. But, I must say, that he kept up with them and returned only early in the morning! Now, we were determined to take our back on them and invited them to dinner again just before they were due to leave. This time, we were well prepared for the rough-house! We wore our old mess-kits, had all moveables removed from the ante-room and we had the ground around the fountain, in front of the Mess, prepared into a wet and muddy spot. The idea was to drag all the officers of the Rajputs, one by one, around the fountain in their mess-kit, after dinner. This we did, and by the time they were free to go they were all covered with mud from head to toe! The roughest and toughest among them all was one Captain Cargill, who had a devil-may-care attitude to life. I met him nearly twenty years later as a Major General, after the Second World War, during which, I believe, he had commanded a Division. I met him this time in Quetta, where he had come as a co-student for the first long course at the Staff College which I was also attending. His attitude seemed to have held him in good stead both during the war and after.

I have mentioned earlier, that a Brevet Lieutenant Colonel had been posted to 5 Sikh in Aurangabad to take over the battalion from our old Commanding Officer, who was due to go. Well this happened towards the end of 1937, but the Brevet Lieutenant Colonel a bachelor, did not last long, as soon after taking over the battalion, he got involved with the wife of his Adjutant, an Englishman, and, as was the British-way, was removed from command and sent home without our knowing it. We, the junior officers in the battalion – mostly Indians- learnt about it in a round about fashion when his furnishings such as his curtains, etc, were being sold in the station. Given that he left in disgrace there were no farewells for him.

By now, I had also done the Signals Course at Poona, and taken over the Signal Platoon, in the Headquarters Company, of which Captain Khanolkar was the Commander. Khanolkar was a strange character, but a very good man. The two of us got along famously. 'Khan Sahib', as he was called by all, including the Commanding Officer and other British officers, because of his bushy moustache, was the senior-most Indian officer (KCIO), 'Kasais' (butchers) as we used to call them in the battalion, and he never let you forget it! To attain an air of distinction, he had cultivated the habit of smoking a pipe. This was the 'done thing' for gentlemen, he would say. And except when on parade, he had a pipe dangling from his lips all the time. And what a variety of pipes he had! Some small, some large, some short, some long, some straight, some crooked and curved, some rigid, some telescopic; each for a particular time and occasion. For use at night, while in training, when even a lighted cigarette was an invitation to the 'sniper's bullet', Khan Sahib had devised a pipe with a hood – a 'convertible coupe' is what we called it!

Now, Khan Sahib had the most volatile temper, which would explode at the slightest provocation; but only momentarily, for once he saw the joke, he would instantly give out the most resonant guffaw. So we always enjoyed pulling his leg. There was a story he loved to tell. It was about a British officer (no names), his contemporary, who had passed below him at Sandhurst, but by a peculiar rule extant at the time, had been commissioned a couple of days earlier than him, thus making him senior to Khanolkar. As luck would have it they were both posted to the same battalion. At the very first ceremonial parade in the battalion, when the officers were asked to fall-in in front of the Commanding Officer in their order of seniority, this British officer took up a position to the right of Khanolkar. Seeing this, Khanolkar came

At Aurangabad with the Khanolkars.

upto the officer from behind and catching him, by the scruff of his neck, pulled him back, knocking him down on the ground and occupied his place. Not a very edifying display in front of the Commanding Officer, and the men on parade! What transpired with Khanolkar afterwards in the Commanding Officer's Orderly Room, he was diffident to mention.

He was the only Indian Commissioned Officer to have married recently and according to the British, rather prematurely. For the custom in the Indian Army (and in the British Army also), was not to marry before the age of 30. Khanolkar was only 27, but as his Hungarian born wife had come all the way to India to marry him, he had had little choice. As his Company Officer, I had the freedom of going in and out of Khanolkar's house, and over time both husband and wife grew very fond of me as I of them. I remember their first child, a girl, was born to them in Aurangabad. We, Indians, now in the majority, made much of Mrs Khanolkar, for not only was she the only Indian wife, but she had taken to Indian ways as a duck takes to water. She had picked up the language; even going to the University of Benaras to learn how to write Hindi, had become a member of the Ramakrishna Mission, and had taken to Vedanta. Something the British did not like!

Every Sunday, we, Indian officers of the battalion, including the Khanolkars, used to visit the Ajanta or Ellora caves, that Aurangabad and its neighbourhood were famous for, or historical sites such as the Daulatabad Fort. I was personally greatly influenced by Mrs Khanolkar who initiated me into Vedanta which she practised regularly. When they left on a posting to the Sikh Regimental Centre at Naushera (now in Pakistan) they both invited me to spend atleast a month of my leave with them and Mrs Khanolkar promised to teach me meditation.

Lieutenant Colonel Ford, who had just come from the Senior Officers' Course at Mhow, and belonged to the Sikh Regiment, took over the battalion. We were soon detailed to go to Razmak, in the North West Frontier Province, and the battalion got busy, under Ford, rehearsing mountain warfare drills. On one such exercise, coaxed by my brother officers, I played a joke on my Company Commander, Captain Khanolkar, which just shows how wonderful relations were between us.

The incident I am about to narrate took place in early 1938. Some of the officers present then with the battalion were: Major Field, Captain Wilcocks, Captain Bamford, Captain Khanolkar, Captain Allahabad, Lieutenants Baghel Singh, Ajaib Singh, Ranjit Rai, Hussain, myself and Hassan, in that order of seniority. Those were the days of horses, and although riding was taboo during mountain warfare, Khanolkar, just to show that as a Company Commander he was entitled to a horse, always wore breeches, whereas the rest of us, including the Commanding Officer, preferred to be in shorts.

As I have already mentioned, because of his opiniated and egotistic nature, Khanolkar was often at the receiving end of practical jokes and pranks. On this particular evening, we had ended the day's exercise by setting up a battalion perimeter camp, with its camp pickets, perimeter defence, in-lying pickets and central reserve. This latter was, as always, drawn from Headquarters Company personnel under the direct command of the Company Commander, that is Captain Khanolkar, and I, as his Second-in-Command. To meet any emergency at night, the reserve was required to sleep 'fully accoutred' so as to be ready to spring into instant action. This meant sleeping with one's full uniform on. But Khan Sahib, whose sleeping trench was always next to mine, would invariably take his breeches off, in the hope that there would be enough time to slip them on if and when the 'alarm' was sounded.

At dinner, in the Field Mess, we youngsters decided that I should that night somehow pinch Khan Sahib's breeches and hide them and then see the fun once the 'alarm' was sounded! After dinner, Khanolkar and I walked back to our trenches together, and it was not long before I took off my web-equipment, loosened my boots and lay back on my bedding. Khan Sahib, on the other hand, seemed to be in no hurry. He sat on his bedding, gently lit his pipe (the 'convertible coupe') and while sucking on it slowly went through the ritual of taking his breeches off, folding them carefully, straightening them and placing them under his pillow. He then decided to go 'round the corner' before settling down for the night. This gave me the opportunity I wanted to quickly remove his breeches and hide them in my valise. I could hardly contain my giggles when Khan Sahib returned, stretched himself on his bedding and loudly hoped that he wouldn't be disturbed by the 'alarm' that night!

The inevitable 'raid' by the 'enemy' came precisely at 3 am in the morning and off went the 'alarm'. I was up in a jiffy and heard Khan Sahib cursing and swearing as he could not find his breeches. He was in a panic and, to the accompaniment of the choicest of abuses, was searching his bedding, but to no avail. He then desperately implored me to help him find his breeches. But since I did not wish to be late myself, I rushed off to my post with the Central Reserve. There I waited for Khan Sahib to turn up, but could not imagine how he could! I waited in vain, for it seemed that Khan Sahib had decided, and wisely so, to stay in his trench.

The Commanding Officer, Colonel Ford, having done his round of the perimeter, came to the Central Reserve and asked for Captain Khanolkar. I made an excuse saying that he was around and had just gone to check the security of the Officers' Mess staff. The Commanding Officer then asked the Adjutant to blow the 'Stand Down' and to send for Company Commanders. I rushed off to Khanolkar's trench and passed him the Commanding Officer's orders. Khanolkar was, however, reluctant to leave the trench and suggested that I should inform the Commanding Officer that he was not feeling too well. I replied that I could not tell a lie, and I was about to return to the Commanding Officer, when Khan Sahib beckoned me to wait, and crouching, followed me stealthily, keeping as close to me as possible, so that he would not be noticed. To my added amusement, I discovered that Khan Sahib was not even wearing a pair of drawers! To hide his shame, he was holding one hand in front and the other at the rear. On arrival, I stepped aside quickly, so as not to stand between the Commanding Officer and my Company Commander. Perplexed, Colonel Ford threw the muffled beam of his electric torch on Khan Sahib, who squirming under the light, apologetically, murmured:

"Sorry, Sir, I have lost my breeches!"

When I left Aurangabad I never imagined that the next time I would visit it would be exactly 50 years later - in September 1988 - when I was invited by the 1st Battalion (Mechanised) the Sikh Regiment (the battalion which I had commanded in Jammu & Kashmir Operations) for the Presentation Parade, when they were going to be presented their new Colours since being mechanised in their new Regimental Centre at Ahmedabad. The nearest airport to this destination was Aurangabad and both my wife and I decided to make a halt here on our return journey. I hoped to show her my old haunts. But lo and behold, the place had changed beyond recognition and I could not even find the house I had lived in very easily! It used to be a brick-house then, especially constructed for the Indian Commissioned Officers. When I finally located it it had been plastered over with cement and white-washed. The wife of the Lieutenant Colonel now occupying it was most kind and let us see the entire house. I showed my wife what used to be my drawing-room and bed-room. The other half of the house, in those days was occupied by Lieutenant Baghel. Then I took her to our old barracks. Here, too, although the barracks had been built anew, our office building was nowhere to be seen. It had apparently been demolished. But I found the British graveyard, which used to be next-door to the office building, still intact. I went round the graveyard and renewed my memory of the old tomb-stones. The graves were mostly of young English children, between the ages of 5 and 7 years, who had fallen victim to either cholera or dysentery. This could be gleaned from the writing on the tomb-stones, made mostly of marble. Then I took my wife to the places we would visit on weekends, the Ellora Caves and the Daulatabad Fort. I had intended to take her to the Ajanta Caves but we were told the 60-mile road was not in very good condition, so we gave up the idea. Instead, we went to the middle of town, which I found over-grown and built up. The shopping centre of old had completely changed, there used to be only one street before; but now there were many. This trip in nostalgia would not have been complete without a visit to what I call the Emperor of Delhi's folly (Emperor Mohammad bin Tughlaq) who moved his capital from Delhi to Aurangabad, and built at Aurangabad a replica of the Taj Mahal at Agra, not in white marble but in white-cement which over time turned blue. In my earlier days at Aurangabad we used to go there for moonlight picnics, using the vast platform of the building. This time we viewed it from a distance, as the authorities had enclosed it with barbed wire and imposed a ticket for entering it. Next we retired to what used to be a fountain of water coming out of an erect wall, providing fresh water to the town. This was apparently erected by the mughals, and water was supposed to come from the hills nearby along a secret passage, which no one could discover, although many attempts had been made to do so. Instead of the fountain, we found a stream of water coming from the hills, and a pool of fresh water next to it. It was a good place to refresh ourselves on a hot day, and we had a cold drink there. By the end of the day it made me think that perhaps I had waited too long to return.

8

NORTH WEST FRONTIER PROVINCE - RAZMAK

The battalion left Aurangabad for Razmak, in the North Western Frontier Province, in early September 1938, under the command of Lt Col Ford. Though it was a long journey, being a troops train, we could order it to stop at convenient intervals - at breakfast, lunch and dinner times. The stop for breakfast was the longest, for we wished to take the men out for a cross-country run before breakfast. It was altogether a very pleasant journey. A longer halt was planned at Jalandhar, where we were to meet the ex-servicemen of the battalion from Punjab. The train finally stopped at Missamari, where we detrained and went to Bannu by road. Another Indianised battalion, 1st Battalion the 14th Punjab Regiment was stationed at Bannu, so we had quite a re-union with some ICOs from IMA, Dehradun, who were with the battalion. We also met other Indian officers, such as Captains Thorat, Vir Singh, Gurdeep Singh Dhillon and Ayub Khan (who was Adjutant of the battalion). We even played a few hockey matches with them, and stayed there for about a week, while transport was being arranged for the battalion, on a Road Protection Day, for going to Razmak.

Officers & JCOs of 5/11 Sikh at Razmak.

Author in full trekking gear at Razmak.

Officers' Mess at Razmak.

The battalion arrived at Razmak from Bannu, in the afternoon of a day in late September. We replaced another Indian battalion. Razmak was garrisoned by a brigade strength of two Indian and one British battalions. Razmak was a perimeter camp, made of a stone (sangar) perimeter, divided into three sectors, each manned by a battalion. It also had permanent pickets in each sector, garrisoned by their respective battalions.

We were initiated into the drill of picketing hills upto the Alexandra Fort. I did not find it entirely new, as I had been introduced to the ways of the Pathans during the Mohmand Operations to which I have already referred. Here, in Razmak, I was commanding the Signal Platoon, and later took over A Company. We were a two-class battalion - 3/4 Sikh and 1/4th Punjabi Musalman.

The battalions in the Razmak Brigade used to take on Road-Protection (RP) duties by turn. The responsibility of Razmak Garrison was to protect the road upto the Alexandra Picket, which was permanently manned by the garrison from the neighbouring camp at Dosali. I can recall three main heights that were required to be picketted by the RP Battalion from Razmak Garrison. The first, from Razmak onwards, was Point 6802 (indicating its height). This was a very tricky picket, meant for the protection of the airfield. There was a craggy height, within small-arms range from it, which was not picketted on the principle that a height needed to be picketted only for the protection of the road and not of the picket. As a result, the local Pathans were in the habit of crawling up this craggy feature and firing a volley of shots at the picket when it withdrew, at the end of the RP Day, and sometimes the picket suffered an odd casualty or two. Then there were two more heights, Dundas and Holly Hocks. It is my experiences with the picket at Point 6802 that I should now like to share with you.

One day A Company, which was under me, was assigned the duty of manning this picket with a Platoon. All went well with the battalion, on Road Protection Duty, except when it came to this last picket. While withdrawing, it was fired upon by snipers from across the craggy height nearby. Soon it was realised that one man had been hit in the head and had been left behind in the picket. A counter-attack was launched and the dead-body recovered. In the hustle and bustle of recovering the body, the rifle of the dead man, which had fallen just outside the wall of the sangar, was left behind. This was discovered only when the final check up of arms was carried out on return to camp at Razmak. Now, on the North West Frontier, losing the screw of a rifle was a big offence, and this was a rifle! I was keen to tell the Commanding Officer the truth, but my senior VCO, Subedar Attar Singh, begged me not to do so, vowing that he would recover the rifle before midnight. He mentioned that producing a rifle was no problem, as he could produce five, if need be, but he would arrange to get the same rifle back. He produced a Havildar, with two men, who were prepared to go and look for the rifle, but if only I would allow them to take a rifle for their self-protection. I was not about to lose another rifle and so refused permission, however, I agreed to them taking a bayonet with them. The Subedar said he would make an arrangement with the 3rd Gurkhas, manning the perimeter in the area, that would allow three of his men to go out and return. I said nothing to the Commanding Officer, and after dinner in the Mess, went to bed in my cubicle, but could not sleep out of worry. However, just before midnight the Subedar came to my room and reported that the rifle had been recovered. I heaved a sigh of relief! Of such stuff was my senior VCO of the Company made! Which reminds me of another incident involving him at Razmak.

Lt Col Ford, a very keen Commanding Officer, had started an Interior Economy competition, between Companies in the battalion. This involved an inspection of the Company barracks and the Company cook-house for general cleanliness, and the checking of stores and articles held in the charge of each Company. The competition was held on the last Saturday of the month. On one such occasion I was being grilled by the Adjutant over the inventory items in the charge of the Company Headquarters and all was going well until we reached the last item which read 'folding ladder, MES'. This was news to me as I had never seen such an item anywhere so far, be it the Company stores, or out in the precincts! Bewildered and bemused, I looked at my Senior VCO, Subedar Attar Singh who was nodding vigorously and mumbling apologies for having loaned the ladder to the neighbouring unit. He promised to have it back by Monday morning for inspection by the Adjutant. That seemed to settle the matter for the time being, but I could not, for the life of me, fathom why I had never seen this ladder. After the inspection, I enquired from the Subedar as to where this ladder was generally kept in the Company lines. He vaguely pointed in different directions and assured me that the ladder would be produced before next Monday. Although I had full faith in Subedar Attar Singh's quiet efficiency, this assurance of his did not fully resolve my doubts.

I arrived in Company lines very early on Monday morning, still doubtful of the Subedar's ability to produce the afore mentioned contraption, when, lo and behold, there in front of me stood a ladder with 'MES' embossed on it in bold letters! I rushed off to bring the Adjutant to have a look at the ladder, and inwardly admired the efficiency and acumen of my senior VCO. The inventory had now been fully checked and was correct and so we were declared the 'winners' of the competition, and there was jubilation in the Company all around.

Within an hour, I was sent for by the Adjutant and shown a report from Brigade Headquarters that noted that a ladder was missing from the MES yard. Could it be, he gently enquired, the same ladder that had been produced that morning? I was aghast at such a suggestion and argued that since there was a ten-foot high expanded-metal barbed-wire fence around the MES Yard, only the Gods could have lifted such a heavy ladder over the fence and carried it to the unit lines, half a mile away, through an area being guarded by neighbouring units at night! I ventured to suggest that it might be a case of misappropriation on the part of the MES themselves, or a wrong entry in their register. I averred that our ladder had been with us ever since we arrived at Razmak and that it was unfortunate that on the day of the Inspection, it had been loaned by my senior VCO to the neighbouring unit without my permission.

Later, I was informed by Subedar Attar Singh (who could tell a lie with the straightest of faces that I have ever seen) that he personally directed the 'operation' and stole the ladder out of the MES yard! As an aside, I might mention, that at the outbreak of the Second World War, in 1939, Subedar Attar Singh became Subedar Major of our newly raised 6th Battalion and rose to the rank of Honorary Captain before retirement after the war. In 1971, after my retirement, I went to visit him in his village near Amritsar. He was living the life of a normal villager, but now had a stub where his left leg had been. It had apparently been amputated as a result of some incurable abscess on his left foot.

Major Field wearing a turban at Razmak.

Capt Baghel Singh at Razmak.

Author out on Column with Signal Platoon.

While in Razmak, in addition to Road Protection Duty, which came to the lot of the battalion twice in the week, we carried out, as the Razmak Brigade, three columns, in which encounters with the tribesmen were inevitable. In fact, this was part of the training of troops. The first was a limited column to the local villages behind the neighbouring feature known as 'Dun' which overlooked the camp at Razmak, and provided the local tribesmen tree and brush-wood cover till they were well within the rifle-range of the camp. The residents of the Razmak Camp were regularly sniped at from that direction, in spite of the presence of a picket in the vicinity. This picket itself often became the target of the snipers, and this despite the fact that it could call for artillery fire from the Garrison-post-gun, located on a mound, in the centre of the camp. These 'fire-works', as we called them, were sometimes less and sometimes more.

To counter this menace, it was decided to take out a column from Razmak Garrison to punish the villages located behind 'Dun'. So a column of three truncated battalions (as some elements from each battalion had to be left behind to man the perimeter of Razmak) from the Garrison was taken out in October, 1938, after our battalion - the 5/11th Sikh - had comfortably settled in at Razmak. I was the Signal Officer of the battalion at the time and distinctly remember two things about this column. Firstly, this was the first time that a portable wireless set had been issued to the battalion and that as soon as we entered the brush-wood area on the hilly feature it stopped working. Secondly, for the first time, we had with us, from the signal stores, a gadget known as a 'Popham Panel', for communicating with aircraft of the Indian Air Force. The 'Panel' consisted of a big sheet of black-canvas, with a large white arrow on it, covered with flaps, and three or four, white rounds of canvas. The 'Panel' was meant to be displayed in an open space, so as to be easily visible to the pilots of the aircraft. The arrow was meant to show the direction of the enemy assemblage, and roundels were to be displayed to the left of the 'Panel', each indicating a distance of 400 yards - altogether a very primitive affair. But, it must be remembered that at the time there was no other way of contacting pilots in the air. The aircraft, too, were vintage - 'Wapities', I think. They were double-winged, and without any bomb-racks, as there were no air-bombs, as such. The pilots were expected to throw a basketful of hand-grenades from the air on the enemy assembled in an area. The Wapiti just had one, small-arms, frontal gun, to engage the enemy.

On this column, we were allotted a section (two guns) of 3.7 in. mountain guns, in support. I still remember the Battery Commander of the guns, by the name of Courtney (an Englishman, as at the time no Indians were enlisted as gunner-officers), as he was attached, for meals, to our Battalion Officers' Field Mess. He was a huge man - both in height and width - and I remember that he insisted on paying double the messing-charges, as, he said, he did, in his own Battery Mess. What an honest man, he was! Another thing I remember of this column is that for a better haul - alive or dead - the tribesmen preferred an English body to an Indian one. Thus whenever a British battalion was out on a column, the tribesmen used to regard it as easy prey, and would assemble against it, in hordes, to the beat of a drum. And, invariably, the battalion had to be extricated out of trouble by a counter-attack by an Indian unit accompanying the column. Consequently, our men used to say: "Why take a British unit with the column at all?"

The second column that Razmak Garrison undertook was to the valley of Nahakki village; while the third went to the village of Patti, in an entirely different valley. I must say something about this last column, as it taught me a lesson, to be remembered throughout my service. And this happened with my own battalion - the 5/11th Sikh - the battalion that had earned a great name for itself amongst the tribesmen, for bravery and steadfastness, and was, thus, feared by them. We issued with this column from Dosali, a built-up camp, which was the Headquarters of the Frontier Scouts. It was one marching-stage short of Razmak. The earlier stage of advance to Patti village was not expected to be opposed by the tribesmen, and the Gurkha Battalion, in the column, was detailed to picket the earlier route during the hours of darkness. Very early in the morning, my battalion, the 5/11th Sikhs, was to take over from them for further advance. I, being the Signal Officer, was marching ahead of the Battalion convoy in the company of my Commander's party, protected by a section escort from the battalion. We were marching along a 'kutcha' road, with the battalion following us, by Companies in columns of four, each led by its respective Company Commander. The morning was intensely dark, and except for the soft sound of the footfalls of the marching men, there was dead silence. Only a moment ago, some men had been seen, surreptitiously moving on the skyline of a neighbouring hill and were taken by some of our men to be the enemy. Therefore, the general atmosphere in the marching-column was most tense. At this moment, a Gurkha Commanding Officer and his party, got up from the side of the road to hand over to the Commanding Officer of the Sikhs. The Sikh soldiers in the Escort Section, who were moving ahead with their bayonets fixed, mistook them for the enemy and went for them, with their bayonets. In trying to stop them from doing so, there was a certain amount of commotion, shouting and shuffling of feet in the Sikh CO's party. This, no doubt, gave the impression to the marching column behind that the CO's party was under attack. Their reaction was, therefore, instantaneous and in a flash they left the road and scampered to the left of the road, to take shelter behind the rocks to save themselves. This I suppose is the normal reaction of human beings when suddenly confronted with a risk to their lives. You may call it 'the fear of the unknown'. But the fault lay with their Commanders, who had not briefed them as to what to expect. There was certainly a lesson to be learnt here. If they had been told of the plan of picketing, and that somewhere on the way our battalion required to take over from the Gurkhas, this instant panicky reaction would not have taken place.

Upon taking over, my CO asked me to get the leading Company Commander. But when I walked back I found that there was not a soul on the road. I was wondering what had happened and called out to the leading Company Commander. For some time there was no response, and then slowly, upon being told that all was well, the marching column fell-in onto the road. They were so ashamed that no one was willing to say what had happened. I recalled at once the maxim: (attributed to the great Captain, Napoleon Bonaparte), "The moral is to the physical as three is to one". I would say, from my own experience, "as five is to one". It was nothing but the 'fear of the unknown' that had caused this debacle with those known as the bravest of the brave. I did learn a great lesson that day: to always brief your men as to what to expect, especially during the hours of darkness.

When I got my first three months leave in Razmak, in the month of November, 1938, I decided, as promised, to spend the first month with Captain and Mrs Khanolkar at the Centre at Naushera. I was keen to learn more about Vedanta from Mrs Khanolkar, who had already given me a few lessons. What I ended up learning was much more and this included the remarkable life story of Mrs Khanolkar, leading to her decision to marry the man who was now her husband.

Mrs Khanolkar's father, at the time of her birth, was a librarian at the League of Nation's library in Geneva. She was the first child of her parents, and as luck would have it, lost her mother at the time of her birth and was thus brought up by her father. He put her in a boarding school which was located on the sea-coast. Parents used to come and visit their children on holidays, but in her case only her father came as she had no mother now. How she missed her! She would sit for hours next to the sea and cry for her mother. She would imagine that the sea-waves were the bosom of her mother and loved to loll on the waves for she felt as if her mother was holding her. Now being a librarian's child, she had every opportunity to read books from her father's library, and somehow she found herself drawn to reading books about India - the 'golden-sparrow' beyond the seas. She learnt that Indians were mostly vegetarian, observed fasts and so on, and since she began to identify so much with the India she read about she herself became a vegetarian, and would not eat eggs or meat any more. She showed me the series of drawings she had made in school. In the first one she had drawn herself carrying a bundle of all her belongings on her shoulder, and going to a pawn-shop to exchange them for a boat. In the second, she was launching the boat in the sea and heading for an unknown country called India. In the third drawing, she had jumped from the boat and was playing with the waves imagining them to be the bosom of her mother. In the fourth, she was uncertain as to what direction to take out at sea, as she had never been to India. In the fifth and final one, she returned to school, disappointed. And that's where the series ended.

One summer, her father took her for a holiday to the Riviera. In the afternoon, after they had enjoyed a picnic on the beach, her father took a stroll and returned to say that since she always talked so much about India, he would show her some real Indians whom he had just met on the beach. The first Indian that she saw in the group, who were taking a break from their course at Sandhurst, England, was Khanolkar. She caught hold of his arm and said: "I love your country; I want to go there; I wish to write to you to know more about your country; therefore, you must give me your address in England." And that's how they started corresponding with each other. Khanolkar returned to India, after doing his course at Sandhurst, and was posted to the 5th Battalion of the Sikh Regiment at Aurangabad. Soon after, he got a letter from Switzerland asking him to meet a certain ship at Bombay. Thus they met again in Bombay and decided to get married. After marriage, Khanolkar brought her to Aurangabad. As already mentioned, she was the first Indian wife in station, and because of her efforts to study Sanskrit and speak Hindustani became very popular amongst us Indians.

I was looked after by the Khanolkars not as a guest but as one of the family. Mrs Khanolkar had a set routine; she would get up early in the morning and walk on the bedewed grass of the Bungalow, barefoot, plucking flowers for her prayer-room, which she showed me the very first day I arrived. It was a cosy room, with a cushioned seat, upon which she sat. She would first sit and meditate, through an 'Ishta' - a stone-statue of her Guru - for about an hour, and then sing a few religious songs to the accompaniment of her sitar for another hour, and then retire to bed. She taught me how to meditate. The technique she employed involved drawing a small black dot on a white sheet of paper, and then sitting comfortably, concentrating on this dot till it disappeared from your sight, and you felt that you were looking at a blank sheet of paper. You could increase the size of the dot, and again meditate until this also disappeared. Finally, you reached a stage when you used a blank sheet of paper and this too disappeared when you meditated. This was the stage of 'samadhi', when you were lost to this world and were in unison with the next world. Well, I tried my best, but I could not reach that stage! Mrs Khanolkar told me that even if she could sometimes get into the stage of 'samadhi' for only a moment, after many hours of meditation, she felt the happiest person for the next 24 hours! Come winter or summer, and in spite of her social obligations - dinner parties and so on - she would excuse herself from whatever she was doing and at 5 minutes to eleven o'clock at night she would go into her prayer-room. And I admired her for it. I stayed with the Khanolkars for a full month, and then went home to spend the rest of my leave there.

As I have already mentioned, during the period of our stay at Razmak, we took part in three real Columns, as they used to be called; one to the Dun feature, another to the Nahakki area and the third from Dosali Camp, to the village of Patti. It was a great experience to go on these columns, as they were mini-wars, and you learnt a lot; and naturally suffered some casualties.

During our stay at Razmak, the battalion had earned quite a name, to the extent that the Pathans hesitated to challenge us on the road during our return journey from Razmak to Bannu. From there, we first returned to Quetta, preparatory to going abroad, and were lodged in the hutments-camp, about seven miles from the station. On the way to this camp, we passed through, what they called, 'Kitchener's Folly', a set of complete cantonment buildings, which were built during the First World War, but had to be abandoned due to lack of water. Ironically, later, a whole stream of 'cruses' (as they were called in the local lingo) were discovered flowing beneath the Cantonment area, but by then it was too late, as the buildings had already crumbled!

We utilised our time in this camp preparing for the War, which we were earmarked for. The emphasis was on physical fitness and it is my firm belief that physical fitness of a soldier contributes 90 per cent to his military efficiency. One last thing we all decided to do before leaving for the field area was to wear, for dinner in the Mess, our Battalion Mess Kit - monkey-jacket, over-all, with calf-boots and spurs, etc. That evening the Mess was decorated with all its silver trophies, silver-ware and cut glass, so that we could have a formal dinner in style for the last time before the Mess Kit was packed and left behind. It was altogether a very festive and scintillating occasion for us all. From now on, because of the War, we would be feeding in the Field Mess, and would eat in our field uniforms.

9

THE SECOND WORLD WAR

Bound for Malaya

The battalion left Quetta, by train through Punjab, on or about the 1st of April 1939. I was commanding at the time a (Majha) Company, and the Commanding Officer feared that some of the men might desert. Sentries used to be posted at the door of each compartment and the Commanding Officer would walk up-and-down the train, enquiring from the sentries if anything was afoot, while we slept soundly in our compartment. The reason was that by now we were all Indian officers who were commanding Companies, and we had established a bond with the men, who had given their word to us that they would not desert! Our confidence in the men who had pledged their commitment was something which the British officers found hard to accept and so they were always suspicious. I am happy to say that our position was vindicated as not a soul deserted while the train was passing through the whole of Punjab.

I might mention here that unlike us Indians, the British officer, whether commanding a battalion or its company (of Indian troops) was completely dependant on the reports submitted to him regarding men

Officers, including Author, at Madras before leaving for World War II.

Author and Capt Hassan.

Capts Gurmeet, Hassan, Baghel and Macdonald.

under his command. These were often doctored to please him, whereas we had the advantage of being able to converse directly in Punjabi with the men and thus had a better assessment of their needs. This is why time and again I have recommended the elimination of the rank of the JCO in Indianised units of whatever arm (see appendix F), as this is a legacy from the days of the British which has become an anachronism.

A Medical Officer, Captain Sahibzada, joined the battalion at Madras. He belonged to the area of Jhang in Punjab. He spoke the Jhung dialect with great fluency and since it was slightly different from the Punjabi normally spoken, he became the centre of attraction! While sitting on the upper-deck of the ship well into the night, Sahibzada used to regale us with his ribald and rustic stories, straight from the rural heartland of Jhung. He soon became extremely popular, both with the officers and other ranks of the battalion. He was a good physician too and we all had confidence in him.

We embarked on a passenger-ship, at the port of Madras, and here again, the Commanding Officer feared that some men might refuse to embark and asked us, Company Commanders, to be vigilant and make suitable security arrangements. But, once again, we took the men at their word and there was no trouble! Captain Baghel Singh, a very fine officer, who had somehow fallen foul of the Commanding Officer left us here for home before we embarked for war. Till then, we had no knowledge of our destination - whether the Middle-East or Malaya. The Captain of the ship had been given a secret envelope which was to be opened only after we had travelled for 24 hours on the sea, bearing south. There was at the time a fear that a German submarine was in the area and so our ship was escorted by two destroyers of the British Navy. When the secret letter was opened, the ship turned east and that is how we came to know at once that our destination was Malaya!

We anchored outside the port of Singapore after a few days at sea without having suffered any mishap, and I remember that Major General Barstow of the 2nd Sikh Battalion, who was now commanding a Division in Malaya, came on-board to meet us. But we were not part of his Division; we were ordered to join 22nd Brigade, up-country. We left Singapore by train for our interim station near the town of Ipoh.

Here we were lodged in temporary hutments. For the first few days, before the Field Mess could be set up in hutments, we fed at a local restaurant and here, for the first time, we heard the Chinese serving us, speak 'pidgin' English, which sounded very funny! It was not long before we made our abode in the hutments, especially built for a battalion of troops. The hutments included a place for the Officers' Mess and cubicles for housing individual officers. Each officer's cubicle had a list of articles provided, such as a mattress, a pillow and a 'Dutch-wife'. In the beginning we could not understand what a 'Dutch-wife' meant, until we were told that it consisted of a 'gowda', meant to be held between the knees while asleep, so as to keep the groin well ventilated in a tropical climate!

The town of Ipoh was not very far from our camp, just about a couple of kilometres away. Ballroom dancing was very popular amongst the populace. What we found peculiar to the place, in fact to the whole of Malaya, was what they called, taxi-dancing. There was a tin-shed hall near every town or town-ship, with a wooden dancing-floor, where Western-style ballroom dancing, with a band, would go on till midnight. This was the entertainment, in which every common man would take part. It was called 'taxi-dancing', because there were 'taxi-dancing' girls sitting around the dance-floor on chairs and you could pick your dance partner from amongst these girls, after buying a ticket and presenting it to her. The band played tunes - may be fast or slow foxtrot, slow or fast waltz, or a tango - for a set period of time, and if you felt like another dance, you had to buy another ticket, and, perhaps, choose another 'taxi-dancer'! The band called it a day at exactly midnight, and, generally, their last tune used to be : 'After the ball is over; after the break of dawn'.

Wherever we were in Malaya, whether on the march, or in camp, because of Japanese air supremacy, the digging of slit-trenches against air attacks, was the order of the day. But we faced two handicaps nearer the coast-line: the slit trenches used to fill up with water when the tide rose; and secondly, they were a trap for the ever so common snakes in the tropics. We knew from experience, that good ninety per cent of the snakes were non-poisonous, but the fear of them was universal. Whenever there were enemy air raids, the men would rush to their trenches where many would get bitten by snakes. Orders were to kill the snake that had bitten you so as to determine its lethality. But seldom would it satisfy the man bitten by a snake that his bite was harmless. There were cobras also in the tropics, the most famous being the 'king-cobra'. Our jungle patrols used to tell us stories of how a king-cobra would dominate a track, or an area, and would not let anybody pass that way. I have seen a king-cobra only in a zoo. It was nearly thirty-five feet long! Besides, in the jungles of Malaya there were pythons galore that one had to be careful of.

I should now like to relate an interesting incident in Malaya that occured before the war started. The Maharaja of Patiala, Yadavindra Singh, visited the battalion at Kuanton. A luncheon was arranged for him in the Officers' Field Mess. We had a very good Goanese cook, by the name of D'Souza, who had been with us for a long time in his civilian capacity. Before we came to Malaya on field-service, he had been made an NCE (Non-Combatant Enrolled), and this brought him under military law. His trouble was that he liked his drink too much and used to get 'sozzled' occasionally, especially when he was most needed! Once he was brought to us by the local military police, having been found lying in a coma-like state in a gutter in the town, next to the liquor shop, with a bag of live chickens (which he had been sent to buy) lying next to him. Therefore, not to take any chances, the PMC, Major Brown, promised the cook a bottle of whisky, but only after the luncheon party was over! In fact, he put a bottle in the kitchen next to him, and at the same time, arranged for a guard to be ready at hand, so as to teach him a lesson. He was to put him in the clink, immediately after the luncheon was over and the chief-guest had departed! So, instead of being handed over the bottle, Mr D'Souza was put under arrest and pushed into a cell, already occupied by Sepoy Basta Singh. Now, Basta Singh was a habitual offender in the battalion and spent most of his time in this cell, which was a temporary structure, built of timber, with little ventilation. Towards the middle of the night, the air in the cell must have become oppressive for D'Souza felt suffocated, and started knocking at the door, calling for the sentry to open it. Basta Singh, who was asleep on the floor, felt disturbed by this pounding and shouted out; "Oh, Barue kiun matha marden; Kade Jailan de darwaza vi khule ne - chup karke paija, te mainu vi saun de", (Oh, nincompoop, why are you knocking your head against a wall;

have the doors of jails ever opened by knocking on them? Go to sleep quietly, and let me also sleep). So there was no question of the door opening! How Mr D'Souza spent the rest of the night in the cell, nobody knows. Out early the next morning, he was seen, in his pith-hat, hoeing the grass next to the Quarter Guard, along with Basta Singh, with a sentry standing guard. They were engaged in, what is commonly called, 'fatigue', meant for prisoners. But, lest you underestimate the potential of these two personalities: Sepoy Basta Singh proved to be a very brave soldier, later on, in a bayonet charge against the Japanese in which he was severely wounded; while Mr D'Souza ended up as the main-'khansama' in the kitchen of Netajee Subhash Chandra Bose, the Supreme Commander of the Indian National Army in Malaya!

The Vickers Barthier (VB) Gun, a replacement for the Lewis Gun, and the Sten (Browni) were issued to us, for the first time, in Malaya, together with a wireless set No 31, just before the war with the Japanese began, in 1940. The same was true for the 3-inch and 2-inch mortars and the anti-personnel mines. No anti-tank mines were issued, as the Japanese were not expected to bring tanks through the jungles of Malaya. There was a macabre joke often told about the anti-personnel mine. While demonstrating the arming of the mine to a cadre, the NCO Instructor (a Havildar from a Local Engineer unit) inserted a live detonator into the mine, instead of the dummy, and blew up the whole class of NCOs from local units! It certainly proved the deadly lethality of the mine! Due to shortage of Bren Guns, we still continued to use Lewis Guns (mounted in twins, on a tripod) as anti-aircraft defence for the airfield at Kuanton, but the weapon always stopped after the first burst and thus proved useless for this purpose.

The Colour Bar in Malaya

One thing that stood out in Malaya, being the colony of the British, was that there was a very strict colour-bar between the white man and the Asiatic; much more than what we had come across in India. Every thing for the white man was exclusive - clubs, swimming pools, buses, railway carriages, and even sheds against rain. These were coloured white for the whites and red for the Asiatics. There was a whiteman's club not very far from our camp, and we always thought that it was because of us Indians (and thus blacks) in the battalion that the British officers with us had not joined the Club. But it was not so, as I shall describe later.

After about a month's stay at Ipoh, we were detailed to move to the east coast of Malaya, to a place called Kuanton. Captain Ranjit Rai, an ICO, was detailed as Commander of the advance party going to Kuanton and he had under him two newly joined British officers. When the advance party under Ranjit Rai arrived at the Ipoh railway station, the local station master, who was, incidentally a South Indian, (I might say here that the railways in Malaya were generally manned by South Indians originally from India) started allotting seats first to the white (British) officers, in the white-coloured carriage, and then to Ranjit Rai in a separate, red-coloured, carriage. Captain Ranjit Rai did not like this a bit and told the station master that it was not his business to allot seats, and that he would do that himself as Commander of the party. He ordered the British officers to travel in the red carriage, and told his orderly to put his bedding in the white carriage. According to the station master, this was all against the rules, and, therefore, he would not start the train. There was an impasse! The station master referred the matter to his British boss in Singapore, who must have referred the matter to the Fortress Commander, the final authority in Malaya, and soon orders came to the station master to let the train go. There were many incidents of this nature when the so-called colour-bar had to be relaxed in view of this new phenomenon of senior Indian officers, who had been recently inducted into Malaya for the war campaign.

I must tell you this story of the colour-bar which has always rankled in my mind. Just about a month before the war started in Malaya, the Raja of Perak, the Malayan State in which we were lodged for the defence of the Peninsula, invited the British officers in Kuanton for a drinks and dinner party to Perak, the capital of his State. Now these Rajas, in Malaya, had the same status and relationship with the British as the Rajas/Maharajas in India, and so the Raja of Perak extended the invitation to the British officers, and British nurses only. But we being an Indianised battalion, had Indians also holding the same position and status (which, I can understand, was perhaps, not known to the local Raja) as the British officers and we expected our

Commanding Officer - Lt Col Parkins - to insist that we also be invited to this party, or else, we expected him to refuse the invitation extended to the British officers alone. On the contrary, Parkins accepted the Raja's invitation and took all the British officers with him to the party and we, Indians, were left behind. What a disappointment! We had never expected this from Colonel Parkins, who was our Commanding Officer. We had always felt that Parkins was a bit of an imperialist, but had never thought him anti-Indian, especially when he had been an Instructor at the Indian Military Academy, Dehradun.

At this juncture, I am inclined to pass an opinion, albeit reluctantly, about Colonel Parkins. I must say at the outset that he was morally and physically a brave man who was always ready to take a risk himself before asking his subordinates to do so. I have seen him standing in the open, with bullets flying around him, ordering his men to attack an enemy position. By nature he was an introvert and extremely secretive. He did not have the courage to tell one off on one's face. I remember an incident in our hutments at Kuanton, when after drinking together in one of their residential cubicles, two young British officers quarrelled among themselves over something and indulged in fisty-cuffs, and all of us, including Colonel Parkins, came to know of it. Instead of sending for these officers in his Office and giving them a 'ticking off', he sent a self-written circular letter, to be signed by all of us, saying that living as we were cheek-by-jowl, we should not allow any unpleasantness to occur amongst us. We called this a 'cheek-by-bowl' epistle, as we were at the time having a little trouble with our field-latrines! As to his introverted nature, even I, as his Adjutant, many a times did not know that he had ordered a certain Company, in the battalion, to carry out an operational task. Although, I must admit that he had a very good tactical sense, and led the battalion well in the Malayan Campaign. He was rumoured to be a misogynist and never married.

The Beginning of the War

It was indeed, strange that the authorities never thought that the Japanese were ever going to attack Malaya. Many British and Commonwealth generals visited us, and gave talks in which they mostly derided the Japanese soldiers as bandy-legged and with poor eye-sight who daren't attack the British! I particularly remember the visit of a New Zealand general who came to talk to us after the defeat of his troops by German para-troopers. He said the same thing about the Japanese! When the Japanese landed and took possession of Indo-China, we were told that that was about their limit, and that they would not dare to come further. There were two floating-aircraft at Singapore - the Catalinas, that used to bring information about the Japanese convoys and landings. When two convoys of ships, escorted by the Japanese Navy, were seen heading out of Indo-China, we were told that they were, perhaps, heading for Thailand but certainly not Malaya. They wouldn't dare! Late in the evening of the 8th of December, 1941, a ship appeared opposite Kuanton on the horizon, with a light on its high-mast. It was seen by the 3rd Garhwal, deployed on the beaches of Kuanton town. Soon, according to the Garhwalis, a line of landing-boats appeared in front of them, and they opened fire with their light-machine guns and beat back the attempt. After half an hour, the light of the ship appeared to turn north, and, it seemed that Japanese troops had landed on an unmanned stretch of beach a few miles north of our position. That evening, Japanese troops had landed at Kota Baru, successfully overcoming opposition put up by a brigade on the beach. They had also landed in a place called Pitani, North of Kota Baru, in territory belonging to Thailand. The strange thing is that despite this a few of the British officers in Kuanton still believed that the Japanese had really intended to land in Thailand and had landing at Kota Baru by mistake. How blind can you be!

By then the unsinkable battle-ship, HMS George V and a Cruiser HMS Repulse - of the British Navy had arrived in Singapore and, it was generally believed, that they would see the Japanese off! We know the fate that these two ships met with in the sea east of Kuanton, when they were proceeding to stop the Japanese landing at Kota Baru. Their demise was mainly due to the fact that there was no air cover from our fighters for them. From our position on the east coast, we heard the sound of battle and saw some unmanned life-boats drift on to the coast.

The fact is that this theatre of war had been given the go-by as far as resources for fighting a war were concerned - while the scanty number of troops there were being fed on make-belief ideas that no war was coming to the Peninsula! The British were too proud of their naval base at Singapore, which, they thought, would scare the Japanese away.

The Peninsula of Malaya was lost because of the poor opinion that the British held of the Japanese soldiers. There is no doubt that the Japanese soldier was brain-washed to die for his country, and that he was ruthless in battle, but this was true of any soldier. I remember the day when the Kuanton Airfield was bombed by the Japanese. Before the war, the crew of the Australian bombers used to brag that they would blow the Japanese to pieces if they ever attempted to land on the Malayan Peninsula, but when they took off from Kuanton on the morning of the 9th to engage the Japanese landing-crafts at Kota Baru, only three out of nine bombers returned, and those too with three wounded crew members. When the Japanese bombers came in a flight of about fifty aircraft to bomb the Kuanton Airfield, on the 10th, the morale of the Australian crew was, as they say, in their boots! In spite of the warning received of their arrival, from the coastal observation post, the Australian crew of Hudson bombers, which had been prepared for take off by the ground staff (all British under a British Squadron Leader), refused to fly. This would have saved them from strafing by the Japanese aircraft. Instead, the Australian crew fled the airfield in a panic. What a poor showing by the Australian airmen! From then on we were busy destroying every thing on the airfield, while previously we had been busy building it up! That afternoon, the Japanese bombers came down on the Kuanton Airfield in flights of nine, bombing and strafing everything on the ground. They set fire to all the aircraft lined up on the airfield ready to take off. Everything was scattered hither and thither. The canteen stores, which had earlier been the envy of Indian troops, were now lying in the open, to be had for the picking! Appropriately, the British Squadron Leader and his boys, who all stayed on the airfield, presented our Company (A Company), which was manning the anti-aircraft Lewis guns on the airfield and had engaged the Japanese aircraft as best they could, the thunder-box of one of the Hudson aircraft which had been destroyed on the ground! I am saying this from first-hand knowledge, as I happened to be at the airfield then, visiting our A Company, who were defending the airfield with twin-mounted Lewis guns, which never worked.

If I were to pass an opinion on the whole of the Malayan Campaign I would say that it was a big fiasco. Some eight airfields had been prepared for occupation, scattered over the whole Peninsula, perfectly well-sighted, provided there had been fighter aircraft to defend them; but these could not be spared for the defence of Malaya. In any case, landings along the entire length of the Peninsula had not been expected from the North. The Japanese troops, on the other hand, made full use of the narrowness of the Peninsula, by getting hold of local 'sampans' (boats) and effected landings, however small, behind the defence-lines and thereby caused panic. They would never attack a defensive position frontally, but instead while demonstrating strength in the front, would always attack from a flank. Besides, they also made full use of small infiltrations behind the lines, so as to interdict (maintenance) convoys. They would fire from flanking trees, at night, along a one-road approach, thereby creating, generally, the impression among their opponents that they had been cut-off from behind! This way they also restricted their casualties while causing greater loss of life to the opposition. They did this time and again in the Malayan Campaign, which was admirably suited for these kinds of tactics. I myself was a victim of one of these ambushes which I will describe later on.

Because of these tactics undertaken by the Japanese, there was a constant demand by higher authorities to withdraw, so as to conform to the general line of withdrawal along the whole Peninsula, there being only one line of communication and a lack of lateral roads. Our troops would constantly complain about these orders for withdrawal when there was no pressure from the enemy. They wanted to see atleast the face of the so-called enemy! We got orders to withdraw from Kuanton as well because there was a likelihood of our being cut-off from behind as the parallel division, from Jitra position, had had to withdraw behind the junction of the lateral road from that front. This would have jeopardised our lines of communication - again a handicap when defending a peninsula with very few longitudinal or lateral roads.

As far as Kuanton was concerned, having landed on the unmanned beaches up north, the Japanese patrols made their way, towards the Kuanton Airfield through the jungle, which was marked on our maps as 'incommunicable by human beings'. Our battalion sent fighting patrols into these so-called 'incommunicable areas', and saw signs of the Japanese patrols having been there, but, on purpose I suppose, they were reluctant to engage our patrols by fire. During this stage, it seemed, they were assembling their forces south of this jungle patch, before they would assault the airfield in strength.

This was the time when, we in Kuanton, were living in a vacuum as far as information about the enemy was concerned. Patrols sent by the Garhwalis towards the beaches to their north were beaten back, with losses. The Japanese Air Force had complete supremacy in the area, and their single reconnaissance aircraft had freedom of action and would engage our vehicles on the road with impunity. In the third week of December, the 2/12 Frontier Force, a battalion which had been part of the Brigade which was defending the beach at Kota Baru, and were dislodged by the Japanese, joined the Brigade at Kuanton. They were at first put on the protection of the lines of communication, and later detailed for the defence of the Kuanton Airfield, relieving A Company of 5 Sikh which came into battalion reserve.

One morning, I think it was in January 1942, a couple of Japanese, with hands raised as if to surrender, assaulted the ferry-post east of the creek, behind the town of Kuanton, manned by 5 Sikh. The latter beat back the attack and held on to the post, but only for about 24 hours, so as to allow 3 Garhwal from the beach (who had by now been completely surrounded by the Japanese) to pass through and proceed to the Brigade lay-back position which was about three miles beyond the airfield, along the single ribbon of a road going to Jeruntut. They were to be followed by 5 Sikh to the same position, as the strength of the Garhwalis had been reduced to about 50 percent, and then the 2/12 Frontier Force on the airfield were to follow. This was planned by our brigade for the afternoon of the 2nd of January.

In our case, although the enemy had managed to penetrate all round, and even behind us, we would have preferred to fight him from prepared defensive positions, rather than being caught on the narrow road behind us.

At the Kuanton Airfield also, the 2/12 Frontier Force were caught unprepared while getting ready to leave. We were waiting in our lay-back position for them to arrive intact, but they never did. What happened, in fact, was that as the battalion had withdrawn its pickets around the airfield, without any sign of the enemy being around, they did not realise that the enemy was waiting for exactly this to happen, and occupied the pickets/barracks as they were vacated. And when the battalion was having its evening meal before leaving the airfield, the enemy from the barracks started lobbing hand-grenades and firing at the men. There could not have been a worse moment of un-preparedness for such an eventuality, and the men had no choice but to run for cover, without their weapons. The Commanding Officer, Lt Col Cummings, got into the nearest weapon-carrier, and along with other British officers who got into the two other weapon-carriers, managed to get out of the inferno. The Japanese had, however, laid an ambush on the road of withdrawal by felling trees. This must have been set up soon after our battalion had passed that stretch of the road. Having thus stopped the carriers, the enemy charged on to the occupants with bayonets, Lt Col Cummings and party fought back and managed to drive the carriers through the obstacle of fallen trees, and reached the lay-back position where our battalion had already arrived. Here, we were waiting for the 2/12 Frontier Force to pass through, as planned. Approach to the airfield, from the main-road, lay through a defile, and soon after the weapon-carriers, with British officers in them, passed through the defile, the invading Japanese fixed a light Machine-gun on the defile and blocked that exist. The battalion was thus boxed in and as none of the other ranks of the battalion could get through the defile they were all captured as prisoners-of-war. This story was told to me by Lt Balwant Singh of the battalion, when I met him later in the prisoners-of-war camp. He railed bitterly against his Commanding Officer, and other British officers, for having left the men in the lurch at a critical juncture. The battalion had suffered quite a few casualties in this action.

On arrival at the lay-back position, which our battalion was holding, the British officers of 2/12 Frontier Force were given a heroes' welcome by the Brigade Commander, Brigadier Painter, and our Commanding Officer, Lt Col Parkins! Lt Col Cummings, the Commanding Officer of the 2/12 Frontier Force, was recommended for and was given the Victoria Cross (the highest award for unprecedented gallantry)! If I had my say, I would have sacked the whole lot of British officers, for dereliction of duty, for they had abandoned their men, and left them in the lurch, at a critical moment. Such were the ways of the British!

A Soldier Remembers

Balwant Singh was of the opinion that had the British officers stayed with the men they could have organised some resistance against the Japanese, who were only a handful in number. Instead, the entire battalion, of over 800 men fell into their hands as prisoners-of-war.

Wounded in Ambush: Evacuated to Alexandra Hospital

The next morning, the 3rd of January, I was sent for by the Brigade Major and asked to reconnoitre the next defensive position for the Brigade that is, what was left of it! I took to the road on a motor-cycle, with my batman, Piyara Singh, in the pillion seat, looking for a suitable place for defence along the road of withdrawal. After examining a position, which I did not like, I proceeded further along the road and fell prey to a Japanese ambush on the road. My head was hit by a splinter of a hand grenade or a mortar for I fell down, with the motor-cycle and the pillion rider, and lost consciousness (this was recounted to me later in the prisoners-of-war camp by Piyara Singh). I came to my senses only seventy-two hours later in Alexandra Hospital in Singapore. By then the surgeon had operated on my head, and put in a silver-plate to cover the gash in my cranium. I was lucky to be alive! From what Piyara Singh told me, the Japanese who had ambushed us had come down from the trees, from where they had lobbed the grenades, and had kicked both of us as we lay face down on the road and finding no response left us presuming we were dead! We were picked up later by a vehicle which was following and first taken to Battalion Headquarters, and then transferred to another vehicle and taken down the road to the road-head at Jeruntut. Before getting there, we had had to cross a ferry, which while being winched across was strafed by Japanese aircraft, and those who could run, left their vehicles, but I lay there unconscious. Although some bullets hit my vehicle, I was unhurt. At Jeruntut railway station, I was attended to by a young captain, a surgeon, who dressed my wound and put me on the train, which also was bombed enroute by Japanese aircraft. Passengers who could run were supposed to have fled the train in a panic, but, of course, since I was still unconscious I knew nothing about it. I am supposed to have been removed from the train on a stretcher, and in so doing the contents of my shift pocket, which contained my identity card, dropped out. This was later handed over to me by the Singapore Intelligence Section, who at one time suspected me of being a spy!

In hospital, I woke up with a start in a room darkened by black curtains, and saw a young girl sitting next to my bed. My first question to her was: "Where am I?", followed by, "What has happened?" and, "Where is my battalion?" I shall never forget her reply, "You tripped over a brick and hurt yourself". While I was resolving this puzzle in my mind, she asked me if I was thirsty, and since I was, she offered me fluid from a small beaker, with a mouth to it. I drank it and went off to sleep again. It must have been a sedative, I suppose. I woke up a few hours later, and this time the girl, who was still sitting next to me, talked to me a little longer. She told me that her name was Miss Lane and that she was the daughter of a serving Lieutenant Colonel, commanding an Indian unit, and that she had saved me! I expressed my gratitude to her for that, but she quickly interjected, "No, not that way. I saved your hair". Apparently the surgeon had wanted to shave my hair while he was operating on my head, but since she knew how much Sikhs valued their hair, as her father was in an Indian unit, she had informed the surgeon accordingly and he had desisted from shaving my hair. I thanked her for this considerate act and went off to sleep again. In this manner, I was slowly brought to consciousness for longer and longer periods in this dark room. It must, I suppose, have been part of the recovery process. The surgeon also dropped in occasionally to find out how I was progressing. After being in the dark room for about two days, I felt fully conscious for the first time, and then they moved me to a double-bedded ward, but kept me on a hard board. Having been unconscious for 72 hours with a serious gash in my cranium, it may indeed be said that I had returned from the threshold of death! I remember feeling as if I had woken up from a deep sleep. I have the memory of a pleasing pink-haze in the sky; a kind of a glow, and I truly felt contented with life. I must confess to not having encountered any lovely fairies or demons, as mentioned in our scriptures! On waking up, my greatest surprise, of course, was at my transformation. From being clad in a dirty and soot-laden uniform in the field I was now dressed in silk pyjamas, bearing the monogram of the hospital on them, and for head wear I had snow-white bandages!

The British girl attending on me stayed almost permanently with me for the first few days. Many a time, during the day, an air raid

A Soldier Remembers

siren would sound, and patients who could move, would go down into a shelter made for this purpose. But since I could not be moved from the wooden board on the bed on which I lay, on hearing the air raid sirens this girl used to run upto me, pull a chair near my bed and sit by my side, all the time assuring me that there was nothing to fear. She had no thought for her own safety. In spite of my repeatedly asking her to leave me and go down to the shelter; she never did. And she was only a voluntary nurse. What a brave girl, so conscious of her duty! My impression is that you will find this only among the British.

The ward I had been shifted into was meant for serious cases that needed medical attention all the time. Soon, a young boy, wounded upcountry in his groin by a mortar shell, was laid out in the bed next to mine. When we started talking, I discovered that he was a newly recruited officer from the 2nd Battalion of the Argyll and Sutherland Highlanders, the unit with which I had done a year's attachment some years ago. I found that he was in a bad way, as gangrene had set into his wound and a foul smell emanated from it. He was clearly in the last stage of his suffering. Many a time, he would mention to me, in what seemed a dream-like state, how much he loved his parents and his young sister, how they used to play together, and how much he would miss not seeing them again. What a tragedy war is! He was soon removed from the ward, and I was told that he passed away the next morning.

The next day I had a new neighbour. He mentioned that he was a fighter-pilot who had parachuted and landed on a tree, from where he had had to be rescued. The doctors had insisted on having an x-ray taken, though, according to him, he had suffered no injury. The x-ray had, however, revealed that he had suffered a contusion to his chest. According to him this was an old injury and so though he was in the Emergency Ward he spent most of his time wandering about. It was only when the doctor came on his morning rounds that he would lie in bed. Sometimes he would feel like having a glass of beer and had worked out an arrangement with the medical orderly (a Britisher), who would bring the glass of beer for him from the canteen, covered in a piss-pot napkin, marked with a red-cross! Early in the morning, he would go and have a shower in the common bathroom, and yet when the nurses came later in the morning he would lie down in bed and have a sponge-bath from them! He was clearly having a wonderful holiday and stayed on in the ward for almost four days before asking for a discharge from the Hospital.

One morning, I think it was the 8th of January, one of the medical attendants mistakenly brought me a cable, addressed to Major Malwinder Singh, from his wife, informing him that a son had been born to them. I knew Malwinder well as we had both been in the same battalion, though lately he had been transferred to the Royal Indian Service Corps. I knew that he was somewhere in Malaya, although I had not met him yet. I had also been told by my elder brother, whose unit, the Jind Infantry was on the Island of Singapore, and who had come to see me at Alexandra Hospital, that Malwinder had been wounded during the Slim river disaster and was reportedly missing. He would never receive the happy news about the birth of a son to him in India. Another of those tragedies of life! Thank God, I was not married then! I later learnt more about what happened to Malwinder in the prisoners-of-war camp. Being an RIASC officer at the time, he was responsible for supplies to the Indian division deployed well in the rear, in an echelon position, just forward of the river Slim in Malaya. The Divisional Headquarters were located in a rubber estate, besides the main road, just beyond the river. On the afternoon of the 4th of January, Malwinder decided to visit the Divisional Headquarters of the division that he was responsible for, and arrived there in his station wagon towards the evening of the 4th. There he met some friends, who insisted that he should spend the night with them, and he agreed. The division was well behind the front-line and it was all peaceful there. Early on the morning of the 5th of January, for the first time, the Japanese brought their tanks on to the main road, and started advancing with them. The tanks, which we later saw on the Island of Singapore, were mere tin-boxes. However, their first appearance in Malaya, created panic in the forward-line of the troops defending the Peninsula. There was a call for the Indian division forward of the river Slim to be on the alert, and Malwinder departed in his station wagon driving along the 'kutcha' road of the rubber estate. As his station wagon came on to the main road, his driver saw a Japanese tank blocking the road in front of them. The Japanese tank had halted there as the bridge in front had been blown up by the detachment of the Royal Engineers, prematurely, I should say, for the forward troops were still ahead of the bridge and, besides, the railway bridge adjacent to the road bridge had already been blown up - as a result of the scorched-earth policy of the British forces. As he saw the tank, the driver of the station wagon swerved to the right in an attempt to return the way he had come. In doing so, he exposed Malwinder, sitting next to him in the front seat, broad-side to the tank. The tank fired two bursts that hit Malwinder in the groin. The driver managed to turn the station wagon away onto the road leading to the rubber estate and out of sight of the tank. He helped Malwinder down from the vehicle and tried to comfort him but Malwinder who was badly hurt and bleeding profusely asked to be left alone. A truck driven by an Indian Army driver appeared on the scene and offered to transport casualties to Kuala Lumpur, that is away from the blown-up bridge. However, Malwinder was in no position to walk upto the truck and he asked his driver to go and leave him alone. And that was the last that was seen, or heard, of Malwinder.

After about a month's stay in Alexandra Hospital, I was transferred to another hospital on the Island, as there was a rush of war-casualties to be accommodated. By now, the mainland of Malaya had been evacuated by our troops, the naval base in the north of the Island had been abandoned and the causeway to the mainland had been blown up. It was learnt that the Japanese forces had landed in the northwest of the Island, in the sector held by the Australians, and were heading towards the town of Singapore, along the Bukitima Road. The Japanese, it seemed, had brought heavy guns and were shelling Singapore. The shells could be heard whistling past over-head. On 10th morning, a party of Japanese soldiers entered the hospital and started shooting in all directions. The hospital staff and patients had no choice but to leave, crouching for safety along drainage-channels lined with bricks.

10

SURRENDER TO THE JAPANESE

In this way, I escaped to the town of Singapore, where the Fortress Headquarters was supposed to be located. My idea was to report to the 2nd echelon of the Headquarters, but when I arrived there it was empty as all military personnel had been mobilised for the last-ditch battle for the Island. I had no choice but to spend the night on the floor of the verandah of the building. It was a night full of noises as there was wide spread looting and intermittent fighting going on in the streets of the town. During the day, Japanese aircraft had a free run of the city, bombing and strafing whatever they saw. On the 14th, orders were issued to households and shops to pour all liquor into the drains, or the sea, so that it would not be available to the invading Japanese Army, and very soon, the whole city smelt of liquor. I decided to leave my sanctuary and go out into the open, to a lawn in one of the city squares. There I laid my bed against a small white hut that sheltered an electric transformer. On the morning of, the 16th of February, Japanese aircraft scattered pamphlets that stated that the surrender of the city had taken place and that Indian prisoners-of-war should assemble at Tyrsal Park, a race-course near the town. British and Australian prisoners-of-war were ordered to surrender at Changi Jail, situated at the eastern corner of the Island of Singapore, involving a march of more than ten miles. The prisoners-of-war were further instructed to carry only haversacks containing provisions for daily use. I still suffered from headaches, sometimes unbearable, but luckily I had a small bottle of aspirin tablets with me and I would occasionally take one to relieve the pain, as advised by the doctor. I decided to walk towards Tyrsal Park, following a stream of uniformed men. Just before arrival at the Grand Stand of the Race Course, where we were supposed to assemble, I met a Sikh Havildar who had a band with the letter F, in red, on his left arm. I asked him what it meant, and he replied: "Don't you know I am a free-man; I belong to the Indian National Army!" At that time I knew nothing about the Indian National Army and so I was rather puzzled.

At the rendezvous, I tried to look for my elder brother, Lieutenant Colonel Gurbakhsh Singh, commanding the Jind Infantry, who I knew would also be there. I spotted him soon enough with all his officers. The men had collected in the rear and the officers were sitting in front, on the ground. There was a lot of activity on the Grand Stand, and people were talking about Mohan Singh and the Indian National Army that he had raised. As Mohan Singh was well known to me from my days at the Military Academy, and I had even met him before the War at Ipoh, my brother asked me to go up to him and ask him what all the talk was about. So I climbed the steps of the Grand Stand, and who do I see but Major Mahabir Singh Dhillon, in his uniform, guarding the door to a small room where Mohan Singh was supposed to be. He asked me what I wanted and on being told that I wished to see Mohan Singh asked me if I had an appointment with him. I said, "No, but, surely, I do not need an appointment to see him! He is my friend." He replied, "No, you cannot see him without an appointment; and I am his Military Secretary". I was aghast and returned to my brother without seeing Mohan Singh.

Soon, a British Officer, Lieutenant Colonel Lunt (I am not sure of the name) spoke to us over the microphone from the Grand Stand, while we officers sat on the grass with our men behind us. He spoke in English, on behalf of his Majesty the King and the British Government, and formally handed us over as prisoners-of-war to the

Japanese Government. After him, we were addressed by a Japanese Major General who, speaking in English, handed us over to General Mohan Singh of the Indian National Army! Mohan Singh, whom I had known as a Captain, had overnight become a General! He now spoke to us and enjoined all prisoners-of-war to join the Indian National Army the purpose of which was to free India from the shackles of the British Raj, with the help of the Japanese. This received a tremendous response from the men at the back, but the response from the officers, sitting in front, was rather subdued and a bit cautious. Mohan Singh noticed this and remarked that the officers sitting in front perhaps did not realise that he had the power of life and death over them. If they did not behave, he could have their badges of rank removed and they would then be treated as ordinary sepoys!

He wound up his speech by ordering us to move to the Bidadari hutment camp next door where we were to make ourselves comfortable. There we would hear more from him, till such time, however, the officers were debarred from talking to their men. The latter, therefore, moved off to the camp under their JCOs while the officers went to Bidadari Camp separately. Prithipal, Sahibzada, Gupta, and I, the only officers from 5 Sikh, attached ourselves to my brother's Jind Infantry, as my brother had his officers' mess, with a week's rations and with mess helpers, all intact. The mess staff was ordered to prepare the evening meal for all of us. So, at the very beginning, we were well provided for. However, the attempt by all prisoners-of-war, was to collect as many edible items as possible for the leaner days that lay ahead. Thus scrounging for provisions became our first priority. But first there is a story to be told.

While all of us Indians collected at Tyrsal Park, as ordered, Dargalkar (a KCIO) and Budwar (an ICO) of the Cavalry Regiment, chose to march all the way to Changi Jail to surrender as prisoners-of-war there, as they considered themselves British officers. I believe, they lined up with the British officers and when the Japanese officer-in-charge found out that they were Indians he slapped them on their faces (as was their custom) and ordered them to march back to Bidadari Camp. They arrived at our camp, a couple of days later, thirsty and famished, with their tongues almost hanging out, and the first thing they asked for was water. We fed them a meal and kept them with us.

It is a common saying in Punjabi (which they both spoke) that you may burn a string, but it never loses its twists! Fancy, considering themselves British! They were to get into trouble with the Japanese once again, for a similar reason, which I will describe later.

11
PRISONER-OF-WAR

The Indian National Army

Propaganda for enlistment into the Indian National Army started soon enough. We were very often asked to assemble in the open, sit on the bare ground, and listen to Mohan Singh harangue us about his plans for freeing India from the yoke of the British. Each time he spoke to us, we could not fail to notice the Japanese Intelligence Officer, Major Fujiwara, standing behind him, like a menacing poker! Besides, members of the Indian National Army's propaganda teams, under Major Mahabir Singh Dhillon, would also address us on the finer and useful aspects of the Indian National Army and on the sincerity of the Japanese. Knowing Dhillon well, I would always get up and ask him questions about the conduct of the Japanese in Manchuria and China. Dhillon would feel embarrassed at these questions, and each time I did this, my elder brother, who usually sat next to me on these occasions would pull me down. He later advised me not to ask any questions but to listen to what they had to say; for, he said, besides the fact that they had the power of life and death over us, they would never listen to reason. He was right and I respected his advice.

To show us the contrast between the life of the Indian National Army personnel and the prisoners-of-war, they placed an Indian National Army unit in barracks opposite the Bidadari Camp, and while we would be lined up by the Japanese as a working party ready to be marched off to work, with a handful of boiled rice as our day's ration, tied up in a piece of cloth and slung over the shoulder, the INA personnel, in the opposite camp, would be doing their morning PT, with hot tea and puries waiting for them at the end of it! But, it had little effect on us, as we had accepted our fate, and decided to remain prisoners-of-war. We were at first used to clean the town of Singapore. This task was, in a way, a blessing for us, as I, for one, was able to collect, free of cost, a big bottle of aspirin tablets for my head injury from a Chemist shop that had been hit from the air by the Japanese, scattering medicines all over the place!

As a young man, I had always felt that good handwriting was a great asset in life, and bad handwriting a great handicap. In my case, my English handwriting was not so bad in school, but when I went to Government College, Lahore, and took up pre-medical subjects, it deteriorated. The reason was that there were no set text books those days in biology, chemistry or physics, and the students were required to take copious notes of whatever the professors had to say on these subjects in the class room. As a convenience, I adopted a free style of writing. For example any word that ended with 'ing' became a straight line, followed by a wriggle for 'g'. And this is how I spoiled my handwriting.

I had always wanted to learn the touch-system of typing to make up for my bad handwriting. Under the Japanese regime in Singapore, so as to be clear of any guilt, the populace had discarded all sorts of articles, such as radios, radiograms (this by order of the Japanese) and in some cases even type-writers at crossroads. So, while engaged by the Japanese, immediately after the war, to clean the streets of Singapore, I got an opportunity to collect two things, namely, a wireless set - His Master's Voice which worked both with a 6-volt battery and electricity - and a typewriter (a Remington, with all the knobs on its keys missing!). As they say, beggars can't be choosers! Little did I realise at the time that both these items would hold me in good stead later as a prisoner-of-war. As I shall describe later, the presence of this wireless set and our ability to listen to news from the BBC, was a great morale booster for us during our days in captivity.

In addition to the wireless set and the typewriter, another discovery I made during this cleaning campaign, which took us all around the city, and which was not supervised by the Japanese, was a building that contained our B-Echelon heavy baggage. It seemed that an attempt had been made to loot the building, and the Japanese authorities had, therefore, put a sentry on guard. It was my intention to recover from the baggage that was stored there our religious book – the Guru Granth Sahib - and 'keertan' equipment. Therefore, to get access to this building, I managed to get a letter from the Japanese officer in charge of our working party, written in Japanese, to the effect that I might be allowed entry into this building. The reason I gave to the Japanese officer was that as we were a very religious people, the Sikh prisoners-of-war were reluctant to eat their food in the absence of their holy book. Fortunately, since the Japanese officer himself was very religious, he accepted this plea. We had trucks driven by our own men which were deputed to carry debris away from the town, and I took one of these trucks with me to this building. I was allowed to enter, and on the first day, I collected the religious articles, but before leaving told the sentry that as I had not been successful in finding what I was looking for I would return again the same time the next day.

The next day I unearthed a complete set of plates, knives and forks, and when questioned by the sentry about their religious significance, I explained that these were the plates out of which we ate reverently after saying our prayers! I do not think the sentry was totally convinced, for he warned me not to come back again! However, my task was done and there was nothing more that I wished to collect from this dump.

Now I must tell you this story about our doctor, Captain Sahibzada, to whom you have already been introduced. He joined us, and the Army, just before we proceeded to Malaya and thanks to his facility with his local 'Jhang' dialect and with Punjabi in general, and his easy manner, he soon endeared himself to all. Captain Sahibzada had hardly any interest in the INA but was very keen to help the country's freedom movement. To this end he offered to broadcast to his people back home, in his village dialect, over Radio Bangkok. He was living with us in the

Bidadari hutments at the time, and occupied a cubicle next to mine. In order to relieve our tense existence and the rather miserable circumstances under which we were living as prisoners-of-war, I decided to play a prank on him, and the opportunity offered itself soon as the 1st of April 1942, was only a day or two away. My plan was to send him a telegram from the Japanese authority, accepting his offer to broadcast over the air from Bangkok. I wrote out a cleverly worded telegram on one of the signal pads, which was easily available in the prisoners-of-war camp. The text of the message roughly read: "Your offer to broadcast from Bangkok accepted by Nippon authorities. A Japanese officer will come to collect you tomorrow, the 1st of April, at 1600 hrs. Be ready to come, on road opposite your camp. APAFULA!" The so-called telegram was delivered to him by hand, on one of these signal forms, and he did not for a minute doubt its genuineness! He was happy and anxious to be off and was ready and waiting, well in time, on the road that ran parallel to our camp. He had all his rather diminutive baggage next to him as he stood there, waiting for the Japanese officer who was to come to collect him by car. Needless to say we were laughing our sides out! When it was past the stipulated time, we asked him to read the telegram again, and see if there was any flaw in it. He would take it out, look at it hurriedly, and then put it back into his pocket. When he finally allowed us to see it I drew his attention to the name at the end of the telegram and expressed my doubts as to whether it was Japanese. But Sahibzada would have none of it, and declared that it was a Japanese name alright! We then asked him to look at the date given for the pick up, but even then he would not accept that it could be a hoax! Eventually, we had no alternative but to tell him that it was an April Fool's joke that we had played on him. Fortunately, being a good sport, he took it in his stride and shared in the hilarity. Not only did this show what a simple nature he had, but also his keen desire, almost an obsession, to get on Radio Bangkok!

Almost every day, there was a gathering of some sort or the other, addressed by Mohan Singh, or a visit by the Propaganda Team, exhorting us to join the Indian National Army. But our argument, i.e. my elder brother's and mine, always was that unless Mahatma Gandhi or Pandit Jawaharlal Nehru made an appeal over the air for every young man outside India to join the Indian National Army to liberate India with the help of the Japanese, we would not join, as we had no faith in its present leadership. At this stage, the Indian National Army High Command decided, I am sure, on the advice of Mahabir Dhillon - their chief propagandist - that we two brothers should be separated, so as to prevent us from consulting each other. Consequently I, along with a few others, was ordered to go to, what they called, a Concentration Camp! The camp consisted of a separate wooden barrack, surrounded by a barbed wire fence, and no one was allowed to contact us. We were five of us in this camp; in order of seniority, Major JKT Bhonsle, Major Gian Chand (both KICOs), myself, Captains AC Ayyappa and Prithipal. The first thing we did was to group together all the edibles that we possessed, so as to run a common kitchen. And we had quite a collection: some tins of porridge, a couple of tins of treacle syrup, two tins of Polsons butter and quite a bit of rice. Prithipal and I, the younger members of the group, undertook to cook the meals. With porridge tins aplenty, breakfast became our main meal. We used to serve porridge in plates, with a bit of butter and treacle, and every one seemed to enjoy it very much. Due to the adverse conditions of living and uncertainty regarding the future, many prisoners in the camp had become quite religious, and started their day with a 'puja', or a prayer recitation, in the morning. So it was quite natural that one of us - Major Gian Chand - should decide to build, in one corner of the barracks, a small enclosure covered with a gunny-cloth, where he would sit and perform his daily 'puja' and prayers. Prithi or I used to serve him breakfast there, leaving his plate of porridge outside this enclosure. One morning, it was my turn to serve him his breakfast. After serving all five of us, I found that there was some porridge still left over and so I decided to distribute it equally once again to every one. As I lifted the curtain of the 'Sanctum Sanctorum', where Gian was supposed to be busy at 'Puja', I saw that he had a tin of Polsons butter half-open before him and, after dipping his finger in it, was busy sucking it hard! Obviously, he had not surrendered this tin of butter when we had collectively pooled the edible items we had with us. I did not mention this fact to any one, as it would have let Gian down, but I did think in my mind what an urge there is in human beings to preserve one's life at any cost!

A Soldier Remembers

From our Concentration Camp, we used to be called up, one by one, to appear before the Indian National Army propaganda team that used to visit our camp. Soon Majors Bhonsle and Gian left us to join the Indian National Army, tempted to command two of their brigades, the Nehru and Azad Brigades, respectively. Ayyappa, Prithipal and I remained unmoved by the propaganda unleashed at us and so after a month of our confinement we were released from the Concentration Camp.

At this time, it was suggested by the Japanese that every morning, as the sun came out, we, prisoners-of-war, should bow down to it, like the Japanese did. However, we refused to do so, as we argued that we had our own religion and our own way of worshipping God. As the Japanese had themselves recently introduced the idea of 'a co-prosperity sphere' in the Far East, they decided not to press the issue. They announced that the local Commander-in-Chief, General Tamashitta would soon be visiting the Indian prisoners-of-war and for the occasion, and in future, all prisoners-of-war would wear, on the left side of their chest, secured with a safety-pin, a miniature replica of the Japanese flag, the Rising Sun. This was to serve as a symbol of our being prisoners-of-war of the Japanese, and we accepted it.

As already mentioned, in the early stages of our captivity by the Japanese, two anglicised officers, belonging to the Armoured Corps, Dargalkar and Budwar, had landed at Singapore with their tank unit only a few days before the surrender (you would recall their turning up at Changi Jail to be incarcerated with the British officers!). In order to avoid the bother of dealing with the Indian National Army at Singapore, they had organised their unit's personnel into a working-party and had managed to go to Bangkok for some work under the Japanese. Along with us, their party too had been asked to wear the symbol of the Rising Sun, signifying their status as prisoners-of-war of the Japanese. However, considering themselves to be British officers they were loath to do so; they would have preferred to wear the Union Jack instead! Their refusal landed these two officers in the clink where they were confined in solitary cells. When this information reached us I personally went to Mohan Singh to have these officers transferred to Singapore. He not only did so, but also, for the first week or so, kept them with him at his house, so as to make up for any nutritional deficiency they had suffered. A very fine gesture, indeed, on the part of the Indian National Army chief!

It is a fact that while residing in Bidadari Camp as prisoners-of-war, we had very little control over our men who lived in wooden huts almost next door. You would recall that during the handing-over ceremony at Tyrsal Park, when we were handed over by the Japanese authority to Mohan Singh of the Indian National Army, Mohan Singh, watching the officers' rather luke-warm reaction to the mention of the Indian National Army, had ordered that officers be separated from their men. According to that order, I did not visit the men's barracks, although the Subedar Major of the battalion, Sucha Singh, used to visit me surreptitiously, every evening, and report as to what was happening in the Barracks. Apparently propaganda teams of the Indian National Army used to visit the men every day and entice them, through promises of promotions, etc., to join the Indian National Army. Subedar Major told me that, as a result of this propaganda, most men were willing to join, except for about 40 men of Malwa C Company (Subedar Major being a Malwa himself) who were resisting the idea and were willing to join the working party of prisoners-of-war. The Indian National Army was, consequently, proposing to hand them over to the Japanese for work. And that is how, Captain Prithipal Singh, Subedar Major Sucha Singh, Subedar Sampuran Singh (a Malwa) Jemadar Harwant Singh (Subedar Major's son) and 40 Malwa men (including Non-Commissioned Officers and Other Ranks) and I joined my elder brother's battalion, the Jind Infantry, to form a working party under the Japanese.

12

DESTINED FOR RABAL ISLAND & THE DEATH RAILWAY; PASSED ON TO THE JAPANESE AIR FORCE INSTEAD

By now, a clear division had taken place between those who had joined the Indian National Army and those who continued to resist it. The latter were known as 'obstructionists' and the Japanese had decided to send them to outside stations as working parties. We were the first to be so selected. Our working party consisted of the entire Jind Infantry Battalion with its two officers, Prithipal and I, three Junior Commissioned Officers and nearly 40 men of 5 Sikh (who had not joined the Indian National Army) and the 3/12 Frontier Force Battalion. We were in all about 1500 personnel.

We were first of all shifted to double-decker accommodation near the camp, built by the British for the evacuation of Singapore civilians. A Japanese guard, about a section strong, was put on us. While we were in the double-deckers, the Japanese section set up their canvas-tent in the middle of this complex, with the back of the tent next to the drainage-channel, meant to drain the camp during the rains. This was a 2½ ft deep drain, lined with bricks, which was now over-grown with grass. The Japanese personnel were the privileged class, and they each had a wooden-box containing tins of condensed milk which they kept under their heads when they slept. We, as prisoners-of-war had been on a scarce diet for some time now, and naturally, the Japanese became the subject of our envy. One morning, a Japanese, who was sleeping next to the drain, found that the box under his head had been stolen during the night, and suspicion, naturally, fell on the prisoners-of-war next door. We were all put in a barbed-wire enclosure, and our rations were stopped. We pleaded our innocence on the grounds that given the circumstances, it was impossible to steal a box from under the head of some one who was sleeping without waking him up. This was surely an accounting mistake. But the Japanese were adamant that the box had been stolen, the question was how had it been done? Eventually they said, that they would be quite satisfied, and exonerate us, if only some one would came forward to show them how the box had been removed from under the head of a sleeping Japanese! A little dark man from Jind Infantry, a 'bazigar', from a community whose profession is to steal, came forward with the admission that he was the culprit. He described how in the middle of the night, he had crawled through the drain, like a dog, collecting a stone on the way that was the same size and height of the box. He had slipped this gently under the head of the sleeping Japanese soldier at the same time as he had removed the box containing the tins of condensed milk from under his head! All this without waking up the soldier! He showed us the box which he had buried. As far as he was concerned there was nothing extraordinary about this feat, as he could perform much better tricks such as jumping through a ring of fire or over a camel's back! The Japanese felt shamed by this incident for it showed that a box could be stolen from under the very nose of their sentry who was supposed to be standing at alert all night long. They stuck to their word, and did not worry us any more about it.

    We were then moved to the Singapore wharfs to await a Japanese ship to take us to the Island of Rabal. But, as luck would have it, the ship never turned up and we were shifted to the railway station to board cattle-wagons, apparently heading for the infamous Death-Railway of 'Bridge Over the River Kwai' fame! Lady luck played another trick and our train was stopped just outside Kluang Airfield and taken over by the Japanese Air Force, who required a working party to clear the airstrip there. It was just one of those lucky turns!

The airfield at Kluang was in a dilapidated state, obviously abandoned in a hurry by the British. There was a lot of scrap lying about, some empty and some partially full 46-gallon tins of gasolene, a dump of abandoned vehicles, a lot of insulated electric wire, some white metal which once had been part of an aircraft, and other such materials which the artisans with the Jind Infantry - carpenters, electricians, etc. – put to good use. They started their own workshops, producing cups, plates, scissors, pluckers, and various other items of utility. We also had with us an Anglo-Indian motor mechanic, to whom we assigned the task of producing a motor car and a motorcycle that worked. He produced one of each in no time, and with gasolene available on the airfield, we were able to use the car and the motorcycle when necessary. The Japanese Air Force, our captors, did not object.

At the airfield, our working party was required to take out stones from the hill-quarry near where our train had been stopped by the Japanese Air Force authorities. They gave us trucks, left behind by the British retreating forces, and asked us to provide drivers. There was some Chinese labour also working on the airfield, who were naturally free to be in touch with the outside world. Their presence proved very useful for we could put the blame for rumour mongering on them once we got our secret radio-receiver working and were able to listen to news about the war and the outside world and disseminate it among our men.

There was a barbed wire fence around the airfield, put up by the British, but which now had many gaps in it and which the Japanese did little to repair. Nor did they exercise any rigid control on the security of the prisoners-of-war as they had a shortage of manpower. So we were, more or less left to ourselves. Upto that time, the secret of the wireless set had been with me and my elder brother, Lieutenant Colonel Gurbakhsh Singh. I had kept the set under the debris of abandoned crates and other rubbish, with just a passage leading to it. At the time I was still using the 6-volt battery which I had collected with the HMV set in Singapore, whilst cleaning the city, as described earlier in this book. One day something went wrong with the set, as it would not switch on; and I was in a fix. I thought of the Chinese labour working with us at the Kluang Airfield, and I suddenly remembered that I had once talked to a radio mechanic, who was now, for lack of work, working as an ordinary labourer. I approached him and asked him if he had an instrument to check the circuit of a wireless set, and whether he was willing to accompany me the next Sunday, which was a holiday for the workers on the airfield, with his checking instrument to wherever I led him. He agreed and so the next Sunday I met him as arranged, and led him through the jungle, along a circuitous route. Near our camp I blind-folded him, and led him through an opening in the barbed wire to my little office room where I had previously placed the set, along with its battery. Only then did I remove the blind-fold. I apologised to him for all the precautions I had to take, including blind-folding him, but as he himself did not wish to know where he was going, he did not object. He checked the set and discovered that one of the 'resistances' had gone 'dis'. However, by by-passing it he assured me that the set would still work. I heaved a sigh of relief, for if a valve of the set had gone 'dis', it would have been impossible to replace. I blind-folded him again and led him out of the camp through the gap in the fence, and back to our original rendezvous. I could not help notice that while blind-folded the Chinese was shaking in his shoes out of fear. However, the job was done without the Japanese knowing anything about it, which was a big relief.

Of course, the Japanese had already made it quite clear that if any prisoner was found missing, the Commandant, who happened to be my elder brother, Lieutenant Colonel Gurbakhsh Singh, would be held responsible and punished. And yet because of this, we were able to take many risks.

Living Quarters at Kluang Airfield

While initially living out in the open in the jungle, near the stone quarry where we worked, a few of us contracted malaria, despite our best efforts to smoke out the mosquitoes in our camp at night. Also, despite our very strict instructions to the men not to drink water from any of the streams, dysentery started in the camp, and since there was no medicine, or proper nourishment, prisoners-of-war started dying like flies. We had had no experience of such an epidemic before, and it was as a result of this, we requested the Japanese to allot us some accommodation. They permitted us to search for it, and we were lucky to find wooden barracks near the airfield which were next door to our place of work. So, the men were accommodated in these barracks and the officers, only ten of us, were accommodated in the Warrant Officer's three pre-fabricated houses, at the other end of the airfield. To get to the men, we had to cross the air-strip and the Japanese raised no objection to this, provided we did not interfere with their flying.

The wooden barracks, with a thatched roof, had two storeys which were more than enough to accommodate us. There was, of course, no question of getting beds to sleep-on so men slept on the floor. Lucky for us, the climate in Malaya throughout the year was temperate - neither too hot, nor too cold. There was no question of bedding either. Most men had managed to get a gunny-cloth which was spread on the ground. As far as accommodation for officers was concerned, the ten of us (two from 5 Sikh; Prithipal and I, and eight from the Jind Infantry, including the Medical Officer - Captain Jawaharlal Puri) were accommodated in houses that had been built for the British Warrant Officers. Each had a sitting-cum-dining room and two bed-rooms, with bathrooms attached. We divided ourselves among these three houses, with one bedroom of the first house occupied by my brother and I, and the other by Major Ameer Singh (a Jat, who was nursing a wounded arm in a sling). We used the main hall of this house as a dining room for all of us - for which purpose, we had a large table with benches around it. Each bedroom had a bathroom attached to it. The second house, behind the first, had one bedroom which was occupied by Captain Jawaharlal Puri, the doctor, (who, unfortunately throughout his time as a prisoner-of-war, suffered from gall-bladder stones). The three Captains: Ajaib Singh, Gurcharan Singh (the Quartermaster) and Jaswant Singh occupied the hall-way of the house, and had a bathroom to themselves. The remaining three Captains, Prithipal, Mohan Mukand and Ram Singh shared the third house. We lived together like a family - the ten of us.

Because of my head injury, that hadn't yet healed, my brother, Lieutenant Colonel Gurbakhsh Singh - the Camp Commandant of the prisoners-of-war camp - appointed me Staff Officer for the camp.

Thereupon, I rigged-up a small room in house no 2, as my office. Here I placed my keyless typewriter on a small table. The first thing I did was to get hold of a clerk from among the prisoners who had learned the touch system of typing. I asked him to draw a plan of the keys on a typewriter for me and then requested the unit carpenter to make the keys out of wood, after which I used an ink pen to label them with the necessary alphabets. The typewriter was now complete and I taught myself the touch system of typing on it. I have felt a different man ever since! Of course, being self taught I do not quite hold my hands and my elbows the right way and neither can I pretend to be a very proficient typist!

Next to the officers' quarters was a big tin-shed, on a wooden platform, built by the British. We used it for staging plays and holding musical concerts, which were so essential to keep up the morale of all of us prisoners. Our Commandant, Lieutenant Colonel Gurbakhsh Singh, had a flair for writing these dramas in Gurmukhi (which the men could read). He chose various social themes suitable for the troops. One of his Officers, Captain Ajaib Singh, who had natural histrionic talent, also proved a very competent director. Since I was a bathroom singer, with quite a melodious voice, I was appointed music director! To play the female roles in these plays Ajaib dressed up young lads in the camp – mostly young 'followers', 'nais' (barbers), etc., from his battalion, the Jind Infantry – in Punjabi dress and they truly looked like girls! One of them, a young fellow, was stricken by pulmonary tuberculosis later on, due to malnutrition, and we felt really sad to have to segregate him first in the camp and then later in the prisoners-of-war hospital in Singapore. But more of that later.

I, as the music director, had managed to collect a group of singers from the other ranks of the prisoners, and we would start every drama or musical concert with a rendition of 'Vande Mataram'. We had collected all the Indian National Army's patriotic songs, of which, I must say, there were many suitable for national occasions. We adopted them all, and observed each national festival with the hoisting of the national flag and singing of a suitable national song at a ceremony, specially arranged for the occasion. In patriotic fervour, we were no less enthusiastic than the Indian National Army!

Another thing we started was composing songs and poems, on national themes. Participation was open to the men, JCOs and Officers, who could recite their compositions in the Assembly in whatever style they liked. On these occasions I usually supplied the first line which was either patriotic in content or reflected on the every-day living conditions of prisoners-of-war. I can still remember the first two lines I gave from the old patriotic songs in vogue in 1919-20, when I was a very young lad. They were:

"Meri duniyan lut rahi thi, aur men para madhosh tha!
Khabarle varna kahe gi duniyan, ke inka koee Khuda nahin hai!"

This was indeed a very good past-time for the prisoners-of-war and many of them got an opportunity to discover their 'hidden talents'.

For these concerts, we would invite the local gentry - who were all South Indians and whom the Japanese had kept on in their old jobs; as chief engineer, officer in-charge civil supplies, etc.. They were very happy to attend and the Japanese authorities seemed to have no objection to their coming. There came a time when the airfield authorities wished to demolish the tin shed that served as our concert hall as it came in their flight path. Naturally, we raised no objections to this and instead shifted the venue of our performances to one of our barracks, nearer to the men. The Japanese at our request left the wooden platform under the tin shed intact and we officers continued to use it as a place to gather and enjoy the evening breeze after dinner and reminisce about our families back home. For example, looking at the moon, some one would say: "I am sure, my wife is also looking at the moon right now". It became a way of establishing communion with one's dear and near ones; so essential when you are forced apart by a war. Sitting there in the moonlight, we would often let our imagination run riot conjuring up things of which we were bereft. For example, I remember a night when we were sitting on the platform and our doctor, Jawahar Puri, asked us collectively to name a sweet that we would most like to eat at that moment. The answers ranged from 'laddoos' and 'barfees' to 'jalebies'. Finally we settled on 'gulab jamuns'. Then he said, "Let us imagine, you have got a plate of 'gulab jamuns' next to you; how would you eat them?" We all went through the motions of picking-up a 'gulab jamun' with the fore-finger and thumb and putting it in our mouth. The fact was that you could really feel the taste of a 'gulab jamun' in your mouth! We also used the time to recognise stars in the tropical sky, which appeared to be so near and clear. We thanked our stars - and our luck - that we had come under the sway of the Japanese Air Force, which was on the whole considerate towards us. They were more concerned with their work being done and other than that left us alone most of the time. They allowed us to look after our own accommodation, modify it as we liked through our own resources, keep our own poultry, scrounge for food, look after our sick, observe our religious days, celebrate our national days the way we liked, and have our own system of passes for going in and out of the camp.

13

EARLY DAYS AS PRISONERS-OF-WAR AT KLUANG CAMP

Learning About Our Captors

The first three months, were spent by the Japanese engineers in getting the airfield ready for their use. They extended the airstrip, metalled it and built a hangar, and after that their bombers moved in. Like the earlier engineers, the Japanese personnel on the airfield were quite friendly towards us. They used to detail a NCO to liaise with us who kept changing, as old detachments moved out and new ones came in to replace them. The Japanese authorities had put their NCO in charge of all prisoners-of-war. We discovered from him that the Japanese forces had all sorts of nationalities and religious groups among them. There were Buddhists, Muslims, Christians and, of course, the Manchukoans and the Koreans. The Manchukoans, we found, were taller than the rest. But, overall we felt that the Christians were better, from our point of view. They were more co-operative and understanding, and most of them spoke English - for language was a big problem between us and the Japanese. Once the Japanese did suggest that they would teach us Japanese, but we had refused to learn their language point-blank arguing that we had our own language, Hindustani, which we all spoke. Their strongest objection was to our speaking or reading English. They called English, 'Dame' in their language, which meant 'bad', and we followed suit; and it seemed to work with them! The language problem was, however, real.

To communicate, we often found it necessary to draw rather than use words they did not understand. So, we kept a blackboard with a chalk for this purpose. There were times when this also worked against us. One morning, the Japanese Intelligence Officer came to tell us about an incident of cow-slaughter that had occured in the neighbourhood of our camp. Only a few days earlier we had drawn a goat for him on the blackboard to illustrate our need for mutton for our sick. So, this morning, when the officer drew what looked more like a goat to us than a cow, we thought that he was asking us if we wanted goat's meat and so we readily agreed! But when the officer took our Commandant to the scene of the slaughter and demanded an explanation, he completely denied that it could have been done by any of our men, for as he explained, eating cow's meat was taboo in our religion. The officer found this hard to believe, but, luckily for us, he laid the blame for the happening on the local Chinese. We later learnt that the men of the 3/12 Battalion had killed the vagrant cow for meat. We thanked our stars that we had escaped!

The blackboard we kept to communicate also sometimes led us into piquant situations. As our diet, which was only rice, was deficient in protein, we were very keen to get some pulses as a supplement. But try as we might, we could not find the word we wanted in the Japanese language. So, we took recourse to our blackboard and tried to draw a grain of lentil on the board with a chalk, describing the colour of the grain as well. We particularly stressed the need for it for the sick amongst us. The Liaison-NCO of the Japanese, seemed to understand what we needed and about ten days later brought us a bag of black-pepper! A commodity which he said he had gone to great difficulty to get as it was very rare. We had no choice but to accept it, and directed the prisoners-of-war to sprinkle it sparingly over rice after it had been cooked.

Japanese Punishments

There is no doubt that the ranks of the Japanese Army and Air Force had been tutored before setting out from their country, on this campaign. They would put their hand next to one of ours and say "Ona ji, ona ji", which meant similar. They had also been told about Gandhi and Jinnah, for the first question they would ask us was whether we were "Gandhika". If you said, "yes", it was alright. If you said "no", you were liable to be beaten up!

We got to know that in their forces, they had only two types of punishment - at least during the war! One was a clout on the face. They had a word of command for it; which would enable the recipient to remove his spectacles (if he was wearing them), stand at-ease (if he were standing to-attention) and thrust his face forward to receive the clout! The second type of punishment was an honourable death called 'Hara Kiri' where the culprit was given a sword to kill himself. For a serious crime, he would be beheaded with a sword. Now in our Army, you were not allowed so much as to touch a man by a finger. So, there were quite a few incidents of serious objection and resentment, when the punishment of 'clouting' was executed by the Japanese on us prisoners-of-war.

A young Japanese recruit, during the period of his initiation, or a newly joined individual in a sub-unit was routinely clouted on the face by the senior personnel, both morning and evening, till he lost a tooth or two! I know of a case, when a Japanese officer was too busy to give the 'clouting' punishment himself so he ordered the defaulter to run to the barracks and receive his punishment from another officer whom he named!

Because of shortage of manpower, the Japanese ruled Malaya through fear and terror. They made it known that the punishment for a crime, however small, would be either death by the sword, or by hanging. They would often make the culprit dig his own grave! At one stage, during the earlier period of their occupation of Malaya, the town of Kluang was governed by a Sergeant of the 'Kambtai' (Military Police) and he had the power of life and death over the residents. We learnt of these events from the Chinese labour working with us on the airfield. According to them, the normal procedure followed by the Japanese forces when they occupied a town, was to first surround it on all sides;

then collect and scrutinise the population and divide them into 'blacks' and 'whites', so designated by the hooded detectives who accompanied the occupation forces. For example, anyone who was sympathetic to the KMT (the Kuomintang - the Japanese enemy in China) was dubbed 'black' while the other Chinese were let off as 'white'. What happened to the 'blacks' one can only guess!

Human rights, even in peacetime, are the most abused commodity. During war, they are generally forgotten. Under Japanese rule, they had no place. I remember, in mid-1942, in Kuanton, seeing a man strung up by his neck to a pole, facing the sun, with a notice on his chest announcing, in Japanese, that he had committed a certain crime. The rope around his neck was tied in such a manner that if he stood flat on his feet he would be suffocated by the loop. Therefore, to keep alive, he had to support his whole weight on his toes. But for how long can one support the whole weight of the body on one's toes? In the end, he had no choice but to die of suffocation. I call this torture of the worst kind. Therefore, where were human rights? This is what I saw with my own eyes. There were many stories of the Japanese executing the worst type of torture, both in the 'torture chambers' of Japanese prisons, as well as in the village and town squares. It was a common sight to see a human head, with a swarm of flies around it, strung up on a pole at one cross-road or another in Singapore. Usually the crime was no serious than daring to raise a hand against a 'Nippon' soldier. This was meant to deter people against committing crimes!

Another example of the worst kind of violation of human rights occurred before my very eyes at Kluang. One morning a working party with packs and shovels was requisitioned from amongst us. I accompanied this party. We were taken to a nearby forest and were asked to dig eight slit-trenches, 3 feet deep, in a line. We thought this was the end of the line for us, for we had heard of the Japanese asking civilian personnel to do this before they eliminated them. However, we had no alternative but to do as we were told. After the trenches had been dug, the Japanese officer in-charge, asked us to sit down a little distance away. Shortly, thereafter, a truck pulled up, with civilians in it. These were mostly Chinese, apparently from the local police lock-up, who had been brought for the purpose of providing battle-experience initiation to young Japanese pilots. The idea was to get them used to killing a man with the Japanese double-handled sword. Only then would they be given charge of a fighter-aircraft. These human targets on which the pilots were to practice were asked to stand in front of the trenches - one to a trench.

Starting from the right, the Instructor would demonstrate the technique to be employed by making a gash with his sword on the left side of the neck, drawing blood. It was not long before the person being practised on would collapse. He would, however, be made to stand up again so that the trainee who followed could practice the same technique. I can never forget the faces of those men, who served as human targets. They stood there without showing any reaction, or expression on their faces, while we sat on one side in a cold sweat! More often than not, the youngster who was being initiated into battle, would follow the steps laid out by the Instructor but as he was a novice would inflict a much larger cut. Bleeding profusely the victim would by now completely collapse into the trench in front of him. The second in line would then be made the next target for practice, and the Instructor would repeat his demonstration, but this time more gently, drawing a line on the neck of the victim with his finger, indicating the exact spot where the sword should enter the body so as to sever off the upper part through the heart, with one stroke. One by one everyone fell victim to this training session and after it was all over, we were made to fill the trenches with earth. It was the most traumatic experience of our lives and after that we felt that the true answer to a Japanese was a Chinese - equally equanimous and no less fatalist than a human bomber or a 'kamikaze' pilot!

Japanese Discipline & Habits

I must say that the Japanese did not spare their own men either. On Quarter Guard duty, the entire guard kept awake during the night, unlike our guards who could sleep in their beds while only the sentries stayed awake, standing or sitting, as required. In the case of the Japanese, their guardsmen sat on a bench in front of a table while the sentries stood at their posts, and the Guard Commander, generally a NCO, sat on a chair behind the table and if any of the guardsmen lolled off to sleep, he would hit the person on the head with a stick!

If a party was to be investigated for a digestive ailment, such as dysentery or worms, etc. they would be lined up in the open, stark naked, and a medical team would come with a glass rod, swabs, and a number of clean glass-slides. The men would be asked to bend over and the glass-rod, after having been cleaned before hand by a swab, would be inserted into the rectum of each man and the sample of the stool taken would be smeared on a slide. Similarly, if a party of men were to be immunised against, say, typhoid, cholera and other tropical diseases, by serum injections, the medical team would give all the injections together and let the men suffer from fever for the next 24 hours, for which they would be given leave. Whereas, in our Army, and I am sure, in other Armies too, each of these injections is given separately, requiring a 24 hours waiting period after each injection. This is how the Japanese saved time on the transfer of personnel from one place to another, again, due to the shortage of manpower, I suppose!

I have already mentioned that the Japanese devolved wide-ranging responsibility on their subordinate staff. At one time, in the beginning, a Sergeant of the Kamptai (Military Police) was in-charge of the administration of Kluang Airfield, and I, as staff officer of the prisoner-of-war camp, had to report to him every morning for the details of the working parties required for the next day. Once on a Sunday, when I went to look for him in the lines I found him sitting on the grass in the middle of the airfield. I approached him, and what do I see but that he was sitting with two pretty girls! He introduced me to the two girls who he said were Geisha girls from Tokyo, who had come to entertain the Japanese troops in station. He appeared to be having tea with them, which was served by two Japanese soldiers who had their mouths covered with white pieces of cloth. These soldiers were known as 'toban', the equivalent of batmen, as we know them, and usually served tea to the Japanese several times a day in their offices. I must say that it was a real treat for me to meet both these pretty girls, especially as I had, as a prisoner-of-war, been deprived of such a pleasant sight for so long! As to how they entertained the Japanese soldiers, I do not know. They may well have sung popular songs in their language as the British and the American singers and movie stars used to do for their troops. The Japanese used to have, in addition, the institution of comfort houses for their troops, which I have described elsewhere.

Sometime later, in summer, while on a similar mission as staff officer of the prisoner-of-war camp, again on a Sunday, I found the

Japanese officer in-charge drunk as an owl, sitting wearing only a 'langoat'. He was drinking some potent wine in a bottle from a small sea-shell container. He insisted that I should also have a sip of the wine from the same container. I was hesitant as I noticed that his teeth were affected by scurvy. He, however, would not take no for an answer and sensing my hesitation went to the extent of using force. I had no choice but to gulp it down. After receiving instructions, I was happy to be rid of the man though for some time the fear that I may have contracted scurvy stayed with me. Such was life as a prisoner-of-war!

14

OUR LIFE AS PRISONERS-OF-WAR CONTINUES

We Maintain a Wireless Set & Get News About the War

1942 was the year of the Japanese. They had crippled, through a surprise naval raid on Pearl Harbour, the American navy, and their army had captured the whole of the Far East, less Australia and New Zealand, where General McArther had taken refuge. Having captured the whole of Burma, their army was knocking at the doors of India. In early 1943, the Allies resurrected themselves a bit and we, as prisoners-of-war, could also notice some activity on the part of the Resistance Groups, mainly made up of Chinese communists. They would destroy bridges on the railway line, etc. Besides, we began to see an aircraft of the Allies fly over the Kluang Airfield at night and circle over an area in the neighbouring jungle. The Japanese who had no night-fighters at Kluang, and had not deployed any anti-aircraft guns on the airfield, could not in any way interfere with this nightly mission. Also, about the same time of the year, the Americans started bombing Singapore and on their way back, the formation of B-52s used to drop the left-over bombs over the Kluang Airfield. This gave us an excuse to ask the Japanese to allow us to build bunkers in a clump of trees near our quarters, to which they agreed. And that is how I was able to move the wireless set, that I had been operating clandestinely, into one of the bunkers.

As a result of these raids, the Japanese decided to move some day-fighters to the Kluang Airfield, as it was ideally located to take on the American raiders as they flew to Singapore. We used to see these fighters take-off as the B-52s headed for Singapore. They would rise to a height greater than that of the bombers, and would wait for them to return. Most of these fighter-pilots were 'kamikaze' volunteers who were ready to crash into a corner of the bomber formation. However, most of their attempts were pre-empted, for as soon as the fighters would near the formation, intense fire would come from the flight-guns and blow-up the attacking aircraft. Invariably the fighters, so maimed, would try to make it to the landing-strip, but would more often crash into the rubber estate on the way to the airstrip. So, the Japanese had these trees cut-off, but even then there were many who crashed into these stumps. A few fighters made it back to the airfield, but their aircrafts were badly damaged and the pilots wounded. We learnt of only one bomber being brought down by these fighters, and that too not within our sight. Let me admit that even though our camp was subjected to frequent bombing by the American bombers, we welcomed their arrival as friendly aircraft! We were also happy that the Japanese fighters could not do anything to them. Soon, we heard over our radio that the Americans had almost destroyed the Japanese navy in the battle of the Gulf of Leyte, and that they had started hopping from island to island and were recapturing the land occupied by the Japanese in the first flush of 1942. So, 1943, was a bad year for the Japanese, as they had started losing the war. We were happy, but dared not ask the Japanese as to how the war was going! Occasionally, to keep up the morale of the prisoners-of-war, we used to pass on information heard over the clandestine radio we were operating.

Since the 6-volt battery that I had got with the wireless set at Singapore soon ran out I had to find a way to operate the set on electricity. As I was the staff officer for the camp, responsible for the well being of the men, I decided to ask the Japanese for kerosene lanterns that we could use to light the way at night so as to avoid snake-bites, and also for an electric connection to which we could attach a high powered bulb. This was to be placed centrally in the camp so as to provide illumination to all. The Japanese officer-in-charge agreed that we could take an electric connection from the main switch board of their barracks but said we would have to do it with our own resources. This proved simple as there was plenty of insulated cable lying around among the abandoned debris. I rounded up a few of the Signal personnel who knew about electricity and managed to get a line to the quarters where we were living. From this line, I was able to take one line to the bulb stuck on a pole in the centre of the camp and another, secretively, underground, to my covered bunker not very far from our living quarters. I was able to do this with the assistance of my nephew, Captain Mohan Mukand Singh, an officer in the Jind Infantry, the only one, besides my brother, Lieutenant Colonel Gurbakhsh Singh, who knew about the wireless set. I managed to fit the set in a 46-gallon empty drum with a wooden board as cover, and buried it under the floor of my bunker. I connected the set to the electric cable in such a way that it was energised all the time.

The connection was so arranged that all one needed to do to operate it was to connect the two negative wires that were situated on top of the drum. When not in use I kept them separate by tying them onto two twigs of wood stuck in each corner of the bunker. The set was permanently tuned to All India Radio for the news at 9 p.m., followed by a relay of the BBC news at 9:30 pm. These timings were most suitable as it was then midnight in Malaya! Even then we were careful not to take the risk of listening to the news everyday. We usually did so at irregular intervals of ten to fifteen days. At midnight whenever I listened to the news, Captain Mohan Mukund Singh would wait outside the bunker and keep a look out for the Japanese patrol which used to visit our camp at odd hours at night.

A few of our men were working as 'toban' (batmen) for the Japanese. They would, sometimes, foolishly, tell the Japanese that they were losing the War, and upon being asked as to who had told them so, would reply, "our officers". The Japanese would, naturally, question us, but each time we would pass it off as a rumour heard from the Chinese labour working alongside us on the airfield! However, this explanation did not fully satisfy the Japanese, and they began to suspect that we had a receiver set. On one or two occasions they brought a couple of clinometers, mounted on tripods, to our camp and tried to bluff us into thinking that with these instruments they would soon find out the exact location of the set. I knew that it was nothing but bluff, for nothing on earth, much less these clinometers, could locate the set unless it was switched on at the time. They did pretend on one occasion to have found out the direction in which the set was located, but when we offered to go there and help them search for it, they back tracked. Despite this, we continued to listen to the latest news about the war effort on the set. For instance we learnt of the landing of the American forces in Algeria, and of the British and American forces on the West Coast of Europe, at Normandy. This gave us hope that the War would end soon and kept up our morale, though it was to go on for another year and a half. We also learnt about the initial success of the Japanese in Burma, against the British forces, and of the deployment of the Indian National Army, under Netajee Subhash Chandra Bose. As for the latter effort, we were doubtful that it would succeed because we had witnessed the non-cooperative and selfish attitude of the Japanese forces.

More About the Indian National Army

In spite of our differences with the Indian National Army, we had kept up good relations with its officers. Mohan Singh had been my contemporary at the Indian Military Academy and I had always got on well with him. Shah Niwaz, I knew, was a very emotional individual and, I also knew, that he had joined the initial Indian National Army, under Mohan Singh, because of some dispute over accommodation for a Muslim Junior Commissioned Officer, whom, he felt, was being unfairly treated. In fact, the reasons for volunteering to join the Indian National Army, at the beginning, were most comic! To begin with, it was mostly the Sikh troops that had volunteered, mainly because Mohan Singh was the Supreme Commander. Within months, as a result, I think, of the promotion of JCOs to the rank of officers, a rumour went around that if the Sikhs, who had a majority in the Indian National Army then, captured Punjab there would be no room for the Muslims! Whether it was a propaganda stunt to get the Muslims in, I do not know, but the fact is that from then on Muslim troops began to volunteer for the Indian National Army in droves. As a result, we lost nearly half the strength of our working party at Kluang, as the Muslim troops, the whole of 3/12 Frontier Force, desired to go to Singapore to join the Indian National Army. Nobody could stop them. In a way it turned out well for us for, as already described, the battalion had earlier landed us into trouble by killing a cow, for beef, just outside the barbed-wire fence of the airfield; and then broken into the Japanese explosives room and stolen some detonators, taking them to be cigarettes! We had barely escaped being severely punished for both these two incidents. So, in the prisoner-of-war camp, we were now left with the whole of the Jind Infantry and about fifty personnel of 5 Sikh, a more manageable and compact group.

As I have mentioned earlier, we had always maintained friendly relations with the Indian National Army, and whenever their detachments passed through the railway station at Kluang, we would go over and see them - and thus get the latest news. Once, while passing through, Shah Niwaz, came over to our camp and brought with him a tin of Polsons butter, which was so much in demand those days, and so very rare! It was indeed very good of him to have done so. This was, of course, during the time of Netajee Subhash Bose, to whom, we were told, Shah Niwaz was devoted.

People, perhaps, do not know that under the Japanese three Indian National Armies were raised - the first, under Mohan Singh; the second under JKT Bhonsle, and; the third and final one, under Subhash Chandra Bose. I was on good terms with all of them, yet did not join any of them. It was not that I was bound by any oath, or that I loved British rule, but I simply was not ready to join an organisation that did not have the approval of the political leadership in India at that time.

Mohan Singh, perhaps, was the only man in the first Indian National Army who was sincere. He, however, seemed to place too much trust in the words of the Japanese underlings. The second Indian National Army, under JKT Bhonsle, was a complete eye-wash. Bhonsle, I knew, had done it to save his skin. He had admitted as much to me. It was only when Bhonsle failed to inspire the new Indian National Army that the Japanese agreed to bring in Netajee Subhash Chandra

Bose. But when he came, towards the end of 1943, it was too late for us - who were by then known as 'obstructionists'. And, I must say, that Netajee accepted this fact with grace, the great leader that he was. But there is no doubt that his arrival and his handling of the Indian Independence League did put zest into the Indian community in the region - unfortunately, the circumstances were against him. I was lucky to have had an interview with him in Malaya, and to this day I have yet to meet a more patriotic and devoted individual earnestly committed to the freedom of his country. If he had lived and come back to India, he would have, undoubtedly, transformed the whole political leadership. What a great leader of men he was!

Netajee Subhash Chandra Bose

When Netajee Subhash Chandra Bose was expected to appear at a public meeting in Singapore, Bhonsle sent for me and my brother to witness the show. It was a grand affair, organised on the maidan in front of the municipal building. A high-stage had been erected, with the map of India as the backdrop with each province highlighted by different coloured roses. Microphones were set up on the balustrade of the building and behind each one of them stood an Indian girl dressed in a tricolour saree, ready to sing the National Anthem. Tri-colour flags (with Charkhas) were draped down each column of the building - in real fascist style - as one used to see during the rallies organised by the Nazis, under Adolf Hitler, in Germany of the thirties. My brother and I were sitting with the Indian National Army personnel. There was tremendous excitement as we awaited Netajee Subhash Chandra Bose's arrival. He was supposed to climb on to the rostrum using a ladder. Right till the end, I was doubtful if it would be the real Bose, the Japanese would perhaps send a double! However, someone arrived in a car, clad in a wnite muslin dhoti and kurta, with glasses on. He looked like Bose all right; and when he started addressing the gathering, there was no doubt that it was him! He first spoke in English and then in Hindustani - and what an orator! When he finished, our friends in the Indian National Army asked us if we had changed our minds? We replied that we had not but that we would like to meet Netajee Subhash Chandra Bose and discuss the matter with him personally. In the end, Netajee asked the audience to contribute whatever they could, for the

Independence of their country and the gathering threw on to the sheet, which was spread out for the purpose, whatever they possessed; cash, gold-rings and ladies gold-ornaments. It was a huge collection and there was general satisfaction all around. There was talk that at last a leader had arrived, and from that moment onwards, Indians started looking up, and putting their all into the Independence Movement. Netajee carried out a whirlwind tour of the whole area and began setting up offices of the Indian Independence League at various places. People flocked around him to get enlisted in the Indian National Army, or 'Azad Hind Fauj', as it was now called. He organised a ladies Regiment, known as the 'Rani of Jhansi' Regiment; set up children's battalions, with wooden rifles, and so on. We learnt all this from the local papers. He went to Tokyo to sign an agreement with the Japanese Government and soon the Indian Independence Movement and its Government was recognised by the Japanese Government.

I must now describe our first, and as it happened our last, meeting with Netajee Subhash Chandra Bose. He sent for us, my brother Gurbakhsh Singh and I, from our prisoner-of-war camp, at Kuanton, to a place called Airhitam, situated on the sea-coast about twenty miles west of our camp. We were taken there, under Japanese escort, in a truck. As we entered the house, I could see tea, with pastries, laid out in the verandah, and I pointed this out to my elder brother remarking that, it seemed, that we were going to get some sweets to eat that afternoon - after having been deprived of sweets for years! This was now the end of 1943. We were made to sit in a small room and told that Netajee, who was at the time addressing a conference of his workers, would be around in a minute. Soon, he appeared at the doorway, dressed in khaki uniform; breeches, with tall, black boots; a khaki jacket (without any badges of rank) and a bare-cap over his head, with a copper-emblem depicting a 'Leaping Tiger' on it. This we learnt was the emblem of the army that he had organised in Germany. He was later to show us his album of pictures of the force he had organised from Indian prisoners-of-war in Germany. As he entered the room, we stood up and greeted him with the salutation of 'Jai Hind', to which he responded before he asked us to sit down. He started by saying that from his briefings he had found out that neither of us brothers had joined the 'Azad Hind Fauj' from the very beginning. He wanted to know our reasons. Since my elder brother was our spokesman he explained that there were two main reasons: one, that no leader, worth the name, had led the INA so far, and second, that we were perhaps not patriotic enough to join such a noble movement and lay down our lives for it. Had we been so, why would we have joined the British Army in the first place, he asked? Now, given our assessment of the war-situation that the Axis Powers, including Japan, were going to lose this war we were even less willing to throw in our lot with the Japanese backed INA. Netajee Subhash Bose appreciated our frankness and admitted that we were, perhaps, correct in our assessment of the war. He said he wanted people in his army who were ready to die for their country. He further said, that if we were not prepared to join him, no one would ever compel us to join against our wish, however, if ever we should change our minds he would welcome us with open arms. Thereupon he asked us to partake of tea before leaving; and that was the last we saw of him. We returned to the camp and thereafter we were never worried by the 'Azad Hind Fauj' again!

An Assessment of General Mohan Singh

As already explained, I just could not bring myself to join the INA on two counts. Firstly, there was no political leadership of any standing at its helm of affairs in Singapore; and secondly, because I had no faith in the Japanese, considering what they had done in Manchuria and China. As for Mohan Singh's leadership of the INA, I had little faith in it, though I did not doubt his personal sincerity. He had been a contemporary of mine at the IMA, Dehradun, and I was aware that he did not have the necessary guile to deal with a wily government like that of the Japanese.

It was quite clear from the beginning that the Japanese were supporting the INA for propaganda purposes. Besides, by handing over 90,000 Indian prisoners-of-war to the INA, the Japanese cleverly absolved themselves of the responsibility of guarding them and looking after them, which they could ill-afford given their shortage of manpower and resources, especially towards the end of the war. A less gullible man would have realised that the Japanese were not sincere as they refused to accord the INA any status in writing. Their word was their guarantee and it could not always be relied upon as Mohan Singh sadly learnt later on.

We heard that at one time they had brought in Rash Behari Bose, Chairman of the Indian Independence League, but since he was married to a Japanese lady, and thus considered a lackey of the Japanese, nobody would listen to him. Pritam Singh of the Indian Independence League, who accompanied the invading Japanese forces, was again not considered trustworthy. It was later announced by the Japanese that he had died in an air-crash. We collectively went to consult Major Niranjan Singh Gill, the senior most Commissioned Officer of the Indian Army, but he seemed to be playing his own game of replacing Mohan Singh as head of the Indian National Army. But Mohan Singh, helped by the Japanese Intelligence Officer, Major Fujiwara, was able to check mate him by inducing Niranjan Singh Gill to accept the appointment of head of the Indian National Army Intelligence set-up at Bangkok. Here the Japanese had their own spy network in the form of girls working as stenos and typists. Gill was fond of drinking whisky and the Japanese provided it freely to him, and so, in this way, the Japanese kept control over the goings on in the Indian National Army set-up.

Mahabir Singh Dhillon, who readily became a member of this set-up, later defected on an elephant, we were told, and was utilised by the British to give talks to the Indian troops on the Indian National Army. His escape, during a reconnaissance of the border with India, seemed to have emboldened Major Gill who sent a personal letter to the Adjutant General of the Indian Army requesting him not to stop the allowance to his family in India, as, although he was employed by the Indian National Army's Intelligence unit, he was in fact working as a double agent! He, apparently, sent this letter through an Indian officer, who escaped to India, like Major Dhillon. Through their own spies, the Japanese learnt about this letter and who was carrying it. At the last moment, they confronted the officer, forcibly removed the letter from his person, and put him in jail. This letter, which, we believe, was personally signed by Major Gill himself, also landed him in a Japanese prison, and even Netaji Subhash Chandra Bose, could not persuade the Japanese to release him. This is what we heard in the prisoner-of-war camp, how far it is true, I do not know.

Mohan Singh was very keen that my elder brother, Lt Col Gurbakhsh Singh, who had the whole of the Jind Infantry behind him, and I, should join his organisation. He would occasionally send for us from Kluang, with the object of showing us the contrast between our lives, as prisoners-of-war, and the comfortable life that the Indian National Army officers and men were leading in Singapore. Whenever we visited, we used to stay in relative luxury in the Indian National Army Mess as guests of the Commanding Officer, a tall Sikh gentleman (I forget his name). And each time inducements, in the way of instant promotions, etc., were offered, obviously at Mohan Singh's instance, though he never asked us directly, perhaps because he knew our views.

I remember an evening when we were asked to a drinks party at Mohan Singh's house. We arrived at the Supreme Commander's (that's how he was called in the Indian National Army) double storied house, which had palatial lawns around it. Here, on the lawns, about one hundred officers were in attendance, most of them, we were told, recently promoted from the rank of JCO to that of officer, and Mohan Singh, in shirt-sleeves, was moving among them like a cock strutting among his flock! A short and slightly built man, he was, literally, walking on his toes as he welcomed one and all to his party with a smile and a shake of the hand. He certainly was king here! Alcohol flowed like water, and one could tell the recently promoted element (from JCO rank) by the way they threw back their drinks and then ended up regurgitating them behind the hedge. Soon, a Major General (of the INA) Mohd Zaman Kiani, who had been my term mate at the Indian Military Academy, and was now Chief of General Staff of the Indian National Army, climbed onto the balcony of the double storied house of his Supreme Commander, where he uttered one sentence: "One Movement and One Leader", and then, with a flourish of his hand removed the cloth that had been covering a large-size photograph of Mohan Singh, stuck on the railing of the balcony. Of course, every body clapped. Feeling disgusted at these goings on we felt that it was time for us to depart, and went up to Mohan Singh to thank him for inviting us to the party. Mohan Singh tried to stand as tall as possible-almost on his toes - and shook hands with us vigorously as if to say: "See, what you are missing!" Thus ended our evening with Mohan Singh. Having lived lavishly in the Indian National Army Mess for two days, we were ready to go home to our prisoners-of-war camp and say good bye to the Indian National Army.

Mohan Singh eventually realised that his trust in the Japanese had been misplaced. He dissolved the Indian National Army and, I believe, took a pledge from his officers, written in their own blood, that they would not raise another Indian National Army. That night the Japanese came to take him away and every one believed that he had been killed. However, the next morning, the very same officers who had signed the pledge, I was told, were ready to re-raise the Indian National Army! In the end JKT Bhonsle succeeded in taking over the leadership and so became supreme commander of the new Indian National Army. I had known him from concentration camp days and so the next time I had an opportunity to go to Singapore I visited him. I was curious to know why he had offered to raise the new Indian National Army. He was frank enough to admit that he did it to save his life! This was in early 1943. I suggested to him that he should some how get Netajee Subhash Chandra Bose over to handle the political side of the movement, and get a written assurance from the Japanese government.

15

FIGHTING ILLNESS AND DISEASE WITH LADY LUCK

Even after we stopped sleeping in the open and found suitable accommodation for ourselves, the mosquito menace continued, and we had many cases of malaria. My brother, Commandant of the prisoners-of-war camp, suggested that I go to Singapore and beg Mohan Singh for some quinine tablets. So I left for Singapore in the Japanese 3-ton truck that went there every Saturday, since the Japanese had no objection if one of us travelled in it. I reached Singapore and looked for the Supreme Commander's office. I went to his ADC's room and I found a young Second Lieutenant there. I enquired of him where the Supreme Commander was and was told that I could not meet him without an appointment. I told him that this was not necessary as Mohan Singh knew me well and would see me without an appointment. I then asked him his name and he answered, "Rattan Singh" (I have known him ever since, and we still occasionally meet him in Kasauli where we both have houses). Soon, I saw a big car arrive, with a huge flag, and Mohan Singh, wearing the badges of a full general, sitting in the back. I jumped up immediately, went up to the car, and catching

Mohan Singh by his arm, told him that I had come to have a word with him. He took me to his office and sat down in his chair. I sat opposite him and stated that though we might not have joined the Indian National Army, we were still Indians and hoped that he would help us get quinine tablets for those in our camp suffering from malaria. He was very polite and considerate and sent for his DMS (Director Medical Services), who was none other than Lt Col Chatterjee, whom I knew. Mohan Singh explained my problem to his DMS and asked him how many tablets of quinine he had? (I might mention here that for medicine, as for every thing else, the Indian National Army were dependent on the Japanese). He answered, "about 4000". Mohan Singh asked him to give half of them to me. Col Chatterjee went off to collect the tablets and I sat alone with Mohan Singh. He asked me if I had made up my mind to join the Indian National Army. I gave him the same answer every time: that I did not accept his leadership as no one in India knew him and that should Mahatma Gandhi or Pandit Nehru announce over the radio that this was an opportune time for every young man outside India to join the Indian National Army I would instantly do so. I remember he flung the same old cliched line at me: "Theirs' not to question why; theirs' but to do and die". Soon Col Chatterjee arrived with 2000 tablets of quinine, wrapped in a bundle, and I departed with them, after thanking Mohan Singh.

The quinine did not last us long, and the need for some cloth to cover each man at night from head-to-foot was still felt. So, my brother and I discussed what could be done. Now the orders of the Japanese were that if any prisoner-of-war was found missing, or tried to run away, the head of the Commandant would be severed with a sword. However, my brother said that he was ready to take the risk, and that I should go to Ipoh, up-country, by train, and get some bolts of cloth, which could be cut into 6-7 feet pieces and issued to each prisoner-of-war against the mosquito menace.

I Leave Camp for Cloth

The decision to send me to Ipoh to get cloth to fight the mosquito menace was announced at a gathering of officers, who, almost all belonged to the Jind Infantry, my brother's battalion, and the two of us from 5/11 Sikh were also present, Captain Pirthipal Singh and I.

I left the camp through a well-known gap in the airfield fence and walked a couple of miles to the next railway station along the railway line. As a precaution, I pretended to be secretary of the local Indian Independence League. I let my beard down, wore a kurta-pyjama and stuck an enamelled Indian Independence League emblem, a tri-coloured flag with a charkha on it, which we had acquired from Singapore, on my chest. At the station, I waited for the train to come and made straight for the First-Class compartment. There were a couple of Japanese officers already there, and I greeted them with salutations, to which they responded favourably. I told them that I was secretary of the local Indian Independence League and had some work in Ipoh. Being quite hot, both of them were bare of body and wore just a loin cloth, as was their custom. They accepted me in the compartment willingly, and even offered to share their meal of rice and a boiled egg with me. I accepted the meal with thanks, as I had not eaten an egg since I had been taken a prisoner-of-war, and it tasted delicious! I took a sleeping berth (no tickets were required for travel in the train those days) and got down at Ipoh the next morning, after thanking my travel companions, who were proceeding further. Since I knew Ipoh, I went straight to the house of the Superintendent of Police, Gurcharan Singh (a clean-shaven Sikh from Punjab, married to an Indonesian), whom I had known before, and who continued to be employed by the Japanese in the same capacity. He was shocked to see my state. I told him frankly that I was a prisoner-of-war and had come to him for help. He said, as far as he was concerned, I was an Indian and it was his duty to help me in whatever way he could. I told him of our requirement for cloth. He said that it would not be a problem as all the cloth merchants in the town were Indians, and at his bidding they were bound to help. He took me in his car to the cloth merchants' market and, almost, ordered each one of them to give a couple of bolts for a good cause! In no time, we collected nearly 60 bolts of cloth of various texture and colour. He made a bundle of them, put it on the top of his car, and took me straight to his house.

Since I was in Ipoh, incognito, I decided to find out a little bit more about Major Malwinder Singh, who was not only from my battalion, but from my home town as well. I knew his wife well and felt that I had an obligation to get more information about his final moments, as she was sure to ask me on my return. You may recall that while admitted at Alexandra hospital I had mistakenly been handed a telegram announcing the birth of his son. I had subsequently been told that he had been hit and wounded by Japanese tank fire and left to die. However, since his body had not been found, he was reported in Army records to be "wounded and missing". While in the prisoner-of-war camp at Singapore I had heard various rumours that suggested that either he had been picked up and saved by the locals or by the local resistance forces of whom he was now a member. Now that I was in Ipoh, which was just a few miles away from the place where Malwinder had been wounded, i.e. the other side of the Sitang river, I decided to investigate. Sardar Gurcharan Singh suggested that I get in touch with a group of Sikh youth who owned motorcycles and were known to transport Indian Army casualties from the Sitang river to clinics run by Indian doctors. I contacted them but they did not seem to have any news about Major Malvinder Singh. I did, however, get the addresses of a few of the clinics where they transported casualties but failed to find Malwinder who had a prominent scar (a birthmark on his face) which easily identified him. The doctors seemed to know nothing about him either so I returned rather disappointed.

That evening Sardar Gurcharan Singh took me personally to the railway station in his car, together with the huge bundle of cloth, and helped me board the train. This time I had a First Class compartment all to myself. I got down at the station, one short of our camp, and dragged my bundle to the Station Master's office, who again was an Indian. Incidentally, the railways in Malaya were all manned by South Indians. I asked him to look after the bundle till I sent a party over from our camp which was just down the line. This was done the same night and the cloth was distributed to each prisoner keeping in mind each one's body size. Thus we were able to solve our malaria problem. We had a doctor with us, but without medicines it was hard for him to manage.

I Leave Camp Once More for Typhoid Serum and Syringes

When typhoid started in the camp, and we lost a couple of men because of it, it was decided by my brother, in consultation with other officers, that I should leave the camp once more and try to get the serum and syringes required to immunise every prisoner-of-war against typhoid, from civilian friends.

 I left the same way as before, pretending to be secretary of the local Indian Independence League with the Indian Independence League emblem on my chest. By this time, luckily for me, Dara, an old friend, had been installed by the Indian National Army as head of a new set-up to look after prisoners-of-war. He had his headquarters at Kuala Lumpur. So, I made straight for his headquarters and found a Japanese guard at the entrance. I pointed at my Indian Independence League emblem by way of explanation, and the Guard Commander asked me to write down my name on a slip of paper, which he sent in. Very soon, Dara, appeared on the balcony of a double-storeyed house and invited me to come in. He came down the steps to meet me and took me up to his living room. The first thing he said when he saw my physical condition was, "good, we must first make up your deficiency of vitamins". I explained why I had come, and he offered to take me the next day in his car to the secretary of the local Indian Independence League, Sardar Budh Singh, who he said was a very nice fellow, always ready to help.

 The next morning, Dara took me to meet Sardar Budh Singh, who was a very venerable old gentleman, with a long white, flowing beard. I made it quite clear to him, at the outset, that I was a prisoner-of-war from Kluang who had come to him for help as an Indian, as we had a typhoid epidemic in our camp. He replied that as a fellow Indian he considered it his duty to help us. He said that he would collect as much serum and as many syringes as possible from Kuala Lumpur, where there were quite a few Indian doctors. But, he suggested I should go over to Kuala Kangsar and meet Sardar Man Singh the next day and ask him for help as well. So I arrived at Sardar Man Singh's residence the next day where I was warmly welcomed and given a room to stay. He offered to do what was required and suggested that I also go to Penang Island, not very far from there. He said he would ring up Doctor Jaggat Singh, who was a very well to do rubber estate owner, and who had quite a few Indian doctors under his sway in the area. So he rang up Doctor Jaggat Singh, and despite his absence, spoke to his secretary and arranged to have me picked up the next afternoon from the ferry-wharf. On my arrival, I saw a Sikh looking for who me introduced himself as Pritam Singh, the Secretary of Doctor Jaggat Singh, and took me by car to a palatial building, where the doctor, my absent host, lived. Two young girls came out of the house to greet me, aged 13 and 15, and introduced themselves as Doctor Sahib's daughters. The elder one showed me my bedroom which was a delight. It had a four-poster bed with a lovely Dunlop mattress and a mosquito-net tied to all four posts. There was even a Grandfather clock next to the bed. She asked me if I would like to bathe and realising that I did not have a change of clothes offered to lend me her father's 'kurta-pyjama'. She also informed me that after the bath, I could, if I so wished, listen to 'Reh-Ras Path', which the Bhai Jee, on the premises, would be reciting in the prayer room situated next-door. I asked for something to cover my head, and she brought me a silk-kerchief.

After a hot bath, I listened to the 'Reh Ras Path' being recited by the Bhai Jee in his melodious voice. I had almost forgotten how soothing it could be! Later, the secretary suggested that the next morning at 10 o'clock, he would take me to various Indian doctors in the area and I could ask them for whatever I wished. I visited all the Indian doctors and made it quite clear to each one of them that I did not belong to the Indian National Army, but was a prisoner-of-war of the Japanese. It seemed to make no difference to them as they gave me both serum and syringes. During my two day stay at Penang, Shri Pritam Singh, secretary to Doctor Sahib, made a special effort to show me everything worth seeing in Penang. This included a journey by the funicular railway to the famous Snake Temple where thousands of snakes were nestling wherever they could. They were all supposed to be harmless and had obviously been doped with opium.

On my return to Kuala Lumpur, Dara insisted on keeping me for another two days and even dressed me in his suit to take me to the Race Course! He also took me to a dance and dinner at the house of one of his friend's. He had a very fine young officer, Mahabub, as his Adjutant. Though I had by now collected, from three places, enough serum and syringes for typhoid injections for nearly 1000 men Dara would not hear of my return to the prisoners-of-war camp. He insisted that I would have to put on some weight and make up for my deficiency of vitamins before he would release me. Consequently, he fed me chicken two times a day! On the third day of my stay, however, he shared his anxiety with me that his Second-in-Command, a Major recently promoted from the rank of a Junior Commissioned Officer, had somehow got to know that I was a prisoner-of-war and would probably inform the Japanese Military Police. He suggested, therefore, that I leave for my camp by train the same evening, and arranged for a car to take me, along with my parcel of medicines, to the railway station. I got down at a station one short of the camp, and this time the parcel was not too big for me to handle on my own. So I proceeded with it straight to the camp where I delivered it to our doctor, Captain Puri. I had been away from the camp for over a week but fortunately no one had asked for any explanations.

The doctor arranged that the injections should be given in batches, so as not to interfere with the daily requirement of labour, and within ten days every one of the prisoners-of-war had been given the typhoid injection. I had also had one, but as ill luck would have it, I developed typhoid fever within a few days of being injected. According to the doctor this happens sometimes. I used to sleep on the floor next to my brother, and although our strict orders were that any one with an infectious ailment was to be segregated from the rest, in my case my brother made an exception and kept me next to him, in spite of the danger to him. He nursed me with great care. However, my immunity at the time was so low that after 11 days, the normal course of the typhoid fever, I had a relapse and suffered with fever for another ten days. After typhoid, I had a bout of beri beri, and did not really recover my health till the war ended. In fact, I came out of the prisoner-of-war camp a sick-man, and on arrival in India, was admitted into the Military Hospital at Ambala with beri beri, and boarded out of the hospital after two months as Category 'E'. Beri beri, they say, is an ailment that you just cannot get rid of, as it recurs. It has been with me ever since.

16

HOSPITAL FACILITIES FOR PRISONERS-OF-WAR AT SINGAPORE

In health-care, we were much better off than the prisoners-of-war at Singapore. Our Commandant, Lieutenant Colonel Gurbakhsh Singh had ordered that looking after the sick would be our first priority, both in terms of care and nourishing food. People with minor infectious ailments such as coughs and colds were segregated from the rest. By adopting very stringent measures, we were able to overcome malaria and dysentery, though after the loss of a few men. Preventive measures, as advised by the medical officer, were strictly adhered to. I have mentioned earlier how we tried to keep up the morale of the men, by disseminating news that we heard over the secret wireless set. We also set up a gurudwara and a temple.

'Keertan' sessions used to be held every Sunday morning at these places. I must say that the Japanese respected our religious sentiments, and did not interfere with our 'Keertans'. Every Sunday morning, when the Commandant had an opportunity, he would address the men on various subjects connected with our welfare as prisoners-of-war, including arrangements for the sick, etc. We were lucky not to have any case of mental illness, which was so common in Singapore, although we could not prevent people from contracting tuberculosis, due to malnutrition. We tried to segregate such cases, but some were so advanced that, against the patients' wish, we could not help but send them to Singapore. We, however, gave them assurance that an officer from the camp would visit them once a fortnight, without fail, and bring them as much succour as possible in the form of green vegetables, etc. This duty generally fell on me, and I saw some ghastly sights at the hospital at Neesson, in Singapore.

This hospital was being looked after by Lieutenant Colonel GS Chawla. Lt Col Chawla was a very dedicated officer who had landed in Singapore just before the surrender of the Island to the Japanese. And throughout our three and a half years' of captivity as prisoners-of-war, his hospital rendered invaluable service to prisoners-of-war in Japanese captivity. I had met Lt Col Chawla earlier in Rawalpindi, when I was doing an attachment there with a British unit. He was then a young Captain. Apart from being a fine man, he had very good relations with the Japanese medical authorities and managed to get various concessions for his hospital from them. The hospital was located near the Naval Base, in hutments built by the British for the evacuation of the Naval Base personnel, in case of emergency. It had a barbed-wire fence around it and a Japanese guard at the main gate. Our sickmen, as I mentioned earlier, were generally admitted to this hospital and so I used to visit it quite often and always stayed with Lt Col Chawla.

The other hospital for the care of Indian prisoners-of-war was situated on the Johore-Baru Road, Lieutenant Colonel Dutta's Hospital. Besides, there was a Rehabilitation Centre, which operated under Major Hari Singh of the Medical Corps, on the Neesson Road in hutments nearer the town of Singapore. Close to the Bidadari Camp, on the same road, Major Surita Chowdhry, a very fine medical officer, also ran a clinic for sick prisoners-of-war.

I still vividly remember the case of a young officer, a Second Lieutenant, who had been wounded by a mortar shell in the latter stages of the Malayan Campaign. His whole face had been blown off and he was admitted in one of the prisoners-of-war rehabilitation centres, located on Neesson Road in Singapore. He had an open wound and was in terrible pain, without any antibiotics available for his treatment. I was truly concerned about his health, and used to visit him each time I came to Singapore from Kluang. He was a Pathan boy and his name was Zahir. He was not older than twenty one years and, obviously belonged to a well to do and loving family. His co-patients once told me that he had refused to take his food, boiled rice, or whatever it was they gave him, saying that he would not eat unless his mother fed him herself! He often reminisced about how his mother used to give him a glass of milk, with her own hands, in the morning, and would feed him all his meals herself (he must have been the youngest of the family to receive such loving treatment!) and now all he wanted was for his mother to feed him. I am glad to say that this young Second Lieutenant lived on and at a recent RIMCOLIAN (old students of Royal Indian Military College, Dehradun) re-union at Delhi, to which a number of Pakistanis came, I had the pleasure of meeting him along with his wife. I was happy to see that his face was almost complete, thanks to the wonders of plastic surgery! He told me that he had gone abroad to have it reconstructed.

The other case I recall was of another young Pathan, tall and handsome, from the old well-known Hong Kong and Singapore Artillery which was the creation of the British, an elite Regiment which only enlisted men - both Sikhs and Pathans - over 6 feet in height. This young man was a member of an anti-aircraft artillery detachment which had joined the Indian National Army. This detachment had been despatched by the so-called Supreme Command of the Indian National Army to an Island near Singapore on anti-aircraft duty against the Allies' bombers that used to bomb installations at Singapore frequently. The Japanese ship by which they were travelling was, I was told, torpedoed by an enemy submarine and split into two, with all the burning oil spread around the wreckage of the ship. The passengers of the ill-fated ship were thrown into this burning sea. The Japanese on-board salvaged a rescue boat and started picking up men but only the Japanese personnel first, leaving the Indians to fry till the oil burnt out! Later, another Japanese ship came to their rescue and picked up those of them who were still alive. This young man was

A Soldier Remembers 151

the only survivor, and the Japanese, seeing the state he was in, dumped him at the prisoner-of-war hospital at Neesson, in Singapore. When I came on one of my visits I found that this young Pathan was presenting Col Chawla with quite a problem. He refused to eat and was determined to starve to death! Col Chawla took me to meet him and what did I see: a man perfect in every way below the neck, but with only a cranium, swathed in bandages on top. I was told that his face and head had been completely consumed by the burning oil at sea. He could only be force-fed through a pipe; no wonder he had decided to die! Was his life worth living? The patient was in agony and had to be relieved of his pain with morphine injections. He eventually started to die - a very slow and painful death - by starvation, after refusing to be force-fed.

It was in this hospital that I met Major Mehra, a surgeon. He took me to his improvised Operating Theatre, which was just a thatched hut with a bamboo table for operating on. Knives and tongs served as his instruments and yet he performed some major operations - such as removal of stones in the gall-bladder, appendicitis, etc. - successfully! He showed me an emaciated man, who had a haemoglobin count of only one and who was to be operated upon for the removal of stones from his gall-bladder! There appeared to be no other choice.

The shortage of medical equipment and medicines was real. I remember the time when Major Surita Chowdhry once mentioned to me that he was receiving a number of prisoners-of-war suffering from tropical sores and whether it was possible for me to get him some sulphur from upcountry. I promised to look for it. While scrounging around, which was the constant past time of prisoners-of-war, I discovered quite close to Kluang an abandoned depot. Here, in the past, they had produced red-palm oil, which, according to our doctors, was a very good medium for cooking, as it had Vitamin A in it. Besides the depot, was a dilapidated room in which, as luck would have it, I found a bag of sulphur which had been opened and a part of its contents spilled. I filled half a card-board box of sulphur and brought it to camp. Instead of taking the air force truck, in which I normally travelled to go to Singapore hospital, I decided this time to take this card-board box of sulphur to Singapore by train so as to avoid any questions about its contents. I later discovered that this was even a riskier proposition as there had been a number of destructive explosions in and around the country-side, perpetrated by the Communist Resistance Group which was active in the area, and the Japanese were on the look out for materials such as sulphur. However, I tried to camouflage the cardboard box as best I could, and on arrival at Singapore railway station, I engaged a coolie to carry it for me, and tried to walk apart from him, in case he was caught by the Japanese Police. In which event I was prepared to disown him. But, foolishly, I forgot to ask the coolie his name, and wondered how I was going to call for him once I was outside the railway station. Fortunately, he spotted me and so I got the box of sulphur back!

I was met at the station by Captain Sahibzada, our old Medical Officer, who had been by then engaged by the Japanese to broadcast in Punjabi, at the Singapore Broadcasting Centre. He had a car and so it was very easy to carry the box and deliver it to Surita Chowdhry, who was so very grateful for it. But I realised later what a great risk I had taken, for the Japanese knew of only one punishment - beheading the culprit!

To reach our patients with tuberculosis at the Neesson Hospital, I had to pass by the barbed-wire enclosure for the mentally sick of whom there were a fair number. I was told that mental illness was very common among prisoners-of-war. A number of them pretended to be some great personality or the other - Hitler, Mussolini, Tojo, etc. There was one Sikh amongst them who was dressed as the King of Club exactly like the one you find in a pack of cards. Where he managed to get the attire from, or the black paint, with which he had made the club-signs, I do not know. He came up to me and said that he was Mohan Singh, the Supreme Commander of the Indian National Army! I just nodded and walked away. Later I met the medical officer in-charge of the enclosure who admitted that such cases were on the increase in the prisoner-of-war camps and that they did not have enough room to cater for them. I suppose mental depression had a part to play. Thankfully we had no such case in our camp at Kluang, as our living conditions, under the Japanese Air Force, were less stressful.

The TB enclosure where our patients were lodged had five wooden-barracks which terraced down a slope. The patients in the first three barracks were able to walk. Those in the next were all lying on the floor, being advanced cases. In the lower most barrack, I was told, were those who were waiting for their end. It was my unpleasant duty to hospitalise a young lad from our camp who had acted in our plays, in a female role, many a time. He had contracted tuberculosis and eventually we had no choice but to take him to Singapore for admission in Colonel Chawla's hospital. I felt sorry to leave him there but promised to visit him often and bring as many provisions as possible with me for him on each visit. One of our patients was already there and so I laid him down next to him. The next time I came to visit they were in the barrack one above the last. I enquired after them and gave them what little I had brought for them from our camp. There were some pieces of beet-root, some tapioca-bread and four eggs – two for each of them. While returning, I was waylaid by other patients, asking for various things which it was impossible for me to bring for them. I particularly remember a request from a Muslim patient, who had a small beard like a 'Maulvi'. He pleaded with me to bring him a tin of Polson's butter; after eating which, he opined, he would be fully cured! I promised him that, come what may, I would try and get a tin of Polson's butter for him, and would bring it for him the next time I came. On my return, as usual, I went in the morning to report to the Japanese officer so as to get orders for the day's work, and saw that in the corner of his room he had a number of tins of Polson's butter lying around. I begged him to let me have one, and he signalled me to take it. I was very happy that I had got the tin that the sick Maulvi had so craved! After nearly a month, I went back again to the hospital, to the TB Ward with the tin in my hand to deliver it to the Maulvi, who had so desired it. But, to my dismay, I learnt that he had passed away only the day before! I felt really bad at having failed to carry out the wishes of a sick man. So I gave the tin to the first man in the TB Ward who I met.

Now the Medical Orderly in charge of the TB Ward told me a story that you will undoubtedly find hard to believe. Apparently, in the lower most barrack of the ward, where patients who were soon expected to die were shifted, when one of them died, the others would roll over and fleece the dead body of all its possessions, and, in fact, fight like vultures over them - such is human nature!

Burying the Dead

Compared to Singapore, throughout our three and a half years as prisoners-of-war, we had fewer deaths from illness in our camp. The majority of deaths were due to dysentery, a few due to typhoid and a couple were caused by accidents. Even then, we found it difficult to arrange for wood, or buy it from the market (as we had no money) for the purposes of cremating the dead. So we decided to bury them instead and found a place next to our quarters where there was a suitable gap in the barbed-wire fence around the airfield. This was a slightly raised portion of ground just beyond the railway-line. We marked the spot where each body was buried with a wooden plaque which bore the individual's name and other necessary details, in case the body was ever exhumed. However, as we were the subject race, after the War, there was no Graves Commission set up for Indians buried in Malaya as was set up for the British and the Australians who collected the remains of their dead and reburied them with proper Christian rites and rituals in the Commonwealth Graves Commission's various burial grounds. During the War there were many who did not even get a decent burial. Their bodies were often thrown in the next-door trench, or left in the open for the enemy to bury, if they so chose, or for wild animals to carry away into the jungles of Malaya. Such was the fate of many of our war casualties. So we had no choice but to leave the buried behind; and I often wonder if their remains are still there. Only names of the Indian dead were collected and Memorials, like the one at India Gate, bear their names. Even after 50 years of Independence, we have yet to set up a Graves Commission. The reason, of course, usually cited is that we cremate our dead, but, let me tell you, that this is not possible in a war where most bodies of the dead have to be buried. It is time that we Indians also, thought of collecting the remains of our dead after a war and giving them a proper funeral.

Laughter as Medicine

About this time, Captain Prithipal Singh, my colleague from 5 Sikh, developed an itch both on his head and on his chin. The doctor diagnosed it as eczema of some kind, for which he had no medicines. So the next time I went to the prisoner-of-war hospital, I took him along with me and had him admitted. There, Colonel Chawla treated him with some ointment and he did get better, but he had to shave his head and beard.

Soon after, we read in the INA paper, which used to be issued to us weekly, that Lt Col Dara of the Indian National Army had been appointed in-charge of all prisoners-of-war on the Peninsula of Malaya, with his Headquarters at Kuala Lumpur. There was rejoicing among us officers, as Dara was an old friend of mine from Government College, Lahore days - we had been in the same class, and had played hockey together for the College. The next time I went to the prisoner-of-war hospital at Singapore, Captain Prithipal was ready to come back with me. He was now clean-shaven and had a short crop of hair over his head, exactly like Dara's. So I decided to play a prank on my camp at Kluang. I told Prithipal not to speak at all, as I was going to introduce him to the officers of our prisoner-of-war camp as Dara! We both met Subedar Major Sucha Singh, of my battalion, just inside the main gate of our camp, and I introduced Prithipal to him as 'Dara San' (San means 'Sir' in Japanese). Prithipal just nodded his head in acknowledgement and the Subedar Major seemed to accept him as 'Dara San' for as we walked towards the officers' barrack he talked to Prithipal in a very polite and respectful manner. As we arrived at the officers' barrack, where we all resided, I introduced Prithipal to every one as Dara San; and they all accepted him as such. I suggested that some tea be offered to our guest, and a pot of tea was produced in no time at all! Every one of the officers took care to talk to 'Dara San' with great respect, and in a subdued tone, although they were no doubt intrigued by his silence. Soon I blew the whistle on our little joke, and every one of the officers laughed his sides out. How much good it did to every one I do not know, but that was the object of it. I always looked for opportunities to introduce laughter into our lives for they helped us release the pent up tensions that we as prisoners-of-war always lived with.

Medical Advice and a Prescription for Survival

Lt Col GS Chawla, full name - Gurbakhsh Singh Chawla, was a man of many parts. Though a doctor by profession, he had a knack for writing. Finding that prisoners-of-war needed medical advice regarding their diet, during the lean days of their captivity, so as to make up for their daily requirement of vitamins, iron and other essential constituents, he began sending us instructions, in the form of a magazine. He suggested collecting plants that grew wild, such as 'arby' (a long leafed plant), and also advised us to grow, in our back-yard, plants such as beetroot, tapioca, etc. which grew profusely in the tropical climate of Malaya. What is more, to make up for deficiency of iron, so essential for keeping up ones haemoglobin, he suggested that prisoners-of-war eat, however unpleasant, the filings of ordinary nails or of any other pieces of iron. We were also advised to cook along with rice, the leaves of 'arbi', and sweet-potatoes - which again grew in abundance in the tropics - but which tasted so bitter that we were inclined to use them sparingly. And, of course, tapioca roots, when dried, made very good flour for chapaties; and we used it quite often. Though, it was only an excuse for wheat flour, which we missed badly!

Along with these dietary instructions, he would include amusing stories in the magazine to keep up our morale. He often asked me to contribute towards his magazine, which he titled 'The Physician', and I, in fact, became his regular correspondent. I reproduce below one of the contributions that I sent to 'The Physician'. I believe it represents my attitude to the whole episode of our captivity by the Japanese.

Laugh, Prisoner, Laugh

Moments of happiness in a prisoner's life are few and far between; what with the adverse conditions of living and restrictions on his movements, mental quietude is to him a thing unknown. He cannot eat what he likes, he cannot do what he likes, he cannot even think what he likes; for his mind is so straitened through constant anxiety and thoughts of home that it is rendered quite insensitive. Books lose their charm for him, friends their value. He feels himself a spent force, both physically and mentally, with little or nothing to do with the outside world; a being apart from it - a resigned soul!

Yet it is not the passive and calculated resignation of an anchorite, but the racked helplessness of a young foal held in yoke. So that, no sooner does a little resuscitation return than the filly-mind is again struggling to be 'delivered'. But a little 'twitch' reminds it of its position of helplessness. Its mental-way now leads to the edge of the fathom-less abyss of despair, and it is a matter of touch-and-go whether it is going to tumble in, and be lost for ever, or check itself and thus be saved for the better times to come. Some sort of diversion, or recreation, at this critical moment is all that decides the issue.

I have been to the edge of the abyss many a time and have found no better diversion than to sit down with pen and paper and write something, and no better subject than the little jokes of every day prison-life. It was at moments like this that I wrote some light-hearted pieces for 'The Physician', which you might have read in its later issues. 'The Physician', as you know, is being circulated by the prisoners-of-war hospital, Neesson. My thanks are, therefore, due to its editor for publishing them in his esteemed magazine. I send this little piece for the same purpose.

And, finally may I remind you, fellow prisoners, to cheer up and keep faith for:

SOMEONE IS THINKING OF YOU!
Although you are miles from the home that you have,
A strange soil beneath you, and a strange sky above;
Morning and evening, and all the day through,
SOMEONE IS THINKING OF YOU!
Someone remembers, somebody cares,
Your name is whispered in somebody's prayers;
Think of the things that are lovely and true, for
SOMEONE IS THINKING OF YOU!
Through danger and weariness, peril and pain,
In moments of doubting when faith seems in vain;
Keep the bright hope of FUTURE in view, for
SOMEONE IS THINKING OF YOU!!!

Of Human Vices and Virtues

It was found in the prisoner-of-war camps that human addictions to tobacco and alcohol are difficult to overcome. As regards tobacco, prisoners were known to run to the barracks of the Japanese Escort and pick up stubs of cigarettes that the Japanese had thrown out of the windows. And some prisoners inhaled the smoke of whatever they could get hold of, such as jute, dried droppings of ponies, or even paper.

Others addicted to alcohol tried to brew their rice-ration at the cost of going hungry! One such prisoner was Major Ghanshyam Singh, a friend of mine, who had started a furnace in Singapore to brew alcohol out of his meagre ration of rice. He was a very likeable individual and very popular with those who controlled the prisoner-of-war camps and hospitals. In fact, he spent most of his time at the Rehabilitation Centre on Neesson Road.

I used to leave Kluang Airfield once a fortnight carrying eatables for our patients in the prisoner-of-war hospital, and would often visit 'Pop-Eye', the nick-name given to Ghanshyam. He once asked me to get a bottle of rice-arrack for him, produced by the local civilians. I bought one bottle and for my next visit to Singapore, tied it up in a piece of gunny cloth. As was my usual practice, the next time I visited, I carried this bottle in my gunny bag to Neesson Camp. Apparently, the Japanese authorities had issued very strict orders to search all those who entered the prisoner-of-war camp at Singapore and so when I arrived at the Neesson Rehabilitation Centre, the Japanese guard stopped me and wanted to check my bundle. I was, however, very reluctant to open it, as it had a bottle of arrack in it. Luckily for me, at the very same time a Japanese Captain came in his car to inspect the Guard. After he had finished his inspection, I went up to him and explained that I had come from up-country and had brought a bottle for my friend in the camp and that the sentry would not permit me to take it in. The Captain accepted my plea, and signalled to the sentry to let me take my bundle in. The sentry, however, insisted, that while I could take the bottle in, as he had to obey the orders of his Officer, when coming out I had to bring the bottle back, full as it was, for nothing had been said about consuming it there! When I mentioned this fact to my friend Ghanshyam, he exclaimed: "Forget about it! How can the sentry issue such instructions"? 'Pop-Eye' and his friends imbibed the contents of the bottle with relish and slept peacefully that night! The next morning, as I prepared to leave the camp, I was hoping that the same sentry would not be on duty. 'Pop-Eye' accompanied me to the gate, and hid himself behind a bush. I went forward and noticed that there was a different sentry at the gate. This sentry was about to let me go, when, from a distance, the sentry who had let me in saw me, and beckoned me to wait. He ran up to me and asked me to open the bundle of gunny-cloth I was carrying and to show him the bottle. I had put in the empty bottle, and when he asked me why the contents of the bottle had been consumed, I said that what I had understood from his instructions was that I was to bring the bottle back, which I had, and that the question of the contents had never arisen. He slapped me on the face (as was their wont) and as a punishment ordered me to stand to attention, until further orders, facing the sun. I could see 'Pop-Eye' behind the bush watching all this and, perhaps, feeling sorry that I had had to suffer all this because of him. Luckily for me, the truck from Kluang arrived soon after, to fetch me, and the Air Force NCO in-charge of the truck asked me to come as quickly as possible, as he was in a hurry. And thus I was released from my punishment. And, I am sure, that 'Pop-Eye', who had been a witness to all this, was also relieved.

On another occasion, during one of my visits to Singapore, I was carrying a rather large parcel of vegetables, etc., for the sick at the Neesson Hospital. The Air Force NCO in-charge of the truck stopped the truck at the T-Junction of the main Jahore-Baru-Singapore road, and asked me to get down and make my way to the hospital on foot, as he was in a hurry. He said he would pick me up at the hospital the next afternoon at 3 o'clock. I had no choice but to walk the distance of six miles along the road to the hospital, carrying the rather heavy bundle on my person. Not only was the weather hot, but being rather weak due to malnutrition, I had barely walked half a mile down the road when I had to sit and catch my breath. While sitting, I noticed a Japanese flag-car waiting on the road-side. When I looked around, I saw a Japanese officer a little ways up, on a hill, examining something. I waited for the officer to come down and then in my broken Japanese told him where I was coming from, and that since I was ill I was finding it difficult to walk to the prisoner-of-war hospital at Neesson. Could he kindly give me a lift to the hospital, I asked? The officer agreed and made me sit next to him in the rear seat. Thus I arrived at the hospital in great style. The guard gave a salute to the officer's car, and I was dropped off within the hospital premises, well past the guard. In fact this created such an impression on the guard that the next day when I left the hospital he let me out without checking me!

Now I describe an incident that shows that despite the ill treatment at the hands of the Japanese, our men never lost their humanity. It was towards the end of 1943, when, as far as the war was concerned, the Japanese were going through a lean period. Our men, of the Jind Infantry, were working on a drain which ran parallel to the concrete strip of the airfield. Due to the shortage of manpower, compounded by heavy casualties, the Japanese Air Force was now employing young Japanese between the ages of 13 to 15 years. They were being trained for bombing in, what we thought, was a very primitive manner. They were supposed to throw, from their two-engine bomber, a tennis ball on to a red rag tied to a pole, about 30 feet above the ground, which was supposed to represent the target. The aircraft would dive upto the target, by the side of the landing strip, and would try and hit the red flag on the pole. There were often clouds in the sky, which would come in the way. One day we saw an aircraft, on training, enter a cloud, and when it emerged, even we on the ground felt that it would find the dive too steep for safety, and we hoped that the pilot would not try to dive. However, the young pilot decided to dive and came on to the target at a steep angle. The worst happened. The aircraft, after hitting the concrete surface with its tail, crashed in front of us. All the Japanese, who were watching the exercise, were told to run away, as after the accident they were expecting the petrol tanks of the aircraft to burst. Nobody warned our men. They saw the bodies of two young pilots writhing in pain and out of sheer humanity, two of our men, rushed forward and pulled the bodies to safety. Soon afterwards the tanks of the aircraft exploded with tremendous force. The Japanese Commander came back to the scene of the accident and asked for the two men who had brought the bodies out of the fire. Removing the two watches (which incidentally were still working) from the bodies of the pilots, who were now dead, he presented them to the two rescuers and said that he would recommend that the authorities at Tokyo issue scrolls of bravery to them. Whether the scrolls ever arrived from Tokyo and were presented to the two brave men, I do not know.

17

THE JAPANESE SOLDIER

'Kamikaze' - The Divine Wind

The Japanese Army, especially the forward troops or ambushing-parties carried their cooked, or semi-cooked rations, for periods as long as a month, on their person, in the form of boiled or half-boiled rice, tied up in a tube-like cloth container (like our 'bansli'), wound round their waist. They had no separate cook-houses; in fact they had no followers (cooks, etc) in their army. In the field, every soldier was supposed to cook his meal himself in his tiffin-carrier.

For fresh supplies, or meat requirements, they depended on local resources. No wonder then that after the hostilities were over, we saw so many three legged cows; one leg having been severed and eaten by the leading party which would then leave the cow behind as meat ration for the party that followed. This brings me to their method of keeping their meat-rations (supplied on hoof) fresh for a period of time, without the services of a refrigerator, which was difficult to come by, in the field. I saw this while we were on detachment duty, as a working party, with a section of Japanese troops as our escort. While we were supplied a handful of rice, supplemented by wild shrubs and under-growth, collected from the jungle, the weekly ration of the escort section came in the shape of a piglet-on-hoof, transported by truck. To keep the meat fresh (without a refrigerator), the Japanese would cut one leg of the animal one day (for cooking), and tie a torque on the stump to prevent bleeding; cut another leg the next day, and so on, for as long as a week, without caring for the suffering of the animal. Their logic was that after all, they had come all the way from home to die for their country, and had offered themselves for 'kamikaze', so what, if animals had to suffer in the process!

I have seen the ground staff of the Japanese, at Kluang Airfield, carry out tank-hunting training, with a squad of six men, two of whom would be given mines to strap on to their breasts. They would quickly run and lie down, serving the purpose of a human mine, on both sides of the 'tank-tracks' and think nothing of being blown up. Such was the spirit of self-sacrifice of the Japanese soldier! A great deal has already been written about the spirit of 'kamikaze' (divine wind) that prevailed among pilots who volunteered to crash dive into targets.

At Kluang Airfield, we were witness, one afternoon, to the departure of such a flight. Kluang Airfield, under the Japanese, was at first an airfield for bombers, it then became an airfield for fighters, and finally, during a rather lean period, in early 1944, it became a bomber-cum-training airfield for kid-pilots between the ages of 13 years and 15 years. The Commander of the airfield at the time was Major Tani. He had been impressed into service from the University of Tokyo, where he had been a Professor of English. So he spoke English well, and would often come to our officers' quarters, mainly to practise his English with us. We found that he was a better type of Japanese officer, as while conversing with us he would very often talk to us on subjects of personal interest. We thus picked up enough courage one day to ask him if he was married - a subject which we usually avoided in our conversation with a normal Japanese officer. He answered 'yes', and, in fact, pulled out his wallet from his pocket and showed us the picture of his pretty wife and two children - a boy and a girl - both very young. We, naturally, asked him if he ever thought of them; and he replied, rather harshly, "Never! I have handed them over to my nation." He further went on to state that he had come to die for his nation, and was a volunteer for 'kamikaze'. Thus ended this rather personal conversation, on an abrupt note.

One afternoon, in early 1944, Major Tani came to our quarters, fully dressed in his dress uniform - medals, tall-boots and all - and said that he had come to say good-bye, as he was leading a 'kamikaze' flight, and soon his life's mission was going to be completed. We, genuinely, felt sorry for him, as he had been one of the nicer Japanese officers that we had encountered. Once, upon our constantly complaining about our meagre rations, he had invited all of us, officers, to his place for a 'Sakiaki' dinner. The meal consisted of raw vegetables, including sea-weeds (which we ate for the first time in our life) and which, I believe, is a regular feature of the Japanese diet. These were all put in a cauldron of steel (like our 'Karahi') and we were each given a china-bowl, with a raw-egg in it, as well as a pair of chop-sticks. The idea was to pick up a piece of raw vegetable from the cauldron and eat it after dipping it in the raw-egg. This was supposed to compensate us for all the vitamins that our bodies had been deprived off! What was more welcome from our point of view was the glass of thick sweet-beer which he subsequently served each one of us. It was also from him that we learnt of the Japanese tea ceremony. It is a custom that is a legacy from the 'samurai' days, when every 'samurai' was a warrior ready to kill and die by the sword. In each house, a special room, with a low-roof (so that a sword could not be drawn in that room) was set aside for visitors who were received and offered tea in a ceremonial manner. This entailed that the visitor drink tea from the side of the cup, opposite to the one offered, so as to show respect for the host as well as indicate his friendly intentions. This man was now ready to die in keeping with the spirit of the 'samurai'.

Apparently, some ships of the British fleet had been sighted west of Sumatra Island and orders for the kamikaze flight, to deal with these ships, had come from the Japanese Eastern High Command, in Singapore. The orders were that seven aircraft were to take off for the job, with the leading aircraft to be piloted by the Major and the other six by Sergeants. All seven aircraft had explosives packed in their noses, and they had all been garlanded, ready for take off. After bidding Major Tani good-bye, we all came out to watch the planes take off. All the pilot-students under training had lined up on both sides of the aircraft, and were waving paper flags bearing the emblem of the 'Rising Sun', their National Flag. The atmosphere was festive, though we were all rather sombre at the prospect of losing a friend. As the planes readied for take off, the Japanese officers on the staff of the Training School under Major Tani, suddenly jumped onto the aircraft and would not get down, as they said they had also volunteered for 'kamikaze' and did not want to be left behind as their Commander was going. Major Tani tried his best to order them to get down, but they would not budge. So there was an impasse of some kind. Major Tani had no choice but to refer the matter to the High Command in Singapore. Soon orders came that he was to leave for the mission, come what may, as otherwise the ships that were to be targetted were likely to disappear. Major Tani then ordered the youngest staff officer - a Lieutenant - to get down and stay behind to man the wireless-set that was to keep communication with him. This officer, reluctantly, disembarked on his Commanding Officer's orders, and we sat with him around the set. Within less than half an hour, Major Tani spoke to say that there were clouds in the sky and, therefore, he could not see the ships. We were, sincerely, glad to hear this news, as we wished him to come back. But, soon he reported that there was a break in the clouds, and that he, and the rest of the members of his flight were going down through them to see if they could spot their targets. He soon confirmed that the targets had been sighted, gave orders to the rest of his flight companions, and finally while preparing to dive into his target, shouted: "Banzai!" (hurrah!) - their war-cry. This signalled the end of the whole staff of the Training School at the airfield. The result was that the young students left behind would wander, arm-in-arm, singing songs, bereft of staff to teach them. This state of affairs lasted for a month, till more staff could be detailed for the school and brought to the airfield. This incident highlights the spirit of self sacrifice of the Japanese soldier.

If a Japanese soldier was wounded and left behind in battle, rather than be captured he would commit 'Hara Kiri', that is kill himself by his sword. I remember the day that the surrender of Singapore to the Japanese occurred and odd parties of Japanese soldiers came into town. They were little men, shabbily dressed in tattered uniforms, and looked like members of an irregular army. Looking at them we felt

A Soldier Remembers

ashamed that we had surrendered to such an Army! Often, one of them would come up to us and raising his hands in front of us would say: "You tall man, you call yourself a soldier; then why did you surrender? There is no such word as 'surrender' in our dictionary; we would rather be killed in battle than surrender!" If you pointed at his torn uniform and suggested that it was a shame that his Government could not afford another uniform for him, he would reply, "I set out from my country with the resolve that I would fight and die for the country in this very uniform, so that I would not be a burden on my nation; and I am determined to stay in it till I am killed in battle". Such was their brain-washing and yet they were not immune from superstition. Many of the Japanese soldiers sported a 'million stitches' scarf around their neck. This scarf was supposed to have been sewed, a stitch at a time, by a million maidens in Japan, and according to the soldiers wearing it, it would bring good-luck and prevent the wearer from being struck by a bullet. I have forgotten what this scarf was called in Japanese, but we used to call it the 'million stitches scarf'.

18

THE STRUGGLE TO STAY ALIVE

Stealing Rations

Although the Japanese, avowedly, said that they had not signed the Geneva Convention, we had an understanding with them that they would not employ our men in the digging of their field-works, etc., and I must say that they stood by it. While they would dig their own field-works for the defence of the airfield, they would use our men only to transport their cooked rations, i.e. boiled rice, cooked pieces of fish, or boiled eggs, and this working-party was the most popular of all!

    The reason, we discovered later, was that there were only one or two Japanese who supervised the ration working-party, and since the prisoners-of-war were usually hungry, this provided an opportunity to them to help themselves to handfuls of cooked rations which were swallowed while on the move. The Japanese were none the wiser! Similarly, another popular working-party was that which required a couple of men to load the Japanese weekly rations from the railway station at Kluang. These rations, sent by train from Singapore, included cases of beer. It appears that this working-party of two men would make sure that there was a case of beer on top of the load. While travelling from the station to the storeroom at the camp, a distance of half a mile, they would ride on top of the vehicle and consume at least two bottles of beer, and would throw the empty bottles away, into the jungle, en route. Later, while unloading the rations, this half-empty cardboard case would be placed underneath the other cases and thus it would go unnoticed. One day, however, things went wrong. The working-party, mistakenly loaded a case of 'sake' on top of the truck, thinking it was beer. 'Sake', a wine, is much more potent than 'beer'. The result was that by the time they reached their destination, the storeroom at the camp, they were completely drunk and were lying on top of the truck in a stupor. The driver of the truck got down and shouted "Oh, India!" (this being their normal way of calling Indians) except this time there was no response! The driver, with the help of a couple of more Japanese climbed up and threw the two senseless bodies down on the ground and beat them with a stick. Not that it made a difference, for the two men being beaten were dead to the world! They then sent for my brother, the Camp Commandant, and we had to carry the two drunken men, now beaten to a pulp, back to the lines on improvised stretchers. The next morning, my brother and I went to find out how these two men were doing, and found them lying on the ground looking well and refreshed! My brother remarked, "Did it not serve you right (to be beaten)?", and they replied, "Yes, but it was like a massage that we would not mind going through every day provided we are drunk!"

Rearing Chickens

In early 1944, although things were looking up for us as far as the War was concerned, we were feeling the pinch of malnutrition. We had been prisoners-of-war for nearly two years and had subsisted during this period on just boiled rice and a few fresh herbs and leaves that we occasionally managed to collect from the jungle. But we had the good fortune of having a Camp Commandant who was always concerned about the welfare of the sick. He collected us one day and outlined a plan he had to run a poultry farm and a vegetable garden in the officers' yard of the camp, whose produce, in the form of eggs, would all go to the sick, who were either in our camp or at Singapore hospital.

The construction of chicken-pens was no problem, as any amount of chicken-mesh and timber was available at the airfield. The initial lot of roosters and hens were collected from the villages around the airfield, in exchange for their weight in rice. Fortunately, the Japanese NCO detailed to liaise with us at the time, was not only from Manchukuo (and thus sympathetic to us) but was also a Christian. So with his help, we collected a sufficient number of birds to start our poultry farm. We used to feed our fowl mostly on weeds and worms collected from the jungle, and also on snails, of which there were plenty in the tropics. There are a couple of stories connected with this farming venture that I must relate.

To get a hen out of the rut of not laying eggs, we used to tie the culprits leg with a string. Once we did this to a hen, and the next morning found it dead. It had obviously been bitten by a poisonous snake, as we could see snake tracks on the ground and some signs of the struggle put up by the bird. The loss of a bird was unbearable, and yet since it had snake venom in it, no one would go near it! Now, I had been a pre-medical student and had done many dissections on animals. I was, therefore, of the opinion, that we should not allow this bird to go waste, but should eat it after taking the heart and other major organs out and after washing the flesh thoroughly. But no one was willing to take the risk. So I decided to cook the bird for myself, after taking the precautions mentioned above. While eating it and after, I was the cynosure of all eyes as everyone was waiting for the poison to take effect after six hours. When I got up the next morning hale and hearty there were many who wished to share the remains of the chicken with me! Such is the urge for survival!

Now for the second story. Once we chased a sow on the airfield, with a young piglet behind her. The sow escaped but we managed to catch the piglet and enclosed him in a coop adjacent to the one that had some newly hatched chicks in it. The piglet must have been really hungry, because by the next morning we found that it had killed and eaten most of our chicks! We decided to hold a court-martial of the piglet (for we had any amount of spare time on hand and a few law books). The court was assembled by the order of the Commanding Officer, complete with a 'friend of the accused' and a representative of the advocate general. Evidence was presented by both the prosecution and the defence, and by the order of the court, the piglet was sentenced to death! It went straight to the cooking pot of the sick in the camp.

Growing Vegetables

For the vegetable garden, we had to break fresh ground. Looking around, we found an open patch near our camp, but it had elephant grass growing on it, may be for centuries, and despite all our efforts- for we were all farmers' sons - we found it difficult to loosen the roots which bound the earth together. Eventually we did succeed, but at the cost of the two youngest among us - that is Lieutenant Ram Singh of Jind Infantry and I. Both of us developed beri-beri soon afterwards. Our calves and feet got swollen and were subject to what is called 'pitting' - a sign of cardiac beri-beri. The only cure for it is Vitamin 'B' injections, which could be got only from the Japanese. I promised my colleague, Ram Singh, that I would one day, request the Japanese officer in-charge of our camp, for these injections. Well, that day came soon, and the Japanese officer was kind enough to hand me a whole carton (blue in colour) which I thought, probably, contained at least a dozen vitamin phials. I put it quickly in my pocket, without looking inside. When I got back and opened the box, I found that there were only two phials in it. And, although, I was disappointed, I told myself that something was better than nothing! I informed Ram Singh that I had managed to get two phials of Vitamin B serum, and that we should take an injection each the next morning. We both turned up, punctually at seven, at Dr Jawaharlal's hut, and handed him the carton with the two phials. As Ram Singh was younger, I asked him to go into the hut and have his injection first. The doctor took one phial out of the carton, filled his syringe and gave Ram Singh his injection. Then he took out the second phial, flicked it with his forefinger to get the serum down, but could see nothing. He came out of the hut to examine the sealed phial again to ascertain if there was any serum in it. Sorrowfully, he declared that there was none. Although, I was naturally disappointed, I could see that Ram Singh, a very fine officer and a gentleman, was equally distressed. Had he been able to do so he would have somehow taken the serum out of his body and given it to me. But let me tell you that this self-sacrifice that had been forced on me had the effect of ten injections, and I immediately felt much better!

Food for the Soul

Now I must tell you of my encounter with Vedanta in the prisoners-of-war camp.

At Klaung Airfield, where we were employed as a working-party, a Japanese officer, by the name of Captain Sato, arrived to command the Station. He had apparently been a teacher of English at Tokyo University before being impressed into the Japanese Air Force. I went one morning to get orders from him for the next day, and I saw on his table the complete works - 8 volumes - of Swami Vivekananda's writings. Upon enquiry, he mentioned that he was a great exponent of Vedanta, and a follower of Saint Rama Krishna. As he was at the time busy translating Vivekananda's work into Japanese he asked me whether I would help him. I was rather surprised that a Japanese should be interested in the philosophy of Vedanta, but then I remembered Mrs Khanolkar, who too had been a foreigner. He asked me, after I mentioned that I had been initiated into Vedanta, to visit his prayer-room at his residence. This I did, and found it to be exactly like that of Mrs Khanolkar's - with a comfortable seat on the ground for meditation with an 'ishta', just a piece of stone, to meditate through. He then gave me the eight volumes of Vivekananda's books to read, and translate. I had plenty of time to go through the books and enjoyed them immensely. I then tried to help him much as I could especially with the Hindi and Sanskrit terms.

19

THE END OF THE WAR

The item of greatest interest to us, that I heard over our secret radio, was the capture of Mussolini and the transfer of Italy's allegiance to the Allies. As luck would have it, the very next day, General JKT Bhonsle, the Supreme Commander of the Indian National Army at the time, arrived with a Japanese Major General in tow, at our camp. He described the War situation thus: the Germans were progressing on both sides of the Suez Canal where they were planning to join up. And added, "Now is the time for you to join the Indian National Army". I took Bhonsle aside and told him the news about Mussolini's capture and Italy joining the Allies, pretending that it was a rumour that I had heard from the Chinese labour working at the airfield. I asked him to go back to Singapore and have it confirmed. The Japanese, of course, did not allow any one to listen to the BBC and so this was news to him as well. He did not have the heart thereafter to ask us to join the INA! After about an hour's visit he returned to Singapore and that was the last I saw of him for he was soon replaced by Netajee Subhash Chandra Bose.

More and more encouraging news came in every day over the radio. The news of the Allies victory over the Axis powers was, of course, most welcome, and we noticed that the Japanese were preparing for the last act. We could not, of course, tell what was going on in their minds. They would always say that they had no such word as 'surrender' in their vocabulary. And then would follow it up by saying "Before we die, we shall kill you all!" Our future, at this stage, was very uncertain.

We, the officers, decided to prepare for a break-out from the camp, should such a need arise. Towards this end we started to collect rifles from here and there and hid them as best we could. Besides, in case we needed it in an emergency, we buried a motor cycle, less its platinum-point (which I still have with me) in a hole below our quarters, lined with corrugated sheets, to prevent it from rotting in a tropical climate. When the War ended we left it where it was.

Then we got news of the Atom Bomb! It was something new, and unimaginable! We heard over the secret radio, on news relayed by the BBC, that the Japanese had been given an ultimatum to surrender by the 15th of August 1945. But we were told that the Far East Commander of the Japanese forces, Count Tra-Uchi, who was located in Singapore, had decided, in spite of orders from the High Command, to fight it out till the very end! The 15th of August passed and yet there were no signs of surrender in Singapore, or Kluang. Count Tra-Uchi, who incidentally was related to the King of Japan, adamantly resisted till the 22nd of August. And then suddenly came the news of the Allied forces occupying Singapore and their landing at Seramban, near Kuala Lumpur, in the North of Malaya. Not long thereafter the Commonwealth War-times Crimes Investigation Party enquiring into crimes committed by Japanese officers visited our camp. By then we had realised that something was a foot as all the aircraft had been flown away and the Japanese were busy destroying secret papers.

The Tables Turn and the Japanese Surrender

This team was headed by a British Brigadier, and consisted of our officers. They arrived in jeeps - vehicles which we were seeing for the first time. We had been told that they were coming, and Lieutenant Colonel Gurbakhsh Singh, the Camp Commandant, had directed that no officer was going to blame any Japanese officer, as, considering the circumstances, the Japanese Air Force had behaved quite decently with us. The team had all the Japanese officers in station line up before us, and asked us to point a finger at any one who might have misbehaved, or tortured us. But we stood still and pointed at nobody. The Brigadier asked once again, but our reaction was the same. The team then left and as already described in the introduction, within minutes, a Japanese staff car pulled up in front of our gate, and the Station Commander, a Japanese Major General descended from it, and asked for the Commandant, my brother. The latter appeared in his normal bed-raggled state, expecting to hear something unpleasant. But to our surprise the Japanese Major General, the Station Commander, came to attention in-front of my brother, and bowing reverently said in his broken English, "You are a bigger man than I am; and I have come on behalf of all Japanese officers in Station to apologise for anything that we might have done wrong." We were all too stunned to respond! The Major General then turned back, walked past his car and went on. Having gone about fifty yards beyond his car, he suddenly came back and bowing in front of Lt Col Gurbakhsh Singh again asked his permission to take out a cigarette-box from the car. My brother nodded his assent and the Japanese Major General bowed his head once more, collected the box of 555 cigarettes from the dashboard of the car, and departed on foot. Such is the national character of the Japanese! This incident also shows how through forgiveness you can win the heart of the toughest enemy! There is a lesson in this for all of us. In the evening, a Japanese Captain, from their Station Headquarters, came to deliver us a complete list of weapons and ammunition vehicles with them, and also brought an offer from his Commander to move into our camp while we moved into the barracks occupied by them. But my brother, the Commandant, refused to move. As for the Japanese men, those of them who did not wish to surrender, had already disappeared into the jungles of Malaya. From among those who remained, we used their services to guard some vital points in the town of Kluang, before proper administration could be established.

It is the curse of war that during the time of no rule, between surrender of one Army and the take-over of the administration by another, there is a lot of restlessness and disturbance in the country. I had had a glimpse of it in the town of Singapore on the 15th of February 1942, and now in the country-side around Kluang. There was a lot of rape, killings and looting, by the unruly elements, as reports from the surrounding villages indicated, and we could do nothing about it. We heard that the communists (mostly Chinese) were busy holding court and killing their opponents outright! Later these Resistance Forces came out in the open in the town of Kluang and put up buntings and banners, declaring deliverance by the British and 'good-ridden' from the Japanese! They did not know English very well, for I remember, in their buntings the word 'emancipated' was written as 'emaciated', and it sounded very funny! We had to issue them a warning to keep out of the city of Kluang, and they quickly packed up and left.

Unexpected Visitors and Welcome Supplies

Last, but certainly not least, a couple of officers, an English Captain and an Australian Lieutenant came into our camp with a wireless set (on the day of the surrender of the Japanese) from Force 136, a secret organisation working in the jungle next door to us. They had apparently known of our location and had come as a result of instructions from SEAC (the South Eastern Allied Command) located at Ceylon. They were in wireless communication with SEAC, and immediately directed that some essential supplies be dropped for us at Kluang, by air. The next day, supplies such as hair oil, tooth-brushes and tooth-paste, vitamin tablets and so on, were dropped at Kluang Airfield. They were warmly welcomed by us!

I must describe a strange incident connected with this air-drop of supplies by the British personnel of Royal Army Service Corps, from Ceylon. Next to one of the containers, I found a watch, with its strap broken but in working condition. I decided to send it back to the owner with a note asking that on arrival he acknowledge receipt. I then delivered it to SEAC Headquarters at Singapore, and described the circumstances under which it had been found. Within a month, I got a reply from the owner of the watch to say how happy he was to have recovered it; and I felt very satisfied!

We Travel up Country

Now that we had a car, left behind by the Japanese Commander, and we had heard of the arrival of the 1st Battalion of the Patiala Forces up North, my brother and I planned to travel by car to meet them and get the latest news. We decided to take Subedar Major Sucha Singh of my battalion with us as well as a mechanic in case we were stranded on the way due to a defect in the car's engine. So, we set off for Kuala Lumpur on the only road that ran along the ridge of the Peninsula. What had once been a metalled road now had weeds growing on both sides of it, due to non-maintenance, and therefore, it was not easy to drive along it. At one spot, after travelling for about a hundred miles, the road suddenly disappeared, and we fell down a slope into a mudbank. The jolt had obviously damaged the car. We soon realised that the bridge on the road had been destroyed and that we had no choice but to wait for help. Within half an hour, a vehicle arrived on the opposite side of the bridge, and as luck would have it they were engineers from the British forces, examining the road! They got to work, and winched our car out of the mud bank onto their side of the bridge, and then off they went, on their four-wheel drive, to complete their mission, leaving us behind with our mechanic to repair the damage to the car. The battery, which had been disconnected, was connected again and the engine of the car started functioning. The connecting-rods of the front-wheels, that had bent, were straightened out with stones, and we were on our way again and arrived without any further mishaps. Here, unfortunately, bad news awaited us as it had just been confirmed that Sucha Singh's son had died in battle in Burma, a few months back. The whole charm of our meeting up with the Patialas seemed to evaporate.

The first thing we asked for, on arrival, from the Patialas, was food cooked with onions which we had not tasted for ages! Of course, we also relished the salt in the meal that we had been deprived of all this while.

The Secret Wireless Set is Out

As for the wireless set that we had been using, I dug it out from under my bunker and found that all the wooden parts of the set had been eaten up by the tropical vermin and only its metal-parts remained which included the inside of the wiring; and yet the set had continued to work. I wanted to keep it as a momento. So I handed it to a shopkeeper in the town of Kluang, and ordered a wooden case for it. When we returned from our trip to the Patialas it was a Sunday, and the train which was coming from Singapore, to take the prisoners-of-war of our camp, had already left for Kluang. I was keen to collect the skeleton of the set in its wooden box before I boarded the train but being a Sunday the shop was closed, and there was no one who knew the shop-keeper's residential address. Therefore, I had no choice but to leave the car, with its keys in it, at the railway station and catch the train to Singapore, leaving the doughty skeleton of a wireless set behind!

20
OF LEADERSHIP & LUCK

I must record here my admiration for my elder brother, Lieutenant Colonel Gurbakhsh Singh, Officer Commanding, Jind Infantry, which was a battalion belonging, at the time, to the Native Indian State Forces of Jind State, and on loan to the British Government, for the duration of the War, as Imperial Troops. My brother was a remarkable leader of men from whom I learnt the art of leadership during our period of captivity under the Japanese in Malaya. He was the embodiment of all the qualities of a soldier, and was a human being of a very high order.

I was ten years his younger and looked up to him as a father figure. He had looked after the affairs of the home, when my father was away in the employment of Jind State. When I was a student at Government College, Lahore, from 1929 to 1933, I used to write to him to send me my college fees and personal allowances, etc. I was lucky to have had him with me in the prisoner-of-war camp, in Singapore, when the surrender took place, and also to have had the benefit of his advice during the creation of the Indian National Army, under Mohan Singh. Throughout this period, he acted wisely and steadfastly. Although

Author's elder brother, Brig Gurbakhsh Singh (1952).

the senior most among the Indian prisoners-of-war, in command of a battalion, he never sought the limelight.

His powers of leadership, and his hold over his men, can be judged from the fact that his was the only Unit, amongst all the Units of the Commonwealth Forces, in Singapore, that stayed together as a battalion, under his command, down to the last recruit. Their answer to the Indian National Army's propaganda teams always was that their Commander was their 'Mai Bap' and whatever he decided would be acceptable to them. No wonder then that the Indian National Army were so keen to have him and his battalion in their midst!

When we were hijacked by the Japanese Air Force to Kluang Airfield as a working party, Lieutenant Colonel Gurbakhsh Singh's powers of leadership came to the fore. He was extremely fair to the men and ordered that all nourishment, rations, etc., even when produced by our combined efforts, must first go to the sick in the camp, or to those evacuated to the prisoner-of-war hospitals in Singapore. He saw to it that the men's safety, honour and welfare came first, always, and every time. To keep up the morale of the men, he organised musical concerts, songs and dramas on social subjects (which, incidentally, he wrote himself in Gurmukhi) in which his NCOs and men participated. We celebrated all National days, holding rallies, when the National Flag (with a Charkha in the middle, at the time) would be unfurled and patriotic songs sung. The latter were borrowed from the Indian National Army. Last, but not the least, a 'Keertan', with the Guru Granth Sahib displayed, used to be held in the camp every Sunday morning, which officers made it a point to attend. At these Sunday gatherings, Lt Col Gurbakhsh Singh used to get up and address the men, briefing them on the latest situation of the War (heard over the secret radio, but given out as rumours heard from the Chinese labour). During discussion with the men the question of joining the Indian National Army used to sometimes crop up. My brother's answer was simple: "We need to stay together. It is up to the majority of you to decide". But the men used to say in unison: "You are our 'Mai Bap'; whatever you decide will be acceptable to us". And the net result was that we stayed out of it. Although it used to annoy me at the beginning, as to why the men should be asked to decide, I later saw in it the great art of leadership. It was the way to induce them to leave the decision to the leader! Being a State Forces battalion, all the officers came from the same State (almost from the same town, Sangrur, which was the capital of the State) and a few of them were interrelated. And so their loyalty and obedience was guaranteed; while I had added just two officers (Prithipal Singh and I) and three JCOs, who were personally loyal to me. Any decision taken by all of us was safe from being divulged. And that's how my brother could take the risk of sending me out of the camp, occasionally.

I attribute our survival as prisoners-of-war to the honest intentions and good will that we had for one another, as well as to luck. Otherwise how could we have escaped from going to Rabal Island from where, I believe, no prisoner-of-war returned alive? There are even reports of the Japanese resorting to cannibalism, because of lack of food there! We sat for three days, in soot and rain, on the wharfs of Singapore, waiting for the Japanese bottom that was to take us to Rabal Island. As luck would have it, it was torpedoed on the way. We were then shifted to cattle-wagons and transported in a newly repaired, and rickety train, destined for the 'Death Railway' of 'Bridge over the River Kwai' fame. However, we never reached as on the way we were commandeered by the Japanese Air Force that had need for a working party at Kluang. Was this not lady luck at work?

I do believe, however, that no matter where we had ended up my elder brother, Lt Col Gurbakhsh Singh's tact and ability to adjust to events as they occur would have seen us through, even in the camp of the 'death railway'! As my brother often told his men, "These are difficult times and we must accept our position as prisoners-of-war of the Japanese." And it was this spirit of forbearance and forgiveness that eventually won the hearts of all who knew him, including the enemy.

Compared to prisoner-of-war camps in Singapore and elsewhere, our camp in many ways was better. We had our own system of passes for leaving the camp. My fellow prisoners-of-war used to call my pass the Magna Carta! Thanks to my secret radio I was able to keep in touch with the latest news about the War and pass it on to others in the camp and to friends whenever I visited Singapore. I was the first to tell them about Mussolini's capture and about the dropping of Atom Bombs on Hiroshima and Nagasaki. At that time, nobody knew anything about such a bomb (the knowledge then about nuclear energy was all theoretical) and at first no one would believe me. They were, of course, very happy and wanted to believe that it was true, as it was going to end the War.

21

COMING HOME

Reunions and Partings

At Singapore, we met our old comrades, the British officers of 5/11 Sikh, and it was quite a reunion. I was particularly close to Captain Russel Roberts, who had shared a hutment with me at Kuanton. While Roberts was incarcerated in Changi jail his wife, who had managed to send their young daughter to safety to England, spent her time throughout the war in a prisoners-of-war camp on the island of Sumatra. As the war ended, he was looking forward to being united with her, but tragically as she was being brought from Sumatra to Singapore by air, she died on the way. Another instance of how tragic war is!

I was invited for dinner one evening by Lt Col Kalah, who was commanding a battalion, and he presented me with a Japanese sword which I still have with me. Unfortunately, Col Kalah got killed in Indonesia later while operating against the rebels there. During this period under the Japanese, we had received no mail from home, nor any welfare parcels from the International Red Cross, which, we believe, the Japanese left lying in Singapore and never distributed among the prisoners-of-war for whom they were meant.

A Soldier Remembers

After spending a few days in the salubrious climate of Singapore and eating nourishing food, we travelled to Madras in a French luxury liner, in the care of nurses and nursing orderlies. There, on landing, we were met by the Governor of Madras. We were then provided clothing, paid our arrears in pay, and sent off to our homes on two months leave. It was good to meet our parents, and near and dear ones, after so long. It was truly a memorable reunion!

Back Home in India

I was, however, not well when I returned from the prisoner-of-war camp, as I was suffering from beri beri, a Vitamin B deficiency. So after 15 days stay at home, I went to report to the Military Hospital at Ambala. There, the physician examined me thoroughly and admitted me into an Officers' Ward. Just before lunch, a nurse arrived with a medical orderly who was carrying an opened bottle of beer. As he tried to pour it out for me, I protested to sister that I was a teetotaller. But she was adamant and said: "The doctor has ordered that you are to consume a bottle of beer before each meal". And while I was drinking the beer I remember her saying, "Major, in a fortnight's time, you will be down on your knees begging for it!", to which I replied: "Sister, that day will never come". While all these years I have stuck to my resolve, it is true that if I am to make an exception it is for a glass of beer now and then! In fact, I started a new drink in the army, which came to be known as my special drink, when I began to take my beer with a little soda added to it. Someone once cleverly described it as a drink that looks like a strong whisky, tastes like beer and has the effect of soda!

Meeting Friends from the INA

While in the Military Hospital at Ambala, I got a message from the Adjutant General's Branch, Army Headquarters, enquiring if I was willing to give evidence against the three Indian National Army officers, viz. Mohan Singh, Shah Niwaz and Dhillon, who were being court martialled. I refused on the grounds that I had been a prisoner-of-war the whole time and knew nothing about the Indian National Army. That seemed to settle the matter. It may be noted that all those officers who gave evidence at the Court Martial of Indian National Army officers, were awarded OBE, by the British. But I have no regrets for I was not prepared to compromise my principles of life for anything. However, since all the senior Indian National Army officers had been very helpful and decent to me, I felt it my duty to go and see them in Delhi, where I was told they were incarcerated. So, after being boarded out of the Military Hospital I took a Chevrolet station wagon from home, and donning my Captain's uniform, departed for Delhi.

On arrival, I went to Army Headquarters to enquire where the Indian National Army personnel were being kept and whether I could go and see them. Going up the steps of North Block, I met Rajinder (commonly known in the Indian Army as 'Dhobi') who told me that while a few of the Indian National Army personnel were being kept in the Cantonment, others were in the Red Fort. So, I went straight to the Cantonment and it did not take me long to find the camp where they were lodged behind a barbed-wire enclosure. I met my friends there: Major Taj Mohammad (of my battalion) and Habib-ul-Rehman (who had been Military Secretary to Netajee, and who showed me the blistered hands with which he had tried to smother the flames that had engulfed the body of Netajee Subhash Chandra Bose, after his plane crashed). I also met, at the gate of this enclosure, Major Mehra, who had come out to meet his wife and 5 year old son. I was surprised to find him there, for, as far as I knew, he had been a prisoner-of-war, posted as a surgeon at the Neesson Prisoners-of-War Hospital. But, apparently at one stage he had signed-up for the Indian National Army, and the British had found his name in some old files. Taj's case was similar. He had been caught by the Indian National Army personnel somewhere in Malaya up-country and had been made to sign up. Upon arrival at Bidadari Camp, when he discovered that I, at the time the senior-most Indian officer of the battalion, had not signed-up, he joined us and stayed on with us as a prisoner-of-war for about six months, and even accompanied us to the Kluang prisoner-of-war camp. However, the Indian National Army (because of his earlier signatures) had caught up with him and had taken him to Singapore. The enclosure I had gone to in the Cantonment was meant for 'White' personnel of the Indian National Army. Upon enquiry, I was told that the 'Blacks' were enclosed in the Red Fort.

So, soon after, I got into my station wagon and headed for the Red Fort. I entered the Red Fort without anybody questioning me. In fact, I asked the British military personnel posted on duty (they looked like military police) as to where the enclosure of the Indian National Army personnel was, and they directed me all the way, without questioning me even once. I was directed across the railway line, which I had not seen before, and as my car arrived outside the barbed wire enclosure, the British guard on duty pulled the barbed wire barring the door aside and let me and my station wagon in. It was not long before I came across the ten-foot high fence enclosing the 'Black' personnel of the Indian National Army. I parked the car to one side, and started chatting with them as a friend would, for these were people, for example Dara, who had been good to me and helped me when I had been a prisoner-of-war. I enquired about Mohan Singh and was told that he was in a cell next-door. So, I went to look him up and enquired after his welfare. Soon I heard shouts of 'Inqlab Zindabad' from passengers of a train that had halted on the line passing through the Red Fort and the Indian National Army enclosure near where I was standing. This, I believe, was a ritual that occurred every morning as the passenger train passed through the Red Fort. The passengers of the train would pull the chain of the train and force it to halt near the Indian National Army personnel's enclosure and would start shouting 'Inqlab, Zindabad'. They were answered by the Indian National Army personnel in similar vein. There was quite a din for good five minutes this time, till the train moved on again. The noise brought the Military Police Colonel out of his office, in the Red Fort. He arrived in his Army car and when he found me standing there, right next to the fenced enclosure, with my car parked nearby, he wanted to know who I was and how I had managed to get in? I gave him my name and said that I was there since nobody had stopped me on the way. He just could not believe it; and looked quite flabbergasted about the whole situation. He said it was very serious; and that I should get in with him in his car, and that he would arrange for my station wagon to be driven to his office.

I accompanied him to his office, where he detailed a middle-aged civilian to take my statement. I told him everything about me, including the fact that I happened to be near the enclosure where the Indian

National Army prisoners were because no body had stopped me on the way. I explained that I had gone there as I had always had good relations with the Indian National Army, in spite of the fact that all the time I was in Malaya I had remained a prisoner-of-war of the Japanese. As they had been good to me I had come to ask them, if in return, I could be of any use to them? My statement was sent to the Colonel of the Military Police, who after reading it asked me to come into his office, and enquired if I knew any body at Army Headquarters. I thought for a moment, and then answered: "Yes, General Savory used to be my Company Commander at the Indian Military Academy. Whether he remembers it now, or not, I do not know?" The Colonel could not believe his ears as I was talking about the Adjutant General of the Army! He immediately rang up the Adjutant General's office, and spoke to General Savory himself. The General remembered me, but since he was leaving his office for home, he asked the Colonel to send me to his house. I arrived there in an Army car, with a Major of the Intelligence Branch accompanying me, and my car following, with another driver. General Savory was sitting in the verandah of his house, and had a cup of tea and a chair ready for me. We exchanged a few words of greeting, having met for the first time since the days of the Indian Military Academy when I was his cadet. Incidentally, he belonged to the same Regiment - the Sikhs - as myself, and, it was at his instance that I had joined the 5/11 Sikh. He, naturally, asked me about the battalion - although, as Adjutant General of the Indian Army, he must have known that almost the entire battalion had joined the Indian National Army and that inspite of that, I had stayed a prisoner-of-war during the entire period. In my defence, I argued that I had done nothing wrong by visiting the Indian National Army personnel lodged in the Red Fort for they had all been good to me during my difficult days and the least I could do was ask after their welfare. In the end he said, "Forget about it; you have done nothing wrong. Had I been in your place I would have probably done the same". He sent the Intelligence Major off, and said that I could go wherever I wished. After this incident I developed a close relationship with General Savory and used to regularly correspond with him when he returned to England. On his retirement in 1947, he was made a full general and was conferred with a knighthood. From then on he became Sir Reginald Savory.

Returning to Normalcy

Towards the end of the year, I managed to get a vacancy in the Unit Commander's Course, at Dehradun. There I met my old IMA friend Chania Atal, with his newly wedded wife, Chandra. And since I had not quite recovered from beri-beri, Chandra fed me with the choicest of fish dishes (which she herself cooked) so that I would put on some weight. I can never forget their kindness. Thereafter, in April 1945, I was posted to the 4th Battalion of the Sikh Regiment, at Cambelpur, beyond Rawalpindi. As Second-in Command of the battalion I spent the summer of 1946 with them. Regrettably, Atal died a few years later of heart-failure and Chandra passed away recently - what a loss of good and kind friends!

I was later selected to attend the first long course at Staff College, Quetta, which commenced in February 1947. I drove all the way to Quetta in my small German car – DKW.

First Long Course at Staff College – Quetta

The journey to Quetta in my DKW was quite eventful. The first part on the first day, was along the canal banks and this caused delay, as the locks on the canal road had to be opened. With the result, I fell short of my destination – Multan – by many miles. Towards the evening I decided to stop at a railway station along the way. As I walked on the railway platform looking for a waiting room in which to spend the night I noticed a railway saloon standing by. I looked in and found that it was occupied by the railway engineer of the region. He had to wait there for the night and kindly offered me a berth in his saloon. It was a godsend, and I readily accepted his offer. Not only was the bedding all laid out, but he invited me to have dinner with him which was prepared in the saloon kitchen by a retinue of cooks! So I spent the night in comfort and left for Multan early next morning, after thanking my host for his hospitality.

At mid-day I arrived at Multan and had to look around for a rest house. I spotted a big provisions store and before taking any further action asked for a list of their customers from among the army officers in station. And whose name do I see but that of Lt Col Keval Rattan, a very close friend, with whom I had studied in school in my home town Sangrur! So I rang him up, and while he was equally surprised to hear from me, he instantly invited me to his house. We met like long lost friends and though I would have wished to stay on longer I had to leave the next day, early in the morning. It appeared that there were two ways to get to Quetta from Multan: one through Lora-Lai, a hilly route, and rather circuitous, and the other through the Sibi desert to Jacobabad and thence along a very good and frequented road to Quetta. I decided to take the second and Keval Rattan's wife very sensibly prepared a tiffin breakfast and lunch for me as I was unlikely to get any enroute. Before I left, Keval advised me to spend the night at Panchnadi and leave early the next morning for my journey through the Sibi desert so that I could make it to Jacobabad by the early evening.

What a journey it was! While driving through the Sibi desert there was no road to speak of, there were just two brick tracks wide enough for the wheels of a vehicle. Many a time I would lose my bearings as the wind would cause the sand to shift and cover the brick tracks. I often had to stop and probe to find the bricks, or having failed to do so, would proceed and then spotting them later on, would have to make my way back over the sand to reach them. Fortunately my car, the DKW, had a front wheel drive and took to sand as a duck takes to water!

The shifting sands of the desert certainly impeded my progress, with the result that I arrived at Jacobabad rather late in the evening and made my way straight to the waiting room of the railway station, where I spent the night. The next day, while covering the last stretch of my journey, I found that the clutch of my car was slipping, perhaps because of the rather strenuous journey through the desert. So I stopped a truck going to Quetta and asked him to tow my car. He left us outside the city limits and I made my way to the main buiding of the Staff College in my car, which though flawed was still working. At the entrance to the main building I met Jungu Satarawala, who guided me to the notice board where information regarding the allotment of quarters was pinned. The room I had been given was in the hutments, next to the main building.

This was the year of India's partition, and of serious disturbances in the Punjab, and other parts of the country. On this course and in station, I met some old friends. Amongst them, the best friendship I cultivated was with Major Latif of Baluch Regiment and his pretty wife, Sarwar, both of whom were from Bahalpur. They had one child - a girl – who was a toddler at the time. Sarwar's mother was also staying with them. Over time, I became very friendly with the family and used to walk in and out of the house at all hours of the day.

Because of communal disturbances and inter-religious killings in Punjab all communications, such as mail and telegraphic systems had broken down. The old lady, Sarwar's mother, was worried about the safety of her son (Sarwar's elder brother) and his family, who were stranded in Simla, where the son was a judge. She used to see me visiting the Latifs almost every day and one day asked Latif if I could be trusted enough for her to share her anxiety with me. And Latif's reply, I believe, was: "If you can trust me, then trust him also". So, one evening, she told me the source of her worry, and I promised to write to my nephew, my elder sister's son, Lt Col Shivinder Singh, the same evening and I assured her that provided my letter got through, he would most certainly do as I asked him to. When I returned to my residence I wrote out instructions to my nephew which involved taking an empty truck with an escort to transport the family and their belongings to safety. I advised him to take them down to Delhi and to put them on an aircraft going to Karachi. In the end I asked him to confirm via a telegram that he had received my letter. I posted the letter the next day and continued my visits to Latif's house. After about a week, the old lady asked me if I had received an acknowledgement to my letter. And since I had not yet received a telegram to this effect from my nephew, my answer was, "No". But I assured her over and over again that if my nephew had received my letter, he would do exactly as I had asked him to do. Over a month passed in this way and each time I visited Latif's house, I had no answer to give his wife's mother who perhaps began to feel sorry for having divulged her son's whereabouts to me! Because of the prevailing conditions throughout the country, our course at the Staff College was shortened by a month, and we dispersed by the end of November that year. And this was how I parted from the Latifs.

I was asked to fly to Ambala ahead of the rest of the students from India, who were expected to follow by train, and to arrange a reception for them there. On arrival at Ambala, the first thing I did was to get hold of a car and drive straight to Patiala to meet my nephew, Lt Col Shivinder Singh, to find out if he had indeed received my letter. Apparently he had, and had done as I had instructed in my letter, but was unable to acknowledge it as no telegrams were going through. He told me the whole story. Of how he had arrived at the judge sahib's residence, who, seeing his Sikh escort, all burly men from the Patiala State Forces, dressed in khaki, had feared the worst, and had secured himself and his family in the house, bolting all the doors and windows. Shivinder, my nephew, had gone knocking from door to door but had received no response. Luckily, he had my letter in his pocket and it was only when he placed it against the window-pane and beckoned the judge to come close and read it, that judge sahib opened the door. They were told to load whatever they wished to take with them into the empty truck and then to sit with it under a canvas cover draped over the back of the truck. This was how they travelled to Delhi where they were put into a plane going to Karachi, their final destination. I was the happiest man to learn of this!

There is an interesting aftermath to this. One day in March 1987, I happened to be sitting on the same sofa as Mr Humayun, the then Pakistan High Commissioner, at Daljit Singh, the Coca-Cola king's house. I mentioned to him that it was a shame that because I had commanded the Indian Forces against Pakistan in 1965, I was not being granted a visa to visit Lahore. He answered, that he was unaware of this. Just then, Daljit, our host, came over to our sofa, and said that he had been in Peshawar the evening before, and that an old lady had come up to him and mentioned that she also had a son in Delhi. Upon enquiry, she answered that he used to be a Major in Quetta in 1947, but now, she believed, he was a big General. Upon further probing, she named me, and told him the whole story. I at once turned to Mr Humayun and said, "Did you hear that? I have a mother in Peshawar, and yet I am not being given a visa by your High Commission to visit Pakistan." His response was instant, "How can this be? You and your wife will get your visa tomorrow to go to Pakistan." And that's how we got our visa to go to Lahore in April 1987.

22

JAMMU AND KASHMIR

First Landing

At Ambala, after meeting the train from Quetta, I was admitted to the Ambala Military Hospital with flu and fever. There was a radio in my ward, so I was able to listen to the news twice a day. On the 29th of October, I heard over the evening news that the Commanding Officer of 1 Sikh Battalion, Lt Col Ranjit Rai, had been killed near Baramula, in Kashmir. I had still not recovered from my bout of flu, but since I was the next in seniority to Rai in the Sikh Regiment, I decided to offer my services to the battalion. So the next morning, I asked the Medical Officer on duty to discharge me from the hospital, which he did, but very reluctantly. He made me sign a certificate that said that I was leaving the hospital at my own risk. I did so gladly.

Immediately on my release from the hospital, I rang up Wing Commander Arjan Singh, Commander of the local Air Force Station, who was a friend of mine, and asked him if he could fly me to Delhi. He agreed, and thus 1 arrived at Delhi and from the airfield itself (Safdarjung at the time), I rang up the Military Secretary's office, to say that I desired to take over 1 Sikh in Kashmir. Colonel Misra, the Deputy Military Secretary at the time, answered that they had been looking for me and that I should immediately report to DEP (Delhi and East Punjab) Command for further instructions. I went straight to Headquarters DEP Command, in Delhi at the time, and met the GOC-in-C, Lieutenant General Russel, who said that I should get ready to leave for Srinagar by air first thing the next morning. I was, however, not to go as Commanding Officer of 1 Sikh, but as Deputy Brigade Commander to 161 Infantry Brigade, being inducted at the time in the Valley. I arrived at Safdarjung Aerodrome at 5 o'clock on the morning of the 1st November and there I met Captain Misra, the Despatching Officer on behalf of DEP Command, who told me that the Brigade Commander, Brigadier Janak Katoch, had been wounded the evening before and had been evacuated to Delhi and that I should go and take over the forces in Srinagar. He said, he was not very sure if the Srinagar Airfield was still in our hands, and that I should first ascertain that and then land. Mine was the first civilian aircraft to leave Safdarjung Aerodrome that morning. Soon after crossing the Banihal Pass, the Captain of the aircraft, a civilian, invited me into the cockpit to assess the situation on the ground, at the airfield, before we landed. He, too, had been instructed at Delhi to land only if he found the airfield still in our hands.

As the aircraft neared the airfield at Srinagar, a pall of smoke could be seen over every village around the plateau of the landing-strip, an unmistakable sign of arson and destruction by the Pakistani Raiders. Therefore, in order to make sure that the airfield was in friendly hands, I asked the pilot to make a trial-run over the landing-strip, without actually touching down. The intention was to wait for hostile reaction from the ground and land only if all was well, on the second attempt. We were able to do this without any untoward incident.

The first Indian Army officer to meet me at the airfield was Lieutenant Colonel Pritam Singh. He described the military situation and handed over to me saying that a battle was raging at the time on the perimeter of the airfield, where about 200 Raiders, having burnt and looted the village of Ilgam, were engaging a platoon strength of his battalion, a mere 30 riflemen. He had, at that time, only one Company defending the entire airfield. As he was briefing me, I noticed

Author saluting the memorial built to honour the memory of Lt Col Ranjit Rai at Baramula, Kashmir.

Assembling guns - J&K Operations, 1947-48.

parts of a mountain gun being off-loaded by some Sikh troops from one of the aircrafts that had landed after mine. I walked up to the young Sikh officer, supervising the unloading of the equipment, and recognised him as Second Lieutenant Jabar Jang Singh of Patiala State Forces, my own nephew! He informed me that his instructions were to deliver these two mountain guns, which were the property of the Indian Army, and had been on loan to the Patiala State Forces for the duration of the Second World War, to the airfield and return with his crew to Patiala. He had strict orders not to participate in the fighting in Kashmir, as Patiala State had not yet decided to merge with India and did not, in any way, wish to interfere with the 'internal affairs' of a sister state - Kashmir. I told him of the fighting near the airfield and, using my influence as his uncle, asked him to order his crew to assemble the guns and pull them behind the only jeep that had come to meet me, to the perimeter of the airfield, where a mere infantry platoon was gallantly facing a much larger force of Raiders. Jabar Jang Singh pulled out of his pocket a written order, signed by the Commander-in-Chief of the Patiala State Forces, the Maharaja himself, which clearly stated that these men of his were, under no circumstances, to take part in the fighting in Srinagar. I read the order, folded the paper carefully and put it in my pocket. This time I pleaded with him and drew his attention to the critical situation near the airfield and hinted that if the Raiders were to gain a foothold on the perimeter of the airfield his departure to Patiala by air would be in jeopardy. He decided to consult his men, and watching them from where I stood, I realised that they did not seem to be interested in embroiling themselves in the fighting. At this stage I had a brain-wave! Walking up to them stiffly and calling them to attention, I shouted: "As Senior Commander in the field area I order you to assemble your guns and follow me". As for the written order from their Commander-in-Chief, I drew their attention to the well-known Field Service Regulation which enjoins that an order given by a Superior Commander can be disobeyed, or altered, by a Field Commander on the spot, provided the latter was fully satisfied that this needed to be done, and could justify it later. Pointing my finger at the young officer, I said: "Should you disobey my order, I will have you summarily court-martialled and shot for showing cowardice in front of the enemy, under the powers I enjoy as a Force Commander in Battle". The havildar with the gun detachment, thereupon, quickly responded that his men were ready to carry out my orders, but, unfortunately, the guns they had brought from Patiala were without their sights and could thus not be used. I explained that this did not present a problem, as the distance to be covered to hit the target, where the Raiders were assembled at the edge of the airfield, was so short that they would be required to only fire 'direct', through open sights! The detachment had no choice but to obey my orders, and once they saw the jumbled enemy and the havoc their shots was causing among the fleeing Raiders, it was difficult to stop them from firing! From my point of view, the gamble had worked! The Raiders, who had had every intention of attacking the airfield, not only dispersed helter skelter, but were also convinced, with the appearance of artillery on the airfield, that their objective was now out of reach. And no serious attempt was made by them, thereafter, to threaten the airfield and our much needed reinforcements of manpower and equipment continued to arrive by air undisturbed.

In accordance with my instructions, Colonel Pritam Singh had already moved the Brigade Headquarters from the airfield to a double-storeyed house half a mile on the road to Srinagar. I arrived there just before dark. There I met the Headquarters Staff and was given a briefing by the Brigade Major, Dilbagh Singh, who described the latest situation. 1 Sikh, which were the first battalion to arrive, and had lost their Commanding Officer, Lt Col Ranjit Rai, in an exchange of fire near Baramula, had been compelled by the Raiders to pull back. They had 'firmed in' on the high-ground outside Pattan, about 10 miles from Srinagar on the Baramula road, but they were soon surrounded by nearly 2000 tribesmen who were pressing on them from all directions. Their physical contact with Brigade Headquarters had been severed by the enemy. Three more battalions: 1 Kumaon, 4 Kumaon and 2 Punjab had been inducted into the Valley by air, in driblets, over the past three days and no sooner did their detachments arrive than they were deployed for the defence of the airfield, or for blocking approaches to the city of Srinagar, in that order of priority. The only reserve available in the hands of the Brigade Commander was a platoon of 2 Punjab, deployed at the time for the security of the Brigade Headquarters.

Very soon the officiating Commander of 1 Sikh, Major Sampuran Bachan Singh, was on the wireless from Pattan and wished to speak to me. He pleaded with me for reinforcements and for supply of ammunition. I promised him the ammunition, even if it was to be 'free dropped' on his position from the air, but as for reinforcements, there were none! I, however, suddenly remembered that the Brigade Major had mentioned, a moment earlier, that one of the Infantry Companies with 1 Sikh was made up of gunners, recently evacuated from Pakistan. Since we had no crew to man the mountain guns from Patiala, I offered these guns to Major Sampuran Bachan Singh, provided he could open the road half-way towards Srinagar from his end, to escort them to his position. He was thrilled with the news of the guns and readily agreed to receive them half-way. I then turned to Pritam who had been listening to my conversation with Sampuran and instructed him to tie the guns behind jeeps and escort them with his own personnel, up to the point where he would meet 1 Sikh. This was to be done the first thing the next morning.

I kept awake long hours in bed that night, thinking about the current situation and future developments. I must have hardly gone off to sleep when I was woken up by Dilbagh, who said that Colonel Kashmir Katoch, Chief of Staff of Jammu and Kashmir Forces, had come with Bakshi Gulam Mohammed and Mr DP Dhar (both civilian liaison officers, helping the Army), to see me, as they had some very serious developments regarding the defence of Srinagar to report. I came down the steps in my pyjamas and met the visitors. Kashmir Katoch narrated that at dusk that evening, one of his mounted cavalry patrols (from the Maharaja's bodyguard) had been fired upon by some hostiles as they approached Ganderbal from the direction of Srinagar. When another patrol was sent to establish and maintain contact with the enemy, it was engaged by small-arms fire, at about midnight, only four miles outside the city. He felt that the hostile Pakistanis would enter the city before first light and wanted to know whether I had any troops to spare to block their further advance from that direction? I deliberately kept silent and did not answer Kashmir's query, as I did not want to tell him in the presence of Bakshi and Dhar, absolute strangers to me, that I did not have a man to spare! I was sure Kashmir would understand the meaning of my silence, but Bakshi, mistaking it for professional diffidence and lack of local knowledge, volunteered to suggest that if I made available three battalions (a word, obviously, picked up by him, since he had been Civilian Liaison Officer) of troops, he would himself lead them to where, he thought, were suitable positions on the three roads leading into the city from the north. Three battalions! We did not have the best part of even one battalion at the time in the whole Valley! I thanked him for his suggestion and assured him that I was fully seized of the situation and that the needful would be done forthwith. I bade them goodnight and a good sleep. After they had left, I instructed the Brigade Major to have the 2 Punjab Platoon, defending the Brigade Headquarters, mounted in civilian buses (the only mode of transport available at the time), after the morning 'Stand-to', and informed him that I would accompany them to investigate the shooting incident on Ganderbal road. It was past 2 am by now and I resolved to have a good three hours' sleep before setting out.

I left my Headquarters with the Platoon of 2 Punjab, commanded by a young Lieutenant (I forget his name), in two buses. Men were sitting everywhere, some inside and some on top of the buses, and while I sat with the driver of the bus that was in the lead, the Platoon Commander sat in the front seat of the bus that was following. Bakshi had, quite naturally, been doubtful about my knowledge of the city of Srinagar. He had no way of knowing that I had roamed through the streets of Srinagar and studied the road map of the Valley quite extensively, during the two summers I had spent in Srinagar, trekking through the Valley as a young officer before the Second World War. So the way that led through the city to Nagin Lake and Ganderbal was quite well-known to me, and I led the buses through the town without a hitch. There was quite a stream of refugees, laden with their personal belongings, on the road from Ganderbal, and they appeared to be as scared of us as of the Pakistanis! As soon as they would spot the soldiers sitting in the buses they would rush off and hide. It was past Nagin Lake that I met a young lad who told me that some Pakistanis in uniform were occupying a solitary house in the fields, away from the road, nearly half a mile beyond. I asked him to sit beside me in the bus and show me the house from the road. This he did from behind a tall tree and I ordered the Platoon to dismount and move towards the house in an assault formation. When we were about 350 yards from the house, I could clearly see that the building was manned by riflemen who had their rifles pointed at us from the roof, through the windows and over the compound wall. I, thereupon, ordered the platoon to go to ground, and was thinking of making an encircling move when a man got up on the roof of the house and waved a white flag at us. I signalled him to come down. He understood the signal and with an escort of two armed soldiers, one on either side of him, made his way towards us.

As the party came nearer, I noticed that they were wearing Jammu and Kashmir Forces uniform and looked like Gurkhas! The man with the white flag was a Subedar. He came upto me, saluted and said that they were the Gurkha Garrison Company of the State Forces posted at Bandipur. Two days earlier, they had been dislodged from their position by the Pakistani Raiders and had taken up a new position at Ganderbal. They had heard rumours that Srinagar had already fallen to the Pakistanis and so the evening before, when a mounted patrol had arrived from the direction of Srinagar, assuming them to be Pakistanis, they had opened fire on them. And since their own position had also been revealed to the enemy in the process, they had decided to quit the post at Ganderbal and to occupy this house, away from the road. However, they had hardly settled in the house when another mounted patrol of what they perceived as the 'enemy' had approached the house in an attempt to encircle it, and they had been left with no choice but to once again fire at them. That morning they were expecting yet another attack from the Pakistanis and had therefore made all preparations to meet it. They were at first quite sure that we were Pakistanis who had come to destroy them and were ready to open fire, but then noticed me, a Sikh, among the troops! The Subedar admitted that it had taken them quite a while, spent in argument, to come to the conclusion that a Sikh could not be commanding Pakistani troops! How well this story tied up with the narrative of Col Katoch! It only goes to show the fluid situation prevailing in the Valley at the time.

As the Gurkhas abandoned their 'Fortress', there was quite a reunion between the Punjabi troops and the Gurkhas. I took the Subedar of the Gurkhas in the bus with me to a place known as Malashahi Bagh, a vantage point on the road from Ganderbal, which could serve

Taking position against the Raiders - J&K Operations, 1947-48.

Author planning strategy in the Field.

as the next defensive position for his Platoon against the Pakistanis. Such was the 'shoe string' and 'tooth pick' manner in which the Indian Army fought its first campaign in Kashmir after partition!

After this episode, I returned to Brigade Headquarters and decided to clear the Raiders from the areas and villages south of the airfield. With this in view, I decided to send two fighting-patrols, a Company strong each, into that area. The patrols were from the 2 and 4 Kumaon who had, more or less, assembled on the airfield by then. The patrols were to leave the airfield before first light on the 3rd of November. The task given to 2 Kumaon Patrol was to make straight for milestone 8 on the Baramula road, searching villages on the way. The second patrol of 4 Kumaon, under the command of Major Sharma, was to search the village of Illgam, where fighting had taken place on the 1st of November, and the neighbouring villages, and then take up a position guarding the approach to the city, near the village of Badgaon. Major Sharma had reported that he had seen a lot of locals hiding in the nullahs, but he had apparently left them alone. These were, in fact, the Raiders who came alive to assault him in large numbers, after he had taken up position on the features over-looking the village of Badgaon.

I had maintained contact with both the patrols till 9:30 am, and all was well with them till then. In my mind I was going over the operational measures that could be instituted to secure the city of Srinagar, for the Raiders were now posing a serious threat to it. I decided to withdraw 1 Sikh from Pattan to the bund at spill-channel across the main Srinagar-Baramula road, at milestone 4. I planned that this should happen on the morning of the next day, the 4th of November. Instead of passing the message to 1 Sikh on the wireless, which could be intercepted by the enemy, who were known to possess the same sets as ours, I arranged that Wing Commander Mehar Singh, commonly known as 'Mehar Baba' (because of his bushy beard) would fly me over the 1 Sikh position, so that I could drop the message for withdrawal. He flew me in a Howard aircraft, the only aircraft available at Srinagar Airfield at the time.

We were lucky to have Mehar Baba for air support, for he was not only a very fine pilot but was also ready to take any risk necessary to provide this support. Realising the limitation of the Howard aircraft, he had taken the initiative to bring in a flight of Spitfire aircraft from

A Soldier Remembers

Delhi, and had landed them on the grassy and limited landing-strip of the Srinagar Airfield. These were later to prove a great asset against the Raiders, as events began to unfold.

After dropping the withdrawal message on the 1 Sikh position, in a Howard flight piloted by Mehar Baba, during which he also used the Howard front-gun to fire on some trucks of the enemy plying on the Uri-Baramula road - which was at the time in enemy hands – we returned to the Srinagar Airfield just before midday. On return, I immediately enquired about the two Company patrols of 2 and 4 Kumaons and I was told that they were progressing well. At about 2 pm, Major Sharma, commanding 4 Kumaon patrol, reported, after having reached his objective, the hill above the Badgaon village, that the civilians, whom he had earlier seen hiding in the nullahs, had suddenly come to life and were engaging him with mortars and Light Machine Guns, and he asked for air support. Mehar Baba responded immediately, but wanted to be shown the exact location of Sharma's position on the map. I remembered that there was a map displayed on the wall in the Operations Room of the Brigade Headquarters and so I rushed there, and with the help of a razor, cut out an one-inch square piece of the area from the map and took it to the airfield, to brief the pilots. Both Meher Baba and I went without lunch that day, as we were fully preoccupied in arranging air support for Sharma's Company. The pilots soon reported that their mission had been successful and that they had managed to disperse the Raiders. I returned to the Operations Room at about 4.30 pm, and who do I see there but Brigadier Bogey Sen sitting with his head held in both hands, in a very morose state. I naturally, asked him why he was sitting that way; and he replied that Major Sharma had been killed. I asked him for the source of this information and he pointed to a small room next to the Operations Room. I proceeded there and found a man lying on the floor, still shivering, in spite of being wrapped up in two blankets. On questioning, he disclosed that he had been with Major Sharma, manning the rear-link with Brigade Headquarters, and had run away because his wireless set had been hit by a bullet. He was too shaky to give a coherent account of the events, so I asked the Mess orderly to give him a hot mug of tea, with a lot of rum in it! This was done, and within half an hour the man was himself again, fit to be asked about the true state of Sharma's Company. It came out that he had only seen Sharma hit by a bullet, and not dead. It was obvious that he had panicked and run away from the scene out of fear. As one could not, therefore, rely on the account given by him, I contacted the Officer Commanding 2 Punjab, on wireless, whose battalion was located just behind the hill-feature held by Sharma's Company. He gave me the true picture. Sadly Sharma had died of bullet wounds, and his Company had suffered fourteen more casualties. I instructed OC 2 Punjab to re-capture Sharma's hill and clear the casualties. This was done and Sharma's body was recovered and sent to Delhi the next day by air.

Naturally, on his arrival, Brigadier Sen assumed command of 161 Infantry Brigade and all the forces in the Valley, and I became his Deputy. The next morning, the 4th of November, we were told at Brigade Headquarters that Sardar Vallabh Bhai Patel and his party were to visit us that morning. They arrived at Brigade Headquarters at about 8 am, and consisted of: Mr Patel, his secretary, Mani Behn Patel (Mr Patel's daughter), Mr Baldev Singh (the Defence Minister), his secretary, Harish Sarin and a British officer, Lieutenant Colonel Billy Short, who belonged to the Sikh Regiment and whom I knew from before. The last I had heard of Billy Short was that he was Civil Liaison Officer in the Punjab. The party was straightaway taken to the Operations Room for briefing by Brigadier Sen. Being of Anglo-Indian descent (a Bengali father and an English mother), Brigadier Sen was an impressive speaker as he had a good command of English, which he spoke with an accent. However, during the briefing, it became clear that he was greatly shaken by Sharma's death and could only paint a very gloomy picture of our forces' situation in the Valley. As his Deputy, I could not contradict him. When we came out of the Operations Room, I took Billy Short aside to ask him what he was doing there, and on being told that he was acting as adviser to Sardar Baldev Singh, the Defence Minister, I asked him if he could arrange for me to have a few words with Sardar Sahib. This he did, and so I was able to quietly tell Sardar Baldev Singh that the situation in the Valley was not that bad; and that he should inform Sardar Patel accordingly, explaining that Brigadier Sen had, perhaps, been adversely affected by the loss of Major Sharma the evening before. Whether Sardar Baldev Singh conveyed my message to Mr Patel or not, I do not know.

However, before leaving by air from the airfield, where we had all gone to see Mr Patel's party off, Sardar Patel addressed Brigadier Sen thus: "Brigadier, you hold on; we shall send you reinforcements!" The build up of force continued by air as far as it could.

Since I was the one who had dropped a message from the air on the 1 Sikh position, asking them to withdraw to the spill-channel at mile 4, generally known as Shelatang, for the defence of the city of Srinagar, before the new Brigade Commander, Brigadier Sen had arrived, I felt it my duty to meet 1 Sikh during their withdrawal and show them their new position on the spill-channel. Therefore, immediately after Mr Patel's party had departed from Srinagar Airfield, I left by jeep to meet 1 Sikh on the road. I went up to mile 7 on the Srinagar-Baramula road and saw 1 Sikh coming through. They had managed to bring all their heavy equipment and spare ammunition by loading it on local tongas (without their ponies, which, the locals claimed, had run away) pulling them themselves - some men in front and some in the rear - and running at the double. Tremendous improvisation! Standing there on the road, and seeing them through, I indicated to each party where to stop - in the vicinity of the spill-channel whose banks ran across the road and formed an excellent high-ground for the deployment of their light machine-guns.

Having seen to their deployment at Shelatang, I returned to Brigade Headquarters and told Brigadier Sen about it. Brigadier Sen, although in command of troops at the time, showed little interest in their deployment, and so I as his Deputy, did everything regarding the conduct of operations there. He did not seem to mind, and stayed most of the time at his Headquarters. It seemed that the Raiders, who were surrounding the 1 Sikh position at Pattan, did not interfere with their withdrawal, as they thought the Sikhs were withdrawing for good. They were more interested in going for the city of Srinagar. So they followed 1 Sikh leisurely and contacted them on the spill-channel at Shelatang, on the night of 5th/6th November and engaged them with small-arms and mortar fire, which was suitably replied to by the Sikhs. The Raiders did not, however, come very close to the 1 Sikh position that night, and by the morning they withdrew. By the 5th evening, 4 Kumaon had been flown in and on the 6th morning, I deployed them behind 1 Sikh, in the area of the abandoned race-course, so as to counter-attack the Raiders in case they came again close to the 1 Sikh position. By the time 4 Kumaon concentrated behind the 1 Sikh position, the Raiders had withdrawn to their lair in Zainkut village, over half a mile away from the Sikh position. So 4 Kumaon were left where they were, in the depth of 1 Sikh, to bide their time and wait for a suitable opportunity.

The Battle of Shelatang: The Turning Point

Their opportunity came on the morning of the 7th, for during the night, the Raiders again closed-up on the 1 Sikh position, and engaged them throughout the night, heavily. By the 6th evening, some armoured cars had also arrived at Srinagar, under the command of Major Rikhye. They had been given the task of patrolling approaches coming to Srinagar from the north, first thing in the morning of the 7th. With the Raiders closing up on the spill-channel, where 1 Sikh were engaging them, the stage was now set for decimating them in the open ploughed-field in front of the 1 Sikh position. By the evening of the 6th of November, General Kulwant Singh had also arrived at Srinagar Airfield, with his GSO-1, Lt Col Bhagat, to take over command of what was to be known as Jammu and Kashmir, or JAK Forces. Since two complete battalions - that is 1 Sikh and 4 Kumaon - were involved in the operation, I asked Brigadier Sen's permission to go to spill-channel and conduct the operations as I knew the area. He agreed. Before leaving, I requested Rikhye, to kindly, ask his patrol of armoured cars, which had left for patrolling the northern approaches to Srinagar, very early that morning, to come along a track leading from that direction to a position adjacent to Zainkut village which would place them behind the Raiders' likely concentration in front of 1 Sikh. I also arranged with our air force to concentrate their patrolling in that area, where they were likely to come across lively targets.

On arrival at 4 Kumaon position, on the race course, I caught hold of their Commanding Officer, Lt Col Pritam Singh and with him, later, contacted the Commanding Officer of 1 Sikh, Sampuran Bachan Singh. A plan was made that while 1 Sikh would engage the raiders frontally, 4 Kumaon at my orders, would attack the village of Zainkut from the left of the 1 Sikh position, and thus would not only cut the Raiders off from their base, but also capture their base. I asked 1 Sikh to have a

Gen Kulwant Singh, Brig LP Sen & Author.

Standing under the Victory Gate erected to commemorate the defeat of the Pakistani Raiders.

Company ready in civilian buses, on the road behind their position. When I gave the signal, they were to rush through along the Baramula road to milestone 7, where I had seen, on the morning of the 4th while watching the 1 Sikh withdrawal, some trenches dug down and left behind by the 2 Kumaon Patrol Company, sent there on the 3rd of November.

What a melée it was that day in front of the 1 Sikh position on the spill-channel! The irregular Raiders tried to get on the high ground of spill-channel, held by 1 Sikh, but were mowed down by the 1 Sikh Light Machine Gun fire. They then tried to pull back their casualties into the hay-stacks on the ploughed maize field hoping to get shelter there from the 1 Sikh fire. But no sooner did they do so, our aircraft spotted them and fired their incendiaries into these hay-stacks setting them on fire. The attacking Raiders were caught in such a cleft-stick that they found themselves helpless. Pritam and I were watching all this, and he was, naturally, pulling at the leash, wanting to go into the attack, but I held him back. At this very time, our armoured cars appeared from behind and opened up on the desperate Raiders from behind. At this stage, I let loose the 4 Kumaonis for their attack on the enemy base at Zainkut. I was told by them that the Raiders who remained had jumped into the Jhelum river and into the adjoining lake - and nearly all perished! A little further from the village of Zainkut, in a clump of trees, the Kumaonis found two abandoned 3-inch mortars, which had been used by the Raiders against us, as well as some ammunition. There was also an Army Ambulance car that had been left behind by the Raiders. At the end of the day, we counted some three hundred bodies. I remember being asked by a plucky journalist, Mr N Sharma, who was milling around there whether he could keep a miniature 'sarangi', retrieved from one of the dead Raiders, as a souvenir!

Never had I seen nor was I to see again a melée like this one! I had the 'rear-link' operating to Divisional Headquarters, and I asked on it for General Kulwant Singh's permission to continue the chase of the enemy. But he countered my suggestion by saying that it was now the Brigade Commander's job to continue with his Brigade, and that he had just asked Brigadier Sen to proceed, and that I should hand over to him and come back to the airfield, as he had some other job for me to do. Very soon, the Brigadier arrived on the scene and took over the chase of the enemy.

Brigadier LP Sen

I must admit that I found Brigadier LP Sen a great puzzle. He did not seem to be interested in life in general and commanding troops in particular. He behaved just like a bystander, who depended entirely on his subordinates or staff, yet this did not stop him from bragging and showing-off whenever the opportunity presented itself. How he won his DSO, during the 2nd World War I do not know. What is more, he rose to be the Chief of General Staff of the Indian Army! 'Bogey the Bogus', was the term generally used to describe him, and which fitted him well.

Much later, he had the temerity to write a book called 'Slender was the Thread', about the Jammu and Kashmir Operations, in which, he claimed to have personally fought the battle against the Raiders on the spill-channel, at milestone 4 from the town of Srinagar. He refers to a culvert (which does not exist except in his imagination) under which he supposedly gave orders for attack. The rest of the description of the battle has been lifted from my notes, as he was not even present there! I, who had planned and conducted that battle, had no choice but to contradict his statements.

His military incompetence can be judged from the fact that when the Raiders were on the run after the battle of Shelatang, described earlier, and he had been given orders to pursue them with his brigade, he stopped at Uri, instead of chasing their broken ranks up to Domel and destroying the bridge over the river Sindh. Had he done so the Raiders would not have got an opportunity to rally round as they did. Nor would the regular Pakistani army have been able to cross the river. Infact we would not have had a Kashmir problem at all!

The blame should lie with General Kulwant Singh, GOC J & K Forces, for knowing Brig Sen's military incompetence one could not have expected better from him. Gen Kulwant Singh should have seen the advantage of going to Domel. Instead, it is said, that he gave in to pressure from the Maharaja of Kashmir, Hari Singh, who was keen that troops be sent to Punch where a relative of the Maharaja's, Brig Krishen Singh of the J & K Forces, was holed up. Thus Brig Sen was instructed to take a column of two battalions from the garrison at Uri to Punch. Down below, in the Naushera Sector too, the objective of the column should not have been Kotli but Kohala bridge – the only bridge on the river Jhelum allowing ingress to Pakistani forces from the south. By blocking both the bridges at Domel and Kohala the Jammu and Kashmir problem would have been solved once and for all. It is surprising that no one in authority, military or civilian, has commented on these omissions which have cost the country so dear.

The J & K Operations Continued

The battle of Shelatang will go down as one of the most decisive battles in the Jammu and Kashmir operations. It tilted the scales completely in our favour by shattering to pieces the main strength of the raiding force, and by wrenching from them forever the initiative which they had gained as a result of a premeditated advance on Srinagar. Any danger to the security of the town was thus entirely eliminated and our forces could now move from the defensive to the offensive. As Deputy to Brigadier Sen, I had the privilege of conducting this battle on the ground.

161 Infantry Brigade, under the command of Brigadier Sen, and consisting of 1 Sikh, 1 Kumaon and 2/17 Dogras (which had only that evening completed its concentration in Srinagar by road and air), with one troop of armoured cars and one troop of 25 pounders (which again had only just arrived by road), started the chase of the enemy at last light on the 7th of November. Small parties of enemy, encountered on the road, were readily destroyed. The enemy was, obviously, in a great state of confusion and disorder, for many of their parties just walked into our hands, while others, regulars in the Pakistan army, voluntarily surrendered. In the absence of any form of transport the pursuit was carried out on foot, and 3-inch mortars, medium machine guns and reserve ammunition, were all carried by the men. Pattan, was reached at about 2 am. Four enemy trucks, which were presumably bringing reinforcements to the Raiders, fell into our hands, while another four managed to escape. Trouble from small parties of enemy, who were engaged in loot and arson in the Valley, was still there. The force remaining in Srinagar, after 161 Infantry Brigade had taken up the chase, was, therefore, organised as Sri Garrison under my command.

23
COMMANDER, SRI GARRISON

The tasks given to the Sri Garrison were:

- Defence and maintenance of law and order in Srinagar;
- Mopping up of the enemy still remaining in the Srinagar Valley; and
- Protection of the line of communication of 161 Infantry Brigade upto Baramula.

Troops under command of Sri Garrison, initially, included those air-lifted from 2 Punjab, 4 Kumaon, 6 Raj Rif, and one troop of 2 armoured cars and one squadron of the Kashmir State Forces' horsed cavalry. The defence of the Valley and maintenance of law and order in Srinagar were easily accomplished. A Srinagar Defence Scheme was put into operation, and law and order in the town was ensured through imposition of curfew and show of force by flag marches, both by Infantry and armoured cars. The mopping up of the enemy also did not present much difficulty. The area of the Valley was cleared of parties of Raiders through deep patrolling by Infantry, supported by horsed cavalry (the Maharaja's bodyguard), with the air force also co-operating in the operations. A convoy system was instituted in the Valley, and the protection of convoys was effected through close escorts and patrolling of the road by armoured cars and infantry in mechanised transport.

In the meantime, things had started boiling up in Jammu also. Raiders from Pakistani territory had crossed into the state all along the border. Pockets of State Forces' troops along the border were either liquidated or pushed back. This was easily accomplished, as the muslim element of the State Forces' Garrisons changed sides and turned against their comrades. Before long, State Forces' Garrisons at Mirpur, Kotli, Jhangar, were surrounded and local refugees had taken refuge with them. 50 Para Brigade was hurriedly concentrated at Jammu. 2 Punjab from Sri Garrison was flown from Srinagar to Jammu, on the 13th of November, to rejoin their Brigade. On the 15th of November, the Para Brigade set out from Jammu along the road leading through Akhnoor, Naushera, Jhangar, Kotli, and Punch, with the object of relieving the Garrisons on the way and linking up at Punch with 161 Infantry Brigade from Uri. Berripattan, 60 miles from Jammu, was reached the same evening without any incident. The fording of Berripattan river, however, took four days to accomplish. Naushera was reached on the 19th of November and Jhangar on the 20th. A small force of a battalion (2 Punjab), with attached troops, was sent to Kotli on the 22nd of November and met with slightly stiffer resistance on the way than heretofore. Owing to the stiffening of opposition and the vulnerability of the long line of communication from Jammu, the idea of advancing to Punch was abandoned, and it was decided not to hold Kotli but to fall back to Jhangar, after evacuating the non-muslim refugees and the State Forces' Garrison positioned there. This was accomplished by the 26th of November.

After the position at Uri had been consolidated, according to orders from the J & K Forces, a two-battalion group consisting of 1 Kumaon, 2/17 Dogras, a battery of 3.7 Howitzers and a troop of armoured cars, set out on 20th November along the Uri-Punch road, with the avowed objective of linking up with 50 Para Brigade from Kotli. 1 Sikh had been left behind for the defence of the Firm-Base at Uri. The Uri-Punch road is a very circuitous and hilly road with innumerable small wooden bridges. The column had nearly 200 vehicles of all types and sizes, which had to negotiate very temporary and difficult diversions round the demolished bridges, within two miles of the starting point. This crossing took much longer than was expected, with the result that a portion of the vehicle column had to halt for the night at milestone 7, away from the main body, which had by last light of the 21st of November, reached Hajipir Pass, at milestone 22. This vehicle column had only a very small infantry escort with it, with a troop of armoured cars positioned at its tail-end. All went well with this column during the night, but it had hardly started on its journey in the morning when around the first bend on the road it came across a road block. As vehicles pulled up nose to tail, fire opened up on them from all directions. The enemy had obviously been sitting up for the column and was holding all the high features in the vicinity. Attempts by the small Infantry escort to capture one of the nearby features failed, with heavy losses. Owing to the bends in the road the armoured cars at the tail-end of the column could not cover the vehicle column. The width of the road did not allow the armoured cars to move up and down the halted column, as was necessary. Moreover, they were themselves heavily invested by fire. One of the armoured cars had its wheels punctured. This armoured car was turned back on the narrow road, with the greatest of difficulty, and despatched to Uri, carrying information and casualties. After subduing all opposition, the looting party of the Raiders, which had been biding its time in a nullah, below the road, all this while, sprang into action and ransacked the stranded vehicles and set them on fire. Before last light the remaining armoured cars, fearing they would be rushed in the dark, also left for Uri, carrying further casualties. That night, the enemy succeeded in burning a wooden bridge on the road towards the Uri side of the column.

Jammu and Kashmir Forces Headquarters (JAK Headquarters) was set up in Jammu, under the command of Major General Kulwant Singh, on the 8th of November 1947. On the evening of the 8th I got a call from JAK Headquarters that Pandit jee, the Prime Minister of India, would be arriving at the Srinagar Airfield at 9 o'clock the next morning and that Sheikh Abdullah and the Maharaja of Kashmir would be there to receive him, and that as Commander, Sri Garrison I should also be there. Mehar Baba had flown in the Maharaja's aeroplane, from Srinagar to Jammu, early in the morning of the 8th, to fetch Maharaja Hari Singh, who was at the time living in his palace at

Author standing in line to greet Pandit jee at the Srinagar Airport, 9 Nov 1947.

Jammu. Maharaja Hari Singh duly arrived in his aircraft at the Srinagar Airfield at about 8.30 am, before the arrival of the Prime Minister. Sheikh Abdullah and myself also arrived at the airfield about the same time. Pandit jee's aircraft arrived punctually at 9 am, and Sheikh Abdullah and the Maharaja advanced to the door of the aircraft to greet Pandit jee. Notably, Pandit jee greeted Sheikh Abdullah with warmth, but cut the Maharaja cold with only a limp handshake. There were other dignitaries also to meet the Prime Minister, and he met them all with pleasure. As Commander, Sri Garrison, I was required to drive the Prime Minister in my jeep, to 'Lal Chowk', where the citizens of Srinagar were assembled to welcome the Prime Minister of India on his first visit to Srinagar, after it had been saved from the Pakistani Raiders' invasion. A stage had been set for Pandit jee to address the gathering. There was tremendous enthusiasm among the populace collected at 'Lal Chowk', and red flags (a symbol of the National Conference of Jammu and Kashmir) could be seen every where. I should mention here that Pandit jee was accompanied by his daughter, Indira Gandhi, and private secretary Mr Zutshi. Sheikh Abdullah first spoke from the stage, followed by Pandit jee. As soon as Pandit jee stepped on the stage, he received a thunderous 'hurrah' from those present, and there were shouts of 'India Zindabad'; 'Pakistan Murdabad'. There seemed no doubt that they were all for India and were happy that the Pakistani plan had been foiled. The meeting over, Pandit jee and party were taken by Sheikh Abdullah to the National Conference office nearby.

The next appointment for the dignitaries was lunch at the Maharaja'a Palace, with its view of the Dal Lake. Here again, I noticed, that Pandit jee hardly spoke to the Maharaja. Thereafter, I took Pandit jee, in my jeep, to the airfield, and he and his party were seen off by all concerned.

Soon after, I got busy organising defences for the protection of Srinagar, with the forces that had been allotted to Sri Garrison. Unknown to me, Brigadier Sen had been diverted, after consolidating at Uri, by JAK Headquarters to Punch, to rescue a relative of the Maharaja's, Brigadier Krishan Singh, who was besieged at Punch. Thus, instead of chasing the Raiders beyond Domel and into Pakistan, when they were demoralised and running, we diverted our strength for a task that could have waited. By so doing, we allowed the Raiders to regroup and they returned to trouble us again around Uri. We did think it an odd decision at the time. The misfortune that the column to Punch met at milestone 7 on Uri-Punch is described below.

Before first light, the main force of the Punch Column, which had halted for the night of 20th November at Hajipir Pass, while approaching the Kahuta Bridge, saw the bridge go up in flames! The Column Commander, Brigadier Sen, naturally thought that the bridge must have been set on fire by the enemy, and rushed his troops forward to save it from being completely destroyed. He later discovered to his consternation that the bridge had been set on fire by the State Forces' troops, charged with its security. The reason given was that the troops had taken the advancing column to be Pakistanis. Whether the information of the advance of a friendly column from Uri had been sent to the State Forces Brigade at Punch and passed by them to the troops at the bridge, is a matter of doubt. It does, however, show the state of panic and low morale prevailing amongst the State Forces troops. By the time the column reached there, the bridge had been completely destroyed by fire. All available hands were, therefore, put to the task of making a ford. In the meanwhile, the news of the vehicle column, having met with a disaster was received by the Column Commander, Brigadier Sen, who, after leaving 1 Kumaon to cross over and join Punch Brigade, rushed back with the rest of the force the same afternoon, the 21st of November. He arrived at the scene of the disaster on the morning of the 22nd.

The information about the ambush of the vehicles did not reach Srinagar until 10 pm, on the 21st of November, when orders were received by Sri Garrison from Headquarters JAK Forces to despatch, as soon as possible, a battalion to the scene of the incident, as a relief-force. 4 Kumaon were detailed for the task, and they left Srinagar by MT at about 2 am on the 22nd, reaching the scene of the ambush at about 10 am the same day, almost simultaneously with the arrival of the column from the other direction. It took two days to clear the road of the burnt out vehicles, and to make a diversion at the site of the burnt-down bridge. Even then, the sides of the diversion were so steep that vehicles had to be winched across one by one. Of the 24 vehicles ambushed by the enemy, about thirteen were recovered. Three of them were cannibalised, and eight thrown overboard, as a total loss. The Punch Column, less 1 Kumaon, returned to Uri on the evening of the 25th of November. General Kulwant Singh, GOC Jammu and Kashmir Division, expressed a desire to go and see the column, and I was detailed to accompany him from Srinagar and that's how I was able to see the mishap that had occurred with the column, first hand. After doing their job of destroying bridges and looting vehicles of the column on the Uri-Punch road, at milestone 7, the Raiders returned to their stranglehold in village Bhatgiran, south of Uri. This village was strategically placed, in a jungle and on a hill, and fully defended against any likely attack. It was from this stronghold that the Raiders inflicted heavy losses on 1 Sikh, having lured them into their lair, during their fighting-patrol action in the area on the 12th of December. An account of this is given a little later. This incident was a testimony once again to Brigadier Sen's dependence on members of his staff, and his personal lack of interest, for he had allowed his units to take a number of vehicles with them on this rather short column, without arranging for their security on the march.

In the meanwhile on the night of the 22nd of November, the enemy, about 900 strong, taking advantage of the pre-occupation of a large proportion of our forces in the area of the ambush, launched an all-out attack on a small isolated picket of 1 Sikh, across the Jhelum river, at Uri. The objective of this attack had been admirably selected. The picket was held by only 20 men under a JCO and was separated from the Uri Garrison by the Jhelum river, with the only bridge over it destroyed. The troops had made a single-plank crossing themselves, in its place. It was however clearly inadequate. It would take reinforcements from Uri at least two hours to reach the picket position, and they too would have to cross over the rickety plank.

The first attack on the picket started at about 11 o'clock at night, supported by very heavy Medium Machine Guns and mortar fire, from close range. The attack was repulsed. An hour later another assault was launched with even greater strength, from three directions, in an attempt to envelope the picket position. The gallant garrison of the picket, only 20 men under a JCO, fought back courageously, holding up the first wave of the assault within 30 yards from its perimeter. Wave after wave of enemy attempted to force the picket, but to no avail. The field guns, down at Uri, which had not had the chance of previously registering the gun-tasks, having only just arrived, responded to the grave emergency and gave support to the picket, assisted by the slight moonlight of a waning moon.

Down at Battalion Headquarters of 1 Sikh, the Battalion Commander's predicament was, indeed, great. He realised the desperate position of the picket, yet with every available man already committed to the defence of Uri, he had no reinforcements to send. The espirit de corps and the camaraderie in the battalion can be well judged from the fact that the Quarter Master, Captain Joginder Singh, and his Administrative Platoon (mostly cooks and sweepers) volunteered to go to the assistance of the picket and after the most hazardous crossing of the Jhelum, over a plank, in the middle of the night, rushed up the hill at record speed. The adamant fight put up by the small Garrison of the picket and the dashing speed of this reinforcing force, which kept shouting war-cries all the way up, so demoralised the enemy that he abandoned any further attempt to force the picket's position and withdrew in haste, leaving behind a 3-inch mortar. This most gallant show put up by a handful of 1 Sikh soldiers, against enormously overwhelming odds, will surely go down in history as an epic. The loss of this picket position of the Uri Camp would have resulted in disastrous consequences for the whole operation.

The period from the 23rd of November to the 11th of December, was rather a quiet one. Activity on our side was mainly confined to local patrolling around the perimeter. The enemy was, however, reported to be building up, especially in the area of the village Bhatgiran, on the high feature east of Uri. A certain amount of re-grouping of the Uri Garrison was carried out and the defences of the perimeter strengthened. 1 Sikh had been withdrawn from the perimeter into reserve and 4 Kumaon had taken their place. 2 Dogra were spread along the line of communication from Baramula to Uri, with their Headquarters at Baramula and a Company strength was deployed in areas of Rampur and Mahura.

Sri Garrison now consisted of 6 Raj Rif and odds and ends of rear parties of 161 Infantry Brigade units and State Forces elements in the Badamibagh Cantonment.

From Uri, on the 12th of December, with a view to ascertaining the extent of the enemy's build up, a fighting patrol of approximately three Companies of 1 Sikh (total strength about 230 men) were sent out to the Bhatgiran area. The Sikhs set out on this patrol in very high spirits and made no attempt to hide their line of advance, or conceal their objective. On the contrary, their war cries could be heard, miles around as they proceeded. The Sikhs had made a great name in this theatre and were feared by the Raiders more than any other troops. Noticing the exuberance of the Sikh patrol, those manning the enemy obstruction posts and outposts, on the way, surreptitiously withdrew to their main position around the village of Bhatgiran, and warned the enemy-garrison there of the Sikhs approach. The enemy force, estimated at about 1000 strong, thereupon laid a clever ambush for the patrol.

The high feature overlooking the village of Bhatgiran was secured by the patrol without any opposition. The Sikhs were, however, spoiling for a fight and decided to advance into the village itself. In so doing they unwittingly ran into an enemy ambush. The enemy intention was to entrap the whole patrol and destroy it in close combat. They had, for the purpose, detailed a force of about 500 men. As soon as fire opened on the forward elements of the patrol, these 500 Raiders pounced on the patrol with swords and bayonets. The Sikhs acted boldly and rushed into the enemy with cold steel. A melée ensued and each side more or less fought to the finish, the Sikhs getting the better of it in the end. The enemy was estimated to have left behind 300 dead. The Sikhs, who had lost 60 men, including Jamedar Nand Singh, VC, and had almost an equal number wounded, withdrew to Uri bringing with them all the wounded and their arms and equipment. As happens in hand to hand combat, especially in a melée, the Sikhs lost the cream of their men. Casualties included one officer killed and three wounded (including the officiating Commanding Officer, Sampuran Bachan Singh), two JCOs killed and three wounded. This was naturally a great set back to the fighting efficiency of the unit as a whole. And it was, therefore, decided to send 6 Raj Rif and relieve the unit which was sent back to Srinagar for some rest. The relief was completed by the 22nd of December; although one of the Companies was still held back by 161 Infantry Brigade at Baramula. Sri Garrison, as such, was now dissolved and I came down one rank and took over the command of 1 Sikh, in addition to carrying out the duties of Station Commander, Srinagar.

24

DROPPED 1 STAR – TOOK OVER 1 SIKH

In addition to commanding 1 Sikh, I was still commanding Sri Garrison, as well as Deputy to Commander 161 Infantry Brigade. Being located in Srinagar, these three appointments were feasible, although they meant added responsibility. But my main concern now was with the battalion that had suffered heavy losses, especially in the senior NCO ranks. In the hand-to-hand fighting with the Pathans at Bhatgiran, the battalion had lost its only VC, Jamedar Nand Singh. If I had been with the battalion at the time, I would have left the VC behind, preferably at the Regimental Centre, and most certainly, at Uri, before proceeding on such a risky mission. However, I was now faced with the task of making up for the loss of JCOs and senior NCOs. I rang up the Commandant of the Centre who sent more men and I then concentrated on training the battalion and explained to the men that we had come to the Valley, a purely Muslim area, as ambassadors of our great country, India, which had itself recently gained Independence. It was up to us to protect and look after our brethren in the Valley and thus show the world that we are a civilised country. At the time of opening the 'Darbar' for any questions, 83 men got up and said that I was their

'Mai Bap' and they would do exactly as I asked them to do, but could I tell them how and where their families were in Pakistan? To this my answer was that their families, like so many other evacuees, would have to leave it to luck. I explained that we should not allow this to interfere with our mission which was to set an example, through exemplary behaviour, of our commitment to the local residents of the Valley, irrespective of their religion. Being intelligent troops, they understood this and thereafter there was not a single incident of misbehaviour with the locals on their part. In fact, later, in May 1948, when we had been in Handwara for nearly two months, and were preparing to carry out the 'Summer Offensive', the local residents went to Sheikh Abdullah in Srinagar, and pleaded with him that Sikh troops should not be taken away from Handwara, as they felt safe with them!

In early January 1948, the days were lovely and sunny in the Valley, and everything seemed peaceful. One day, the Subedar Major of the battalion, who had been visiting the local gurudwara in the city, told me that he had seen some Sikh orphan boys, begging in the gurudwara, uncared for, with lice in their hair. "Can we do something about this?", he asked. I readily agreed and we discussed the matter. I might mention here that there is nothing that cannot be done between a sensible Subedar Major and an understanding Commanding Officer! We decided to collect the orphans and put them in a separate barrack in Badami Bagh, where we were residing as a battalion, and to provide them food, clothing and bedding from our own resources. We started a school for them and it soon became an ideal institution that we could be proud of. We even invited Sheikh Abdullah to visit the school and observe the boys being taught. He was greatly pleased with the effort of the battalion. I was later able to arrange a 'Home' for them which the Sikh Regimental Centre agreed to run and so the boys were eventually transported to the Centre in an empty returning aircraft. They were known as the 'Kashmir boys' in the Centre and when they grew up the Centre managed to send them to the National Defence Academy. A few of them became officers in the Indian Army!

Uri had its first snowfall in the middle of January. It was a heavy one, resulting in the Uri front getting more or less frozen for the time being. Activity on both sides was thus confined to local patrolling only. Banihal was a headache to all. It was the only life-line to the forces in the Valley. The success of operations, indeed the very existence of the troops, in Kashmir depended on the pass being kept open during the winter months. Yet, like an irreconcilable monster, it defied all efforts of military as well as civil engineers and remained at times closed for as long as a month. The anxiety of Headquarters Jammu and Kashmir Forces, whose responsibility it was to 'feed' the Valley, may well be imagined. The fact that the troops were well fed throughout, speaks volumes for the organisational ability of the Forces Headquarters and the pluck and grit of the auxiliary services. By now, the middle of winter, the Valley was completely swathed in white. With Uri sufficiently secure and other entrances into it snow-bound and impassable, the residents of the Valley thought that they could relax without any fear of the Raiders, at least during the course of winter.

With life pretty dull, I decided to enliven it a bit and wrote the following, rather funny poem, and sent it to Brigadier Sen, the Brigade Commander in Uri:

OC ONE SIX ONE

>OC One Six One, what a son of a gun!
>Nineteen forty seven, on November one,
>While basking in the sun, he was called to the gun.
>OC One Six One, what a son of a gun!
>
>There was a job to be done, Kashmir to be won;
>Without a lorry or a gun, he was up for fun.
>OC One Six One, what a son of a gun!
>
>Fortune played him a pun, Badgaon hardly was fun;
>Further hopes there were none, he thought all was done.
>OC One Six One, what a son of a gun!
>
>Then came Shelatang, what fun! What fun!
>He had Badu on the run; he could vie Wellington.
>OC One Six One, what a son of a gun!
>
>Many battles had he won,
>But at Mile Seven, he had in the eye done
>By the old Pathan; and wasn't he on the run!
>OC One Six One, what a son of a gun!

When he's had a tot of rum, May be too many one;
He will tell you for fun, how the last War he won!
OC One Six One, what a son of a gun!

He is man among men, the rarest of gems;
Isn't he, Good old Sen; Bogey of Shelatang!
OC One Six One, what a son of a gun!

One thing I must say for Brigadier Sen, he certainly had a sense of humour. I give his reply below:

SRI GARRISON BY URI

With a yellow coloured jerkin lined with wool from Kashmir sheep,
In a well upholstered limousine he flashes down the street;
Six feet two in height our handsome hero's always in a rush,
Who is he? You ought to know - you've hit the mark - HAIRBRUSH.

Now our HAIRBRUSH is a soldier of good fortune and renown,
And to ladies he's a Rajah with jewel studded crown;
In the Srinagar Valley, he's the darling of the girls,
Who gaze with admiration, when he with skill, his beard curls.

Irresistible to cameras and newspapermen of Hind,
His protest at seeing his portrait into everyone he's dinned;
But then, HAIRBRUSH is Commanding SRI GARRISON in style,
And you cannot blame our pressmen who stalk him at every mile.

When the Valley was assaulted by the Raiders and their gangs,
As the 2IC of ONE SIX ONE he suffered all our pangs;
When at Shelatang they fought us and we killed them by the score,
Our HAIRBRUSH showed his mettle in the battle from the fore.

When on we went, our 2IC we had to leave in rear,
He had a mammoth job to do to keep our life line clear;
How well he organised it, is known to one and all,
For supplies and ammunition we never had to make a call.

We organised a Garrison and called it SRINAGAR,
And housed it in a mansion which he called Kalah Jagah;
With carpets, heaters, beds with quilts and almost every outfit,
He told his staff, I am sorry, its War, we've got to rough it.

One day the clouds got slightly dark, the locals said it would rain,
HAIRBRUSH, he called a meeting and began to wrack his brain;
"Now, VAS, come here, switch on our lights and fire a few embers,
And signal URI camp at once, to send us all their timber".

Said, VAS, "I think the telephone will be the answer, Sir,
These chaps in URI just don't know our plight and distress here;
I'll say one truck, three tons of wood, is wanted here for warmth",
Our HAIRBRUSH said, "One is no good, say three, by crack of dawn".

A clear-the-line call came right through to URI in the night,
A voice said, tell your Sunray that our Sunray's had a fright;
It looks like rain, our Sunray says out with all your might,
And send it up to SRINAGAR for fires big and bright.

All in reserve were woken up and took up to cutting logs,
We didn't spare an effort, although we worked in bogs;
The cry went up in URI, SRI GARRISON wants a fire,
And we will send them all we can no matter how we tire.

The Sunray and his staff in SRINAGAR must be cold,
So don't let's spare ourselves one bit every man was told;
We sent them wood, logs, coal and then one hundred massive trees,
And SRI GARRISON is now as warm as a toasted cheese.

On twenty two November at Milestone eight, we halted by a ridge,
When returning from column we found a broken bridge;
SRI GARRISON were not found lacking for column they did send,

Under KHANNA 4 KUMAON, with orders - RELIEVE THEM AT THE BEND!!

The column came, milap was made, and there three days we tarried,
Two stranded airmen, found in PUNCH, some 60 miles we'd carried;
Our hero, with the airmen, was exchanging notes and capers,
A camera clicked, he had been tricked - once more in India's papers.

Our HAIRBRUSH and his staff all still roughing it we're told,
We feel very bad about it, but then, we know its cold;
Don't worry SRI GARRISON and HAIRBRUSH have no fear,
We'll always do our best for you, CHEER UP, a bright new year!

And our reply was:

POOR SRI GARRISON

Poor Sri Garrison, the mote in the eye of every one!
Should you ask for our arise, that's not a question wise;
We only know of our demise, for we were never really born!!
Poor Sri Garrison, the mote in the eye of every one!

You may ask for our est, well we're half a man at best;
Could there be a bigger jest, we are of Sen's boys torn.
Poor Sri Garrison, the mote in the eye of every one!

Neither is our status clear, some say we are Jak Div Rear;
Others 'No Demand Fear', you are part of One Six One.
Poor Sri Garrison, the mote in the eye of every one!

We in personalities abound, such as never could be found;
Should you get the world around, where were such specimens born!
Poor Sri Garrison, the mote in the eye of every one!

The head is a common old 'horn', who keeps piping all day long;
Never would he leave alone, he is OC crazy gone!
Poor Sri Garrison, the mote in the eye of every one!

The G II is a man of letters, weren't he one it would be better;
Would've been long a 'bola hatter', were it not for his poetic renown.
Poor Sri Garrison, the mote in the eye of every one!

Our 'Q' was once Sallik, with always 'fair enough' on lip;
An' he soon made the usual 'bollick', it's nearly a week since he's gone.
Poor Sri Garrison, the mote in the eye of every one!

You would at Velu scarce laugh, he's said to have told the Brigadier off;
And wasn't he scared half, when his pip was nearly torn!
Poor Sri Garrison, the mote in the eye of every one!

To meet our CLO is a 'treat', for all you see of him are teeth;
Every thing for him is 'thck', no matter what you say he'll own.
Poor Sri Garrison, the mote in the eye of every one!

Of comfort most we're accused, of having 'power-that-be' abused;
Of comfy gadgets having used, they say we sleep from dawn to dawn.
Poor Sri Garrison, the mote in the eye of every one!

We have a roof over our head, well that's the most that could be said;
May be, we have a springy bed, they say we live like Mountbatten.
Poor Sri Garrison, the mote in the eye of every one.

We have a carpet or two, perhaps a curtain hanging too;
What if long baths and heaters few, they say we are beautifully adorn.
Poor Sri Garrison, the mote in the eye of every one!

We do sometimes go to Club, or pay a visit to a Kashmir pub;
Do hail at Soni, 'old tub', but that's only off and on.
Poor Sri Garrison, the mote in the eye of every one!

How we envy the chaps ahead, who are rum and chicken fed;
And recline on an earthy bed, lying in twos between the fawn.
Poor Sri Garrison, the mote in the eye of every one!

These are some of the 'repartees', bad as they are, that kept us going in the winter of 1947.

Field guns in action in Handwara in February 1948.

The Author planning the offensive for the liberation of J&K.

The Author gathering information from the locals.

25

GILGIT

The trouble on the western border of the state had its repercussions in the northern region also. A revolt flared up in Gilgit sometime in the beginning of November. The Gilgit Scouts in the area staged a coup-dé-tât by imprisoning Brigadier Ghansara Singh, governor of the place, and turning on the Hindus in the State Force Garrison. The Muslim element of the Garrison, who had been in league with the insurgents, joined hands with them at the first opportunity. The whole of Gilgit, being predominantly a Muslim area, thus passed into the hands of the insurgents, without almost a single shot being fired.

The insurrection at Gilgit posed a serious threat to Baltistan and Ladakh, adjoining territories to the east. The only forces available in the area were State Forces detachments, scattered in penny-pockets in places such as Dras, Kargil, Leh, Skardu, Rondu, etc. The State Forces posted at Rondu, which were guarding the bridge over the river Indus, on the road from Gilgit to Skardu, having, as already mentioned, been attacked by their Muslim comrades, the way was now open for the Gilgit insurrectionists to invade Skardu.

The Garrison at Skardu consisted, at the time, of approximately one Company under Major Thapa, based in a small Fortress. As soon as trouble started in Gilgit, the Hindu residents of Skardu area flocked to the Fortress and took refuge under the Garrison. The protection of the Fortress and the refugees inside it now became the paramount responsibility of Major Thapa, and he prepared the Fortress for a long siege during the coming winter, when he knew he would be completely cut off from Srinagar.

It was not very long after the fall of Rondu that the Scouts from Gilgit, under the command of Col Mata-ul-Mulk, son of the Mehtar of Chitral, attacked the little Fortress of Skardu also. This was about the middle of December. Soon afterwards, the Zojila Pass, the only entrance into the Valley from Srinagar, closed due to heavy snowfall, and this precluded any hope of sending reinforcements to the besieged Garrison. The much needed ammunition was, however, dropped into the Fortress, now and then, by our Tempests. In response to repeated requests from Major Thapa for reinforcements and supplies, a relief/supplies column was sent up, under Brigadier Faqir Singh of the State Forces, to hazard a passage through the Zojila Pass, towards the end of January. Having made it through the Pass after a superb effort, the column fell prey to a nasty ambush about two miles short of their destination and all arms, ammunition and supplies with the column were lost, besides many lives. Brigadier Faqir Singh was himself wounded by a mortar bomb. The news of this mishap to its relief column must have come as a great blow to the Garrison at Skardu. Nevertheless, the undaunted Garrison, under the gallant command of Major (now made Lt Col) Thapa, held out gamely against heavy odds for many months to come. The next attempt to reinforce the Garrison was made in the month of April, and the fate of that effort was equally dismal - but of that anon.

26

1 SIKH OFFENSIVE – WINTER OF 1948

It was on the 7th of February - in the middle of winter - that the news of a 'mass' invasion of the Valley from the west, over Phurkian-ki-Gali, reached Srinagar like a bolt out of the blue. According to this report, brought in by the remnants of a State Forces picket based at Shulur, a large force of Raiders numbering 'thousands' had that morning surprised the Kashmir militia-post at Trahgam and successfully persuaded them to change sides. They had then fallen on the small State Forces Garrison at Shulur and forced them to abandon their post. The whole of Trahgam Valley had thus passed into the Raiders' hands, and a path was now open for them to capture Handwara and Sopor and advance on to Srinagar. A state of near panic prevailed in Government quarters! The only troops available, to meet this threat, were 1 Sikh, less one Company at Baramula. 1 Sikh, as will be remembered, were supposed to be resting at Srinagar after the Bhatgiran incident.

Orders were passed on to me, as Officer Commanding 1 Sikh, at about 10 o'clock on the night of the 7th, to move out at the earliest and 'deal with the threat'. There was no information about the enemy beyond what has been related above. A troop of armoured cars, 7 Cavalry, from Baramula was supposed to meet me, I was told, at the road junction 7 miles short of Baramula in the early hours of the morning of the 8th. They were to provide support only. The battalion was lined up to start just after 1 am and I made off in a jeep ahead of the convoy in order to make arrangements to meet the armoured cars at the road junction, and to find out from the locals the state of the road beyond Sopor, as well as any further information about the enemy.

The first opportunity I had of studying the map and thinking over a plan of action was in the jeep during the journey from Srinagar to Sopor. I made out the following plans:

- Battalion Rear to be based at Sopor and to be responsible for the security of the town.
- Battalion with armoured cars in support, to advance beyond Sopor, tactically and establish a firm base at the area Watawian 3648 - ring-contour 373500, where nullah Pohru came nearest to the hill and formed a natural barrier for defence.
- Company less a platoon, in Mechanised Transport, supported by a troop of armoured cars was to carry out a patrol to Handwara and try and get as much information about the enemy as possible.

The battalion convoy from Srinagar arrived at the road junction at about 4 am - and had to wait for the armoured cars which did not fetch up till 6 am This time was, however, utilised in putting Junior Commanders in the picture and in giving out to them the outlined plan as described above.

The armoured cars from Baramula having 'married up' at the road junction, Sopor was reached at 7 am and a further advance resumed at 8 am, leaving the Battalion Rear behind. The road beyond Sopor was under one or two feet of snow and, therefore, only 4x4 vehicles with anti-skid chains could move on it.

Messrs DP Dhar and Nazir, representatives of the National Conference, had accompanied me from Srinagar as Civil Liaison Officers. The National Conference representative at Sopor, Mr Soofi, was contacted for information, but he seemed to have none beyond the rumours known at Srinagar. The advance to the Firm-Base was uneventful and the base was secured at Watawian by 3 pm. I personally took out the patrol to Handwara, of a Company less one Platoon and a troop of armoured cars, from the Firm-Base, at 3.30 pm, and returned to Base at 6 pm, without any incident. Handwara was found to be clear of the enemy, though excitement and panic amongst the population was noticeable. The Civil Liaison Officers, DP Dhar and Nazir, stayed behind at Handwara, to reassure the local population and to watch further developments. Much against my wish, the armoured cars, having completed their patrol to Handwara, returned to their base at Baramula for maintenance - a place at least four hours distance away from our Firm-Base, given the snow. No amount of protesting to Brigade Headquarters at Uri, on my part, availed. The night/early morning of 8th/9th February was utilised in strengthening the perimeter defences of the Firm-Base, and a plan was made to carry out a strong patrol, the next morning, in the direction of Wodhpur and secure the next Firm-Base in that locality.

At first light on 9th February, Messrs Dhar and Nazir brought the news that the enemy had occupied Handwara after last light on the 8th of February - a couple of hours after our patrol had returned. This news was to some extent welcome as now we knew where the enemy was and instead of groping in the dark, we could deal with him. The operational plan made overnight, was thus modified. A Company under Major Suri was despatched at once to secure the suspension bridge on the way to Handwara. It was appreciated that as soon as the enemy came to know of the presence of our troops in the area, he would try and secure this bridge at the first opportunity. The Company was therefore ordered to lie low and capture some prisoners alive, so as to get definite information about the enemy, which was so imperative at this stage. A plan was worked out at the same time to surround the village of Handwara during the night of the 9th/10th February, and deal with the enemy there at first light. A troop of armoured cars was asked for, and promised by Brigade Headquarters at Uri, for this operation They were to arrive at Handwara bridge at 7 am on the 10th of February.

The road to Handwara passing through the Firm-Base was very narrow, with a hill-side on one side and deep snow on the other. Owing to the absence of any parking place away from the road, all tactical vehicles with the battalion were parked on this road. This left very little room for the armoured cars, which were expected to arrive on the morning of 10th February, to pass. All hands were, therefore, engaged throughout the afternoon and till late at night, right up to the starting time of the Handwara operation, in making a way for the armoured cars. The troops had thus to go straight into night operations without a moment's rest. At 5.30 pm, on the 9th, a party of the enemy, who had apparently come to secure the bridge, as was expected, were surprised by our post there and 15 of them were captured alive, including an officer. However, two or three of them managed to escape. These prisoners, especially the officer, yielded some very useful information about the strength, organisation, arms and equipment of the enemy and their future intentions.

The enemy in the area, the officer told us, was the 1st Battalion of the Azad Kashmir Forces, about 800 strong, organised and equipped more or less on the lines of a regular Pakistani Battalion. His Commanding Officer's name was Lt Col Nausherwan Khan, a Pakistani Army officer. I might mention here, that Nausherwan Khan was an officer, junior to me, from the 5th Battalion of the 11th Sikh regiment, the battalion to which I belonged before the Second World War. I therefore knew him well. In the unit we used to call him 'jangli', for his boots were size 12, a size more than that of any other officer.

The prisoner also gave the names of all his Company Commanders and said that most of the senior officers in the battalion were regulars of the Pakistan Army. He further gave the exact location where the Headquarters and men in Handwara were to spend the night - the police station and tehsil respectively.

On receipt of this information, the starting time for the night operation was advanced slightly in order to block all exists from the village of Handwara before first light, and two shock parties were organised to deal a 'coupe-de-main' to the enemy while it was still dark. A good proportion of the men, who constituted these parties, were those who had been in the village with our patrol on the evening of the 8th of February and therefore knew the location and 'lie' of the two objectives – the police station and the tehsil. This information was supplemented by a detailed description of the buildings by the locals.

Guides were also detailed to accompany these parties. The expected arrival of the armoured cars, in the morning, was tied up with the plan and a confirmation was received from Brigade Headquarters, late that night, that the armoured cars would be at the suspension bridge at the appointed hour.

The night-march for the Operation from the Firm-Base commenced exactly at midnight of the 9th/10th of February. The troops started off in excellent heart, assured of victory! The bridge, where we had a Company in position, was reached at about 2 am. The Company at the bridge reported that they had seen, about an hour earlier, a small party of the enemy approach the bridge. Sensing that the bridge was held, the party had run away in fright leaving behind a tin of kerosene oil and a few bundles of swabs. They had apparently come with the intention of setting fire to the bridge. The flight of this incendiary party and the escape of a few of the enemy patrol on the evening before, were not a very happy augury for the night operation now in progress. Doubts began to assail our minds as to whether we would find the enemy asleep, as we had hoped. Was it more likely that he would be 'sitting up' waiting for us, having been forewarned? Or, would he have escaped by the time we got there?

One of these forebodings came true. I was with the leading troops. Just as our first stop-party was getting on to the bridge north of the village, the most likely route of escape for the enemy, running footsteps were heard on the bridge and a few men were seen disappearing in the haze of the night. The contact was so close that one of the enemy actually got hold of the arm of the JCO leading our party and, pulling at it, enjoined him to run shouting: "enemy, enemy!" It was no use opening fire. So our party quickly took up position and silently awaited the arrival of some more enemy troops. None came. Soon it was discovered that it was the tail-end of the escaping enemy that we had encountered. I therefore decided to take up the chase along the road, to intercept him at Wodhpur, where the road and the track along which the enemy had escaped - converged.

The track ran almost parallel to the road to Wodhpur via the suspension bridge, and was separated from it by a wide nullah and some marshy ground, then under deep snow. The distance between the road and the track varied from 1500 to 2500 yards. It was thus outside the small arms range, and any move on foot off the beaten path over the snow was impossible. At first light, soon afterwards, we found ourselves and the enemy running parallel to each other and both making for the same vital objective - the bottleneck near Wodhpur. The snow was deep and the going was hard. There was no transport available and everything, including 3-inch mortars and ammunition, was being carried by the men. The distance to the objective along the road was about half a mile longer than along the track.

We were hoping against hope that the armoured cars would have arrived at the bridge, as pre-arranged. However, as we passed the bridge, we were told that they had not arrived. I left word behind for them to follow us on arrival. They did not do so, and thus missed bagging one of the biggest trophy's they could have ever hoped for!

There was no faltering on our part in this race with the enemy. Having got a head start on us, however, and because of the lesser distance, they beat us to the objective. Before we could reach Wodhpur the enemy's covering party had taken up position in the houses overlooking the road and on the hills both sides of the bottleneck. A battle ensued. By the time we were able to dislodge the enemy, he had succeeded in covering his retreat - a very hurried one, no doubt, but without any major loss of life, except for a few wounded. We had two seriously wounded, including Maulvi Mohd Saed, our Civil Liaison Officers, Dhar and Nazir having been evacuated. As a result of this action, the enemy was forced to abandon all his heavy baggage and equipment, including a No 62 wireless set, with a generator, and some ammunition. He had been split up into two parties - one retreating towards Magam and the other, the bigger of the two, moving towards Kupwara. It was about 3 pm by now and we were too tired and hungry to keep up the chase that day. In the absence of any snow-traction vehicle or porters, there was no possibility of the 'administration' keeping up with us either. Even the armoured cars, on which we had counted so much, and which could have played havoc with the enemy, entrapped as he was, had failed to turn up. Besides, before such a hazardous operation could be undertaken a little appreciation of the situation was essential. It was, therefore, decided to withdraw a major portion of the battalion back into the Firm-Base for rest with the intention of taking up the pursuit early next morning.

The Company at the bridge under Major Suri was detailed to carry out a search of Handwara village. A large dump of enemy heavy baggage and bedding, including rations, etc, was recovered from the Tehsil in the village. A torn Pakistani flag flying atop the building was also collected. After repeated appeals to Brigade Headquarters, a troop of armoured cars was sent to us sometime towards the evening of that day - only 12 hours too late! The crew felt sorry, when they were told of the excellent opportunity they had missed. If they had arrived that morning, as had been arranged, we would have, without any doubt, destroyed or captured the whole of the enemy force and there would have been no 'Handwara front' for some months to come – at least during the winter months!

An Appreciation

The enemy was a full battalion strong and we were a battalion less a Company - and a weak one at that, after the loss at Bhatgiran. We had a great advantage, however, in terms of morale over the enemy, who had been badly shaken by our recent operations and had been split into two parties. He had further lost practically all his heavy baggage and bedding - a very important factor in winter - and some of his reserve ammunition. He had also lost a No 62 set, probably his only means of communication with the home-base - contributing no doubt to his feeling of isolation. We had a little superiority in weapons also, in that we possessed some 3-inch mortars which the enemy did not. Under these circumstances, for us to take a certain amount of risk was considered justified. A party of the enemy having withdrawn towards Magam, the establishment of a firm base at Wodhpur was felt essential, in order to secure the line of communication of the pursuing force against any threat from that direction. In the absence of any means of traction over deep snow and owing to the non-availability of porters, it was not possible to move any rations with the pursuit parties. As for blankets, each man would have to carry his own. The presence of a 3-inch mortar with the pursuit-party, in addition to its ammunition, was considered important and this again had to be carried by the men.

The pursuit was taken up early the next morning, the 11th of February by a force consisting of Battalion Tactical Headquarters and two Companies supported by two armoured cars. The third Company was left behind to establish a firm base at Wodhpur, with a platoon to protect the suspension bridge near Handwara. Snow on the road was at least 2 1/2 feet deep resulting in very heavy going for the armoured cars. Progress was consequently slow. On reaching Arampura at about 10 am, it was found that the decking of the wooden bridge there had been dismantled. The enemy had not, however, had the time to damage the load-bearers. The decking was replaced with the help of local labour (the same people who had only an hour earlier been employed by the enemy to dismantle it!) and our advance resumed. To slow us down, the enemy had felled trees all along the road. The clearing of these caused considerable delay with the result that Dragumula, only 4 miles from Arampura, was not reached until 4 pm. Here one of the armoured cars got ditched, and it took over an hour, and all available hands, to get it back on to the road again. There was less than an hour's light at hand, and it was, therefore, decided to go into bivouac at Dragumula for the night. There had so far been no encounter with the enemy, who, the locals reported, was fleeing only just ahead of us!

A report was received just as we were getting into a perimeter camp that the enemy was engaged at that very moment in cutting down the bridge at Kupwara. This was a very important bridge, over a big, deep nullah, and the securing of it intact was of vital importance to us for any further advance. A Company was, therefore, despatched post-haste to capture the bridge as soon as possible. This Company moved in the dark at record speed. There was a spirited encounter with the enemy at the bridge. The bridge had been set on fire as the Company arrived and was well covered by light machine guns being fired from a house on the opposite side. The Company managed to secure the bridge and extinguish the fire. It speaks well of the morale of the troops when one considers that the action took place in the middle of the night and in the extreme cold of mid-winter. That the enemy had suffered casualties could be seen next morning from the trails of blood left behind on the snow. We suffered one casualty.

The pursuit was resumed in the early hours of the 12th of February. In view of the damage caused to the bridge by fire, the armoured cars were left behind at Dragumula with a platoon of infantry as close escort. Kupwara was found completely deserted. The enemy, it was discovered, had retreated from the village in haste in the middle of the night, leaving behind some more blankets and woollen shawls, apparently snatched from the locals.

The chase was resumed without loss of time, Trahgam was reached without incident at about 2.30 pm. Some dead bodies of local civilians (Kashmiri Pandits), including women and children were seen littered about on the road-side. These, we were told, had been shot by the enemy. The going all along over deep snow had been hard, more so with the extra load that every man was carrying. The blankets had been abandoned at Dragumula with instructions for them to be sent up later with local porters, if possible.

The enemy, it was reported, had only just evacuated Trahgam, taking all his wounded and sick with him. He was stated to be in a bad way and terrified! We too had received orders from Brigade Headquarters to abandon the chase and return to base at once. So, in order to scare the enemy still further, a Company was pushed straight through to pursue him up to the village of Guglus, while the remainder of the force engaged themselves in settling down for the night at Trahgam. We had been well received by the public at Trahgam, especially by the President of the local National Conference, who gave us assurance of the fullest co-operation from all. The problem of procuring rations for the troops was solved by the capture of a large quantity of enemy supplies in the village, including ground-nuts and almonds. The latter were particularly welcome to the rather hungry troops and were consumed in inordinate quantities - killing much of the appetite! This was supplemented by 'chappaties' of maize-flour, prepared by the men themselves, using shovel-blades as iron plates - quite a novel idea! The 'chappaties' cooked in this manner were somehow especially tasty!

The Commander of the 1st Azad Kashmir Battalion, which had occupied Handwara, as already mentioned, was Nausherwan Khan. A fact confirmed by our search party which recovered a valise with his name on it. I have already referred to his large shoe size and lo and behold, while running, in haste, from Handwara, he had left one of his boots behind! We were told by the locals that as a result of this he had to perforce ride a pony during his retreat ahead of us. Therefore, I decided to do him a good-turn and carry his extra-large size boot with me so as to return it to him, when the opportunity arose. On arrival at Trahgam, I asked Nazir Ahmed (if I remember his name correctly), the local President of the National Conference, to arrange for a local who would take a message from me, along with the over-sized boot, to the Commander of the enemy force, withdrawing ahead of us. He produced an old man, with a long beard (a local goldsmith), who was willing to do so, but who wanted a rifle, for his own protection. I refused to give him a rifle (as I did not want to lose a weapon) and in the end, Nazir managed to get him a local shot-gun. The messenger left Trahgam but did not return the same evening. However, I had done a good-turn to my erstwhile colleague, Nausherwan, from the Indian Army battalion, the 5/11 Sikh. If I did not get a letter of thanks from him, it was of small consequence, given the circumstances!

To keep ourselves warm at night was a real problem. Some of the pickets and sentries were right in the open. They were given priority for great coats, which only a few of us had. The remainder had to be content with a shelter of some sort. The firewood, however, was plentiful and fires were kept burning in the open and in the rooms the whole night. In spite of that, I do not think anybody could have had a wink of sleep that night. I know, I did not. It was one of the most uncomfortable nights I have ever spent! All I had on me was an Angora shirt and a jersey pull-over. The night passed uneventfully and everybody was up very early next morning, looking for the sun.

The agent sent after the enemy the evening before had not returned. This looked ominous. However, before withdrawing to base, as ordered by Brigade Headquarters, it was decided to take out a strong patrol up to Shulur so as to give the illusion of the pursuit being kept up. A platoon was left behind to hold the fort, so to say, at Trahgam, and the remainder of the force (two Companies, less a Platoon), plus the Gurkha Platoon, and a 3-inch mortar, moved out at 7 am on the 13th of February. A Firm-Base was established on a ridge a mile short of Guglus and a Company, plus the State Force Gurkha Platoon, were despatched forward to carry out 'recce in force'. The Company was to advance along the main track and the Gurkha Platoon was to take the side-track to Shulur, branching off the main track just short of Guglus.

No sooner had the Gurkha Platoon branched off to the left than the Company on the main track came under very close-range heavy fire from the ridge and from the village. At the same time an enemy party of about 50 tried to charge the Company from behind a hedge a few yards to their left, with loud shouts of 'Ya Ali'. As luck would have it, the charging enemy, while they were wading through knee deep snow, came under close range enfilade-fire of the Gurkha Platoon, whom they had not spotted. Practically, the whole of this charging enemy was nearly wiped out. Not less than 40 were left killed or wounded in front of the Gurkha Platoon position. Very few managed to escape. The Company fought in a spirited manner, supported by the 3-inch mortar left behind from the Firm-Base, and drove the enemy out of the village. In this action, the Company lost one Non-Commissioned Officer. Having broken action, we withdrew back to our Base at Wodhpur without further incident. In this last day of operations alone, the troops had advanced four miles from Trahgam, seen action, withdrawn a distance of approximately twenty miles, carrying on their person a 3-inch mortar with its ammunition, reserve small-arms, ammunitions and other stores over terrain covered in deep snow. It was a remarkable feat of fitness and endurance!

14th of February was spent in regrouping and readjusting dispositions and in local patrolling. The dispositions of the Battalion now were as follows:

Two Coy Bn Plus HQ One Coy	- Wodhpur
Gurkha Platoon and Tp Armd Cars	- Suspension-Bridge

Towards the evening of 14th February, a party of the enemy was reported to have arrived back at Dragumula, obviously encouraged by our withdrawal from Trahgam. Owing to inclement weather, operations were confined mostly to reconnaissance and fighting patrols in the direction of Dragumula and Magam. No serious engagement with the enemy, however, took place. A section of 25 pounders had arrived and the guns were placed in position at Wodhpur. It was decided, on 19th February, to carry out an advance that night and surround Dragumula by first light the next day. The night operation was carried out as planned, but only to find that there was no enemy there. A firm base was established there and a Company patrol sent to Kupwara. The patrol reported Kupwara clear of enemy. Kupwara was secured at 7.30

am on 21st February, and a Company of 7 Sikh, which had joined the battalion a day earlier, was established there. During his withdrawal from Dragumula the enemy had destroyed all bridges, big or small, on the road to Kupwara. These were repaired by local labour. The next day was spent in patrolling the area from Wodhpur to Kupwara. No enemy was encountered. A section of 25 pounders was, therefore, moved from Wodhpur to Dragumula.

At 5.30 am, on 23rd February, just before first light, an enemy party of about 300 strong, mostly locals, attacked a picket of 7 Sikh Company at Kupwara. The enemy had approached under cover to within 50 yards of the picket position on three sides, with a bren group as near as 25 yards from one of the posts. In spite of repeated assaults, the picket succeeded in holding the enemy at bay, until the break of dawn, and the arrival of reinforcements, when the enemy was forced to withdraw. Three dead were left behind, along with large quantities of ammunition. The inspection of the ground soon afterwards revealed many trails of blood as the wounded and the killed had been dragged away by the enemy over soft snow. In this action, the 3-inch mortar detachment with the picket was obliged to fire at a range of 150 yards from its position and lent valuable support in repelling the attack. Local patrolling was carried out on 24th February and it was confirmed, both by the patrols and local agents, that the attack on our picket on the 23rd morning, if not instigated, was certainly led by some bad elements from the village Hyahom. This village which is about four miles from Kupwara is purely a Pathan village, the headman of which had already joined hands with the Raiders and two of his sons were Commissioned Officers in the Azad Kashmir Forces.

It was, therefore, decided to carry out a punitive operation against this village. An advance on the village began on the morning of the 25th of February and the village was surrounded without incident by 11 am. A search of the headman's house revealed some Sten Magazines and ammunition hidden in the roof and about 20 complete sets of uniform in a box. There were also huge stores of looted articles. The rooms were too dark from inside to permit a thorough search and it was, therefore, decided to set fire to the house. This completed, the force returned to Kupwara, taking the family of the headman, consisting of his wife, daughter-in-law and her husband, who was later discovered to be a deserter from the Kashmir State Forces, as hostages.

Some local patrolling was carried out on the 26th and the 27th of February. 1 Sikh Battalion was relieved by 7 Sikh. One Company of 1 Sikh was, however, detained in the area as a reinforcement to 7 Sikh. The rest of the battalion withdrew to Srinagar.

I Temporarily take over the Brigade at Uri

In early March 1948, Brigadier Sen went on medical leave for ten days, and I as his Deputy, was asked to take over the Brigade from him at Uri. On arrival at Uri Camp in the morning, I enquired from the Brigade Major the timings for morning and evening stand-to, and was informed that they had none. I was surprised and asked him to organise a perimeter-defence of the camp at once, giving responsibility, by Sectors, to the Units located in the area. I announced that I would go round the camp that evening, checking its perimeter-defence - a normal drill in a hilly camp. I was surprised that Brigadier Sen, a seasoned soldier, should not have organised this. I did not expect the Staff who were new at Brigade Headquarters to know about this. I then asked the Brigade Intelligence Officer to show me the pickets around the camp, by numbers. Imagine my surprise when I discovered that he did not know how many camp pickets there were! There was one locality, north of the camp, I was told, which indulged in sniping the camp every evening. I enquired from the Brigade Major, if we had any picket in the Area, and we replied that he did and that it was held by the Jat Battalion. I decided to visit the picket the next morning, and asked the Brigade Intelligence Officer to accompany me with an escort of two riflemen who would move ahead of us for our protection. We had hardly gone one third the distance to the picket, when I noticed that the Intelligence Officer was lagging behind; obviously, he could not take the climb, being unfit. So I asked him to take one of the riflemen with him and go back to camp, and I continued my advance to the picket with one rifleman.

When I reached the picket, as they knew I was coming, they were standing-to, as is the normal practice in the Army. I met the JCO in-charge; shook hands with him and asked him to stand-down the picket, and he did. The JCO had a blanket spread on the ground to receive me. The sun was just coming out, and the JCO remarked: "Aaj to do suraj charhne chahien, kyon keh Brigade Commander Sahib padhare hein!" (Today, we should have two suns coming out because Brigadier Commander sahib is visiting the picket). Apparently they had never been visited by any one from Brigade Headquarters before. I was aghast! Such was the situation at 161 Infantry Brigade Headquarters at Uri.

I was told that the Brigade Commander spent most of his time, during the day, sitting in a small room next to his Headquarters, basking by the log-wood fire. The walls of this small room were covered with soot, and so long as I was there, I banned entry into that room. I, myself, preferred to sit in the open, in the sun, which I found enjoyable. After ten days, Brigadier Sen returned to Uri and relieved me.

Back to the Offensive

One Company of the battalion, it will be remembered, was still at Baramula under 161 Infantry Brigade and had been there from the very beginning. The disposition of 7 Sikh, with one Company of 1 Sikh, a troop of armoured cars and a section of 25 pounders, under their command, was roughly as follows:

Battalion HQ and two Companies	- Kupwara
Company (less one Platoon Section Field Guns)	- Dragumula
One Platoon	- Wodhpur
One Company	- Handwara
Company 1 Sikh (reserve)	- Suspension-Bridge and a troop of armd cars

The activity of our troops in the area owing to cold and snow was mostly confined to local patrolling. This rather passive policy encouraged the enemy to spread out and come closer and closer to our forward posts. The sniping of Kupwara was in those days a daily occurrence. Patrols issuing out from Handwara also reported increased activity on the part of the enemy. About this time the Company Commander of the Company at Handwara, Major Karnail Singh, whilst on a patrol, was seriously wounded in a sharp engagement within two miles of Handwara. Company 1 Sikh, which was in reserve at the bridge, was utilised to comb the valley and establish a picket at ring contour in the area, called 'Nagi Picket'.

Kupwara too continued to come in for a lot of attention from the enemy, whose base of operation was reported to be at Trahgam. It was decided to liquidate this base after a night advance. Two Companies of 7 Sikh set out from Kupwara at midnight. As they were passing near the village of Pethahir in the early hours of the morning, they came across a little boy who led our troops to the houses in which the enemy was supposed to be asleep. The houses were cordoned off and the enemy was asked to surrender. He, however, chose to fight it out and thus lost about 34 men, including an officer, while 7 men were taken prisoners. 36 rifles, two revolvers and a large quantity of ammunition were recovered from the houses where they were living. This was a signal for the enemy garrison at Trahgam to evacuate. Advance to that base was, therefore, abandoned and a Company post was established instead at a place called Pethahir. Patrols from Pethahir reported Trahgam and beyond, up to Shulur, clear of the enemy. A Company post was, therefore, established at Shulur.

The front of 7 Sikh having thus been extended, Headquarters 1 Sikh and the only company with it at Srinagar, were ordered out to Handwara. The Handwara-Kupwara area was now divided into two sectors between 1 Sikh and 7 Sikh, with all inclusive Wodhpur-Magam-Tartpura, to 1 Sikh, as Inter-Battalion boundary. The two Battalion Headquarters were located at Handwara and Kupwara respectively.

The Company 1 Sikh which had been attached to 7 Sikh, now reverted to its own battalion and 1 Sikh less two Companies, with a section of field guns under its command, were roughly disposed as follows:

Battalion HQ	-	Handwara
(Company Less two Pls)	-	Handwara
One Pl State Force	-	Handwara
Section Field Guns	-	Handwara
One Platoon	-	Nagi Picket
One Platoon	-	Wodhpur
One Company	-	Lachh

With the enemy frustrated in his attempt to concentrate and attack the Uri defences from the high ground to the east of the camp, in action at Bhatgiran with 1 Sikh on 12th December, the Uri front came almost to a stand off. The enemy now decided to by-pass Uri from the west and harass its line of communication. In late January and early February, parties of the enemy were reported across the river, opposite Mahura, moving with the avowed intention of destroying the powerhouse. This move of the enemy was countered by posting pickets on the high hills across the river in that area. The enemy then adopted the tactics of infiltrating through these pickets at odd hours and sniping the road to Uri. This became a real menace by the middle of March. The enemy was reported to be operating from the villages situated behind the range running along the river and west of it.

It was, therefore, decided to comb this area and trap the enemy in between the arms of two pincers closing in from the north and the south. A certain number of the enemy in the area was expected to be flushed out in the direction of the Kashmir Valley over the Kazinag range. A Company of 1 Sikh from Srinagar, under the command of 161 Infantry Brigade, was posted at Panzul in the Valley to give him a hot reception. While the combing operation was successful in so far as it cleared the area, most of the enemy managed to escape. Two parties, each about 150 to 200 men strong, had crossed over to the Valley and with luck on their side, had just escaped the 'welcome' awaiting them. While this combing operation was going on, we were in patrolling-touch with our Company at Panzul from our post at Lachh. The Company at Panzul informed us one morning, in late March, that they had chased a party of the enemy in the direction of Lachh. Our post at Lachh was, therefore, all ready to receive them. In the evening an agent reported that the enemy had just passed through Naugam and was proposing to spend the night at Mankal. Company less a Platoon, at Lachh, was detailed to carry out a night march and surround the enemy in the village of Mankal by first light. I had gone over to Lachh from Handwara to supervise the night operations. A guide was procured from the Civil Liaison Officer, Mr. Nazir, who himself decided to accompany the troops on this mission. Hopes were high and every one was certain of a big catch.

The elements were, however, against us. Punctually at starting time (midnight) a violent rain storm hit the area and raged throughout the night. And to cap it all, the guide lost his way and decided to take a short cut through a nullah. The night was pitch dark and the ground extremely slippery. Most of the way the troops had to 'two-chain' each other, as one of them jocularly remarked, causing delay. The objective was reached an hour after first light, but it was too late. An old man in the village informed them that the enemy had left just half an hour earlier. Hard luck indeed!

An amusing incident occurred here. The old man informed Mr Nazir, the Civil Liaison Officer, that on hearing of the arrival of the Raiders the residents of the village had run away into the jungle. Nazir thereupon set out in search of them, accompanied by two Sikh sepoys as his escort. He was wearing militia uniform and was walking ahead of his escort in the jungle when he spotted these poor evacuees and beckoned them to come near and around him. The villagers crowded in front of him with their backs towards the approaching Sikh sepoys whom they had not noticed. Nazir told them, light-heartedly, that he was the Commander of the Pakistani troops and wished to know what arrangements they had made for the reception of their brethren? The villagers were rather taken aback at first, but, after a moment's pause, all of them spoke with one voice and said that the Pakistanis being their muslim brothers were most welcome and that all they had was at their disposal. Nazir asked them if they had ever heard of the 'Kafir' Abdullah. "Kafir, indeed", they all agreed, "Maha Kafir", who had imported those savage Sikhs to perpetrate untold atrocities upon poor Muslim Kashmiris! By then, of course, the two Sikh Sepoys had also arrived, unnoticed. Nazir then asked them if they had actually seen these Sikhs and experienced their savagery. They replied that they had not, but said that they had heard a great deal about them. "I will show you some", said Nazir, pointing towards his escort, "have a look", and as they all looked back and saw these two Sikh stalwarts, standing with their bayonets fixed, they literally collapsed! The escort enjoyed the joke more than Mr Nazir himself!

For this operation I had moved my Tactical Headquarters to Lachh and was following the fortunes of the patrol on the wireless set. Just as I heard of the bad luck they had had, our agent came in with a report that at that very moment another party of the enemy were having their meal at the village of Naugam, and that they too were bound for Mankal. I passed on this information to the patrol on the wireless and told them to lay an ambush for this enemy party. To hasten affairs, I sent a detachment of mortars from the Lachh post, half a mile to a flank, and instructed them to fire a few bombs into the village of Naugam, to scare the Raiders out off the village. This worked, and the enemy was soon on his way into what looked like the 'Jaws of Death'.

The patrol had already informed me that they were ready to receive the enemy and I commenced a running-commentary with the wireless operator at the other end. The enemy, I was informed, had last been reported walking 'right in', only 300 yards from the ambush, when something terrible happened. A local lad, upon being suddenly challenged by our 'stop' behind the ambush, got hysterical and ran down the hill through the jungle, shouting and shrieking at the top of his voice. There was no way of stopping him. Shooting would not have helped. The Raiders hearing his cries, smelt a rat and took cover at once. On hearing what the young fellow had to say, they scattered and ran for their lives! The patrol tried to give chase, but it was of no avail in the jungle. The troops returned to Lachh in the evening tired, hungry and soaked to their skins and what was worse, despondent at their extremely bad luck!

The troops may have found a little consolation in the report that the enemy mortally scared after the day's events had resolved to take, against all counsels, the most hazardous escape route over Bod Bangas via Bangas Gali and had perished to the last man in a storm of hail and lightening, a phenomenon for which Bod Bangas is notorious. This report was later confirmed by government sources as true.

7 Sikh had stretched their necks out a bit too much by holding Shulur, and this post of theirs was getting plastered by the enemy. 1 Sikh was asked to establish a Company post at Sonamul, on the flank of Shulur. This was done without difficulty.

It was here one morning that I saw 'Range Practice' going on. I was visiting the picket at the time and was asked by the Commander if I would care to see some 'Range Practice'. I was led to a tree and from behind it watched one of our sentries stand up in a slit-trench with a red flag in his hand. There was a shot from an enemy sniper. It hit somewhere to the right of the trench and the sentry signalled with the red flag, "Wash out - right". There was another shot and this time the signal was, "Too high". So this was 'Range Practice'! It was foolhardy on the sentry's part, in a way, but I did not say anything. These things, there is no doubt, have a great salutary effect on the morale of the troops.

The 1 Sikh post at Kralpura could not help Shulur much and the latter was getting more and more into trouble every day. With the whole of the Trahgam Ridge in enemy hands the position held by 7 Sikh Company below it, at Shulur, was tactically an unsound one. It was under small arms fire all the time from higher ground and its line of communication to Pethahir, running as it did along the foot of the Trahgam ridge, was constantly threatened. The provisioning of Shulur was, consequently, becoming increasingly difficult and costly in terms of lives. Each time it entailed a full-fledged operation by at least a Company supported by field guns and weapon carriers. A Company of 7 Sikh while on such a mission was once very seriously engaged by the enemy, who succeeded in destroying, or looting, most of the pony-convoy of supplies escorted by the Company. It was with the greatest of difficulty that the Company managed to make its way back to Shulur. The enemy followed up this success by completely investing the Shulur Garrison. The relief of the Garrison, now of two Companies, therefore, became imperative. And this required a full-fledged operation. The plan roughly was:

- A force of two Companies of 7 Sikh to carry out an enveloping night advance on to the highest point on Trahgam Ridge, which was known to be strongly held, and after securing it by first light to press down along the ridge towards Shulur.
- Another Company of 7 Sikh supported by a troop of armoured cars, and a section of weapon carriers, to advance along the road at first light.
- A Company of 1 Sikh at Sonamul, supported by a section of weapon carriers, to demonstrate from that flank.
- Shulur Garrison to usher out and meet the thrust along the road as far forward as possible.
- A Section of field guns at Pethahir was to support the operation throughout.

In early April, 1 Sikh was asked to make a Company of theirs available to 7 Sikh for this operation. The Company at Panzul was, therefore, withdrawn. It reached Handwara after a march of 20 miles at 8 pm and was straightaway pushed in mechanical transport to Pethahir to take part in the night advance starting at 11 pm. The advance entailed a climb of over 5000 feet over a very difficult single-man track and was led by 1 Sikh Company. At first light, the leading Platoon of this Company surprised an enemy post engaged in saying Namaz and wiped-out a complete section, capturing four rifles and large quantities of ammunition. The rest of the enemy put up stiff resistance before being driven out. The objective was secured by 9 am. The resistance offered by the enemy to the troops of 7 Sikh advancing along the road continued to be stiff, until the capture of the Trahgam Ridge. The operation generally went according to plan. The Garrison at Shulur was contacted and the post evacuated, bringing in all supplies and stores. The forward-most post held by 7 Sikh now was at Pethahir.

With the Shulur Garrison withdrawn, the 1 Sikh post at Sonamul became infructuous and it was, therefore, decided to withdraw it to Magam. The orders came rather suddenly one morning and withdrawal was to be completed before last light the same day. The Garrison had been supplied with 10 days' ration only the day before and it had quite a lot of reserve ammunition. There were about 20 bundles of barbed wire that also needed to be carted back. It was not possible within that time to get the requisite number of ponies or porters for this purpose. The track to Kralpura was narrow and 'kucha'. Only Dodges or jeeps could have made it. All 8 Dodges belonging to the troop of armoured cars and the Engineers Company at Handwara were, therefore, commandeered for the purpose.

A convoy of these vehicles, escorted by three weapon carriers, arrived at the post at about 3 pm and was ready and loaded, to start on its return journey, when a shower of rain came down and wetted the track. The enemy had also come to know by now that something was afoot and had started sniping at the convoy. Within a few hundred yards of the start point one of the 7 Cavalry vehicles slid off the road. All attempts at winching it out failed, yet the vehicle could not be abandoned. The light was failing fast and the enemy, appreciating our predicament, was trying to encroach on the convoy as much as it could. The Company escorting the convoy were ordered to form a 'box' round the convoy so that the recovery operation could go on in the dark.

Another Company of 1 Sikh from Handwara was rushed forward as reinforcements. Night fell, but the enemy knowing the Sikhs was too chary to come near, although he kept up intermittently sniping at the convoy throughout the night. Local efforts to recover the vehicle had failed. An Engineer officer was sent for early in the morning, from Handwara, for expert advice and the vehicle abandoned only when he said it was unrecoverable and that too after all the essential parts of the engine and the spare wheel had been removed. The baggage was transferred to other vehicles and the convoy was ready to start again at 9 o'clock the next morning.

The enemy too had gained in strength by now, having been reinforced, and had begun to show his teeth. He came out with the usual drum-beat and attempted to charge one of our pickets. His attempt was, however, foiled mainly by close range enfilade fire from a neighbouring picket. He attempted to charge twice again from different directions and each time he was repulsed with heavy losses. The guns from Pethahir were now brought to bear on the targets in the area and lent invaluable support. Another mishap happened to the vehicle convoy when one of the bridges collapsed under the weight of a weapon carrier. The other carrier when yoked to pull it out had its track come-off. The ditched carrier was in the end winched out with a Dodge, helped by all available hands. What took time was making a diversion for the remainder of the vehicles to pass through. It was not until 3.30 pm on the second day that the convoy reached Magam. The enemy attempted only half-hearted pursuit, presumably due to the losses already suffered by him. The withdrawal was completed by 5 pm that evening, and a Company post established at Magam.

This had been a very hazardous operation and 1 Sikh had come out with flying colours! Never had the spirit of mutual assistance, selfless devotion to duty and dogged determination been more prominent than in this little operation, and it contributed greatly to the high morale of the battalion. The enemy took our withdrawal from Shulur and Kralpura as a sign of weakness and started encroaching more and more on our ground. Sniping at our forward posts at Nagi picket, Magam and Pethahir became a matter of daily routine. The latter place was paid special attention to by the enemy who at one time more or less invested it. He burnt all the bridges on Trahgam road beyond

Sheikh Abdullah & members of the Civil Administration with the Author & other officers.

Sheikh Abdullah addresses troops. The Author is standing behind him.

Pandit jee takes the salute at a Guard of Honour. To his left is the Author.

Pethahir and two bridges on the near-side of it. Contact with Pethahir post could not be established without first opening the road by force. The place was showing signs of turning into another Shulur when the summer offensive commenced in May.

In late March, a threat had also appeared to Gulmarg over the Pirpanjal range. The Commanding Officer of 1 Madras, Lt Col Menon had been ambushed and killed by the enemy on this route only a few miles from Himan Buniar. The Company of 1 Sikh with 161 Infantry Brigade at Baramula was at this juncture despatched to look after Gulmarg.

Pandit jee was scheduled to come to Srinagar in early May to attend the 'Independence Week' and the question of giving him a guard of honour arose. I implored General Thimayya that this signal honour should go to 1 Sikh, who had so far, without doubt, borne the brunt of the fighting in the Valley. The General agreed with me but in view of the widely scattered commitments of the battalion pointed out the difficulty of relieving a hundred men for the guard. I undertook to bear the responsibility for this. And it is now not a very dangerous secret to divulge that the hundred men who presented the guard of honour in full dress to Pandit jee on the oval in front of the Military Hospital formed the entire Company from the Gulmarg front! The evacuation of the defences had been carried out secretly, and for a period of 24 hours the entire defences of Gulmarg were manned by only seven signallers (armed with wireless sets) who constantly passed fake messages on their sets to simulate normal activity. Nothing succeeds like success!

The disaster that occurred to the reinforcement column sent to Skardu under Brig Faqir Singh in the month of February has already been mentioned. This had acted as a fillip to the enemy, who now intensified his efforts against the beleaguered garrison of Skardu. An opportunity to surrender was offered to the Garrison by the Commander of the enemy forces in the area, Prince Matah-ul-Mulk, brother of the Mehtar of Chitral. The offer was rejected by Lt Col Thapa, the Commander of the Garrison, with derision. Appeals from Col Thapa over the wireless for reinforcements were, however, pressing and constant. It was, therefore, decided, in early March, to send a Battalion of State Force - 7 Kashmir Infantry - as a relief column under the supervision of an Indian Army Observer. My 2IC, Major Sampuran Bachan Singh, was selected for the job and given the rank of a local Lt Col. The defence platoon of the battalion, 1 Sikh, was despatched with him as his personal escort.

The first element of the column set out from Srinagar on 3rd April 1948. Owing to the limitations imposed by the size of the staging camps on the way and the narrowness of the track, 7 Kashmir Infantry was despatched in batches of a Company or less at a time. On 2nd May the column was disposed off along the line of communication from Dras to Parkutta in batches varying in strength from a platoon to two Companies, Lt Col Sampuran Bachan Singh had the major portion of the column, approximately two Companies, with him at Parkutta, only two stages short of Skardu. Further advance was, however, held up owing to non-availability of either porters or ponies. The enemy having failed in their attempt to liquidate the Skardu Garrison had, in the meantime, decided to by-pass the Fortress and capture the various staging camps along the line of communication.

A well planned surprise attack was launched by the enemy on the various posts between Dras and Skardu simultaneously. The State Force Garrisons in these posts were caught completely unaware and were either destroyed or driven out without much opposition. The elements of 7 Kashmir Infantry who were at the time staying in these camps were also taken in the sweep and it was the end of the relief Column. Lt Col Sampuran Bachan Singh managed to escape to Leh with the survivors of his personal escort.

The fate of the Skardu Garrison was now sealed. The consequences of this debacle were potent and far-reaching. A threat had developed to Srinagar Valley from two entirely new directions, namely Sonamarg and Bandipur. Indeed, within a few days of the disaster both these places were threatened. It was the more unfortunate coming, as it did, on the eve of the projected summer offensive. Newly arrived reinforcements had to be diverted to meet this threat. 1 Patiala were sent to block the approach from the Sonamarg side and the Biharis (Bihar Battalion), to deal with the threat from Bandipur. The latter were soon relieved by Grenadiers. The Leh Garrison was completely cut off from Srinagar by the land route.

With the opening of the Handwara front and the arrival of 7 Sikh in the Valley, a newly raised Brigade Headquarters, called 'Z' Brigade, under Brigadier Lakhinder Singh, was set up at Srinagar in the second week of February to take charge of the operations in the Valley, and the Ladakh area, ie, Handwara - Bandipur - Skardu - Leh. Its Headquarters was stationed in Srinagar and was later named as Headquarters 163 Infantry Brigade, with the following Infantry units under its command:

- 1 Sikh
- 7 Sikh
- 1 Bihar
- 7 Kashmir Infantry and State Forces Garrisons, manning the various posts in Ladakh.

Upon Brigadier Lakhinder Singh's promotion to Major General, the command of the Brigade was taken over by Brigadier KC Katoch, on 22nd March 1948.

27

GENERAL THIMAYYA TAKES OVER SRINAGAR

In April, the forces in Jammu and Kashmir were reorganised into two separate entities to be known as JAI Division and SRI Division, under the overall command of Western Command. Major General Kulwant Singh, the erstwhile Commander of these forces (JAK Forces) was appointed Chief of the General Staff of the Indian Army and the command of JAI and SRI Divisions was given to Major Generals Attam Singh and Thimayya respectively. General Thimayya arrived in Srinagar with his Headquarters on 4th May 1948. With the opening of the Banihal Pass, after the winter freeze, fresh reinforcements had started pouring into the Valley. 77 Para Brigade, commanded by Brigadier Nair, arrived on 5th May 1948, along with some field artillery units and anti-tank units and other ancillary units to make up the complement of a Division.

There was so much military activity in Srinagar in the month of April and early May that there could not have been any doubt in anybody's mind that something was afoot. When and where, were the two potent questions, the answers to which were not yet known. The first inkling of the projected operation came at the Divisional Commanders' Conference on 13th May 1948. I attended the Conference as a representative of my Brigadier, Commander 163 Infantry Brigade, who was indisposed. At this Conference, the Divisional Commander, General Thimayya, outlined his ideas on the offensive, what he was out to achieve and how he hoped to do so. His main thrust was going to be along the Uri-Domel road, and he proposed to relieve for the purpose 161 Infantry Brigade, which had been in the area from the very beginning of the campaign, under Brigadier Sen. 161 Infantry Brigade's commitments in Uri were to be taken over by the newly arrived 77 Para Brigade. Prior to the main thrust, 163 Infantry Brigade, in Handwara area, was to carry out a diversionary push in the direction of Tithwal, in order to draw as much of the enemy reinforcements from Muzaffarbad as possible. There was to be a two to three days' interval between the start of the two operations. As Officiating Commander 163 Infantry Brigade, I was asked to submit a 'very short' appreciation and outline plan for that diversionary operation.

The three Brigadiers, Sen (161 Infantry Brigade), Nair (77 Para Brigade) and I (163 Infantry Brigade), and all available Commanding Officers of the battalions taking part in the summer offensive, were taken for an air reconnaissance over the area in a Dakota aircraft sometime in the second week of May. The aircraft flew along the main Srinagar-Domel road and returned via the Tithwal-Handwara area. This reconnaissance gave us a good idea of the ground over which we were to operate.

Before the formation of Headquarters SRI Division, 163 Infantry Brigade, it will be remembered, was in charge of the operations in the areas Handwara-Bandipur-Ladakh. In view of the impending operations, Bandipur and Ladakh sector were taken over by Headquarters Srinagar Division. This left only two battalions under 163 Infantry Brigade, those in the Handwara-Kupwara area - 1 Sikh and 7 Sikh. 7 Sikh was swapped over with 3 Royal Garhwal Rifles from Headquarters 161 Infantry Brigade, on the 10th of May, and 1 Madras joined the 163 Brigade, at Handwara, on the 15th of May, only two days prior to the D-Day. I took over command of 163 Infantry Brigade officially on 6th May from Brigadier Katoch, who was indisposed. 77 Para Brigade was detailed to take over all the commitments of 161 Infantry Brigade by the 13th of May '48. Having been thus relieved by 77 Para Brigade, 161 Infantry Brigade was to concentrate in the Uri area, preparatory to taking part in the impending operations. And D-Day for the diversionary push by 163 Infantry Brigade was fixed as the 18th of May, and for the main thrust, by 161 Infantry Brigade, along Uri-Domel road, as the 20th of May.

My assessment was that the enemy in the area in front of me was about 1650 strong - a mixture of Swaties, Mahsuds and ex-Pakistani Army personnel and locals. The enemy was divided roughly into two sectors - Trahgam and Handwara, with Sector Headquarters at Panzgam, and Dogarpur respectively. A portion of him was scattered along the line of communication to Tithwal. Tithwal was the main base of the enemy.

For an irregular force, the estimated strength of 1650 was quite considerable. The enemy was, however, known to be scattered in small parties and, provided a complete surprise was obtained, he was not expected to put up any organised or concerted opposition. Once he was on the run, it was speed, and not strength, that was required on our part. So it was not the numbers that were opposing us in the area that were as important as the strength that might be thrown against us at Tithwal after its capture. It was appreciated that at least three Battalions would be required to hold Tithwal and secure its immediate rear against any threat that might develop from the direction of Muzaffarabad. Another battalion was required to guard the northern flank and protect the 40 mile long line of communication. That is why the 4th Battalion was considered necessary and asked for.

28
ADVANCE OF 163 INFANTRY BATTALION TO TITHWAL

We had hoped to achieve surprise by taking the most difficult, and thus to the enemy the least expected, route for our main advance. We also intended to use the hours of darkness. The thrust along the main Trahgam track, under an obvious handicap of ground, was meant to lure the enemy to stick on and thus be entrapped.

The difficulty of terrain and the line of communication dictated that the troops would have to carry all the provisions they needed for a week on their person.

I had been exercising my mind as to what type of emergency food, that would be nourishing and filling, could be best carried on the person of each man. It would have to last for the duration of the operations, at least a week, until such time as some kind of administrative system could be established on reaching our destination, Tithwal. My mind went back to my College days. Each time I went home on leave, I used to bring back a tin full of 'panjiri ladoos' to the hostel. Not only did they last me for months, but they were very filling and nourishing as well. So I ordered the Sikh Battalion to prepare 'panjiri ladoos', three pieces for one day, to be taken three times a day with a mug of tea at each meal. That is 21 ladoos per man. And when the Madras Battalion joined my Brigade, just a couple of days before we left for the operations, I asked the Sikh Battalion to teach them also how to make 'panjiri ladoos'. An additional advantage of this preparation was that all the ingredients were issued to the men in the normal course as ration. Once the Madrasis tasted the 'panjiri' they simply loved it! This solved the problem of emergency ration for the duration of the operation. For the tea-ration, each Section was asked to carry tea-leaves and condensed milk.

Initially, since there was a shortage of troops that could be spared for this, so called, 'Divisionary' thrust, Chowkibal was given as the ultimate objective for me to occupy. For these operations, I had planned for the Garhwalis to attack Trahgam Ridge frontally from Pethahir, while the Madrasis and the Sikhs were to carry out a night advance and cut off the raiders from behind, issuing from Handwara. To maintain the secrecy of operations, ponies required for the administrative train were collected from distant areas and kept under secret cover in the Handwara area. A sand-model was prepared of the whole area and was made available to the battalions so as to familiarise each man with the ground over which he was to operate. Orders were given by me down to Company Commanders on the same sand model, on the morning of the 16th of May. Each man was to carry, in addition to the week's 'panjiri' ration, one ground-sheet, or a water-proof cape and a blanket in his pack. Half of the blankets, of unit strength, were to be carried by the follow-up ponies.

All preparations, including administrative arrangements, were completed before the morning of the 17th of May. That morning, and in the afternoon, enforced sleep-rest was ordered in assembly areas for the men taking part in the night-operations. About two hours before the time of start, I paid a visit to the assembly areas and found the officers and jawans full of cheer and confident of success.

About this time, an hour and a half before the time of start of the Handwara Column, a hare was raised by Officer Commanding, 1 Madras. He had just had a report, he said, from his platoon at Nagi picket that the enemy was registering, with 3-inch mortars, the road through the defile, half a mile short of Zachaldor. He had fired as many as ten bombs in the area. Since 1 Madras were to lead the advance and the route lay through this defile, the Commanding Officer suggested that the route of advance upto Zachaldor be altered via Nagi picket. This would have entailed a very steep climb of at least 1500 feet from the road level upto the picket, and an equally steep descent on the other side, over an almost non-existent track. I assured the Commanding Officer that this so called 'registration' was no registration at all, for I knew that it had occurred many a time before. All that the enemy was trying to do, I pointed out, was to bomb Nagi picket from the feature on the opposite side of the defile, and the bombs that fell in the road-area were only a few 'shorts'. Nevertheless, to assure the Commanding Officer further, I promised to send a couple of bren groups from Nagi picket, which was to be my Tactical Headquarters, on to the edge of the defile so as to cover the column through. As a precaution against odd mortaring, orders were issued to the column to increase intervals between sections while passing through the defile.

In view of the distance involved for the night advance, the column had to start half an hour before last light. I saw the column start off from Handwara at 6.30 pm on the 17th of May and drove ahead in my jeep with my Tactical Headquarters, which were to be established at Nagi picket by 7 pm. Col Biji Kaul, Commandant, Jammu and Kashmir Militia, had come over to watch the progress of the operations during the night and was accompanying me. It was just getting dark when we started climbing up the Nagi picket, leaving our jeep on the road. The picket was at the time being heavily sniped at from a small feature 500 yards to the east. It did not, however, worry the picket, nor did it in any way interfere with the advance of the column on the road below, of which I do not think the enemy was aware. Had my Rover set walked into the hands of the snipers, as it nearly did, but for our shouts, it would have indeed been unfortunate. For, during our climb up to the picket the signallers manning the Rover had lagged behind and, in the dark, were making straight for the feature from where the enemy party was sniping!

The sniping stopped at 8.30 pm and about the same time, I sent a couple of brens with a section, from Nagi picket, to the near edge of the defile, with orders to lie low and see the column through and, if perchance, something should open up from the opposite side, and they could spot flashes, they were to let them have it! Col Kaul and I stood in a slit-trench with our eyes and ears straining hard for any signs of the column moving on the road below. Nothing could be seen or heard. It had been estimated that the column would pass the defile at 9 pm It was well past that time. The section sent to the defile, to cover the column through, had not returned either. We were getting rather anxious when some men were seen advancing towards the picket. It was the section coming back. The Commander reported that although he had not distinctly seen, or heard, the column go through, he had sensed their passing. A few rifle shots were heard at a distance coming from the direction of the route the column was supposed to take. This was followed by a few odd explosions here and there in the countryside, obviously caused by some jittery enemy sentries. All seemed to be going well - and so it did - throughout this advance. A complete surprise had been achieved. The few rifle shots that we had heard were fired by our protection picket who had caught a few of the enemy asleep at an observation post. I thought that they might have spared the bullets! A wireless silence was to be observed till first light, except in the case of an emergency, for which contingency my Rover set had been kept on listening watch. Contact could not however be established with the column until 2.30 am. The column reported that all was well, except that the going had been hard and that they were lagging behind. The objective - Dogarpur Ridge - was not reached till after mid-day. The enemy, who had been completely surprised, offered no opposition and was reported to be fleeing in small parties.

Things were not so rosy on the other side. The 3 Royal Garhwal Rifles, two Company columns, bound for the feature behind Trahgam, who were scheduled to leave Kupwara at 11 pm on the 17th were delayed by an hour owing to the delinquency of the civilian guide. Their route also lay cross-country, along nullahs, etc. Nothing was heard of them till 12 noon the next day, when the forward element of 3 Royal Garhwal Rifles, advancing along the Trahgam road from Pethahir, established wireless contact with them. This column had given us some very anxious moments and the news that came through about them was also quite disturbing. They had had rather a tough time since the morning, having been surrounded by the enemy.

This is what happened. The column having been delayed by an hour in its start from Kupwara and finding the going - cross-country - very much more difficult than expected, found itself at first light, when they should have been on the objective, still about a mile short of it. All had gone well with them till then. This was, perhaps, responsible for lulling the Commander of the column into a false sense of security and for causing him to commit a tactical error by failing to take the necessary, all round precautions, covering themselves over dead ground, searching villages en-route, or on flanks, etc - in their advance on to the objective in day light. As it happened, realising that they were much behind time, the Commander tried to rush through, headlong, to the objective, taking a short cut through the village of Guglus, without at first searching the village, and literally 'woke-up' the enemy who happened to be residing there.

The enemy allowed the first wave to go through unmolested and ambushed the second wave inside the village, and simultaneously opened up from behind on the first wave which was by now climbing up to its objective on the ridge. This did not deter the first wave who continued to press on, if anything, at a faster pace, until a section of the enemy's Medium Machine Guns opened up on them at close range from Shulur, from a flank, taking them in enfilade and causing heavy casualties, which included their Commander, Captain Kang. The fire was so effective that it restricted all movement and the advance to the objective was completely held up. It was a pity, for the objective was only a short distance away and there was not a soul there at the time!

Our troops, down in the village, fought gallantly and drove the enemy out of the houses from where he was firing. Enemy reinforcements had by now, arrived and taken up positions all round the village. By now the ridge had also been occupied by the enemy. The Commander of the column, thereupon, decided to withdraw all troops and casualties into the village and take up a perimeter defence around it. The enemy made many attempts to rush the position, our troops, however, fought back gallantly and held out against overwhelming odds. In this action the column lost 8 men while 14 were wounded, including the Company Commander. Although the column had failed to capture the objective assigned to it, the presence of this force behind the enemy position had, without doubt, contributed a great deal in turning the enemy out of his very strong defensive position on the Trahgam Ridge.

A Company of 3 Royal Garhwal Rifles supported by two troops of armoured cars and a section of weapon carriers, commenced their push from Pethahir along Trahgam road, according to plan, at first light on the 18th of May, under the direct command of their Commanding Officer, Lt Col Kuman Singh. Pethahir, it will be remembered, had been more or less in a state of investment for some time, with enemy positions very close and all round it. A very stiff opposition was, therefore, encountered from the very start. The enemy was in well-dug positions, and every inch of ground had to be fought for. Progress was consequently slow. It was further retarded by the need to make diversions at all the bridges/culverts on the road which had been destroyed by the enemy. The guns in position at Pethahir came in for much plastering by enemy mortars, causing casualties. Inspite of their very accurate fire, the crew of the guns did not leave their guns even for a moment and lent most consistent, effective and valuable support throughout the operation.

As it happened, General Thimayya, General Officer Commanding the Division, also happened to visit the Garhwalis at the time, and came under mortar fire. As I was going to this sector in my jeep and passed his jeep on the way, he shouted out to me: "A hot reception is awaiting you!".

The Garhwalis pressed on against stiffening opposition with great determination. The knowledge that their night column had been surrounded by the enemy, egged them on to many an act of collective and individual gallantry. They neutralised the enemy opposition, post by post. The feature overlooking Trahgam was captured by them just after midday. This completely broke the back of the enemy defences on the ridge and further advance by our troops was carried out thereon without much opposition, enabling contact with the beleaguered Companies at Guglus at about 3 pm.

Here I witnessed a miracle. Knowing that these beleaguered Companies had sustained many casualties, I had arranged for the Commanding Officer of my Field Ambulance, Lt Col Lobo, with a medical detachment, to move forward with my Tactical Headquarters, to afford immediate medical aid to the wounded at Guglus. While the identification of those killed was being carried out, two men were found with some life still in them, though they were as good as gone. Blood plasma was administered to them in my presence and it was an experience to watch life being infused into near corpses. There was at first just a slight movement of arms, which soon turned into a wriggle and then, lo and behold, their eyes opened wider and wider like the resuscitation of a dying flame and soon, very soon, they started to talk, and even smile! Both these men, whose names I have forgotten, I know, are now alive and kicking. After this experience, I issued orders to all my Company Commanders that in every action, no matter, however small, a medical officer with bottles of plasma will be made available to casualties as far forward as possible, and I shall relate later on, in this account, another instance of this nature where lives were saved by administering plasma to the wounded during a patrol action in Tithwal area. By 6.30 pm that evening all casualties had been attended to and evacuated and a Company post established at Trahgam Ridge as a Firm-Base. The remaining troops and armoured cars withdrew to Pethahir for the night.

To revert to the other front. As already mentioned, 1 Madras had reached Dogarpur Ridge after midday on the 18th. A search of Dogarpur village revealed signs of the enemy's hasty withdrawal. 1 Sikh, who now passed through 1 Madras, found their way to the objective, Karmil R, completely devoid of tracks and the going, cross-country, over a series of ridges and nullahs, most difficult. Only a couple of small enemy parties were encountered on the way and suitably dealt with. Towards the evening the Sikhs bivouacked for the night somewhere on their way to the objective, Panzgam. Company 1 Sikh, now established on the track coming from Tartpura, nearly brought off a very good ambush. A party of fleeing enemy walked into the Company position when they were not quite ready to receive them. The enemy turned back and escaped rather lightly, but terribly scared!

Two of our fighter aircraft came over the area at about 7.30 pm on the 18th and engaged parties of enemy withdrawing from Shulur Valley and trying to escape towards Parkhian-ki-Gali. Much use of air support, could not, however, be made owing to the absence of a contact-car. In fact, air support, although promised before the start of the operation, did not materialise until after the 19th when an aircraft paid another visit to the area, but to little avail.

The blocking of the two exits from the Shulur Valley and the elimination of the enemy base at Panzgam, commenced on the morning of the 19th of May. An armoured column, consisting of two troop armoured cars, a section of weapon carriers and a platoon of 3 Royal Garhwal Rifle, in APVs, set out from Pethahir at 8 am on the 19th of May. They travelled on the Trahgam road, which ran along the bottom of the ridge, which was now in our hands. Shumanag bridge was found to have been completely destroyed by the enemy. There was a fairly deep and fast stream of water flowing through the nullah and making a diversion through it took nearly three hours to complete, despite all the engineering resources and spare hands available. Another hour was taken by all the vehicles to pass through. Advance was resumed at about 1 pm. The position at Shulur was found to be deserted, except for an old man, who, upon arrival of the column, tried to escape. He was captured and turned out to be an enemy agent, presumably left there to watch the movement of our troops. The advance was kept up along the road to Panzgam. Progress continued to be rather slow owing to the narrow road and weak bridges on the way, as well as due to the fact that all villages and houses on the way had to be searched. A 3-inch mortar, with a lot of ammunition and large stocks of small arms and ammunitions and signal stores, were collected from a house in Shulur village.

As we were nearing Panzgam, a number of small enemy parties were seen to be fleeing over the ridge behind the village, and were effectively engaged by armoured cars. The enemy made no serious attempt to interfere with our advance, except for a certain amount of sniping from a ridge on our right flank. Panzgam was reached at 4 o'clock that afternoon, and found to be completely deserted. A large dump of enemy supplies was captured in a house in the village. Contact with 1 Sikh from the other direction was established at 5 pm, and the valley of Shulur was now completely surrounded, although, unfortunately, most of the enemy had managed to escape. He was, however, reported to be completely disorganised and fleeing in great disorder. His forces were split into two - with some escaping via Pharkian-ki-Gali to Keran and others via Karmil R and Nasthachur Pass to Tithwal. Chowkibal was reached by 1 Sikh without any further opposition, and 1 Madras was pushed through for an attack the next morning on Nasthachur Pass. Working out artillery support for them on the map, I discovered that from Chowkibal, even if the guns could reach there on a non-existent track, the target was out of range of the field guns (25 pounders) by about 400 to 500 yards. The Battery Commander, Major Bawa, suddenly remembered that he had two brand new guns in his battery which were over-shooting by 400-500 yards! And that was just the extra distance we needed, benignly arranged by providence!

Thus guns were ordered up to Chowkibal to be in position by first light on the 21st of May, so as to be able to support the attack on the Pass by 1 Madras that morning. How the gunners managed to move those big guns over the very narrow, circuitous and slippery road, as it then was, has always been a miracle to me. It does, however, reflect the keenness of our gunners to help their infantry comrades at all cost, and speaks well of the co-operation and fellowship existing in our Army. The keenest of them was their Commander, Major Bawa, who asked me again and again if he could dismantle a gun and manhandle it to Nasthachur Pass, from where he assured me he could support our advance right up to Tithwal. The advance to Nasthachur by 1 Madras, was resumed at 10 am on 21st May. Time was taken in the morning to tie up artillery support and other details pertaining to the attack on the Pass. Artillery support by field guns at Chowkibal, owing to the uncertainty of wireless communications, was arranged on a timed programme, while the Mountain Battery with the Madras Column was detailed to take on impromptu targets.

The attack on the Pass started at about 1 pm on the 21st of May and the Pass was in the hands of 1 Madras after an hour. The enemy put up only a token resistance. He was believed to have been completely surprised and demoralised by Bawa's shells, which we later saw had landed plonk on enemy positions on the Pass!

1 Sikh was pushed through, while 1 Madras held the Pass, and before last light secured the village of Naichian, situated at the end of the Nasthachur defile, 6 miles beyond. The night of 21st/22nd May was spent without incident. Orders were issued that night for 1 Sikh to resume its advance at first light the next morning, with 1 Madras less a Company (to be left at the Pass), to follow on behind as reserve.

Nasthachur Pass is over 10,000 feet high and even in May still extremely cold. It is further notorious for a piercing and ceaseless wind. The discomfort that the troops - and mostly Madrasis at that – had to put up with that night, without any great coats and blankets, is hard to imagine! The Sikhs slightly lower down, the other side of the Pass, had spent a comparatively comfortable night.

On the afternoon of the 21st of May, Major Rajindra Singh, GOC's ADC, brought a DO letter for me from General Thimayya. In it the General said that the operations on the Uri front were not going on as well as expected and that he was thinking of diverting 77 Para Brigade on to this front. His question to me was, would I push on to Tithwal and secure it at all costs? We were already on the move. Nasthachur Pass, half-way to Tithwal, had been in our hands since 2 o'clock that afternoon, and my Tactical Headquarters were about to move forward. I asked my Brigade Major to reply to the letter on my behalf and to say that the orders would be complied with.

1 Sikh led the advance the next morning, the 22nd of May, with 1 Madras behind them in immediate reserve. Opposition throughout the day was almost negligible, except for sniping here and there. Precautions, however, could not be relaxed and the advance was carried out tactically. An hour before last light of the 22nd of May, the forward elements of 1 Sikh had secured the defile beyond Chhamkot, still about 5 miles from Tithwal along the track. Chhamkot was considered to be a good place for rest before carrying out a night advance on to Tithwal. Besides, Tithwal was from here within easy range of the mountain guns, which could, therefore, go into position to support the attack on Tithwal the next morning.

The plan for the capture of Tithwal was simple:

- 1 Sikh were to carry out a night advance along track Chhamkot Saltal - north of Dhana - mostly running along the water-shed, so as to secure the spur overlooking Tithwal by first light of the 23rd of May.
- 1 Madras was to advance along the main track and secure, after first light, the high-points south of Tithwal, assisted by 1 Sikh from across the nullah.
- Mountain Battery was to support the operation from their position at Chhamkot.

Author supervising the Battle of Tithwal.

The Author speaking to local residents.

The operation went according to plan. The Sikhs, after a hazardous march over a steep, narrow and most difficult track, which caused some delay, secured the ridge overlooking Tithwal by 9 am on the 23rd of May. The enemy was completely surprised. Upon appearance of our troops from this unexpected direction, he evacuated his positions around Tithwal without a fight, except for some sniping, and withdrew across the river. 1 Sikh entered Tithwal at 9.30 am on the morning of the 23rd of May. Soon afterwards, 1 Madras also arrived and occupied, according to plan, features south of the village.

29
THE CAPTURE OF TITHWAL

The village was in ruins as a result, we were told afterwards, of sacking and burning by the Raiders during their initial invasion. Huge stores of enemy foodstuffs, including canned supplies, were captured. They were a godsend to us as we had been almost starving for the past two days, having outstripped our administrative-echelon ponies.

The enemy was reported to have thrown all reserves of arms, ammunition and equipment into the fast flowing stream of the Kishanganga river before fleeing. Some important documents were, however, captured, including an 'Intelligence Summary', dated the 13th of May, which gave correct details of the change of command carried out by us recently, and the regrouping of our forces in Jammu and Kashmir.

The villages in the Tithwal Valley on our way, we found, were completely deserted, except for an odd, very old man, here and there. I made it a point to speak to each one of these old men and asked them where the residents had fled and why. They all said that they had been told by the retreating enemy that the 'bearded savages', the Sikhs, were coming in large numbers and would eat them up alive. The poor locals had, therefore, hidden themselves in the jungle. I assured them that our mission was to liberate them from the Raiders and no more, as they could see for themselves from the conduct of our troops, and advised them to ask the populace to return to their homes and resume their normal living. Within a few days the Valley was once again astir with life!

The story of the Hindu population, most of whom had been converted to Islam, was different. They had run away to the jungles not out of fear of the Indian Army but of the retreating Raiders, who, in their desperate flight, wreaked havoc on these innocent 'infidels'. And this element of the population did not have to be persuaded to return from the jungle as we arrived. They came out in flocks - men, women and children - to greet the troops with folded hands and tears of gratitude flowing down their cheeks. Their happiness at this 'deliverance' knew no bounds, and they had some woeful tales to tell. We arranged a temporary relief camp for them and sent them to Srinagar in batches with the returning convoys of ponies.

My Tactical Headquarters reached Tithwal a couple of hours after its capture. Our positions around the village were consolidated by 2 o'clock that afternoon. So far, all attempts to get in touch with our relay-set at Nasthachur Pass on my No 48 Rover had failed. There was no means of informing Divisional Headquarters at Baramula of the capture of Tithwal and of getting instructions for further action. I, at one time, had thought of sending an officer back for liaison; but since every one of them, I could see, was tired and famished I did not have the heart to ask. I knew how tired I was feeling and they had done much more than I had. Besides, I thought that nobody could put the Divisional Commander into the picture at this stage as well as I could. I, therefore, decided, to the horror of all, to walk back to Nasthachur Pass, 16 miles away, that evening by myself. This, I felt, was most imperative. I could not afford to wait for my 62 set, which was in the administrative echelon, to arrive; and who could tell if I would be able to get through on it to Divisional Headquarters.

My mind was made up and I was not going to take an escort with me either, for the troops, I knew, were too tired. Besides, I hoped to walk faster without it. All the officers implored me not to go alone, for this was, they said, the evening when in the dark, the enemy parties, who might have been lying low during the day, would try to escape, and suppose I walked into one of them? They were perhaps right, but I was not going to be dissuaded. Upon their insistence, I agreed to take one of the officers, Captain Gopal Singh, an Artillery officer, who was keen to go home on 10 days' leave with me.

Gopal Singh and I set out from Tithwal for our backward march just after 4 pm on the 23rd of May. After about a couple of miles of almost level walk along a nullah bed, we came to a couple of miles of rather steep climb. We had been moving at a fast pace and the strain of the climb, especially towards the end, was beginning to tell on my knees, and yet our destination was still 12 miles away! Gopal, I noticed, was also straining equally hard, though neither of us would admit it to the other. Soon afterwards we came across our Mountain Battery column in the Administrative Echelon on the track and Gopal suggested that we should take a couple of ponies from them. I jumped at the suggestion.

This column of ours was worth seeing. It was the Brigade Administrative Echelon which had been trying to keep up with our advance for the past six days, from the very start, and at a pace that did not permit any stops for taking a rest, cooking food for the troops, or for grazing the animals. In fact, as the rations had finished three days earlier, there was nothing to cook. They had managed, I discovered, to cook a chappati per man out of some maize flour captured at Nachian. The last 24 hours, I was told, had been 'Mastana', as one of the Sikh soldier's in the column remarked. So they had every reason to cheer when I told them that we had captured large quantities of enemy food supplies at Tithwal!

What was worth remarking about this column was that it looked more like a gypsy caravan than a military convoy. It was a motley crowd of porters, ponies, donkeys, buffaloes, cows, and even goats - all laden with bulging loads and looking absolutely tired and famished. They were trudging along, some in line and some in groups, with one object in life - to get to the other end! There was much to be desired in this column, regarding military formation, security, discipline and so on. It would have been no use my shouting orders at them, for they seemed quite incapable of reacting! So I hailed them with cheers and their response was ten-fold. It is really amazing to see how long a man can subsist on that single commodity - morale! Their morale, I could see, was on top of the world! Reinforcing the gypsy like image of the convoy, was the presence too of cackling fowl; a chicken had been tied up by its legs on top of a load. The loot of war, I presume! The presence of buffaloes, and so on in the column, could be explained by the number of pony corpses we saw on the way. These animals had been 'commandeered' as substitutes on the way.

Our pace now was very much faster. We had also taken a mounted Sowar with us and he was doing our 'point man' as we trotted along the track. Some suspicious movements were noticed at two or three places, but those might have been local villagers trying to snoop into their houses. By 6.30 pm we were past Nachian village, 10 miles from Tithwal, and only six miles from the Pass. It was just getting dark, and the track, from then on, entered thick jungle.

The sky was dark with clouds, and it was darker still inside the jungle. We, however, jogged along the slightly discernible track. The track seemed to become less and less distinct as we progressed, until we came to a dead-end. In our path was a huge, fallen tree. Two of us got down and tried to look for the track on the other side of the tree, but to no avail. I had a map with me and tried to consult it, but I had no light. Neither did any of my companions. Not even a match - as we were all Sikhs! How I wished that I had smoked at that moment! I suspected that we had gone wrong near a bridge immediately after entering the jungle. We trotted back to the bridge, and took, from there, what, we thought, was a different track, although owing to the darkness there was no question of distinguishing one from the other. Soon, to our great consternation, we reached the same fallen tree. I wished I could consult my map. Memories of my scout days came back and I tried to light a fire by means of striking two stones, but without success.

On the way down, I remembered, that we had had a nullah flowing to our immediate right, and we could hear, at some distance, another one to our left. I had no doubt in my mind that the track we used in the morning, on our way to Tithwal, ran along the left bank of a nullah. Could it not be the distant one? There was no alternative but to try it. We went cross-country, through the jungle, passing felled trees and boulders. There was no question of riding our chargers over that ground. They were snorting and shying at each step. With the greatest of difficulty we arrived at the edge of the nullah. Wading through the knee-deep icy cold stream, at that hour of the night, was no pleasure, and our disappointment can be well imagined when we found no signs of the track we had expected on the other side of the nullah. We must have wandered around in circles looking for it in the jungle for over an hour. It was now past 10 pm. There was no alternative left but to retrace our steps to the old track - the same frightful journey on foot through the nullah and the jungle!

We had on our way that evening met an old man, who had come out of a house in the village of Nachian to greet us. I suggested that we should go back to the village and use the old man as a guide. In any case, we were bound to get enough light there to read the map. Captain Gopal Singh pointed out the danger of our walking into the hands of some enemy party who might be resting there for the night. But the chances of that, I thought, were too remote, for fleeing enemy would never rest in a village so near the track. On the way back, we heard a party of men coming from the opposite direction. Upon hearing the hooves of our horses they scampered into the jungle on either side of the track. I was on the leading horse. Instinctively, I whipped out my revolver and held it loaded in front of me, while continuing at the old pace, hoping for the best. I was expecting a volley of shots any moment. Nothing happened. We wondered if that had been an enemy party! If so, they had lost the chance of their life! It was nearly midnight when we reached the village of Nachian. There were no signs of life in it. We first went to the house, the old man had come out of. He was not there. We searched through or knocked at (for some of them were closed from inside) all the houses but without a response. We saw a light moving on the hillside. I shouted and moved towards it. It ran further away from us, faster and faster. Was it, what they call, a will-o'-the-wisp, I wondered?

The night was still dark, but we noticed a haze of light from behind a hill towards the east. It was the half moon coming up. I had the bright idea of waiting for the moon to rise so that I could read my map by its light. The idea was mostly dictated by the completely exhausted state of my body and mind, which needed rest. I wanted to lie down for a minute. For security reasons, we moved slightly away from the village and alighted from our horses. Captain Gopal Singh and the orderly took upon themselves to stand sentry in turn while I, most selfishly, I must admit, went into a deep slumber. The horses indulged in their much needed graze in a maize field closeby. I was awakened by Gopal at about 1 am, when there was moonlight. I tried to read my map but could make nothing of it. The light was not nearly enough. It suddenly occurred to me that I could use the eye-piece of my binoculars to concentrate light on the map. Necessity, as they say, is the mother of invention! And it worked wonderfully well. With its help Gopal and I memorised the whole route, by paces, for we knew that our friend the moon would desert us inside the jungle!

Soon we were on our way again, strictly according to the map. And, would you believe it, we came to the same fallen tree across the track again! But this time we were certain that we were on the right track. Leaving the horses with the orderly, Gopal and I carried out a 'groping' reconnaissance beyond the tree and to our great joy discerned a streak of a track issuing from it on the other side. The track was so indistinct that most of the way through the jungle we had to lead our horses on foot. And inspite of that we almost lost the track on three more occasions, at least, before we got to the open basin at the foot of the Nasthachur Pass. Here we were challenged by a sentry, of 1 Sikh pony-convoy, who were resting there for the night. Upon recognising me, the sentry led me to the Quarter Master of 1 Sikh, Captain Joginder Singh, who very kindly gave us a couple of blankets each to keep ourselves warm and a handful of Panjiri (emergency ration) to eat! Both these were most welcome! We rested there for a while and then started on our way to the Pass, about a mile of very steep climb beyond. We fetched up at the Pass at about 4 am, completely exhausted and frozen. I lost no time in getting in touch with Divisional Headquarters over the wireless, and asked the General Staff Officer-I, Lt Col Uberoi, to come to meet me at the Pass as early as he could make it that morning.

The exhaustion in my case was so complete that I felt my endurance had reached its limits. As soon as I lay down under two blankets I started feeling feverish and within an hour my body temperature had shot up. Symptoms of extreme exhaustion were apparent in the traces of blood in the urine that I passed.

The GSO-1, Lt Col Uberoi, arrived at the Pass at about 11 am on the 24th of May and we discussed the possibilities of sending a battalion column, supported by a section of mountain guns, from Tithwal to Muzaffarabad, by the shortest route over the top of the ridges. The distance involved was only 18 miles and once having arrived on top of the water-shed, the going according to the map appeared to be fairly easy and level. The operation was to be called 'Surya'. The code names of its various stages, and places on the way, were also fixed by us, and the details of air supply to the column arranged. Colonel Uberoi suggested that it would be a good idea if I went and discussed the plan with the Divisional Commander, General Thimayya also. I was feeling much better now, although still slightly feverish, and so I decided to accompany him to the Divisional Headquarters that afternoon. It meant an 8-mile walk for me, before we could pick up a jeep near Chowkibal. We arrived at Baramula, late that evening and I went over the plan with the General Officer Commanding, General Thimayya.

I had to reach Tithwal at the earliest. So, I left Baramula very early the next morning, the 25th of May, in a jeep. I took on a pony from Chowkibal and reached Tithwala the same evening. During the ride I had thought out, in my mind, the stages of the operations that would precede 'Surya'.

In order to ensure security of Tithwal against any counter-attack from the direction of Muzaffarabad, the high ground south-west and south of it, that is Richmar Gali, Pir Sahiba and Mir Kalsi, would have to be secured at once. This would require at least two battalions less two Companies to hold. At least two Companies would be required for the immediate defence of Tithwal itself.

To make a Battalion available for 'Surya', the third battalion of the Brigade, the Garhwalis, who were at the time, employed on the protection of the line of communication, were to be relieved and concentrated at Tithwal. This I had fixed up with Divisional Headquarters. Already, in anticipation, on my way to Divisional Headquarters, the day before, I had ordered 3 Royal Garhwal Rifles, less two Companies to move to Tithwal forthwith, so that they would be there by the evening of the 25th.

A sufficient supply of ammunition of all kinds, especially 3.7 Howitzer, and rations for 'Surya', were to be dropped from the air before the operation could be undertaken. The provision of a sufficient number of ponies and porters was a must.

On arrival at my Headquarters in Tithwal that evening I was told that the enemy was reported to be rushing regular Pakistan Army forces towards Tithwal. He had already put up a covering party somewhere half way on the Tithwal defile, beyond Tekiwal. I issued orders the same evening for 3 Royal Garhwal Rifles, who had only just arrived, to secure the high ground across the river Kishanganga the first thing the next day, the 26th of May. 1 Sikh were to send a Company patrol and secure Richmar Gali. 1 Madras were to be responsible for the perimeter defence of Tithwal.

The action, as it transpired, had been taken in the nick of time. The enemy had arrived on the Ring Counter and Point 7229 when the Garhwal assault went in. He tried to resist but was driven out and positions secured by the evening. The Sikh patrol bound for Richmar Gali was, however, finding its going over precipitous and difficult ground, entailing a very steep climb, very hard and had only reached half way to its objective by last light that day. It had established a firm-base there for the night. The enemy, it was reported by agents and by our own troops at Point 7229, had already started digging in on Mir Kalsi hill and Pir Sahiba Ridge, in order to block our further advance along the track through the Tithwal defile, where the river Kishanganga flowed. A frontal assault on this position through the defile, I realised, would be suicidal. I was convinced in my mind that the only way to take this position and secure the southern exit of the defile was to capture Richmar Gali first and then descend on the enemy along the ridge. For this purpose, 1 Sikh Company was already on their way. In order to draw the enemy's attention towards the approach along the defile, and away from Richmar Gali, I decided to demonstrate in strength the next morning along the main track through the defile.

A big column of troops and animals was marshalled at leisure on the morning of the 27th of May, in full view of the enemy position, and the advance commenced along the track at about mid-day. It was, on purpose, carried out as slowly as possible, so as to give it the character of extra caution, and thus lure the enemy into moving as much of his strength as possible on to the lower slopes of the ridge to oppose this 'attack'. Our post at Point 7229 was told to demonstrate forward towards the defile in conformity with the advance along the track. The enemy opened up when we were well out of his small arms range. An incident occurred here that I must describe.

It was my practice, as Brigade Commander, to have a small party comprising one Lance Naik and two men, from 1 Sikh, as my personal escort, and they generally moved ahead of me during my visits to pickets or detachments on isolated hills. In this case, while I was demonstrating to the enemy a frontal attack along the track running through the Kishanganga river defile, we reached an open space next to the village of Alikoh. In this open area I was, purposely, giving orders for further advance in the open, for the enemy to see. Through my binoculars, I could see some men in uniform on the feature of Pir Sahiba. Before the Order Group could disperse a couple of Medium Machine Guns opened up on us. I ordered every one of the Order Group to take cover, but since the Machine Guns of the enemy at Pir Sahiba were well out of range from where we were standing, the bullets were falling around us like pebbles (being fully spent). I thus continued to stand in the open, having ordered every one of the Order Group to take cover, as I considered the fire from the out-of-range Machine Guns quite harmless. Seeing this, the Lance Naik in-charge of my protection party, ran up to me, and standing between me and the direction from where the fire was coming, said: "Sahib, mere piche arrh lai lo, kithe thode goli na lag jai". I was so touched by the act of this Non-Commissioned Officer that I held him in my arms, and affectionately said: "Bacha, main nu is fire da koi dar nahin, tun fikir na kar". I could not help but appreciate his bravery and extent of commitment to his task of protecting me even if this meant laying down his life for my safety. Such is the material of which our rank and file, in the Indian Army, is made!

It was about 4.30 pm now and the column gave the semblance of having been 'checked' by the enemy. Soon I gave orders to slowly withdraw to Tithwal, to make the enemy believe that the attempt had failed. We withdrew back to camp just after last light on the same day.

The Sikh patrol, sent earlier, had arrived that evening just below Richmar Gali and was proposing to assault the objective at first light the next morning. I ordered the rest of 1 Sikh to also join up with their company at Richmar Gali as soon as possible, and capture the ridge, Pir Sahiba-Mir Kalsi, from that direction. They were given a Forward

Observation Officer, while artillery support for the assault was laid on with the Mountain Battery in position at Tithwal. The Sikh patrol captured Richmar Gali, early morning on the 28th of May. They had only just beaten the enemy patrol to it, who, carelessly, walked into them and had 5 of their men killed. This was apparently the enemy's usual 'dawn patrol'. The enemy quickly reacted to the knowledge of our having captured Richmar Gali on his right flank, though not in strength until the next day, possibly due to the fact that after our last day's 'failure' he was expecting us to make another stronger attempt along the defile. The whole of that day the enemy made half-hearted attempts to retake the height overlooking Richmar Gali, but was each time repulsed with losses. The rest of the Sikhs, after a superb effort, had reached Richmar Gali later on that evening and made plans for an assault on Pir Sahiba the next morning.

1 Sikh assault on Pir Sahiba feature commenced on the morning of the 29th of May. It met with very strong opposition from the beginning. The advance lay, for most of the way, along a knife-edge which was well covered by a nest of enemy Light Machine Guns from behind built-up defences. Every inch of ground had to be fought for, resulting on a few occasions, in hand-to-hand combat. The enemy who were regular Pakistan Army troops belonging to 3/12 Frontier Force Rifles, put up a very stubborn defence. Each enemy post had to be eliminated by close-range fighting and many acts of heroism were witnessed on both sides. Artillery support on many occasions had to be called for by the Forward Observation Officer with 1 Sikh, within 25 yards of our own troops. The accuracy of our gun-fire was the talk of the troops for a long time. Pir Sahiba was not completely secured until late that afternoon. The bodies of 43 enemy dead were actually collected on the field of battle, apart from many who were known to have been dragged away by the enemy. The position was consolidated by 1 Sikh by last light that day and preparations for the next day's assault on Mir Kalsi started. Jemadar Gulam Mohd, of 3/12 Frontier Force Rifles, was wounded and captured. Although severely wounded in the head, he was able to give us some very useful information.

Pakistan Army forces in the area - both on the Uri and Tithwal fronts - consisted of a Division strength, under the command of Major General Mohd Nazir. A Brigade of this force, had been rushed forward to Tithwal recently and a battalion of this Brigade, 3/12 Frontier Force Rifle, was opposing 1 Sikh. The Brigade Commander, Brigadier Atta Mohd, had been on a visit to his Battalion Headquarters at Pir Sahiba when the Sikhs attacked, and he was himself conducting the operations. The position was lost because of a surprise attack by the Sikhs from a flank. In this action the Brigade Commander and the Battalion Headquarters were nearly captured. The enemy JCO was running along with the Brigade Commander's party when he was hit in the head. Owing to the danger of being caught, all officers had removed their badges of rank. His battalion Commander was just ahead of him, and in a hurry had dropped one of his shoulder badges, which he (the prisoner) had picked up (this had been recovered from his pocket and was responsible for the false report that a Lt Col of the Pakistan Army had been captured). Other battalions in the Brigade were 2/8 Punjab, 4/12 Frontier Force Rifles and two Companies of 13 Punjab (Medium Machine Guns). He was not sure if 5/12 Frontier Force Rifles were also there.

Mir Kalsi Ridge was captured by the Sikhs the next morning without any opposition - not a single shot was fired. The enemy had apparently had enough. With the whole of this feature, upto Richmar Gali, Pir Sahiba and the Ring Contour on the other side of the defile, in our hands, I was confident that Tithwal had become a little fortress. Nothing could touch it! That morning a section of Mountain Guns was moved forward, behind Mir Kalsi feature, in order to get extra range in front of our position. Two Companies of 3 Royal Garhwal Rifles across the river - at point 7229 and Ring Contour - were relieved by 1 Madras with the object of concentrating the Garhwalis in Tithwal.

With the capture of Richmar Gali and Pir Sahiba feature, the stage was now set for operation 'Surya'. The column could concentrate behind cover of this feature one night and debut forward on the next, so as to reach the nearest point on the water-shed, along which the column was to proceed, unnoticed by the enemy (during the hours of darkness).

The feature of Mir Kalsi close to the river Kishanganga, along which the main track lay, was held by a platoon of 1 Sikh. The feature was absolutely bare and rocky on the top and on the east side of it, thus rendering it rather difficult to prepare for defence. The west side, towards the enemy, was, however, full of plantation, affording good cover right upto the position. The feature thus lent itself to easy assault from the enemy side. Besides, it stood there like a sentinel on the western exit of the Tithwal defile. No wonder then that the enemy selected it as its first objective for counter-attack. Our gun positions behind this feature, protected by a Company less a Platoon of 1 Madras, as close escort, may have been an added attraction for the enemy.

On the morning of the 1st of June (a Friday), when Mir Kalsi platoon had stood down from their 'stand to' and were having their morning tea on the leeward side of the hill, a sudden and heavy artillery and mortar concentration opened up on the position. Every one lay flat on the ground, wherever he was, and waited for the bombardment to stop. After about 15 minutes, a red light was seen fired from amongst the plantations on the enemy side of the hill and only about a 100 yards from the picket position. This was apparently a signal for the artillery concentration to stop. Instinctively also, it acted as a signal for the picket-garrison to rush to their alarm posts! It was a race with the enemy, who was trying to charge the picket position from the other side. The Sikhs just managed to beat him to it. Standing up in their defences and, shouting challenges at him, they turned the enemy back from within 25 yards of the position.

The enemy left behind 18 dead in front of the position, including an officer who had received a direct hit to his face from a 2-inch mortar bomb. The Platoon Commander, Jemadar Harchand Singh, immediately sent a section forward to chase the enemy. Our only casualty, besides minor injuries from bombardment, was a sepoy out of this section, who stepped on one of our own A/P mines by mistake. A Bren, a pistol and a number of rifles were collected from the enemy dead.

After the failure of their attack on Mir Kalsi, the enemy took up position on a feature across Panjokot nullah on the opposite side of our picket position, but within 300 yards of it. Both these positions were at a level in height and equally exposed to each other. Life in these positions for the next few days, when nerves were rather frayed, was simply hell! Nobody could move out, even to attend to a call of nature, without attracting a bullet. I remember visiting this position immediately after the attack. Even the slightest of exposures was not spared. Crawling up to it and over it was the order of the day. However, the next time I visited this picket, after about three days, I noticed that the Jemadar Sahib was standing up on the crest and was signalling to me to walk right ahead. It was apparently their 'truce' period, and this is how it came about.

One morning, when they had had enough of it, the enemy post stuck up a white towel on a twig near one of their posts. Our picket did not, at first, understand the meaning of it. Then slowly and cautiously a man on the enemy side, straightened himself in his trench in full view of our sentry, while our sentry held fire. This man got out of his trench and started walking about leisurely. This was repeated by his other comrades as well. It was then that our sentry understood the meaning of the white towel and put up one himself! There was a hand wave from the other side as if to acknowledge the understanding arrived at! There was not a single shot exchanged, and both sides attended to their normal duties. From then on, both these posts allowed themselves an hour off for the call of nature in the morning, another hour off at both meal-times and on odd half hour off now and then for tea or when a VIP happened to be visiting the post. A gentleman's agreement indeed!

After the enemy's attack on Mir Kalsi feature, the section of guns in the lee of the picket position was moved to a higher and safer site near 1 Sikh Headquarters at Alikoh. This further effected a saving of troops required for their close protection.

Realising the impregnability of the Sikh position in the front, the enemy started paying more and more attention to the 1 Madras position north of the river. He was reported to be crossing over to that side over a rope bridge in the area of Nausada. It was quite probable that he might come along track Balgiran-Jargi feature and, after crossing the Kishanganga over the suspension bridge near Mirpur, appear at our back. So an Engineers Detachment with the necessary explosives, and a platoon as escort, were despatched on the morning of the 16th of June to blow up the bridge at Mirpur. They returned to base the same evening, after having accomplished their task. Local reports later indicated that we had beaten the enemy to the bridge only by a few hours. They also confirmed that the enemy was milling about in front of our positions, at Ring Contour and Point 7229 with a view to attacking 1 Madras. The positions were, therefore, prepared for such a contingency. The Madrasis were given priority for defence stores, such as barbed wire and anti-personnel mines, etc., of which we were so far in very short supply. Bunkers were also ordered to be made shell-proof.

The attack came on Ring Contour in the early hours of Friday, the 8th of June, after the usual morning Namaz. It was a well planned attack. A party of enemy came close up between Ring Contour and Point 7229, with the primary object of containing the latter picket and started demonstrating on that flank with firing and shouting. In the meanwhile another party of enemy tried to charge the Ring Contour position from the opposite direction along the spur, preceded by a very heavy concentration of artillery and mortar fire and closely supported by four Medium Machine Guns in a nest. The enemy Medium Machine Guns took on the neutralisation of our forward bunkers one by one, and succeeded in doing so to a great extent by killing or wounding all the occupants in a few of the bunkers. These bunkers were, however, readily reinforced by 1 Madras, while still under heavy fire, and the enemy assault was beaten back. The barbed wire fence and anti-personnel mines had played their part in stemming the attack. No less than 15 anti-personnel mines had gone up and blown ten men of the enemy to pieces on the spot. This had a decimating effect on the morale of the enemy, who soon turned back and fled shrieking with fright! 1 Madras chased him with a patrol. 22 enemy dead were collected from in front of the picket position, besides two Bren guns, 10 rifles and some stens and ammunition. 1 Madras had lost 8 men while 10 were wounded. This was the first major battle the Madrasis had fought under my command and they had, without doubt, come out with flying colours. A healthy rivalry existed among the three battalions in my Brigade, and each one of them had had an opportunity to show their mettle. The Garhwalis, at Trahgam Ridge, the Sikhs at Pir Sahiba and Mir Kalsi; and now the Madrasis. Well deserved messages of congratulations were received by 1 Madras from the other two battalions.

We had by now realised that Friday was considered an 'auspicious' day for the enemy to attack. This was doubly confirmed by the actions at Mir Kalsi and Ring Contour. Both these attacks had taken place on a Friday. In future, therefore, Friday for us became a day of caution. Reminders would be sent out to battalions every Thursday to post double sentries that night and to be generally on the alert.

As a result of our sudden push from Kupwara and the elimination of the enemy from the Shulur Valley, a party of Raiders were trapped in Lolab Valley east of Kupwara, with little hope of escape. Their base of operations was reported to be in the village of Khumrial in that Valley. 4/8 Gorkhas had two serious engagements with this party of the enemy in early June before they were able to drive them out. 4/8 Gorkhas who had been responsible for the protection of the line of communication from Handwara to Nasthachur Pass were, in the second week of June, relieved by 1 Battalion Jammu and Kashmir Militia under the command of Lt Col Amar Singh of the Indian Army. Danger to the line of communication was now negligible and the armoured cars in the area were, therefore, withdrawn to Baramula.

The main thrust of the summer offensive along the Uri-Domel road had come to a stand-still just short of Chakothi, within 10 miles of Uri. The Divisional Commander felt that there was a possibility of Tithwal offering an opening in the enemy's defence line covering Muzaffarabad. He sent for me at his Headquarters, to discuss the possibility of implementing operation 'Surya'. I was, however, sceptical of its efficacy at this stage because of the reported heavy concentration of enemy in front of Tithwal. Before, therefore, giving my final answer to the Divisional Commander's proposal, I expressed a desire to carry out a reconnaissance-in-force in front of the 1 Sikh position in order to find out the real strength and extent of the enemy defences.

On 10th June, I returned to Tithwal and on the 11th morning I took with me Lt Col Kuman Singh, Commander 3 Royal Garhwal Rifles - who was to carry out the operation - and his Company Commanders to Pir Sahiba position with the object of having a look at the ground and making out the plan for the operation envisaged. Commander 1 Sikh joined us on the position.

30

RECCE-IN FORCE BY 3 ROYAL GARHWAL RIFLES

The plan that was roughly drawn up was as follows:

3 Royal Garhwal Rifles, less one Company, were to concentrate behind the 1 Sikh position at Pir Sahiba by first light on the 13th of June and would remain under cover during the day.

They were to leave the Sikh position after last light on the 13th of June and were to carry out a night advance up the Buni Ridge, and after leaving a company and a detachment of Medium Machine Guns and a 3-inch mortar at Takia Seru, as a firm-base, were to assault the Mussargutte feature, which was known to be held by the enemy, along the spur from behind. Medium Machine Guns, 3-inch mortars and reserve ammunition were to be carried by porters. As many prisoners as possible were to be captured, alive.

A company of 1 Sikh were to be ready behind Mir Kalsi Ridge at first light on the 14th of June, and if need be, they were to attack the Mussargutte feature from the front, and thus squeeze the enemy.

The section of Mountain guns at Alikoh were to support the operation throughout. Air support was laid on for the morning of the 14th of June. It would be on call.

3 Royal Garhwal Rifles left the Sikh position according to schedule at last light on the 13th of June. Their route lay along a very steep and narrow track down to Panchkot nullah and thence upto Buni ridge. The going was found to be very much harder than expected and progress was consequently slow. Panchkot nullah was not reached until 1 am and the advance up the Buni Ridge was resumed soon afterwards.

At about 3.30 am the forward platoon, while engaged in surrounding two adjacent houses in Takia Seru, with a view to searching them, was challenged by an enemy sentry from within one of the houses. Short shrift was made of him with a bayonet. The rest of the enemy in that house, numbering about 9, offered to surrender and came out with raised hands. While our men were preparing to round them up one of the enemy lobbed a hand grenade into our ranks, causing casualties. The restraint on the Garhwalis was broken and before their Commander could intercept, seven of the enemy had been 'khukaried' dead, one was severely wounded, and only one survived unscathed. He was the sole prisoner that morning. The second house had about 25 enemy men in it (a platoon less a section). They resisted and were thus killed to the last man.

The enemy had been completely surprised and had apparently woken up out of a deep slumber. As if by magic, the whole of the countryside started resounding with fire. No less than 8 enemy Medium Machine Guns were in action from various ridges and their traces could be seen criss-crossing in the air like fire works! Signal lights were floating all over the place. The din was intense. The enemy layback positions, right up to Muzaffarabad, had also joined in. Muffled thuds of gun-fire could be heard in the far distance. A lot of shouting was going on in the enemy lines, obviously out of nervousness.

The Garhwalis rushed headlong up the spur, shooting from their hips, and drove the enemy out of Buni village. The enemy, who had been taken completely by surprise, ran out of the houses leaving everything behind - arms, ammunition and even boots. It was light by now and the Garhwalis took up a defensive position around this village, expecting a counter-attack by the enemy any moment. They could hear it brewing behind the next feature nearby. It came at about 8 am and was successfully repulsed. A second attempt was made half an hour later, and that too was easily foiled. The third assault was led by a fair-coloured, hefty-looking, officer who came brandishing his stick and shouting words of encouragement to his men. This attack nearly succeeded until the leader of the assault was hit by a burst from a Light Machine Gun and fell in full view of our position. This resulted in the enemy breaking ranks. Attempts to take the officer's body away cost the enemy many lives. We lost four men trying to drag the body in our direction.

Our troops were by now running short of ammunition as the porters with the reserve ammunition had all disappeared. Orders were, therefore, issued to the Garhwalis to withdraw. Withdrawal was carried out without any interference from the enemy. One of our Tempests came over the area about this time and engaged targets with good effect. The enemy was estimated to have lost at least 50 men while many more were wounded. The Garhwalis lost 8 men while 14 were wounded, a few only slightly. I had a grand-stand view of the whole battle from the 1 Sikh position.

The climb from Panjkot nullah to the Sikh position at Pir Sahiba, was very steep and the track narrow. Carrying casualties on this track was extremely difficult. Two of our wounded were in a rather serious condition owing to loss of blood. They were thus quite incapable of making that climb. Recourse was made to that life-infusing blood-plasma and, as usual, it worked wonders, and the wounded were able to make that climb on their own feet!

The sole prisoner of the operation was completely terrified when he was brought to me. The Garhwalis had apparently been threatening him. After he had been given some hot tea and something to eat, he came out with some very useful information. He belonged to 3/12 Frontier Force Rifle and confirmed the statement of the previous prisoner that they were in the area, along with the elements of the following battalions - 2/8 Punjab, 3, 4 and 5 Battalions of 12 Frontier Force Rifles and 15 Punjab (Medium Machine Guns) Battalion. He also told us that the officer who had been killed, leading the counter-attack, was his Commanding Officer, Lt Col Sardar Khan. He further stated that the route to Muzaffarabad over the water-shed, which was proposed as the route for 'Surya', was strongly guarded. I passed this information on to the Divisional Headquarters and operation 'Surya' was postponed indefinitely.

The Sikhs reported that the whole of the next night, the enemy was very jittery. He had repeated the 'fire works' of the night before many a time under cover of darkness. It was now definitely known that the enemy had occupied Point 9444 - the highest point west of Ring Contour and over 2000 yards away from it. From that ridge he had opened up once or twice on our aircraft who were dropping supplies for Tithwal. This necessitated the shifting of our dropping zone. Further, it was reported that he was trying to haul a gun up to Point 9444 with the obvious intention of shooting at Tithwal. (The 'Gun' was later discovered to be a 4.2-inch mortar). Upon this information, the camp in Tithwal was thinned out and administrative installations shifted to the leeward side of the Tithwal Ridge, under cover from the enemy post at point 9444. Reports had also come in that, having failed to make a wedge in the Tithwal defences, the enemy was now thinking of reoccupying Keran and thus a threat from the north to our line of communication was developing.

In order to secure Keran against this move of the enemy, my plan was to send two converging columns on to Keran, one from Tithwal along the Kishanganga river and the other from Shulur, via Pharkian-ki-Gali. Having secured Keran, the force was to establish a Militia Company position there, to hold and guard the bridge. A column consisting of one company 3 Royal Garhwal Rifles and a Detachment of Engineers, under the command of Major Kanwar Singh, 2IC of 3 Royal Garhwal Rifles, left Tithwal for Keran after last light on the 15th of June, with instructions to capture Keran in co-ordination with the thrust from Shulur. They were given orders to blow all the bridges on the Kishanganga river on the way up and return to Tithwal via Shulur. Owing to the proximity of the enemy position which overlooked the track, the first part of the advance, over the most difficult and narrow track along the river, had to be done at night. The column from Shulur consisting of one Company of Jammu and Kashmir Militia, and a party of the Civil Administration, started for Keran on the 17th of June '48. The Tithwal column having accomplished its mission, after establishing the Militia Company at Keran, proceeded to Shulur.

The civil administration, I knew, were very chary of blowing up the 'very expensive' suspension bridges over the Kishanganga river. So the order to blow up the bridges between Tithwal and Keran was my responsibility alone. I got a message from the General Officer commanding my Division, just after the capture of Keran, that in view of increased activity by the enemy in Kagan, west of the Kishanganga river, he hoped, that I had destroyed the bridge on the river. I promptly signalled back to say that the orders had been already complied with. Bridges between Keran and Shardi still remained, affording access to the enemy from that flank. I was ordered by Divisional Headquarters to blow up these bridges also. I utilised 3 Royal Garhwal Rifles Company, which had just reached Shulur, after Keran, for the purpose. The Company column, under the command of Captain Gulati, set out from Pethahir, on the 19th of June and returned to base after two days, having accomplished the task uneventfully.

Tithwal camp lay in a deep hollow with the hill features to the west and the south and the east of it rising precipitously to great heights thus defending it from any gun-fire from the direction of enemy positions to the south of the Kishanganga river. The enemy had made repeated attempts to hit the camp from that direction but found their shells either shooting overhead or hitting the shoulder of one or the other hill, on both sides of the Tithwal defile. The enemy guns could not be moved across the river Kishanganga in the absence of a suitable bridge. With the capture of Point 9444, over-looking the Tithwal camp, although at a distance of 4000 yards or more from it, the enemy saw possibilities of achieving his objective. And it was here that a 'gun' was reportedly being hauled up to the post.

We had taken note of this possibility and had reacted accordingly. The camp had been thinned out and bunkers strengthened against shell fire. A mortar bomb from that great height was expected to take longer in its flight than normal, thus increasing the time lag between the receipt of the report of its firing and the arrival of the missile. We, therefore, instituted an 'air warning' system. The first bomb from this mortar was fired on the 23rd of June. The warning whistle blew and everybody took cover, except for the two clerks of my command post who kept sitting in the open under a tree, trying to be brave! As luck would have it, the bomb, the very first one, landed in their midst, killing one outright and wounding the other. The lesson learnt proved very costly to them!

I was called up to the Divisional Headquarters on the 22nd of June and told that Brig JC Katoch, Commander, 163 Infantry Brigade, who had been indisposed, and from whom I had taken over, had returned, and that I was now to hand over the Brigade to him. It was with a heavy heart that I received this news, for I had become very attached to the Brigade and they had done me proud in the recent operations. It was perhaps good for me that I should now hand over the Brigade to another Commander, for I had not been feeling quite well lately. The inordinate exertion that I had indulged in in the early stages of the Tithwal operation, had had a telling effect on my health, and had brought back the old symptoms of beri-beri, contracted by me in my days as a Japanese prisoner-of-war. I needed the immediate attention of a specialist. Brigadier Katoch and I travelled to Tithwal together on the 23rd of June. I handed over to him the line of communication units on the way, and the Brigade, on arrival at Tithwal. I returned to Srinagar on the 26th of June, 1948.

Receiving an Equestrian award from Dr Rajendra Prasad, the first President of India.

The Author with the Commandant & Staff at the IMA.

Farewell to IMA. The Author being pulled out on a wooden cart.

31

DEPUTY COMMANDANT, IMA

On return from Jammu and Kashmir, I was posted as Deputy Commandant to the Indian Military Academy (IMA), Dehradun. The Commandant was Brigadier Mahadev Singh. The post of Deputy Commandant had been lying vacant for some time, and I was very happy to accept it despite the fact that I had to come down one rank - from Brigadier to full Colonel. It was nice to be back at the Academy, where I had once been a cadet.

I was well aware of the responsibilities of the Deputy Commandant, which besides general administration, included allotment of accommodation, etc. Therefore, on the very first day, I visited the bungalow that used to be the Deputy Commandant's residence and was surprised to find that, for some reason, it had been allotted to two Captains' families, and that the house was in a bad state with its grounds neglected. The pool in the compound, which in my days as a cadet had been in perfect condition, was now utterly chocked with weeds. So I decided to shift the two families occupying the bungalow to their authorised accommodation and occupied the bungalow myself with the intention of restoring it to its former glory!

I also noticed that the grounds of the Academy were not well-kept. In my day, we were not allowed to walk on the grass-lawns, whereas now, due to laxity in this regard, there were foot tracks all over the lawns which served as shortcuts to walkers, cadets and the public in general. I, therefore, brought back the order of yore that did not allow Gentlemen Cadets and others to step on the grass, and had the foot-tracks dug up and sown with grass, while notices were put up warning passers-by to keep off the grass. The horticulture staff were pulled up and given the task of planting fancy shrubs and flowers so as to make the grounds of the Academy more attractive, as they had been in the old days.

Another thing I noticed, and also knew from my own days, was that Gentlemen Cadets (GCs) drank hard liquor on the sly. So I allowed drinkers to officially consume a bottle of beer each on payment, if they so desired, provided they only drank on the apron of grass, near the cricket ground, on Sundays, when a picnic lunch would be served to them from the Cadets' Mess, which happened to be next door. This was meant to give the Gentlemen Cadets a certain amount of freedom as future officers of the Indian Army. I know that it went down well with them. I was unmarried then, and used to very often have meals with the cadets, and saw to it that the standard of the Officers' Mess was maintained. I would also on occasion visit the morning sick parade of cadets, to find out if there were any malingerers among them. I was also keen to see to the welfare of members of the staff and their families, which was very important for keeping up their morale. I did all this as tactfully as possible so as not to rub anyone up the wrong way.

Another thing I was keen on teaching the cadets was punctuality. For any event, I made it a point to turn up five minutes before the time stipulated, so as to set an example for the GCs, be it an official or unofficial event. Any late arrival was strictly dealt with. Other than this, I encouraged the officers-staff to be as natural with the GCs as possible, so as to make them feel at home. In fact, I was trying to smoothen the rough-edges of Academy-life as I remembered them from my days as a GC. I like to think that I succeeded. However, I did not stay in this appointment for long, as in April 1949, I was detailed by Army Headquarters to head an Inter-Services Team, to carry out a study of the difficulties faced by our troops, in the Jammu and Kashmir Operations, in the way of equipment and rations. I had in this team representatives from the Navy, the Air Force, all branches of the Army Services, Ordinance Factories and a Chemist and a Physicist (the latter two from Delhi University).

The farewell given to me by the officers and their families at the Indian Military Academy was unique. Besides the usual drink and dinner party held in the Chetwood Hall of the Academy, punctually, at mid-night, when I wished to take leave of my hosts, I was led outside the Hall; and what do I see below the steps, but a steam-roller! They made me sit on it and drove it to the swimming pool. We were all in our blue jacket mess-kit, but this did not deter the officers who took me up to the diving-board and from there pushed me into the pool, full of water. Struggling out of the water, it was my turn to pull in my hosts as well, sparing the ladies. There was quite a melée in the pool! I then invited them all to my house, which was next door, and seated on the front-lawn we drank champagne. This was, however, not the finale.

Next morning, as I was due to depart, they brought to my house, from God knows where, a wooden cart, with ropes for pulling. They made me stand in the cart, and placing a decorated 'dupatta' on my head - like a bride - and pulled me in the cart all the way to the car that was waiting to take me to Delhi.

32
INTER-SERVICES SCIENTIFIC TEAM – FOR J&K OPERATIONS

The Inter-Services Scientific Team that I led, had its headquarters in Srinagar, and submitted periodic reports to the then scientific adviser to the Ministry of Defence, Mr Kothari. I made the Team visit every picket on the cease-fire line and listen to the various problems faced by those actually experiencing them. This entailed a march on foot, from Srinagar to Leh, which was undertaken in stages. This walk was both fascinating and scenic. The idea was to visit every picket en route. In Dras, for example, a post held by our troops throughout the winter of 1947-48, the temperature there, in winter, went as low as minus 40 degrees Fahrenheit. We were told that even beer froze in bottles, apart from all the medicines and mixtures. During that winter the troops at the Post had no kerosene oil to burn in their bukharas. There was no other local substitute that could be burnt for providing heat, as even a blade of grass did not grow in the area! We were told of an individual who, to get some warmth, put 30 blankets on himself, and yet continued to feel cold. Men at the Post complained that they found it difficult to sleep during the winter and would be waiting, from early morning onwards, for the sun to rise, and provide them some warmth. This was the Post, about a platoon strong, which we discovered had suffered the most from cold during that winter. The Team was set up for the period of a year, and at the end of it, it produced a report that was submitted to the Scientific Adviser. The report was, thereafter, circulated to all concerned, for whatever action was considered necessary. At the end of this appointment, I was posted as Brigadier General Staff, Western Command, then under Lieutenant General Srinagesh.

33
BRIGADIER GENERAL STAFF WESTERN COMMAND

The Sikh Regimental Centre

The Sikh Regimental Centre had just been transferred from Ambala to Meerut. In early 1952, unfortunately, the Colonel of the Sikh Regiment, Major General Khanolkar, who was area commander Calcutta, passed away in the train on his way to Calcutta. I, being the next senior in the Regiment, was elected to be the next Colonel of the Regiment.

The first thing I did, having belonged to the 5th Battalion of the Sikh Regiment which had been disbanded by the British after the Second World War as most other ranks had joined the Indian National Army in Malaya, was to re-raise this fine battalion. Luckily, the new government of independent India was favourably inclined towards the Indian National Army and I was given permission to convert the newly raised 7th Battalion of the Sikh Regiment into 5/11th Sikh. As Colonel of the Sikh Regiment, it was my proud privilege to hand over the flag, in the Red Fort area, to Lt Colonel Manchanda, the Commanding Officer of the newly raised 5/11th Sikh.

Besides, using my influence with Army Headquarters, I was able to send one of our battalions – 1 Sikh – to what was then a popular destination, the Gaza Strip. I had at the time a very energetic commander of the Sikh Regiment at Meerut, Lt Colonel Gurbaksh Singh, and with his cooperation we were able to outfit our regimental band with brand new uniforms, both for summer and winter, and they too accompanied 1 Sikh to Gaza. However, the intention was to send them on to England to participate in the Edinburgh Festival, where I had arranged funds so that they could buy the newest and latest musical instruments.

The Commandant of the Edinburgh Festival, a serving brigadier of the British Army, liked the notes of our buglers so much, that he selected them to play the 'Reveille', the 'Last Post' and the 'Retreat' twice a day at the festival. This was a signal honour. The Commandant wrote to me informing me about this and also asking for permission (which I readily granted) to use our buglers for ceremonies both in England and abroad. He also suggested that our band play for the public at White Hall in London; which it did and for which I received many congratulatory letters from ex-British officers of the Regiment.

During my tenure as Colonel of the Sikh Regiment (which lasted some twenty years!) we were able to build a gurudwara, a home for orphans, a unique war memorial and a stadium at Meerut. The latter was named after our first recipient of the Victoria Cross, Nand Singh. It would be remiss of me if I did not mention the generous financial support we received for all these projects from the honorary colonel of the Regiment, Lt General Yadavendra Singh, the Maharaja of Patiala. I should also like to acknowledge the good work put in by the then commandant of the Regimental Centre, Lt Colonel Gurbaksh Singh.

In early 1967, while Lt Colonel Gurbaksh Singh was still the Commandant, and I the Colonel of the Regiment, four new colours were presented to four Sikh battalions of the Regiment at a Presentation Parade attended by the then President of India, Dr Zakir Hussain. I had invited General Sir Reginald Savory, a senior officer of the Regiment who had served as Adjutant General during the British days, and to whom reference has already been made in this book, for the occasion, I am happy to say that after the Parade, over a cup of tea, General Savory announced that this was the best parade that he had ever seen!

The Author with his 'Canadian' bride on their wedding day, 2 March 1952.

Matrimony

For a long time, Captain Mit Singh, who had at one time commanded the Jind Infantry, had had an eye on me for his daughter. When I returned from Malaya after the Second World War, my family put a great deal of pressure on me, as it was considered a good match, and so I finally agreed to marry her in April 1945. Unfortunately, when I saw her for the first time, I discovered that she had a serious defect in both eyes for which reason Captain Mit Singh had not allowed us to see her before hand. I was immediately repulsed and refused to have anything further to do with her, though for many years I paid her a maintenance allowance.

Towards the end of 1951 I met a beautiful girl from the village of Ranike (not far from my own village of Badrukhan) who had come from Canada, for the first time, with her mother who was a Grewal girl from Sarabha, near Ludhiana. I got permission from the government to marry her and did so on 2nd March, 1952. Soon thereafter, Mit Singh also found a match for his daughter, an army officer, and so my obligations to her came to an end.

Growing Differences with General Kulwant Singh

After General Srinagesh was appointed as Chief of the Army Staff Lieutenant General Thimayya took over Western Command. He had not even been there a year when he was personally selected by Pandit Jawaharlal Nehru, the Prime Minister of India, to head the International Commission for Korea, under the auspices of the United Nations. General Thimayya told me before leaving that he had arranged for me to stay on as BGS Western Command till he returned. Lieutenant General Kulwant Singh was appointed to officiate in General Thimayya's absence.

Differences between General Kulwant Singh and me had already started during the Jammu and Kashmir operations, as already mentioned. To cap it all an incident occurred at General Thimayya's house, 3 Race Course Road, New Delhi, for which it seems General Kulwant Singh never forgave me. Mrs Thimayya was a very kind and compassionate person, and to say the least, very frank. My wife and I were at that time newly married and we were living in the hutments of the Sangli hostel, which were a furnace in summer. We were expecting our first baby, and were not looking forward to the approaching summer of 1953. Mrs Thimayya, being the considerate person she was, suggested to my wife that in their absence we move into their house at 3 Race Course Road. As a goodwill gesture, she decided to leave everything in the house as it was.

The evening before General Thimayya was due to leave for South Korea and Mrs Thimayya for her native place at Coorg, my wife and I went over to bid them farewell. Coincidentally, General and Mrs Kulwant Singh also came to visit and from the way Mrs Kulwant Singh began to visually inspect the house it became obvious that they were expecting to move in. Mrs. Thimayya was quick to observe this and in her usual straight forward manner informed Mrs Kulwant Singh that she was not going to get the house as it had already been promised to us. She went on to say that they should make temporary arrangements to live at 'Shanti Bhawan' (the MES bungalow in the Delhi Cantonment). It seemed that General Kulwant Singh held this against me and consequently working with him became difficult. I asked for a posting to a brigade and was soon posted to 19 Infantry Brigade at Damana, near Jammu. I was very happy to get this appointment, in a new place, under Major General Henderson Brooks.

34

COMMANDER 19 INFANTRY BRIGADE, DAMANA

Our Paths Cross Again: Gen Kulwant Singh & I

Soon after, General Kulwant Singh, in his capacity as officiating Army Commander, Western Command, came to visit army formations in Jammu and was staying at the government dak bungalow. As his ex-BGS I felt it my duty to call on him one evening. In the field area, all the jonga jeeps in which the formation commanders rode had a red light fixed on them. So, I arrived that evening to visit General Kulwant Singh in a jonga which, I was unaware, had a red light flashing on it. It was summer, and General Kulwant Singh had had a table laid out with drinks on the lawn of the bungalow where he was staying. I, therefore, alighted from the jeep at the gate of the bungalow and walked the last fifty yards to the lawn on foot. I greeted the general and was about to sit down when he sarcastically remarked, "So, you are the President of India!" I was naturally taken aback and wondered what I had done wrong. He was soon, however, to make it clear when he said, "It seems you cannot move without a red light on your vehicle!"

I tried to explain to him that this was not of my choosing but was a practice followed in the field area. Unfortunately General Kulwant Singh was a man with a narrow, and I might say, a petty bent of mind. This was not, however, the end of it; something worse was to follow.

Western Command announced that it planned to hold an exercise, in Jalandhar, under the auspices of the armoured division stationed there. I was detailed to be there as part of a syndicate comprising three local brigadiers and headed by a major general, General Uday Dube, who was commanding 25 Infantry Division at Rajouri. We were all sent papers for the exercise, and the instructions made it clear that the problem regarding the deployment of artillery was to be attended to by the leader of the syndicate in his own time. On the very first day of the indoor exercise, the Armoured Corps had laid on a tea for the participants, and I was told that it was at this tea that General Kulwant Singh hatched a plan to catch me out. He issued instructions that the first problem was to be addressed to our syndicate and asked General Uday Dube to appoint me to answer it! When General Dube mentioned this to me, I reminded him that according to the exercise instructions, the problem was his to answer as he was leader of the syndicate. I argued as such on the appointed day, but the Army Commander intervened to say that I should come to the rostrum to answer the problem. It was now quite clear to me that he had initiated the action but luckily for me, out of interest, I had studied the problem and so was able to give an answer that agreed with the staff solution.

An Assessment of General Kulwant Singh

General Kulwant Singh was not a military strategist. I remember an incident involving the Maharaja of Kashmir's ex-ADC, Brigadier Faqir Singh, who was in Srinagar during the winter of 1947-48. Despite his designation, he had had no experience of soldiering. General Kulwant Singh was aware of this and yet chose him to lead a column carrying arms and ammunition for the relief of the garrison at Skardu. Predictably, given his inexperience, the column met with a terrible disaster en route and lost everything it was carrying. General Kulwant Singh then decided to send another column under the command of another lieutenant colonel of the J & K forces, Kishan Singh. Major Sampuran Bachan Singh, my second-in-command, who was a favourite of the general, was promoted to the post of lieutenant colonel and assigned to the column as military adviser without my knowledge. In a similar fashion, again without telling me, General Kulwant Singh took away my defence platoon for his immediate protection. Unfortunately, this column too met with disaster because of the rivalry between the two lieutenant colonels. I have no hesitation in calling these General Kulwant Singh's two great follies in the winter of 1947-48. This is in addition to his unfortunate decision to stop short of occupying the bridges at Domel and Kanuta, which were so vital to the defence of the state of Jammu and Kasnmir, and which could have been secured so easily in the early stages of the J&K operations.

General Kulwant Singh's jealousy knew no bounds and this was especially apparent when he had had a drink too many. I was at the receiving end of many of his verbal tirades when he would declare that he hated my guts and would one day take his revenge on me. I generally chose to disregard his insulting behaviour as he was my senior. Not surprisingly he was hated and despised by nearly all his subordinates and there was jubilation when he was posted to Army Headquarters as Chief of General Staff under General Cariappa, who also happened to dislike him.

As ill luck would have it, I happened to be sitting in General Kulwant Singh's office one day, after the epic battle at Tithwal, when General Cariappa rang him up to enquire about something. On learning that I was there, he immediately assumed that I was trying to cosy up to General Kulwant Singh, and changed my Tithwal award there and then from Mahavir Chakra to Vir Chakra. I was the unwitting victim of a fight between two big bulls!

In the aftermath of the 1965 war with Pakistan, in which we had captured the near bank of the Icchogil canal, I had requests to visit the canal from military men and civilians. If the request came from a military general, serving or retired, who would generally ring me up, I would arrange transport as well as guides. One morning my chief of staff came to my office and said that General Kulwant Singh (who had by then retired) was on the line and wished to visit the front. I casually answered that it would be better if he rang me up directly. I had every intention of providing him with a staff car and a guide and of offering him some hospitality. But he never rang me up, thinking perhaps that it was below his dignity. I knew his nature well and did not hold this against him.

I still remember the Sunday morning when I, as Army Commander, Western Command, was staying at 'Shanti Bhawan' guest house in the Cantonment. I was rung up and told that General Kulwant Singh, who was staying with a nephew in the Cantonment, had passed away. I went straight to the house to pay my respects and found Mrs Kulwant Singh sitting besides the body of her husband. During the course of my conversation with her I discovered that she had been trying in vain to contact the defence secretary so that her husband could get a full military send off. As army commander I assured her that this would be done and instructed the local area commander, Major General Bhagwati Singh, who was also a good friend, to lay on a ceremonial funeral for General Kulwant Singh. I offered to take full responsibility should any questions be raised by the Ministry of Defence. So General Kulwant Singh had a ceremonial funeral and I felt that this was the least I could do for an old general who had at one time also been my army commander.

35

THE IMPERIAL DEFENCE COLLEGE COURSE, LONDON

After three years' command of the Brigade, I was posted to Army Headquarters in the capacity of Director Infantry for a few months before proceeding to the Imperial Defence College, in London, in November 1957.

General Kumaramangalam (then Major General) and I were together on this course. There I met, for the first time since our days at the Indian Military Academy, Dehradun, Lieutenant General Habibullah Khan Khattak, who was then Lieutenant General and Deputy Commander of the Pakistan Army and the senior-most student at the Imperial Defence College from Pakistan. He was a fine man, without any prejudice against India or the Indian Army. Earlier, I believe, there had been some tension between the students from India and Pakistan attending the Imperial Defence College; so, the first thing General Habibullah Khan did was to caution the students from Pakistan, five in number (one from the Foreign Service; one from the Civil Service and three from the Services), not to wash the dirty-linen between the two countries on any public occasion at the Imperial

Defence College. As a consequence, we had the friendliest of relations with the Pakistani students, especially with Habibullah and his family, during our stay at the College. Furthermore, he and I sat in chairs next to each other (which was obligatory only for the first fortnight so that one got to know each other) throughout the course - and very soon students started calling us both 'inseparable'.

I was the first to be informed by him, in the morning, that Ayub Khan had taken over the presidency of Pakistan from Sikander Mirza and that he had been appointed deputy to Mussa, who became the Commander-in-Chief of the Pakistan Army. On his return to Pakistan, I learnt, that he did not get on well with Mussa and resigned from the army and started his own business and did very well in it. He lost his first wife in a car accident, in which he was also very badly injured. He married again, and came to Delhi with his second wife. He rang me up from the Oberoi Hotel one afternoon and asked my wife and I over for tea that afternoon. We later invited them both for dinner to our house, for which he gave me a list of people he desired to meet. So we had a grand re-union of old friends at our house. This was in 1990. He and his wife visited Delhi several times after that, and each time we met over dinner. He had commanded a Bihar Battalion before partition, and attended, at his own request, the Bihar Regimental Golden Jubilee Re-Union at Dinapur in 1994. He passed away in December 1996 and I lost a very dear friend.

36

PROJECT JYOTI

After the Imperial Defence College course, I was posted to command 26 Infantry Division at Jalandhar, in the rank of Major General. I stayed in command of this Division for about a year and was then transferred to the command of 5 Infantry Division, in the same station. We had been given the task of building accommodation for officers and JCOs' families under the name 'Project Jyoti' at Ferozepore, where 5 Division had a Brigade. My family and I stayed on in Jalandhar in the same house, though the new job entailed my travelling to Ferozepore twice a week, to plan and supervise the Project. I travelled to Ferozepore mostly by air. My other two Brigades were located at Jalandhar and at Amritsar. The building project was completed towards the end of 1960, and I must relate an amusing incident that occurred during the completion ceremony.

The completion ceremony was presided over by the then defence minister, Mr. Krishna Menon, while General Daulat Singh was my Corps Commander. For this ceremony, we had prepared a special marble plaque bearing the name of the defence minister, Mr Krishna Menon. During the ceremony, after unveiling the plaque, Mr Krishna Menon turned to me and asked, "What's this?" Seeing my look of surprise he elucidated: "Do you call Shakespeare, 'Mr. Shakespeare'?" And I immediately answered: "I see, what you mean, sir, it will be corrected." And so the next day, we had the word "Mr" removed from the plaque. Such was the ego of Mr Krishna Menon!

Chief of Staff Western Command

Towards the end of 1960, Lt Gen Daulat Singh, our Corps Commander who had been posted as General Officer Commanding-in-Chief, Western Command, then located at Simla, sent for me and asked if I would agree to be his Chief of Staff. I agreed and so at the end of 1960, I became General Daulat Singh's Chief of Staff at Headquarters Western Command, at Simla. General Daulat Singh was a fine gentleman and we got on well together.

In early 1961, Lt Gen Biji Kaul took over as Chief of General Staff under General Thimayya, almost by force, it was said, as he was then Mr Krishna Menon's favourite (and I should add Pandit Nehru's too). Mr Harish Sarin was the Defence Secretary. For some reason, the Ministry of Defence (egged on by the Defence Minister, Mr Krishna Menon, I am sure), started to implement, along the cease-fire line with the Chinese, what was known as the 'Forward Policy'. And the Divisional Commander concerned started getting orders directly from the Chief of Staff (Biji Kaul) to place platoon strength pickets, at places behind the Chinese positions; in areas that were isolated in every sense of the term. Naturally, the Divisional Commander of Jammu and Kashmir objected to these direct orders, which, he thought, were tactically and administratively unsound, and approached the Army Commander to intercede in the matter with Army Headquarters. General Daulat Singh did take up these complaints with the Chief of the Army Staff, but before anything could be decided, the Chinese attacked our posts along the cease-fire line, on both the eastern and western fronts, in NEFA and Ladakh, simultaneously. The immediate provocation for this attack could well have been the statement made by Pandit Nehru, just before taking off for Ceylon, by air: "I have ordered our forces to throw the Chinese out of Indian territory." The result of the Chinese attack, at least in NEFA, was that the leading Brigade of 4 Infantry Division, which was deployed on the Namkachu river, under the command of

Brigadier Dalvi, was completely smashed by the Chinese army and many Indian soldiers, including Brigadier Dalvi and his staff, were taken as prisoners-of-war. When this happened, General Thapar, the Chief of the Army Staff at the time, rang up General Daulat Singh in the Operations Room of Headquarters Western Command, where we were busy tackling the situation at Daulat-Beg-Oldi (our northernmost position in Ladakh), to ask if he could spare me to take over 4 Corps from Biji Kaul, who had fallen ill. And, in fact, persuaded him that I should leave for Delhi the first thing in the morning, this being the 21st of October 1961.

37

COMMANDER 4 CORPS

On the morning of the 22nd of October, I flew to Delhi from Chandigarh and was briefed by the officiating Chief of General Staff, Lt Gen Joginder Singh Dhillon. I also met Lt Gen Biji Kaul, who was lying sick in his house. The next morning, the 23rd of October, I flew to Tezpur, where 4 Corps Headquarters was located. There, I discovered that till then Headquarters 4 Division had not been separated from Headquarters 4 Corps, although the former was fighting a battle of its own. So I ordered this to be done at once, and also warned the Divisional Headquarters to be ready to move into the battle-area forthwith, although I was yet to decide on its actual location.

The next morning, the 24th of October, I flew in a helicopter to Drang Zong on the line of communication to Sela, a prominent position, behind 4 Division, which was fighting ahead. Here, after I landed, I met Major General Niranjan Prasad, Commanding 4 Division, whose forward Brigade was still involved in fighting with the Chinese and questioned him as to what he was doing there when his troops were involved in fighting over a hundred miles away?

Drang Zong had served as a base for 'Beacon' (an organisation responsible for building roads in NEFA). Not only did they have all their silver on display in their Mess, their heavy equipment was still with them. I told the Commander, a Lieutenant Colonel, that he should clear out of Drang Zong as soon as possible for it was likely to be the next objective of the Chinese as tracks by-passing Sela, from both sides, converged there. I then asked him to drive me to Sela in his jeep, which he did. I was carrying loaves of bread and biscuits with me, as, I felt, that I was bound to meet hungry soldiers on the way running away from positions over-powered by the Chinese. I did meet them, and they were in the most bedraggled state, famished and despondent. I tried to give them as much succour as I could. In the Sela complex there was a dropping-zone, at a place known as Senge, where our aircraft dropped supplies, such as barbed-wire, blankets, etc. I found a Major of the Army Services Corps incharge there who was supervising the hauling of supplies to the road. I asked him to put up a barrier on the road and suggested that he give these stragglers from the Forward Brigade food and use them as labour, to collect the supplies dropped from the air. Having given these instructions, I proceeded to Sela. There I met Brigadier Lall, who had replaced Brigadier Dalvi, who had been taken prisoner-of-war at the Namkachu position. I also met, on the march, 3 Sikh Light Infantry Battalion, which had been sent from Tezpur to reinforce the forward Brigade. On the way, we saw arms, ammunition and stores scattered, on both sides of the road, obviously, by retreating troops. Brigadier Lall put me in the picture.

The bridge at Jung, a few miles ahead, had been blown up and the Garhwali battalion of his Brigade was deployed in a lay-back position about a mile ahead of the Sela Pass. 1 Sikh Battalion had just come in, after spirited action by one of its platoons at Bumla. I met their Commanding Officer, Lt Col Mehta, who reported that his battalion was fully intact and in high spirits. After going around the Sela complex, Brigadier Lall, Col Mehta and I felt that with 4 Division, less a Brigade, the complex could be converted into a formidable Defended-Area. With the Dropping-Zone of Senge included, it could be made self-sufficient in every respect, independent of road communications. The next ground of strategic importance, keeping in view the Chinese tactics of infiltration, was obviously Bomdila, and it could be held by the third Brigade of the Division. The position at Sela would be safe enough to be maintained by road from Tezpur, as long as road communications were not cut off by the enemy. I considered Drang Zong the 'well of death', to be avoided at all costs! Knowing the Chinese tactics of infiltration, I was convinced that they would by-pass the Sela position and make for Drang Zong, and try to cut-off road communications to Sela from that position. But with our assured supplies from the air, it would be a question of: 'Who behind whom?' I made all the officers and JCOs sit down, from where they could see all the features, and explained the plan to them.

All this while, Major General Pathania who had been sent by Army Headquarters to replace Major General Niranjan Prasad, was with me. On my return journey to Drang Zong, I left Pathania at Senge, to make himself comfortable there for the night and start his reconnaissance for the defence of the Sela complex first thing in the morning. I returned to Drang Zong rather late that night and flew back to Tezpur by a helicopter early the next morning, the 25th of October.

I held my first Staff Conference at my Headquarters (Tezpur) on the evening of the 25th and explained to the Staff my idea of deployment of 4 Infantry Division and urged them to build up reinforcements and supplies for the Division. The Division was to be maintained by road as long as it was safe and the road available, and then we were to be prepared to maintain the Sela-Senga position by air support alone. In the meanwhile, Army Headquarters was busy re-organising and re-grouping 4 Corps. The NEFA area which was so far held by a Brigade of 4 Division, was reinforced by another Brigade (under the command of Brigadier KMS Buttalia) and put under the operational command of a newly formed (and as yet un-named) Divisional Headquarters under the command of Major General MS Pathania. The only position with which the Chinese had established contact, so far in this area, was Walong, held at the time by 4 Sikh Battalion (ex 4 Division) under the command of Brigadier Hartley.

I discussed the defence strategy of the Walong-Huiliang area with the Divisional Commander, Major General Mohinder Pathania, on the evening of the 25th and came to the conclusion that since there was a direct track from Kibtu (under the Chinese) to Huiliang, by-passing Walong, the main burden of our defence in the area should lie on

Huiliang (where, incidentally, a new airstrip was almost ready), and Walong should be used only as a 'covering position'. I, therefore, vehemently countered the Divisional Commander's idea of reinforcing Walong.

I received instructions from Army Headquarters that the Home Minister, Mr. Shastri, would be addressing a public meeting at Tezpur, on the afternoon of the 26th, and that I should receive him at the airfield that afternoon. Therefore, before the arrival of the Home Minister's aircraft, I decided to visit 4 Division's Administrative Area at Tezpur, particularly as I had been told by Lieutenant Colonel Mehta, Officer Commanding, 1 Sikh at Sela, when I had met him there on the evening of the 24th that he had many men held up in the Administrative Area, and that he needed them urgently. Apart from 1 Sikh personnel, I found many other details awaiting despatch to the forward area and ordered their move forthwith. Later that afternoon, I went to meet the Home Minister's aircraft at the airfield. Mr. Shastri, the Home Minister, told me that he was going to visit my Headquarters after addressing a public meeting in the town of Tezpur. The Minister and his entourage (which included, Mr Chaliha, the Chief Minister of Assam) visited 4 Corps Headquarters in the evening and were explained the latest military situation on a map. Mr Shastri had with him a bundle of currency notes and gold ornaments which, he said, had been donated by the Tezpur public assembled to hear him. They had responded to his appeal to do something for the troops defending them. I requested him to take that bundle of notes and ornaments with him to Delhi and donate them, on our behalf, to the National Relief Fund. He appreciated this and asked me what was our immediate need. When I told him that our immediate requirement was 4x4 gear jeeps for the maintenance of troops in the forward area, he rang up Mr Ray, the Chief Minister of West Bengal, at once, on my operational telephone, and asked him as to how many jeeps, with trailers, he could send immediately to Tezpur? The answer was 300, and thanks to Mr Shastri, they arrived within a couple of days. These jeeps proved very handy for providing logistic support to our forward troops. Mr Shastri seemed to have been very impressed with whatever he saw at Corps Headquarters at Tezpur, and is alleged to have said so at the next meeting of the National Defence Council.

The next day, the 27th, I left early in the morning, by air, to visit Walong and to reconnoitre the area of Walong-Huiliang. I could fly by a Dakota only to a certain point. For the last leg of the journey to Walong I had to wait for nearly two hours due to an 'adverse wind', a peculiar feature which often developed over the temporary airstrip at Walong. Besides, only an Otter, which could carry only ten fully accoutred personnel at a time, was available and could be used for the purpose. This, I considered, to be a very unsatisfactory state of affairs and it further reinforced my view that Walong should not be held in strength and that it should only be a 'covering position' for the main defended area at Huiliang. When I landed at the Walong airstrip, in due course, I noticed that a portion of the Company of Gorkha Battalion had been flown-in that morning, as reinforcements for the Walong Garrison, while the rest of the unit were to follow. This was clearly against my orders to the Divisional Commander, and I ordered these troops to march back to Huiliang, which, I explained to the Company Commander, was going to be the main defensive position of the Brigade. I then visited 4 Sikh Battalion and found them in good spirits.

On return to Corps Headquarters, I sent for Major General Pathania, the Divisional Commander, and took him to task for ignoring my instructions regarding Walong. He, it seemed, was not quite convinced of my strategy for the defence of the area! This was confirmed by the fact that when I left the Corps on the 30th of October, and Biji Kaul took over the command of the Corps, Major General Pathania, with the permission of the new Corps Commander, managed to push in a whole Brigade at Walong, and turned it into his main defensive position with disastrous results!

I utilised the 28th and the 29th of October to carry out a whirlwind tour, by air, of other parts of NEFA and our forward posts. On my return from a trip on the evening of the 29th, I was surprised to find General Kaul sitting in my chair at the Evening Staff Conference, which I generally used to address on my return from forward visits. I thought he had come to visit the Corps, as the new Chief of General Staff, an appointment General Thapar had assured me he would be lured into. Therefore, imagine my shock when I was told by him that he had re-taken his Corps! My offer to brief him as to the latest situation was turned down. When I came out of the Conference Room to go to my room, I found my batman signalling to me that my bed had been shifted into a smaller room, the main and larger-room having been taken over by the new Corps Commander. Soon I heard Biji Kaul come in to the main room, followed by a special surgeon who had been sent with him from Delhi to look after his health!

I rang up Air Marshal Engineer, Air Officer Commanding Tactical Air Force supporting the Corps, and arranged to leave for Delhi the next morning. I desired to have it out with General Thapar, who had given me every assurance that I would remain permanently in command of 4 Corps and that he would induce Biji Kaul to accept the appointment of his Chief of General Staff. En route to Delhi, when the aircraft was approaching Lucknow, there was a call for me from Army Commander, Central Command, asking me to touch down at Lucknow, but I refused to do so, saying that I was headed for Delhi. The next message said that the Chief of Staff of HQ Central Command was coming to meet me at the airfield, and that I should at least touch down at Lucknow and meet him, as there was an important message for me from Army Headquarters. I landed at Lucknow, but asked the pilot to keep the engines of the aircraft going, as I was determined to return to the aircraft at the earliest. The Chief of Staff, Central Command, Major General KC Khanna (who was a friend of mine) brought with him a signal from Army Headquarters that said that since a national emergency against the Chinese had been declared in Sikkim, I should proceed to Siliguri post-haste and take over 33 Corps which was being assembled there. In view of this, I decided to disembark from the aircraft, and made for Siliguri the next morning, by air.

38

TAKING OVER COMMAND OF 33 CORPS AT SILIGURI

On arrival at Bagdogra Airfield, I was met by Brigadier Jagjit Singh Arora, Brigadier General Staff of 33 Corps, who told me that he had come ahead of the Corps, which should be arriving in a day or two. I took his jeep and proceeded straight to Nathu La Pass. There was a Jat Battalion deployed on this pass and the neighbouring pass. I noticed that there was a Company deployed on each of these passes for their defence. At the time, we were holding the crest-line of the ridge, and the stone put up, in honour of Pandit Nehru's visit to the State of Bhutan, through this pass, was displayed near the crest of the Nathu La Pass. I returned to Bagdogra the next day and found that the Corps troops had started arriving. For lack of accommodation, we occupied, temporarily, a portion of the hutments (made of hollow-bricks) of the University at Bagdogra, which was supposed to be opening soon. We found these hutments, completely uninhabitable, as they were leaking, and I had to order the men to go under canvas. One day, the Governor of West Bengal, Ms Padmaji Naidu, arrived with her retinue, including the prospective Vice-Chancellor of the University. They complained that they could not open the University, as we were occupying its accommodation. I replied that we would vacate the University hutments by the evening, and they could start the University immediately. It took the wind out of their sails. I was there for the next two years and the University was yet to start! Such are the ways of the civil!

Kalimpong on the track to Jelep La, was a nest for the Chinese population and their spies! I had ordered that no civilian would be allowed to cross the passes on the International Border, ie, the two passes I have mentioned above. But we found that every morning a postman would cross over Jelep La with a pony laden with mail and Indian newspapers, and go over to the Chinese side, and return with almost empty bags in the evening. The postman said that we could not stop him as he was taking the mail as per International Agreement! We took the matter up with higher authorities in Delhi, but nothing happened. And the mail, and with it, I am sure, intelligence reports by Chinese agents at Kalimpong, continued to flow over to the other side, without any hindrance.

I had taken over 33 Corps with effect from the 31st of October, 1962. As already mentioned, I had gone straight to Nathu La and Jelep La to study the situation there against the Chinese. I was told by Army Headquarters that the defence of Bhutan, along with Sikkim, was also my responsibility. For the defence of Sikkim, I had a division deployed forward of Gangtok, the capital of the state, besides the defences at Jelep La and Nathu La. The ruler of the state, known as the 'Chogyal', was an old man at the time. India had a political officer from the foreign ministry, at the Chancellery in Gangtok, by the name of Bahadur Singh who was married to a Bengali lady, who claimed to be the grand-daughter of the famous Nobel laureate Rabindra Nath Tagore. The Indian Chancellery in Gangtok was situated in a huge compound, with a barbed-wire fence around it, and a big iron-gate for entry. It had a guesthouse within the compound, for visiting VIPs. Whenever I visited Gangtok, accompanied by my family, I had an open invitation from the Special Political Officer to stay with him, and I took advantage of Bahadur's hospitality quite a few times. Bahadur was also Special Political Officer of the State of Bhutan. There was a difference in the status of the two states, in that while Sikkim was under India, like any other native state in India, Bhutan was an independent sovereign state, with a king as its ruler. However, while in Gangtok we came to know that, by custom and usage, all land-rights, including the right to fish in various lakes in the state of Sikkim, belonged to the Maharaja; as did the income from 'guchhies', mushrooms that grow on the hill-sides below the snow. Consequently, we, the new army in the state had a lot of trouble fishing in the lakes. But all this must have changed since, now that Sikkim is part of India.

The old 'Chogyal' of Sikkim was very fond of painting imaginary pictures of the abominable snowman or 'Yeti'. When I went to meet him at his palace, in my capacity as general officer commanding the Corps in the area, after the customary exchange of scarves, he led me to his bedroom, and related to me the story of his encounter with a 'Yeti'. He described how the 'Yeti' had entered his bedroom, through a window, and how he had grappled with it and over-powered it. He had painted his impressions on a canvas. The painting he showed me looked more to me like that of a woman wrapped up in flimsy clothing than a monster! However, it was not for me to comment, and so I went on agreeing with him, impressions and all!

The 'Chogyal' passed away while I was still with my Corps, and I attended his last rites. I was surprised that, according to custom, his body was kept in a supine position, in a specially made cubicle, covered with a dome. Thereafter, his heir-apparent (his only son) became the new Maharaja or 'Chogyal'. The first thing he did was to marry an American girl, whom he had courted in Darjeeling, where he had studied at Saint Paul's School. The wedding took place in Gangtok, where he had a hotel specially constructed for this purpose. He had invited all the dignitaries in the neighbourhood for his wedding, as well as the Maharajas of Patiala and Jaipur. It was my responsibility to receive these dignitaries at the Bagdogra Airfield, and despatch them to Gangtok. While I sent the Maharaja of Jaipur to Gangtok by helicopter, I took the Maharaja of Patiala, Yadavindra Singh, with me in a staff car, along the road running parallel to the Teesta river. Yadavindra Singh was lodged for the occasion in the new hotel. As he was honorary colonel of the Sikh Regiment, I had detailed a Junior Commissioned Officer of the Sikh Regiment to be his ADC and to assist him in whatever manner possible. The first challenge arose with the beds at the New Hotel, which were far too small for the person of the Maharaja who was 6 feet 4 inches tall. So he was accommodated on two beds, placed diagonally. The wedding ceremonies, performed according to local customs, were indeed very intriguing. Hospitality was generous, and liquor, including champagne, flowed like water. I met the royal couple later, in the palace, and had difficulty understanding what the new bride had to say as she seemed to have cultivated a voice that was more a husky whisper – probably it was in fashion those days!

I might mention that not many years after I left command of 33 Corps, to take over Western Command, the Chogyal died. Soon after, his eldest son, the heir apparent, also met a tragic end in a car accident. It is the younger son now who is the 'Chogyal' of Sikkim. Before I leave the subject, I must make mention of the younger sister of the then 'Chogyal', known by the nick name of 'Cuckoo'. She was married, according to custom, to an aristocrat in Lhasa, the capital of Tibet, and had a couple of male children, whom she had left behind to visit her brother, the heir-apparent, who later became the Maharaja of Sikkim. This was in 1950, when the Chinese took over Lhasa. She was unable to return and often mentioned to us, in 1962, that the last she had heard about her family was that her husband, being an aristocrat, was in jail while her sons had been seen begging on the streets of Lhasa. What a human tragedy!

Another Division of my Corps was deployed in the area of Binaguri, with a Brigade Group (including a Regiment of armour) positioned just south of the India-Bhutan border, for the defence of Bhutan, should an occasion arise. Soon, the King of Bhutan expressed a desire to visit Indian troops, and he was taken to inspect the Brigade Group deployed just south of his state border. This was towards of the end of November, 1963. The King was accompanied by his son - the present ruler of the state - who was only ten years old. The son was so interested in the tank he saw (which he was, perhaps, seeing for the first time in his life) that he was hopping in and out of the turret all the time, or examining the gun from both ends. We had arranged lunch for the king's party in the Field Mess of the Brigade. The King, I noticed, was very strict with his son. During lunch, the young prince asked for a 'puri' but left half of it on his plate. Noticing this, he addressed his son, in their own language of course, and made him eat the remaining half.

The King, we learnt later, was very fond of playing football, and used to play in his capital, which was nearly at a height of 6000 feet. He sometimes played two games, one after the other. He would also often invite premier football teams from Calcutta to play against him and his team. By doing so, he is supposed to have strained his heart, and was, accordingly, sent to Switzerland to recover. It was in the month of July 1963 (if I remember correctly) when I had just returned to my hut, after dinner in the Mess, at Bagdogra, that I got a telephone call from the Commander of the Brigade Group, just south of Phuntsoling (in Bhutan), informing me that the Prime Minister of Bhutan, Mr. Jigme Dorji, had just been shot in the chest. His assailant was an unknown miscreant, who had shot him at the rest-house at Phuntsoling, while he was playing bridge with his staff. I remembered that our Mobile Surgical Team was in the area and so I asked the Brigade Commander to arrange for the Team to go immediately to Phuntsoling and do whatever they could. The surgeon, I believe, arrived on the scene, with his team, within minutes, but could not do anything, as the Prime Minister had been shot in the chest, with a lethal revolver, at close range and had literally drowned in his own blood. I promised to arrive there by air, the first thing in the morning, as I expected some trouble, as a sequel. Unfortunately, the King of Bhutan was away at the time in Switzerland, and, therefore, through the Ministry of Defence, the King was requested to return to his state post-haste. I stayed there until he arrived. The Ministry of Foreign Affairs sent Mr Apa Pant, who had earlier been the Special Officer incharge of Bhutan. He knew the King well and enjoyed his confidence. The King and Mr Apa Pant left for Drang Zong, together in the same helicopter, and, I believe, the King went straight to his palace without seeing anybody at the airfield (Drang Zong was the capital of Bhutan before it was shifted to Thimphu). Mr Avtar Singh, the Special Officer, detailed for both the states of Bhutan and Sikkim, but who lived at Gangtok also arrived in Drang Zong. Soon, it was revealed that the King's mother had had a hand in the goings on. The trouble had really been started by second wife (known by her nick name, 'Yanki'), who was jealous of the senior wife, the younger sister of the State's Prime Minister, Mr Jigme Dorji.

It was customary in the state of Bhutan for the king to have two wives - one from the west of Bhutan and the other from the east. The wife from the west was the senior wife, sister of the Prime Minister, and 'Yanki' was, naturally jealous of her. The latter, the younger of the two, got on well with the Queen Mother, who was estranged from the first (senior) queen. 'Yanki' had connived with the queen mother to win over the Chief of Staff of the Bhutanese Army, so as to arrange for Mr Jigme Dorji, the Prime Minister's murder during the King's absence in Switzerland, on medical grounds. The Chief of Staff had detailed an Army Sergeant to do the needful and so, at the first opportunity, he had apparently shot Mr Jigme Dorji at very short range, with a .45 revolver, through a window. The Sergeant had then disappeared into the jungle. On his return, the King dealt swiftly with the matter. He could not do anything to his mother, nor to his younger wife, but ordered his Chief of Staff to see him in his palace. In these autocratic, and medieval, states the residential palaces are made to a pattern, and such was the case with the palace at Drang Zong. The drawing room was on the first-floor, approachable only by a narrow, dark and circuitous staircase. At each bend in this staircase there was a narrow door that led to a small cubicle. Any culprit, difficult to arrest otherwise, would be pulled into the cubicle, through a door so chosen, by strong men detailed for the purpose. And that's how the Chief of Staff was apprehended. He was, subsequently, made to face the firing-squad, in the presence of the disarmed personnel of the armed forces of the state - and, I am sure, in the 'purda' presence of the queen mother and his younger wife. I stayed at Drang Zong, for part of the time, with Mr Avtar Singh, our 'Special Officer' detailed for the state. While there, I took the opportunity of calling on the King in his palace, and also paid my respects to the dead-body of the Prime Minister, which lay-in-state in his own ancestral village nearby.

Although I had been posted to 33 Corps, I still kept a tab on the happenings in 4 Corps, which was in the neighbourhood. In early December, 1962, I was told that the Corps, under the command of Biji Kaul, was in a desperate situation, the Chinese having infiltrated into its position from all directions. During this time, General Thapar, the Chief of the Army Staff, visited the Corps and sat there at Corps Headquarters, closeted, I believe, with Lt Gen Sen, the Army

Commander, since the Corps Commander, Biji Kaul, was not in his office. Desperate calls were coming in at the time from Brig Gurbaksh Singh, Commander Bomdila Brigade, for since the Corps Commander was unavailable, there was no one to give him orders. The Chief, at the time, was accompanied by Director of Military Operations, Brig Palit (nick name 'Monty'). Seeing the hopeless situation of 4 Corps, the Chief returned to Delhi, and being the honest and well meaning man he was, went straight to Pandit Nehru, the Prime Minister, on his return and submitted to him his resignation from the Army. I feel he was wrongly advised. If I were in his place, I would have held both the Army Commander, Lt Gen Sen, and the Corps Commander, Biji Kaul, responsible for the debacle. I would have sacked them and taken over the command of the Corps myself, until a suitable relief could be found.

In the meanwhile, Biji Kaul had written directly to the Prime Minister (having that rare privilege), asking him to seek American help. Soon, we saw the American C-130 aircrafts deployed on field airfields in NEFA and a high-level team of American Army officers, with General Adams at their head, appeared at our Headquarters. This team promised a lot, but gave little. However, it does show our desperation. This was the time when General Thapar's resignation had been accepted and General Chowdhary, who was on the verge of retirement, took over from him.

33 Corps, which I had taken over and whose responsibility was to defend the states of Sikkim and Bhutan against the Chinese, was deployed for its operational role in an entirely new area, where there was no accommodation for the troops. Besides, a tropical climate prevailed in the area, and there was no question of the troops living in the open. Luckily, I had a very practical and experienced Chief Engineer in my Headquarters by the name of Colonel 'Bhalloo' Kochhar. We had a discussion and decided that although initially the troops, perforce, would have to stay under canvas, the tents would be erected on wooden platforms built on stilts. These would be built to the size of a barrack, so that they could later be converted to floors of the barrack. This was done and we were thus able to accommodate two Divisions worth of troops - one Division, in Gangtok and beyond; and another, earmarked for the defence of Bhutan (according to agreement,

Accompanying the Governor of West Bengal, Ms. Padmaji Naidu, on a visit to the forward area. The Author is in the driver's seat.

John Kenneth Galbraith, US Ambassador to India, with the Author at a forward area after the 1962 war. Standing in the middle is the driver.

troops could enter Bhutan only when the threat to its security was imminent from the north) - in the plains of Binaguri. As regards the latter, a complete Cantonment was built, as Operational Task, at Binaguri. It was later discovered that the Teesta river was subject to spate, and that the road to Gangtok and Lungthu, the two areas in which troops were deployed for the defence of Sikkim, could not be depended upon in the rainy season, and winter rains were due. So I sent for my intrepid Chief Engineer - Colonel Kochhar - and asked him to plan the building of a road from Binaguri to Algara, on the way to Lungthu, and beyond to Gangtok, and to let me have an estimate of the time required for the purpose. He came to me with an estimate of six months. Since the winter rainy season was due soon, I gave him six weeks and informed him that I proposed to travel on the new road in a jeep in six weeks time. 'Bhalloo' demurred a bit, but put himself to the task, and lo and behold, the road was ready in six weeks. He met me at the appointed time, on the road, with the usual sweets in hand. 'Bhalloo', as my Chief Engineer, did me and the Corps proud in many ways, and I had full confidence in his ability to perform. This Binaguri-Algara bypass came in handy during the ensuing winter rains, as the road running along the west bank of the Teesta river was totally washed away. Thanks to this bypass we were able to maintain constant contact with our troops at Gangtok and beyond.

Our occupation of the quarters of the University of Bagdogra, mentioned earlier, did not in any way jeopardise our relations with the Governor of West Bengal, Miss Padmaji Naidu. She was very kind and considerate to the troops, and helpful in many ways. She often visited the troops in the forward areas, and always had encouraging words for each one of them. She was kind enough to give my family and I the use of a bungalow within the compound of the Governor's residence in Darjeeling. She was also a very fine orator in English as I discovered when I accompanied her on her many visits.

On the 20th of December, 1962, the Chinese declared a unilateral cease-fire, to suit their convenience as their line of communication to Tibet, which served as their base, was getting clogged with snow. India, no doubt, heaved a sigh of relief! Soon, the Indian Parliament met in a special session, and discussions there led to the ouster of Krishna Menon, the Defence Minister, and sounded a death-knell for Pandit Nehru, who died of a stroke in June, 1963.

Biji Kaul, realising that the troops blamed him squarely for their misfortune and could not be appeased, resigned from his post as General Officer Commanding 4 Corps and went on to retire in Delhi. General Manekshaw took his place.

In June 1964, there was a rumour among officers of the Corps that I was due to be posted as Army Commander, Eastern Command, to Calcutta. This soon changed to Western Command, at Simla. The reason for this change, I was told later, was that the Defence Ministry suspected that the Chief of the Army Staff, General Chowdhary, and the Army Commander, Western Command, Lt Gen Manekshaw, his buddy, were conniving together to perform a coup against the Government!

Area & Corps Commanders of Western Command.

39
ARMY COMMANDER WESTERN COMMAND

On the way to Simla, I called on the Chief of the Army Staff, at his office in Delhi. Over a cup of tea, General Chowdhary mentioned that I had been specially selected to fill this post, despite my being too young for the job. I drew his attention to the age at which he had become Army Commander, but he replied that his was a special case as he had had an extraordinarily brilliant career. From that moment on, I was destined not to see eye-to-eye with him, but more of that later.

At Simla, the Chief of Staff, Western Command, was Major General Joginder Singh, who had been a great favourite of the earlier Army Commander. He was a typical ranker, who would get his superior commander under his thumb, for some reason or the other, and then become all in all in the set-up. During a briefing of the operational tasks given to Western Command, I did not agree with the instructions lately issued by Headquarters Western Command (obviously with his stamp of approval on them) and wished to change them. The Chief of Staff did not like this; so, I took it upon myself to draft a new set of

Operational Instructions. From then on, I lost all confidence in his tactical judgement and hardly ever consulted him on operational matters. He seems to have held this against me as is evident in a book he later wrote on retirement. I did not bother to reply to his allegations, but my ADC at the time, Captain Amarinder Singh, the present Maharaja of Patiala, without even mentioning it to me wrote a rejoinder in the press, contradicting the statements made by Major General Joginder Singh in his book.

I have found that people like Major General Joginder Singh, when they fall foul of their immediate Commanders, work hard at cultivating good relations with those higher up and exploit such relationships. Major General Joginder Singh thus went out of his way to develop a close personal relationship with the then Chief of the Army Staff, General Chowdhary. At one stage in his book, he talks about a plan, that I am supposed to have ignored, that of taking up a position beyond the Ichhogil Canal. This amazes me as he never moved out of Ambala, nor asked to visit the front-line even once during the course of the 1965 Indo-Pak War. I spent most of my time during this War with the front-line troops, and had hardly any time to come back to the Main Headquarters at Ambala. In my absence I expected my Chief of Staff to hold the fort for me, and especially, to preside over the Army-Air Force Close Support Organisation at the Command Main Headquarters. But he failed me in this also. I later learned that he connived with the Chief of the Army Staff, without my consent, to move fighter planes, from the forward airfields to the rear, with the result that there was no close air support for the forward troops. I sent numerous messages to him, through my ADC, on the Rear-Net, but he took no action on them. And I, in turn, could not give an answer to our forward troops who were crying for air support, and who were wondering why our close air support was not functioning. Nor could the Forward Formations, because of this deficiency get any aerial photographs so necessary for operations. We were even denied the benefits of early-morning Tactical Reconnaissance from the aircraft. I hold my Chief of Staff, Major General Joginder Singh, squarely and personally responsible for this deficiency.

The Author's wife with His Holiness the Dalai Lama at a meeting of 'Save the Children's Fund' in Simla in 1965.

The Author welcoming the President of India, Dr S Radhakrishnan to Simla.

The Author watching cricket with Kanwar Dalip Singh (former Chief Justice of Punjab) & Mr YB Chavan, Defence Minister, at Simla.

The Author playing golf at Naldera with Generals 'Jungu' Sataravala, Ooni Candeth, P Kumaramangalam, PS Bhagat and others.

Social Life in Simla

In early 1965, when I was Army Commander, Western Command, in Simla, my wife and I came across an organisation called 'Save the Children's Fund'. It was a British organisation, headed by a retired Colonel. The organisation was looking after the welfare and education of displaced Tibetan children, and my wife and I tried to help them as much as we could. Thus, we became quite friendly with the British Colonel and his staff. Once they invited His Holiness, the Dalai Lama, to visit the children, and my wife and I were lucky to have an audience with His Holiness face to face. It was an experience never to be forgotten. The Dalai Lama looked so pious, serene and dedicated to the cause of Tibet. We were happy to be photographed with him in a group and these pictures are now our prized possessions.

The Advanced Studies Institute lodged in the old Viceregal Lodge in Simla (what a beautiful building!) was inaugurated that year by the President of India, Dr S Radhakrishnan. My wife and I were invited to the ceremony, and we shall never forget the inaugural address given by our President. It was so well thought out and delivered. Doctor Niharanjan Roy, a brilliant scholar, was the Institute's first Director, and we became quite friendly with him. There were many other scholars, carrying out research in the new Institute, and we had the pleasure of meeting them over time.

The other dignitaries in town were, first and foremost, Kanwar and Kanwarani Dalip Singh. Kanwar Dalip Singh had at one time been the Chief Justice of Punjab. We were also on friendly terms with the three successive Governors of Himachal Pradesh, Mr Bhagwan Sahai, Lt Gen Bahadur Singh and Mr Vishwanathan, as well as with Mr Parmar, Chief Minister of the State and his elder brother. They and their families made our stay in Simla very pleasant and enjoyable indeed.

The Beginning of the 1965 Indo-Pak War

The Indo-Pakistan War of 1965, I think, was the greatest event in my service life. It provided an opportunity to me to utilise all my prowess and skill, single-handedly, in a war, without any interference from the top, except for occasional hindrances here and there caused by the Chief of the Army Staff. These did not, however, bother me as I was clear in my mind, as to what was required of me, and that I was doing the right thing.

Readers may be interested to know, that the Chief of the Army Staff, throughout the duration of the War, visited my Main Headquarters, only thrice, that is on the 10th, 14th and the 20th of September 1965, and that too in Ambala, at least a hundred miles from the Front, with a covey of fighters to protect his aircraft against a negligible air-threat. I requested him, many a times, to come to Raja Sahansi Airfield, near the Front, but he refused to do so, considering it to be too dangerous. Yet, he was the first one to have his photograph taken on the Ichhogil Canal, early morning, on the 23rd of September, after the cease-fire, and had it published in the press!

The 1965 War with Pakistan though short and limited was nevertheless, packed with intense activity and heavy fighting. I had been fortunate to have served, since 1947, in various command and principal staff appointments in Western Command and had seen the evolution of successive plans as the build up of armies progressed on both sides. This gave me an insight into the problems of the theatre seldom available to a Commander.

Military confrontation with Pakistan started as far back as October 1947 when Pakistan, in spite of a Standstill Agreement with the Maharaja of Kashmir, let loose into his State thousands of tribesmen from its North-Western Frontier, led and guided by officers from the Pakistan regular Army. They were joined by the Muslim element of the Jammu and Kashmir State Forces who were on border duty and who turned against their erstwhile comrades as soon as the invasion started, on 22nd October 1947. The object of the Raiders was to occupy the State by force.

By the 26th of October, the Raiders had captured and ransacked Baramula, only 32 miles from Srinagar, on the Rawalpindi-Srinagar road, and were preparing to enter the Valley of Kashmir with the airfield and the town of Srinagar as their initial objectives. Concurrently, Mr Jinnah was celebrating the victory at Rawalpindi and was getting ready to drive into Srinagar and proclaim the State of Jammu and Kashmir part of Pakistan. It was on this fateful day that the Maharaja of Kashmir signed the Instrument of Accession to India and a decision was taken by the Government of India to despatch the Indian Army to the Valley to contain the Raiders. Early the next morning, a hurriedly assembled battalion, First Battalion of the Sikh Regiment, started landing on the 'kacha' airstrip of Srinagar Airfield and a column was despatched towards Baramula to stem the advance of the Raiders as far away from the town of Srinagar as possible.

Along with this advance towards the Valley, an invasion by paramilitary forces, backed by Pakistan, had also started along the entire border of the State. The story of the Indian Army operations to checkmate this invasion is a long and complex one and has been mentioned in an earlier chapter of this book. Suffice it to say that by the time the cease-fire was declared, through the intervention of the United Nations Organisation, we were holding the so-called cease-fire line. This was followed by years of parleys between India and Pakistan through the good offices of the United Nations Organisation, but there was no satisfactory conclusion. In the meanwhile, partial peace was maintained by the United Nations Observers stationed on both sides of the cease-fire line, without much change in the hostile attitude of the two armies that faced each other.

With the induction of military aid to Pakistan, given by the United States of America, the equivalent of four Divisions worth, not only was Pakistan able to modernise its army, but it was also able to modernise the equipment of its so-called Azad Kashmir Forces in the occupied portion of Jammu and Kashmir. In addition, it raised a large number of para-military forces in the form of Muhajirs and Razakars. This was done with the object of settling scores with India sometime or the other. The infiltration campaign was inaugurated by Pakistan in the year 1965, with a series of cease-fire violations, the intensity of which gave a new twist to the prevailing uneasy truce. As the year progressed the number of cease-fire violations shot up alarmingly. Almost simultaneously, in February 1965, Pakistan launched an unprovoked attack in the area of the Rann of Kutch with its regular forces, equipped with American arms. This was clearly a part of Pakistan's Master Plan to later seize Jammu and Kashmir by force through a large scale infiltration across the cease-fire line. The idea was to induce the Indian forces to get entangled in the Rann of Kutch, where they would be on a limb, so to speak, and this would give a free hand to Pakistan's nefarious designs on Jammu and Kashmir. I am glad to say that the powers that be resisted the temptation and very few troops were committed in that strategically unfavourable area of Kutch and a major portion of the Indian Army was subsequently available to frustrate Pakistan's misadventure in Jammu and Kashmir.

India's reaction to the Rann of Kutch episode, was to concentrate its regular forces opposite the Punjab border, which compelled Pakistan to do likewise, and it had to agree to accept a settlement of the Kutch affair. Pakistan was keen that the confrontation between the two regular forces along the Punjab border should be settled, so that it could go ahead with its Master Plan in Jammu and Kashmir. The regular forces of both the countries withdrew from their respective border areas in the Punjab in early July 1965, and on the 5th of August 1965, Pakistan launched its infiltration campaign into Jammu and Kashmir.

Although intelligence reports from across the cease-fire line had given indications, from time to time, of the raising and equipping of para-military forces in Pakistan Occupied Kashmir, no clear assessment of Pakistan's intention to launch a large scale infiltration campaign into Jammu and Kashmir was ever made by our intelligence agencies. Therefore, the presence of large batches of infiltrators on the home side of the cease-fire line on the evening of the 5th of August 1965, was a surprise. This is not to say that we were caught off guard, for there had been an increase in the intensity of firing across the cease-fire line, and small raiding parties had been sent into our territory, for carrying out sabotage and spreading consternation amongst the local population, since the beginning of the year. This had sufficiently alerted us and we were ready to meet any emergency.

It is now possible to tell, from hind-sight, that Pakistani infiltrators entered the State across the cease-fire line at several points along the periphery simultaneously, so as to create an all pervading law and order situation for the civil administration of the State. The intention was also to pin down the Indian military and para-military forces earmarked for the security of the cease-fire line, all long the periphery, as also scatter any reserves of such forces that might have been kept centrally located. In addition, especially trained agents and saboteurs entered Jammu and Kashmir for mass scale subversive activities. The infiltrators were equipped with Pakistani arms, and fully briefed and rehearsed, in their various missions, which consisted of destruction of bridges and ambushing of vehicle-convoys, with a view to disrupting the lines of communication; raids on military headquarters, civilian installations and administrative centres; distribution of arms and ammunition to local civilians, across the cease-fire line, and enrolling them as Razakars; creating situations which would result in paralysing the Jammu and Kashmir administration and would encourage an open rebellion in the State.

While the State was to be thrown into utter disorder and lawlessness by these measures, a strong task force of infiltrators, which had its base in the Hajipir salient, was to make its way to the town of Srinagar, so as to mingle, unnoticed, with thousands of people due to congregate in the town to celebrate the festival of Pir Dastgir Sahib on the 8th of October 1965. The next day, which coincided with the anniversary of the first arrest of Sheikh Abdullah, in memory of which the Action Committee of the Plebiscite Front had arranged a procession in the capital, the raiders proposed to sneak into the procession, fully armed, stage an armed revolt and capture important installations such as, the radio station, the telegraph and telephone offices, the police headquarters, and so on, in Srinagar, as well as the seat of the Government in Jammu and Kashmir. This done, they planned to constitute a 'Revolutionary Government'; proclaim it as a lawful government and broadcast an appeal for recognition and assistance from all countries, especially Pakistan. This was to be the signal for Pakistan's armed forces to walk into the State.

I shall not trace the course of events as they unfolded as a result of this infiltration, but shall restrict myself to say that in a contingency of this nature, rather than chase each and every infiltration party, we had planned, as a counter measure, to capture, from both Uri and Punch directions, the base of the Hajipir salient, and in so doing not only hoped to neutralise the Pakistani main base of infiltration but also break physical contact between the infiltrating forces and Pakistan. Therefore, with this plan in view, as soon as vital areas and installations, in Jammu and Kashmir, were sufficiently secure against infiltrators, on the 25th of August 1965, we launched our two pronged attack on Hajipir Pass.

40
THE 1965 WAR WITH PAKISTAN

With the capture of Hajipir Pass, on the 28th of August, there was a distinct fall in the tempo of attacks launched by the infiltrators in the Valley, and Pakistan's nefarious designs were completely check-mated. This was later authenticated by Pakistan launching a desperate attack with its regular forces, equipped with American equipment, in the Chhamb Sector, on the 1st of September 1965. This was the beginning of a regular war with Pakistan.

The area of attack by Pakistan regular forces in Chhamb Sector was cleverly selected, because it was plain country wedged in by rough mountainous terrain on the west and had a formidable obstacle, river Chenab on the east. Therefore, Pakistan could use its armour and heavy artillery in this area, where as due to United Nations restrictions and a weak-bridge over the Chenab, at Akhnoor, we would be unable to induct our own armour and artillery into the area; it allowed the nearest distance to the bridge over the Chenab at Akhnoor, a vital bottleneck on our communications with Rajouri and Punch. Besides, from Akhnoor, operations could be developed towards Jammu and our lifeline to the Srinagar Valley could be completely blocked; the area lay at the junction of the cease-fire line and the international border, between the districts of Sialkot and Jammu. By crossing its armour over the international border, where the terrain was favourable, Pakistan could claim to have only violated the cease-fire line; the area was governed by the cease-fire agreement and we could station only limited forces there.

Therefore, on the early morning of the 1st of September, Pakistan launched a full scale attack in this area with a whole Infantry Division, with two Regiments of Tanks (Pattons), against a truncated Infantry Brigade. Initial success in such a case was inevitable.

Our answer to such an offensive, as I insisted, could only be a fullfledged assault across the international border in Punjab, so as to compel Pakistan to withdraw from the Akhnoor Sector.

Upon Pakistan launching its attack in the Chhamb Sector, on the 1st of September, the Chief of the Army Staff wanted me to meet it forward of Akhnoor, but I asked him to get me the Government's permission to cross the international border, towards Lahore. The Chief was hesitant. I, however, insisted on it, saying that if the Chief was not inclined to ask the Government, then I should be allowed to see the Prime Minister, Mr Shastri, to point out to him that the Government had announced over All India Radio that any attack across the ceasefire line in Jammu and Kashmir would be considered an attack on India. Eventually, on 3rd of September, I was given the 'go ahead' and I had 48 hours in which to launch the offensive across the border. During the three days, since Pakistan's attack in the Chhamb Sector, I had not been sitting idle. In order to dupe the enemy into thinking that we were going to meet his offensive forward of Akhnoor, I ordered the engineers to start repair activity on the Pathankot-Akhnoor road and to strengthen the bridges over the Jammu Tawi and over the river Chenab, just short of Akhnoor. Whether this 'engineered' activity had any effect on the Pakistani plans or not, it is difficult to say. But the fact is that our going across the international border, towards Lahore, took them completely by surprise.

At about 11 pm, on the night of the 3rd of September, Lt Gen Kumaramangalam, the Deputy Chief of the Army Staff, rang me up on the secret telephone, to say that General Officer Commanding XV Corps had been on line from Udhampur to the Chief of the Army Staff,

General Chowdhary, and wanted my permission to withdraw 41 Mountain Brigade, engaged, at the time, with the Pakistanis in the Jaurian position, during the night. Now I must explain, that the General Officer Commanding XV Corps, Lt Gen Kashmir Katoch, was a great favourite of General Chowdhary and used to ring him up directly, which as Army Commander I did not like. Therefore, I questioned Kumaramangalam as to what business my Corps Commander had to ring up the Chief directly? If my Corps Commander was seeking my permission, he should ring me up directly. After saying this I put down the telephone. Within a minute, I got a telephone call from Kashmir Katoch, whom I knew quite well, and he repeated his request. First of all, I took him to task for ringing up General Chowdhary directly over an operational matter, and then discussed with him his suggestion of withdrawing the Brigade, actively involved with the enemy, that very night. "Was it feasible?" I asked. In the end, I decided that the Brigade would stay where it was, and that I would arrive at Jammu Airfield at nine o'clock the next morning, and that he should be ready to accompany me to Akhnoor, in a helicopter.

As an aside, I might mention here, the close call I had on the home front soon after this telephone conversation on the 'Ulta' telephone, which directly connected me to the Chief of the Army Staff. My wife and I had been sleeping in the same room, in our Simla house, and just as I got up from bed to answer the phone, she had given a couple of hearty sneezes, obviously a precursor to a cold. I, immediately, decided to shift my bed to another room, to escape catching it - and that's what saved me. For not only was it a common cold, but in the days that followed it was diagnosed as German measles, which is extremely contagious. It would have been difficult for me to explain why I had fallen sick at that time. People would have indulged in all kinds of speculations. Thank God I took some timely action and saved myself acute embarrassment!

I arrived at Jammu exactly at 9 am and flew with the Corps Commander to Akhnoor. There we met Major General Chopra, Commander 10 Division, who reported that all was well with the Mountain Brigade at Jaurian. I asked him to ring up the Brigade Commander ('Bhaiya' Rajwade), whom I knew quite well, and to tell him that I had arrived and that he would get his orders for withdrawal by 2 o'clock that afternoon, from his Divisional Commander. I also asked him to get the latest news about the Brigade. The reply was that all was well so far, but that the Pakistanis were making preparations for an attack on his forward Companies. I ordered him, through his Divisional Commander, to be prepared for a counter-attack with reserve companies, should the Pakistanis attack and succeed in overcoming his forward defences. Both the attack and the counter-attack happened, and by 12 noon the situation was restored. In the meanwhile, a message came from 39 Medium Battery of Artillery (this was part of a Sikh Battalion converted into a Medium Artillery Regiment and the message was meant for me as Colonel of the Sikh Regiment) that the personnel of the 161 Artillery Regiment, deployed next to them, had deserted en-mass, leaving their guns, with stacked ammunition, and wagon-line (vehicles) behind. They wanted them collected, lest they fall into enemy hands. Despite the desertion, they averred that the Medium Battery, in position, would continue to support the forward Brigade. Upon receipt of this message, I ordered the Divisional Commander, Major General Chopra, in the presence of his Corps Commander, to muster as much manpower and as many electrical mechanical engineers from his Division, as he could, and arrange to collect the guns, the ammunition and the vehicles. Having done so, he could then order 41 Mountain Brigade to withdraw that night. The orders for withdrawal were to get to the Brigade by 2 o'clock that afternoon, so that the Brigade Commander could plan his withdrawal properly. Thereafter, General Kashmir Katoch and I left Akhnoor, by the same helicopter in which we had come, and flew back to our respective Headquarters. The next morning, the 5th of September, my Chief of Staff was rung up by General Officer Commanding 10 Division to say that the Brigade had come back safely, with all its equipment and ammunition. But before congratulating the General Officer Commanding for this successful operation, I asked my Chief of Staff to check up from the General Officer Commanding if the guns had also been brought back. His reply that they could not be brought back made me furious. I ordered his Corps Commander to hold a Court of Inquiry for this lapse. As a result of this inquiry, General Chopra was sacked from his appointment.

By attacking across the international border of the Punjab, we had definitely achieved complete surprise on all fronts. Our plan of attack was quite simple. The idea was to advance up to the Ichhogil Canal (which had been built by Pakistan for the defence of Lahore), on a wide front of four axes and to capture the Canal from Ranian, in the North, Dograi on the GT Axis, Barki, on the Khalra Axis, and its termination opposite Ferozepore and turn it into a defence-line against Pakistan and thus save our troops for further operations. My idea was to keep the additional force, including the 1st Armoured Division, in the reserve for the first phase of the operations. And when the Ichhogil Canal was secured, to launch this force, including the Armoured Division, against Sialkot, crossing the river Ravi in the area of Nainakot, an area already in our hands. For this purpose, we had carried out an engineering reconnaissance of both banks of the river. We could even, in our own time, put up a temporary bridge over the Ravi, since the river was in Indian territory. But the Chief of the Army Staff had other plans, of which I had no idea. Unknown to me, he had formed another Corps, under the command of his favourite, PN Dunn (whom he promoted out of turn), and had launched it from the direction of Samba, leaving me in the Punjab without any reserves during my offensive towards the Ichhogil Canal! It was bad planning, but there was little I could do for it would have meant going against the wishes of the Chief.

However, the surprise on the Punjab fronts was so complete that we had almost free-sailing until 10 am of the 6th of September, the day of the attack. After 10 am, the Pakistani Mass-Artillery, which was till then sojourning in the Lahore Cantonment, was hurriedly deployed in a pre-prepared position, just behind the Resin Factory, on the GT road, towards Lahore on the Ichhogil Canal. They fired their first salvo against 1 Jat, which had just that morning secured the bridge at Bhaini Dhilwan (near Ichhogil Utter) in the Ranian Sector. The truth is that after the capture of the objective, having faced no opposition, the Jats became lax and sent for their Mess truck and started having their breakfast in the open. The Pakistan Mass-Artillery hit the area where the officers were having their breakfast and the Battalion, consequently, scattered running helter-skelter! There is an object lesson in this: that before a war, the officers and Other Ranks must be put through 'Battle Innoculation' and should be generally oriented to battlefield conditions, however easy the victory might be.

As a consequence of this, it took two more attacks, by different battalions, and heavy casualties, before the objective, the bridge over the Ichhogil Canal, could be regained.

The Mass-Artillery of the enemy, then took on Dera Baba Nanak and caused a break-through over the bridge, by armour and some infantry; and later still, concentrated its fire power against 15 Infantry Division position on the GT Axis. But, until mid-day of the 6th of September, all that was opposing 15 Infantry Division on the GT Axis, was just a company of the enemy's Reconnaissance and Support Battalion, which had been sent ahead to oppose the Indian Offensive. This Reconnaissance and Support Battalion had been introduced into the Pakistan Army by the Americans, at the scale of one per Corps. It was fully mounted on jeeps, armed with formidable firepower: 12 Recoilless guns and 12 Medium Machine Guns per Company. A Company came up to the Canal and started firing aimlessly and this is what made Niranjan Prasad believe that he was being counter-attacked by 'two Divisions', as conveyed in his message.

I was pleading all the time that an offensive, across the international border, towards Lahore, would compel the Pakistanis to pull back their Pattons from the Chhamb Sector. This was confirmed by a message sent by the Pakistan Army and picked up on the morning of our offensive. Another ruse I played to lull the enemy was not to move my Headquarters down to Ambala till the afternoon of the 5th of September. What is more, I accepted, and asked my senior Staff Officers to accept, an invitation to lunch, at Kanwar Dalip Singh's house, in Simla, on the 5th of September, just a day before the offensive started. That afternoon, I had a helicopter waiting for me at Anandale, Simla, which flew me, after lunch, to Jalandhar, where I had arranged to pick up General Officer Commanding XI Corps, Lt Gen Joginder Singh Dhillon, before proceeding to Amritsar to see the various formations going into the attack. Besides, I had requested Mr Ashwani Kumar (Senior Superintendent of Police, Amritsar) and the local Deputy Commissioner to meet me at Tactical Headquarters of 15 Division, on the GT Axis, at midnight of the 5th, as I had something important to tell them, and that's when I broke the news of our attack across the international border, for the first time, to the civilian Government of Punjab.

On our way to Amritsar, the Corps Commander and I met military convoys of vehicles, both army and civil (we had requisitioned thousands of civilian trucks to make up for our deficiency of vehicles in the army), moving along the GT Road smoothly, and without lights, as ordered, and well to the left of the road, keeping their stipulated distance between vehicles. The orders for them were not to cross the line of the river Beas, before it was dark. At about 11 o'clock that night, we arrived at Tactical Headquarters of 15 Division. There, both of us, listened to the plan of attack of the Divisional Commander, Major General Niranjan Prasad, as he explained it on the map. Later, at midnight, I saw both Ashwani Kumar and the Deputy Commissioner and asked them to announce in the streets of Amritsar that we were going on the offensive against Pakistan and that people were not to panic if they hear thuds or saw fire. I also requested them to keep the local jail half empty so as to accommodate any civilians that we might capture. Lastly, I asked them not to allow any civilian vehicles to leave Amritsar by road, as we needed the road free for military traffic.

From there, we went down the road, first to 7 Infantry Division (Major General Kishan Sibal), on the Kalra Axis, and then to 4 Mountain Division (Major General Gurbakhsh Singh) and found them both ready to go into the offensive at 4 o'clock on the morning of the 6th of September. At the 7 Infantry Division front, at Kalra, I looked through my binoculars (there was moonlight) and saw Pakistan Rangers sleeping in their mosquito-nets, oblivious of the fate that awaited them in the next two hours. By 3 o'clock in the morning, both General Dhillon and I, were back at the forward Corps Headquarters, at Raya, and I requested every one not to disturb me till 6 am, come what may, as I had busy nights ahead and needed some sleep. Punctually at 6 am, I was told that our assault had gone on well on all fronts. Soon, the Corps Commander and I drove up to the XI Corps Tactical Headquarters, which was nearer the Front. There, a map of the whole area was displayed on an easel, and the Brigadier General Staff of the Corps, Brigadier Parkash Singh Grewal, was manning, in a trench, the Forward Wireless link to the various Divisions.

Here we listened, over a small dry-battery wireless set, to the broadcast made to the nation by Field Marshal Ayub Khan, the President of Pakistan. He seemed to be terribly nervous and was

A Soldier Remembers

stammering. The gist of what he said was that the die had been cast; that India would get what it had asked for; that it would be a cakewalk to Delhi and that he had declared war on India! Just after 12 noon, Brigadier Parkash brought a wireless message from General Officer Commanding 15 Division, on the GT Axis, where initially there had been reports that their leading Brigade had crossed the Ichhogil Canal. He said that his Division had been attacked by two Divisions of the Pakistani Army and that his leading Brigade had withdrawn to Gosal Dial, 7 miles behind the Ichhogil Canal; his flanks were exposed and, therefore, he had decided to withdraw behind the border. I was stunned to receive this message and asked Brigadier Parkash to let the General Officer Commanding 15 Division know that he would not move back an inch from where he was, and that I and the Corps Commander were coming to meet him. I drove the Jonga in which we travelled. It was not long before we saw the havoc that the enemy air had caused on the GT Road. Vehicles were burning here and there, while there were craters on the road, and enemy aircraft were still flying over head. We saw 15 Division Administrative Echelon vehicles abandoned on the road, the drivers having run away, leaving some of the engines still running. We saw an armoured carrier standing in the middle of the road, with its keys still in it. I had it removed off the road. We were directed by the Divisional Military Police to the General Officer Commanding, Major General Niranjan Prasad, who was hiding in a recently irrigated sugarcane field! He came out to receive us, with his boots covered with wet-mud. He had no head-cover, nor was he wearing any badges of rank. He had stubble on his face, not having shaved, contrary to the custom before the start of an operation. Seeing him in such a state, the first question I asked him was whether he was the General Officer Commanding a Division or a coolie? Why had he removed his badges of rank and not shaved, I asked? Of course, he had no answer. We were standing in the open, and, naturally, the men of his Headquarters had formed a circle around us, though at a distance. At one stage a couple of enemy fighter planes flew over head, strafing vehicles on the road, and Niranjan Prasad tried to pull me to safety under the cover of a bush nearby. I had to shout at him to explain that the enemy aircraft were not interested in us, nor could they see us. What they were after were his vehicles that had been abandoned on the road, head-to-tail. I asked him where his reserve Brigade Commander was. He shouted: "Pathak, Pathak" and Pathak came to us, his face as white as a sheet. I asked him where his men (F Group) were, and he answered that they were following, but they were inoperative, because they had suffered very heavy casualties from enemy aircraft. I, naturally, asked him how many casualties they had suffered, and he replied, "Nearly 30 wounded". I said, "30 out of 4000 (the strength of his Brigade) and you say your Brigade was inoperative!" I asked him to pull himself together and then gave him his orders, on the map and on the ground, for the next phase of his advance. He was to take his Brigade along the distributory, shown on the map, and on reaching the Ichhogil Canal, to turn left and re-capture the bridge on the GT Road near Dograi. In order to give his Divisional Commander another chance, I asked Niranjan Prasad to "keep an eye on his Brigade, and report to his Corps Commander, in the morning, regarding the progress of the operations".

I had known Niranjan Prasad for a long time. He had already, on two occasions, acquitted himself badly while commanding a Division. The first time was in NEFA and then later, while commanding 25 Infantry Division, at Rajouri. I was also aware that each time he had written a representation against his senior Commanders. I had found him deficient in command of 15 Infantry Division as early as June that year, and had said as much to General Chowdhary when he visited XI Corps during an Exercise. But the Chief chose to disregard my suggestion for according to him Niranjan Prasad had very close political connections with higher-ups in Delhi! So, this time, sensing that I might remove him from command, General Niranjan Prasad had apparently already written out a representation against me in his note book which he kept in his brief case along with some other secret and confidential papers. I now state what was revealed in a Court of Inquiry which General Officer Commanding XI Corps ordered, to go into the circumstances that prevented General Niranjan Prasad from visiting his Reserve Brigade, under Brigadier Pathak, who had been ordered by me to carry out a certain operation, which Niranjan Prasad had been ordered to supervise. The story goes, that on the morning of the 7th of September, Niranjan Prasad sent for an officer to lead him to the Brigade's position, and set off towards it along the distributory, which was marked on the map. He was in the Jonga in front, with his ADC, while two jeeps, with his escort in them, were following him. As he progressed along the distributory, he was fired at by a distant Medium Machine Gun. Both he and his ADC abandoned the Jonga and took cover in a field of crops nearby, as did the escorts. A little later, Niranjan Prasad decided to return to his Headquarters and asked that the last jeep be turned around for this purpose. Both he and his ADC took off in this jeep, leaving the escort to make their way back on foot. Thus he left the brief-case he was carrying, with all the papers in it in the Jonga, which apparently also had his formation flag and star plates on it. This Jonga, along with his brief-case (and papers) was subsequently captured by the Pakistanis, who started broadcasting the contents of his brief-case, including his representation against me over the air! On the basis of the proceedings of the Court of Inquiry, General Officer Commanding XI Corps wanted to try Niranjan Prasad by a Court Martial, but the Chief of the Army Staff, General Chowdhary, sent for Major General Niranjan Prasad, and, we later learnt, asked him to resign.

After the altercation with General Officer Commanding 15 Division and the despatch of his Reserve Brigade to regain the ground lost, peace prevailed in the area. On the return journey, with General Dhillon sitting next to me in the Jonga, while I drove, I remember turning to him and remarking that it was the hand of God that had sorted out everything! And he agreed. Soon, we saw a vehicle proceeding towards Lahore with a European couple sitting in it. I thought it was odd that the vehicle had been allowed to cross the Divisional Barrier, put up just adjacent to the 15 Division Main Headquarters on the GT Road. So I turned my Jonga around and speeded behind this civilian car. Eventually, I caught up with it, and pushing my Jonga ahead of the car, blocked its path. I then got down and asked the gentleman what he was doing there. He said he belonged to the Swiss Embassy in Delhi, and that he was going to Lahore to spend some time with his friends there. I told him firmly that he could not go by road, and that if he and his wife wished to spend some time with their friends in Lahore, they would have to go there by air. Seeing his hesitation, I pulled out my revolver and asked him to turn back and travel ahead of me. The couple was, indeed, puzzled, but all the same turned their vehicle back. On reaching the Divisional Headquarters barrier, I questioned the Police Havildar in-charge as to why he had permitted a civilian vehicle to go through? He had no answer. The civilian vehicle, I noticed, was now well ahead of us.

After crossing the Barrier, I turned into the 15 Division Main Headquarters, as the stupidity of the message I had received that morning from General Officer Commanding 15 Division was still rankling with me and I wished to warn the GSO 1 of the Division not to let such a senseless message go through. The statements made, namely, "Two Pakistani Divisions are attacking me", "both my flanks are threatened" were totally inaccurate, as we had ascertained, while the belief that safety lay in "withdrawing behind the border" was simply ridiculous. There is no border behind which one can withdraw to safety in a war.

At Amritsar, we met crowds of people excited over the fighting that was going on in the air between our fighter aircraft and those of the Pakistani side. I warned them not to let any civilian car go through to the Front, and mentioned that the war was going in our favour; which raised their enthusiasm even further. As I was telling General Dhillon about the Japanese motor cyclists, in the Second World War in Malaya, who would come hundreds of miles into your territory, undetected, by lowering their hats over their eyes and following one of our own vehicles, we suddenly spotted a motor-cyclist, in uniform, heading towards Beas. I decided to stop him and ask him for his identity. He said he was Captain Grover, a Gunner, who had been on leave and who had heard about the war with Pakistan over the radio, and was now rushing back to join his Artillery unit. He wanted to know where he could find it! I referred him to a Military Police-Post, a few miles ahead, which would help him locate his Unit. I would like to mention here the case of a Commanding Officer of one of the Gorkha battalions, who, again on his own volition, returned to his Gorkha Battalion, deployed on the GT Axis, from leave which he was spending in the United Kingdom. He had heard of the War between India and Pakistan, and wanted to return to his Unit, to resume command. I still remember his name: Lt Col Tugnait. He, if I am not mistaken, was a heavyweight boxing champion of the Indian Army. His return had such a salutary effect on his battalion that not a single man deserted afterwards. I, as Army

Commander, in the field at the time, owed him a debt of gratitude, for having acted as a true soldier. Yet another example of a patriotic son of India returning to his call of duty, without being asked to do so, was that of Captain Amarinder Singh, the son of the then Maharaja of Patiala, Yadavendra Singh. He returned, after having been discharged from the Army, on the advice of his father. However, there were a good number of officers on leave, who upon being sent a telegram to return, did not do so. Also, during the early stages of the Operation, there were a substantial number of troops who deserted from battalions that had weak or officiating commanding officers. As a result, I had to give our tanks, which were already in the rear, orders to shoot at men trying to escape in twos and threes through the fields of cotton and fodder. This phenomenon was particularly common among the Gorkha battalions.

But now to return to the further sequence of events. Travelling on, we saw a Jonga, with Sahib Singh Kalah in it, coming from the opposite direction. He had a very important message for us. The Brigade Commander at Dera Baba Nanak had rung up to say that a couple of squadrons of AMX tanks of the enemy, with some Infantry, had rushed through the bridge, which, incidentally, was supposed to have been in our hands since the morning. Raya, Corps Tactical Headquarters, was not very far from there, and we decided to deal with the situation on arrival. The final information, as it transpired, was that only a few AMX tanks had broken through, and without any Infantry! The Brigade was told to counter-attack and recapture the bridge. This was done during the night and the enemy left their tanks in our hands and escaped across the river. A foolish move indeed!

This was not, however, to be the end of a very eventful day. I had hardly returned to my Main Headquarters, at Ambala, at about 11 pm when I learnt that Pakistan had played its ace card and dropped paratroopers. These were special service troops, with special equipment, supplied by America for the purpose of eliminating airfields. I must admit that we had not anticipated this. This was the ace card which Field Marshal Ayub Khan must have had up his sleeve and hoped to use, when he had declared that morning in his address to his countrymen that they would have a 'cake-walk' to Delhi. The paratroopers, it seemed, had been launched in a hurry, without much preparation, as they all dropped far away from their targets. There was not much action required on our part as they were suitably dealt with by the villagers near where they dropped. They were unable to cause any damage, as intended, to our Forward Fighter airfields at Pathankot, Adampur and Halwara. A little bit of shooting was reported in Halwara Airfield, between aircraft-pens, but that was a response out of sheer panic on the part of 'Lashkars', a civilian set-up, employed by the airfield for the protection of the parked aircraft.

There was no risk to the aeroplanes taking off from the airfield. And yet, out of fear, the Air Force authorities withdrew their Fighter Planes from the forward airfields at Pathankot, Adampur and Halwara, without my knowledge. I believe, that they got permission to do so from the Chief of the Army Staff, with the connivance of my Chief of Staff, Major General Joginder Singh. This greatly upset our communications and arrangements for close-air-support to the troops at the Front. Several calls from the Front had no effect on Major General Joginder Singh, who was supposed to be manning the Close-Air-Support Organisation at my Main Headquarters, at Ambala.

Air support to our troops fighting on the ground, from our fighter planes, which were taking off from Agra, and beyond, without any briefing by the Air-Contact teams, which had been left behind at the Forward Airfields, was, at its best, only spasmodic and ephemeral. The troops on the Front, who had to bear the brunt of enemy attacks from the air, complained bitterly about the absence of our planes. A situation that I found very difficult to explain. I, of course, kept on asking my Chief of Staff, through my ADC, the reason for this lack of air support, for I did not then know that our planes had been removed to Agra, and beyond, by the Air Force, without asking me. A most deplorable state of affairs, to say the least! The result was that during the critical period of early operations, the troops at the Front had no air-support, while Pakistani planes, taking off from Sargoda Airfield, pounded them mercilessly!

In the early hours of the morning of the 8th of September, I received a very alarming report, in the form of a hand-written letter, through a special courier officer, from General Officer Commanding, XI Corps, who had visited 4 Division on the afternoon of the 7th of September, 1965. Following is the text of the original letter:

CONFIDENTIAL

HQ XI Corps
C/0 56 APO

07 Sep 65

My dear Harbakhsh,

I visited 4 Mtn Div this afternoon from 1415 to 1615 hrs & met the GOC at his HQ. Most of the officers in the HQ and the GOC were wearing long faces. The troops I saw on my way to the HQ appeared slack and generally uninterested. On enquiry I came to know the following :

The strength of the six infantry has been reduced to an overall strength of about three and a half bns in 24 hours of action commencing 0400 hrs 6 Sep. This reduction was partially due to enemy action but mostly due to desertion.

The rot started with 13 Dogras, who without orders, left the position allotted to them without any enemy pressure except perhaps shelling. GOC 4 Mtn Div halted them as they were coming back. During night 6/7 Sep they all disappeared except the 5% and the CO's party. This rot quickly spread to other inf units.

4 Div have the following bns and units at present :

18 Raj Rif	1/9 GR
4 Grenadiers	9 J&K]
7 Grenadiers	13 Dogras

Of these only 4 Grenadiers & 1/9 GR are intact. I am told by the GOC that the CO of 9 J&K left his posn, without orders on the night of 6/7 Sep taking a coy of inf with him. 7 Grenadiers are only about two coy strong. 18 Raj Rif has about 10% deserters & the GOC thinks that this unit is cracking up. I am further given to understand by the GOC that deserters are restricted to inf units only & no other arm or service in the Div is affected.

Because of the above situation not a single task given to 4 Mtn Div in the current operations has been carried out. No bridge on the 1 GC in 4 Div sector has been blown. The GOC had to request the posn of the Div on the night of 6/7 Sep & again on the afternoon of 7 Sep. When I visited him today he was arranging the preparation of a def sector in the Asal Uttar area.

The morale of the Div being what it is, it is my considered view that any defences held by the present inf units in 4 Mtn Div cannot withstand even slight enemy pressure. This is a most serious situation in the present stage of the Operations.

I recommend :

That 4 Mtn Div be immediately replaced by some other fmn for carrying out the orders given to them.

Except for 4 Grenadiers and 9 GR, the four inf units of 4 Mtn Div as given in para 4 above should be disbanded.

I request that you pay a visit to this formation at your earliest convenience to see at first hand its state of morale & the competence of its commander.

It was a privilege & an honour to have you here on the epoch making day – 6 Sep 65.

With warm regards

Yours ever
Jogi

As can be seen from the letter, the General Officer Commanding XI Corps had recommended that the Division be replaced; and all its Infantry Units, except two, be disbanded. There was, of course, no question of doing this. And that's when I felt the necessity of having some reserves, which could have been availed of if the Chief of Staff had agreed to my suggestion of crossing the river Ravi, in our own territory, at Nianakot. Because of the Chief of the Army Staff's insistence, 1 Corps, the only reserve I could have counted on, had been deployed in the Sialkot area.

Upon receipt of this letter, the first thing I did, in the morning, was to proceed to 4 Division area. On arrival, I found that although the situation was pretty serious, it did not call for recourse to the recommendations made by the General Officer Commanding XI Corps. In any case, the change over of the formation, in close contact with the enemy, was clearly out of the question. We had no reserves available for this purpose, nor was it sound tactics to break contact with the enemy at this stage. I told the General Officer Commanding 4 Division that these things happen in war, but that so long as he was holding the Asal Uttar road-junction, there was nothing to fear. I enjoined him to strengthen that position as much as he could, by sowing mines in the maize and cotton fields around it, and to get the troops dug-down in trenches. If the Patton tanks were to attack at night, he had to just tell the men to keep their heads down in the trenches and let the tanks pass over them and then engage them from behind. He said he needed troop reinforcements; but there were none. I assured him that as long as he held the Asal Uttar road-junction the tanks could not stay for long in his position. He was to just not let their soft-vehicles, with petrol and ammunition, marry-up with them. I then visited Tactical Headquarters XI Corps, and told the General Officer Commanding, XI Corps, Lt Gen Dhillon, that I had visited 4 Division area, and that every thing was all right there, and that the General Officer Commanding there was sure that he was in control of the situation. I asked the General Officer Commanding XI Corps to flood the area in front of the Divisional dispositions, according to a plan already made by the Enginers, and suggested that 2 Armoured Brigade be made available to 4 Division at once. This was done the same night, and the Armoured Brigade, under the command of Brigadier Theog Raj, played a very distinguished role in defeating Pakistan's Ace Division of Pattons in the battle west of Dibipura the next morning, the 9th of September.

The reason for the 4 Division disaster was the fact that the leading Brigade, which had the Ichhogil Canal as its objective, stopped short of it, mistaking a small nullah, flowing short of the Canal, as its final objective and took up a defensive position on its near-bank. Through lack of knowledge, we did not know that the Pakistanis had built an under-canal passage (a siphon) for their tanks under the Ichhogil Canal. If the leading Brigade of 4 Division had reached its correct objective, the bridge on the Canal, they would have noticed the siphon, and would have had an opportunity to contest the passage of armour through it, and that of the Infantry and soft vehicles over the bridge. As it was, they stopped short of the Ichhogil Canal, and were, the same afternoon, attacked by an overwhelming force of Armour (Pattons) and Infantry, and dislodged from their position, resulting in panic and irregular retreat. It seems that the Pakistani forces used for this counter-attack, were also hustled into it, without the preliminaries so essential for such a counter-attack, and thus they met their Waterloo at Asal-Uttar.

Our offensive in the Sialkot Sector was launched on the evening of the 8th of September, and although it met with initial success, there was not enough time, before the cease-fire came into effect on midnight of the 22nd/23rd of September, for it to develop its operations fully. In the meanwhile, after having been battered in the Khem Karan Sector, Pakistan was able to transfer a major portion of what was left of it's Ace Armoured Division (Pattons) to oppose our forces in the Sialkot Sector.

When the cease-fire came into effect we had a distinct advantage over the enemy, and I have no doubt that if the hostilities had gone on we would have certainly shown more worthwhile results, and Pakistan would have had to eat humble pie!

The first and foremost lesson we learnt, as a result of the infiltration campaign launched by Pakistan, was that our intelligence set up had failed to measure up, in so far as they had been unable to give us any warning of the impending events. I am sure, this lesson will have been well learnt, and that our intelligence will in future come up to the mark.

On the morning of the 9th of September, when I was sitting in my Operations Room, and ruminating in my mind as to how to reinforce 4 Mountain Division in the Asal Uttar area, where, I felt, they were rather thin, my ADC, Captain Amarinder Singh, came in to say that a Major from 17 Sikh wished to pay his respects to me (I being Colonel of the Sikh Regiment). As the officer was ushered in, I asked him what he was doing there? And he replied that he had come to Ambala with an Advance Party of 17 Sikh, as Ambala was going to be their next station. I felt this was a godsend! I then asked him about the strength of his Advance Party, and its composition. He answered that it had two Officers, three JCOs and about 80 NCOs and Other Ranks. I welcomed the information and asked him to organise his personnel into a Company and to be ready to leave for the Front, to be under 4 Mountain Division at Asal Uttar. They were to be ready to leave by 1 pm in the mechanical transport that I was going to arrange. He saluted and left my office forthwith. The transport arrangements were finalised, and the 17 Sikh Company left for Asal Uttar punctually at 1 pm as planned. I had, in the meanwhile, informed Major General Gurbaksh Singh, Commander 4 Mountain Division, that this Company of 17 Sikh had been despatched to reinforce his position at Asal Uttar. He welcomed their arrival and put them right in the middle of his forces defending the road-junction at Asal Uttar.

For the night of the 9th/10th of September, and the next day, when 4 Mountain Division was hard pressed by the Pakistani Ace Armoured Division (with Patton tanks, that had night-vision sight), the Sikh Company (17 Sikh) played a stellar role, against the Pakistan armour, in the defence of Asal Uttar road-junction. For this, their battalion (then 17 Sikh) won the Battle-Honour of Asal Uttar - a unique distinction! By the evening of 10th September, the leading Company Group of Pakistan's Ace Armoured Division had been completely defeated, and some 26 officers and other ranks of Pakistan's 4 Cavalry surrendered voluntarily during the night of 10th/11th, including six Majors and the Commanding Officer of 4 Cavalry. They were taken as prisoners-of-war.

During this battle on the 10th of September, at about 2.30 pm, one of our Artillery Observation Posts picked up a wireless message from the enemy (it is to be remembered that Pakistan was using the same wireless sets as we had) to the effect that Pakistan's Divisional Commander was coming ahead, along the road, to find out what was delaying the Armour advance. Our side got ready to receive the party, and the General Officer Commanding and other Officers with him in the jeep, which was completely smashed, were either killed or wounded. The wounded General Officer Commanding Pakistan Division was taken away by the Pakistan Armour, while we picked from the area the body of the gunner officer with him, his Commander Artillery Brigade, Brigadier AR Shammi, along with his cap and personal diary. The next day when I was present in the area, and at my instance, his dead body was given a military funeral in the field. This was the battle in which Havildar Abdul Hamid of 4 Grenadiers won his Param Vir Chakra.

Late at night on the 9th of September, the Chief of the Army Staff, rang me up to say that he had read Corps Commander XI Corps' letter sent to me, and that his advice was that to save the whole Army from being cut off by Pakistan's Armour push, I should pull back to the line of the river Beas. I was aghast at this suggestion and said that since it was a tactical order, he had to come to the Front with me to give it, or else he had to issue an Operations Instruction, as is the custom in the Army. His reply was that I should stay put at my Headquarters till the next day as he was coming to see me. The next morning, at about 10 am, I went to meet the Chief at the airfield at Ambala, and was surprised to see that his aircraft had a fighter escort. I remarked on this to the Air Force Station Commander, pointing out that our forward troops were crying out for these aircraft every day. The Chief and I went straight into my Operations Room, and we had a very heated discussion. He got so excited at one stage that I suggested that I get him a bottle of beer from the Mess - as he was going to have lunch with us, in any case. He welcomed this, but I had already made it quite clear to him that if he wanted to give me a tactical order, then he would have to come to the Front with me, and only then would I decide whether I would carry it out or not. He left for Delhi by air after lunch and I left for my Operations Room, to follow the Divisional Battle with Pakistan's Armour.

Early on the morning of the 11th, I left in a jeep for the 4 Division area. I had a camouflage coat on, over my uniform, and was driving the jeep myself. Just beyond Bikhiwind, I noticed a couple of artillery vehicles, standing nose to tail and camouflaged with a net. They were loaded with artillery ammunition, and were on fire, having been strafed by the Pakistani planes, which were still flying overhead. As the ammunition was on fire, shells were exploding all round. I observed a few Sikh peasants hoeing the cotton-crop near by and decided to warn them of the danger they might face from exploding shells. After I delivered my warning, the eldest amongst them looked at me and said: "Sardar Sahib, you seem to be new to this place; for this happens every day here". He then asked me if I was a farmer's son. If I was, then I should know that the soil was just wet-enough for hoeing that day and that by tomorrow, it would be hard as stone. "Please do not worry about our safety; you do your work and we shall do ours," was his parting shot. I was wonder-struck at their attitude, and felt a sense of awe. I returned to my jeep, and a little further on saw a farmer pulling a 1000 lbs air-bomb (a dud it seemed) behind a pair of bullocks. Upon being questioned, he said that the Pakistanis had dropped this on his field, and since he needed to plough it, he was moving it near the road, where the Government, to whom the thing belonged, could take it away! As I watched, he unhitched the bomb and left it near the side of the road! While entering the village of Dibipura, where the battle with the enemy armour had taken place earlier, I noticed a few peasants sitting on charpoys in the courtyard of the village. I went up to them and they all stood up to receive me and offered me a seat, and would not sit down until I had. I asked them how they were still there considering the big battle that had been fought in their neighbourhood. They answered in unison, "How could we leave our village; yes, of course, we sent our families and children away, but there was no danger for us while your troops were next door to us." In fact, they had seen the entire battle that had been waged between opposing tanks from the roofs of their houses. There had been a lot of noise, but at no point had they felt personally threatened.

I bade farewell to them and went over to the Headquarters of the Cavalry Unit (Centurions) that had inflicted the most damage on the Patton tanks that had been ranged against them. I met their Commanding Officer, Lt Col Calif. He showed me the Patton tanks that they had captured intact and brought over to our side. The Sikh Dafedar who was showing me the Patton tanks and who later offered to give me a ride in one of them, was like a child with a new toy. He could not stop talking about the computer, the range-finder, the electrically movable turret, and so on, in the Patton tank. When I jokingly asked him how he had beaten such a formidable machine with his old Centurion, his reply was, "It is true, this tank, the Patton, is a Rolls Royce and my tank is a T-Ford. I might not have a computer or a range-finder in my tank, but my training in the Centurion has been such that I can hit a fly at a 1000 yards range, and these Pattons came out of a sugarcane field only at 500 yards range!" Consequently, he explained, he was able to put two shots into each one of the Patton tanks even before they could train their guns on him. And he was absolutely right. I have never seen so many tanks destroyed, lying there in the battlefield like abandoned toys. As I was walking through the fields and looking at these destroyed tanks, with Calif and many others behind me, a young man, dressed in civilian clothes – a pair of blue trousers, a blue-chequered shirt, with the top button open and a blue tie tied loosely around his neck (in the American style)–suddenly

Abandoned Patton tanks standing in the fields.

The Author, Gen Joginder Singh Dhillon & others standing next to a captured Patton tank.

The turret of a tank overlooks the Ichhogil Canal.

emerged from the crops, saluted me and said that as I seemed to be a very senior officer he had come to surrender as a prisoner-of-war. I asked him his name and he replied: Sawar Anwar-ul-Haq of 4 Horse, Pakistan Army. I then asked him why he was dressed as a civilian? He pointed to his tank standing near by and explained that since the leading tanks after being hit had caught fire, he had abandoned his tank fearing that the same fate awaited him. "And, as you know, Sir", he continued, "as a Muslim I did not want to burn to death, so I changed in the tank into civilian clothes hoping to escape. But since I find that I am surrounded on all sides, I have come to surrender." He further mentioned that the Pakistanis believed that we (Indians) had a certain 'Baba' (holy man) who had 'keeled' (consecrated) the shells in our tanks in such a manner that when they hit steel they burned right through it. The 'Baba', of course, was Bhabha, the Chairman of the Atomic Energy Commission! As I had no desire to change his belief, nor that of the rest of the Pakistanis, I kept this information to myself and instead all I said in reply was, "Oh, so this fact has also reached you?" On my return to Dibipura, after inspecting the battlefield, I saw that the Pakistani prisoner-of-war had become the centre of attention. There was a circle of men sitting around him and he was being fed with puries and tea. I pointed this out to Calif and asked: "Is this the way to treat a prisoner?" I asked that he be blind-folded and sent to the rear.

Later, the same morning I moved to Headquarters 4 Division. As it was quite obvious that the enemy's Ace Armoured Division had received a real bashing, I wished to exploit the situation by pursuing the defeated forces, by encircling Khem Karan. But Commander 4 Division had no fresh troops to do the job. I, therefore, asked General Officer Commanding 7 Division to spare 4 Sikh, which had the previous night captured Barki, and so 4 Sikh were placed under the command of 4 Division for these operations. I left it to the General Officer Commanding 4 Division to plan the operation. What was not realised at the time was the fact that 4 Sikh had, for the capture of Barki, spent the previous two nights without any sleep, and had, besides, suffered heavy casualties during the operation. But their Commanding Officer, Lt Col Anant Singh, whom I had sent for to ask if he could undertake this hazardous operation, was such a fine soldier that not even once did he raise the question of fatigue among his men, nor of the number of casualties that his battalion had already suffered. He, on the other hand, undertook the night operation planned by General Officer Commanding 4 Division on the same night, that is the 11th of September. As luck would have it, the next morning, while it was still dark, he and his battalion walked into enemy armour, taking it to be their own. There was, naturally, no news from the battalion, and General Officer Commanding 4 Division got worried and informed me. I rushed forthwith to 4 Division area, trying to get some news of the battalion. Eventually, in the afternoon, Captain Dalip Singh of the battalion appeared with some 40 men, who had managed to slip out of the enemy's grip. I gave these men assurances that nothing untoward had happened, as these situations often occur in a war, and cited examples from the Second World War to prove my point. I asked Dalip to take his men, along with other details that were left behind and concentrate at Bikhiwind, and re-raise 4 Sikh.

I was concerned about the re-raising of 4 Sikh Battalion, as I was Colonel of the Sikh Regiment. Therefore, on return to my Headquarters, rather late that evening, I rang up the Sikh Centre Commandant, at Meerut, and asked him to send as many reinforcements to 4 Sikh at Bikhiwind as he could, describing the situation there to him. As to who would be their Commanding Officer, my mind went to Lt Col Karnail Singh Sidhu, who, I knew, had once commanded 4 Sikh. Col Sidhu was at the time commanding our TA Battalion at Delhi, as he had suffered an injury to one of his legs, and had been categorised, by a Medical Board, as Category E, that is unfit for active service. I, however, rang him up in Delhi, and mentioned the dire straits in which 4 Sikh found themselves, and asked if he felt fit enough to take over command in the field. His reply was: "Of course!" So, I instructed him to take a jeep from his unit and take command of 4 Sikh at Bikhiwind, as soon as he could, and report to me directly, within 48 hours, as to whether 4 Sikh were ready for war again in every respect. I mentioned to him that I had already spoken to the Commandant of the Centre, and that he would be receiving reinforcements soon. Within two days, I received a call from Col Sidhu that 4 Sikh were ready for operations in all respects! I must mention here the name of Captain Shamsher Singh Minhas, who had been wounded in his thigh as Adjutant, 4 Sikh, in the Battle of Barki, but being the good Regimental soldier he was, had refused to be evacuated beyond the battalion Air-Post, as he wished to stay with the battalion. I asked Col Sidhu to appoint him (Captain Minhas) as his Second-in-Command in the battalion, in the rank of a Major. There is an aside to this. When the Chief of Army Staff came to know of this appointment made by me, he rang me up to object and said that I could promote him, but that he would not get the pay of a Major. My rejoinder was, "Over my dead body! Since he will be doing the job of a Major in the field, he must get his pay." I am happy to report that Major Minhas did get the pay of a Major.

While on this subject, I might mention, that at one stage in the War, a vacancy for the appointment of a Brigadier arose, and I asked Colonel Karnail Singh Sidhu, of 4 Sikh, to put on the badges of rank of a Brigadier, as I felt he was fit for the job in all respects, and ordered him to take over the Brigade. Once again the Chief of Army Staff raised an objection to this promotion, as the Selection Board had already rejected his case for promotion to the rank of Brigadier thrice. I pointed out to the Chief that this was war, and that I had found the officer fit in every way for the command of a brigade in the field. I added, that if he felt it was necessary, he could re-assemble the Promotion Board, and upon my recommendation from the field, pass him fit for a Brigadier's rank. I did not hear anything further about this.

What was particularly heartening about this War was the way in which the people of the country, especially the Punjabis, had risen as one. The whole province was electrified to a man. There were no reservations in offering help for the cause. On the second night of the War, the Pakistanis had, quite unexpectedly, dropped paratroopers to eliminate the forward airbases at Pathankot, Adampur and Halwara. Luckily for us, the paratroopers landed away from the airfields, and were thus unable to cause any damage to the aircraft. We did use limited force to deal with them, but the fact is that they were mostly dealt with by the local peasants, who went to the extent of bulldozing their ripening crops so as to weed them out.

It is also amazing what the power of self suggestion can do. The Air Commodore in-charge of the airfield at Ambala, reported to me, over the telephone, that he could see parachutes coming down to land on the east end of the landing strip, and claimed to be counting them as they descended, before his very eyes. His tally was fifteen and more. I found this hard to believe, as it made no sense. Why would paratroopers land so far away from the Pakistan border with no chance of escape? However, I instructed my Chief of Staff to arrange for two truck-loads of soldiers, and ask them to drive, with full lights on, along the airstrip to look for the parachutes. For, I was sure, the paratroopers were bound to leave their parachutes behind. The troops in the trucks scanned the whole airfield, but found no sign of a parachute, let alone of a paratrooper! It just goes to show how fear can make you imagine all sorts of things. The Air Commodore, who spoke to me on the telephone, had perhaps taken a few low clouds to be a group of descending parachutes!

To continue with the wonderful support we received from the public. We had to requisition some civilian trucks, from Punjab, to carry ammunition to the leading troops. They were required to dump the ammunition at the Frontline and return. But none of them wanted to leave the troops, and continued to stay, saying that if the troops could bear the bullets of the enemy, why couldn't they? They learnt road-discipline and how to camouflage their trucks and themselves. They were also very good at disposing of vehicle casualties – whether they be ours or the enemy's. Once I was visiting I Corps, when I saw a civilian truck, fully camouflaged, standing by. The driver of the truck, a civilian, was carrying the complete rear axle of a vehicle on his shoulders. When I enquired from him as to what he was doing, he mentioned that he had taken it out of an enemy vehicle, as it fitted his own, and he would keep it as a spare with him!

Bridges and culverts on the GT Road were guarded by villagers, and I remember, being stopped on the road, for purposes of identification, by NCC cadets at all odd hours. While the peasants did not give up performing their chores right up to the international border; boys and girls from the Punjab had set up stalls of milk, lassi, prasad and puries at every crossroad and would force troops going to the Front, or returning, to partake of their wares. If a vehicle carrying troops was in a hurry and could not stop, they would throw biscuits and fruit into it. Normally, I was always in a hurry and did not stop. Once, however when I was returning from the front, the girls formed a chain across the road by holding hands and forced me to stop my jeep. They insisted on serving my party and I puries and prasad on 'patals' (made of leaves). As I was eating, I saw a bus standing by, with some Pakistanis in uniform in it, they were being fed by the girls like every one else. The Pakistanis, the girls told me, were prisoners-of-war being taken back. I saw a JCO, with some men, obviously their escort, standing nearby. I signalled to the JCO to come and see me and asked him why the prisoners-of-war had not been blind-folded. He said that they had been, but that the girls had demanded that the bandages over their eyes be removed so that they could eat comfortably. I reminded the JCO of his responsibility and asked him to blind-fold them again before moving off. Such was the hospitality and fair-mindedness of the Punjabis!

Ambala, as my Main Headquarters, I felt, was too far behind from the Front, to enable me to control the battle as well as attend to my Headquarters. I had no choice but to leave the management of the Main Headquarters entirely in the hands of my Chief of Staff, Major General Joginder Singh, including the management of the Air-Support, as I was mostly busy conducting the battle from the front.

During the war, whenever I was in my Main Headquarters, at Ambala, I used to ring up my family who were in Simla. One day my wife mentioned that air-alarms had begun to sound very often in Simla, and with two school-going girls (my daughters) with her, what was she to do? I told her not to bother about these alarms as there was no danger of Simla being bombed by the Pakistanis, and asked her to let this be known to friends, should they ask. Once I visited my family in Simla, and there was a message waiting for me from the Loretto Convent (my children's school) that the 'Sister-General' wished to see me and would come to the house whenever I happened to come to Simla. My reply was, "Surely, 'Sister-General' cannot come to a Lieutenant General's house, I must go to her." So I rang up the Loretto Convent and fixed a visit with the 'Sister-General' at the Convent. When I arrived, tea had been arranged in the Convent parlour for me, and how beautifully clean every thing was - the room, the rug and the linen. The 'Sister-General' (an Irish woman) met me and wished to know if she should close down the school, because of the War with Pakistan, and send the girls home? I replied: "Nothing of the sort; there is no danger to the Convent, or Simla for that matter, from the Pakistanis. The school should continue as normal."

1 Corps was launched early on the morning of the 8th of September in the Sialkot Sector. The idea was to establish a 'bridge-head', by a Brigade of 14 Infantry Division, to serve as a spring-board for launching our main strike element - the 1st Armoured Division - with the object of capturing the bridge on the spill-channel (which supplied water to the Ichhogil Canal), behind Sialkot, as soon as possible. Simultaneously, 26 Infantry Division were to attack Sialkot town frontally, so as to engage the Sialkot defences, and protect the right flank of the Armoured Division's advances, while 14 Infantry Division were to capture Zafarwal. 1 Armoured Division broke-out of the bridge-head punctually at 6 am on the 8th of September, but the 43 Lorried Infantry Brigade Group was grounded to a halt in a vast quagmire created by a heavy shower of rain the previous day. After a couple of miles advance, 1 Armoured Division came across some armour and an anti-tank nest, and having cleared them, got involved in some internecine encounters and soon limped to a dead-halt with the mishandling of armour both at Brigade and Divisional levels. The Armoured Division which was supposed to penetrate deep and to the rear of Sialkot, through mistakes on their part, had only advanced 4 miles after break-out from the bridge-head, when there was very scanty armour opposition ranged against them. There was no doubt that due to incompetence of command a great opportunity had been lost!

Having suffered a rebuff in the Khem Karan Sector, the enemy's Ace Armoured Division of Pattons was able to transfer, by railway, two regiments of Pattons, through the plains of Lahore, without any interference from our Air Force (you would recall that the fighter planes had been withdrawn from the forward airfields of the Punjab, without my knowledge, to rear bases). They inducted these into the Sialkot Sector. The result was that our 1 Armoured Division was now faced by Pattons. 1 Armoured Division, after the initial melée on the 8th of September, had gone into a harbour behind village Phillora for the next three days, and it became difficult to get them going. I could not visit this Front till the morning of the 12th of September, because of my close involvement in the Khem Karan Sector. Seeing the mix-up in which I Corps had got involved, I took the General Officer Commanding I Corps to task, on the telephone, for not getting the I Armoured Division going. He said he had received instructions from

General Chowdhary, over the telephone, not to stick his head out too much forward! I was aghast and had it out with General Chowdhary, saying that he had no business to give instructions to the General Officer Commanding I Corps as he had been placed under my command. He apologised for this. The General Officer Commanding 1 Corps made a further mess in handling his Forces, and thus Chawinda could not be captured, despite many attempts made by us, and the incurring of heavy casualties, till the cease-fire came into effect.

I must mention here certain names and incidents, as they not only vindicate the choice I made of certain persons for certain jobs, but throw light on the acumen and soldierly qualities of the persons so selected.

Major Megh Singh. This officer had been commanding a battalion, in the rank of a Lieutenant Colonel, when something happened and he was court-martialled and brought down to Major. He was removed from the command of the battalion and posted to the Training Branch in Headquarters Western Command, at Simla. About a month before the War started with Pakistan, in August, 1965, I was sitting in my office, at Simla, and ruminating over the increasing incidents of violence in Jammu and Kashmir caused by Pakistani personnel who had infiltrated behind the line, when Megh Singh appeared in my office with a request. He mentioned the dare-devil escapades for which he was known in the past, and asked whether, before retiring from the Army, he could offer his services as an infiltrator behind Pakistani lines. I decided there and then that I would send him to the Corps Commander, Jammu and Kashmir, Lieutenant General Kashmir Katoch, to organise a force of volunteers of his choice with the intention of infiltrating behind the Pakistani Line and carrying out some raids, as a counter to their infiltration, behind our Line. He was very happy with the assignment, and I promised him that if he was successful and showed good results, I would be the first to pin the rank of a Lieutenant Colonel on his shoulders. He left very happy, and after I spoke to Kashmir Katoch he was asked to report to him. Before he left, I told Megh that I wanted to keep in touch with him, and that, with the permission of his Corps Commander, to whom I had already spoken, he could contact me directly on the telephone if he needed any help in collecting personnel of his choice. Within a few days, I received a telephone call from him saying that he wanted my permission to enrol Major Bhawani Singh, the Maharaja of Jaipur, in his force. Apparently Bhawani Singh had already signified his willingness to do so. I, however, thought that becoming a member of the infiltration Force, under Megh Singh, was too great a risk for the Maharaja of Jaipur to undertake and so I over-ruled Megh Singh. Incidentally, till date, I have never mentioned this to Lt Col Bhawani Singh, who is now retired from the Army and back in his State.

The 'Megh Force', as it came to be called, performed many daring feats behind the enemy lines, which pleased the Corps Commander, Kashmir Katoch. So, when the latter accompanied me to Akhnoor, on the morning of the 4th of September, 1965, and Megh Singh had just returned there, with a bullet in his thigh, from one of his many escapades behind enemy lines, in the presence of his Corps Commander, I pinned the rank of a Lieutenant Colonel on his shoulders.

Brigadier Pritam Singh. He was under a cloud and was lined up to be brought down to Lieutenant Colonel. This was just before the War. I was worried about who would replace the Brigadier in-charge of Dera Baba Nanak, who during a local Exercise had stumbled into one of our own bunkers and broken his back.. I recalled my meeting with Pritam Singh at Dera Baba Nanak, way back in the 1950s, when I was Brigadier General Staff Western Command and he was commanding a Guards battalion there. He had at the time explained the layout of the sector of Dera Baba Nanak to me. So, I sent for him and explained that I was willing to keep him in his present rank of Brigadier if he would go and take over the Dera Baba Nanak bridge. He was only too happy to do so. And though, he did not particularly distinguish himself there, and retired from the Army as a Brigadier, I had the satisfaction of having helped an acquaintance.

Colonel Bharat Singh. He was Colonel A at my Headquarters at Simla. It was the first day of the War with Pakistan, when I got a report that the Commander, 1 Horse, with 15 Infantry Division had not been well, and as a result, he had issued an order to his Tank Regiment in writing, not to take their tanks nearer than 2000 yards up to the Ichhogil Canal. He warned that the Pakistanis had Patton tanks, which had better range and a better calibre of gun compared to the Shermans which 1 Horse possessed. I intended to replace this officer, when Colonel Bharat Singh trooped into my office and volunteered to go and take over 1 Horse, which he had commanded once. I considered his rank of a full Colonel, and also thought of the five AMX Tanks (brand new) which had been left behind by the Pakistanis, in their foolish dash over the Dera Baba Nanak bridge. I offered to send him as a Force Commander, of the armour in the area of the GT Axis, including 1 Horse and the 5 AMX tanks belonging to the enemy, provided he found the crew for them from 1 Horse. He was to lead his tanks himself right up to the Ichhogil Canal!

Captain Shamsher Singh Minhas. He was Adjutant of 4 Sikh during their attack on Barki, and was wounded in his thigh by a bullet, during that action, but had refused to be evacuated beyond his Battalion Aid Post. Within two days the battalion had a mishap in the Khem Karan Sector and most of them, including the Commanding Officer, were taken prisoners-of-war. I appeared on the scene and asked Shamsher Singh to put on the badges of rank of a Major, as Second-in-Command of the battalion, and to assemble as many of his men as he could at Bhikhiwind, until I had thought of a new Commanding Officer. I did this as I was Colonel of the Sikh Regiment at the time.

Lt Col Karnail Singh Sidhu. In an attempt to find a new Commanding Officer for 4 Sikh, after their mishap in the Khem Karan Sector, on my return to my Headquarters that night, I rang up the Commandant of the Sikh Regimental Centre, at Meerut. Putting him in the picture, I requested him to send as many reinforcements as he could, of officers, JCOs, NCOs and men, from any battalion, to Bikhiwind, post haste. At the same time, I also rang up Lt Col Karnail Singh Sidhu, at that time commanding the Sikh TA Battalion in Delhi, who I knew had commanded 4 Sikh before, and asked him if he was ready to take over 4 Sikh. And although categorised by the Army Medicos as Category 'E', he said, he was feeling well enough to take over the battalion. So, I asked him to take a jeep and reach Bhikhiwind as soon as possible, and report to me direct, on telephone, within 48 hours, that 4 Sikh were ready for action. And he did so. Within a month a vacancy occurred in one of the Brigades in the Akhnoor area, and I asked Karnail Singh Sidhu to put on the badges of rank of a Brigadier and take over that Brigade. And he did.

41

GENERAL CHOWDHARY, INTELLIGENCE EMPIRES & AWARDS

I feel an assessment of the then Chief of the Army Staff, General Chowdhary, is called for.

I will be the first to admit that he had a very sharp brain, and could speak and write well, in English. His greatest failing was that he had an exalted opinion of himself. He often passed smart alec remarks and doubted the intelligence of every one around him. As a soldier, I regret to say, he left much to be desired. How else can you explain that throughout the duration of the War with Pakistan, he visited my Headquarters only thrice, that is on the 10th, the 14th and the 20th of September. And yet, on the early morning of the 23rd of September, soon after the cease-fire was announced, he was the first one to go to the Ichhogil Canal, with a photographer, and have his photograph taken for the press? Subsequently, to prove that he had participated fully in the War he had a book written by a well-known journalist which was completely fictitious.

During the war, I believe, General Chowdhary used to issue handouts about what was happening in the war without ever having visited the frontline. Every evening, he would ring me up, and my set reply was: "nothing to worry about; all is well". Once he suggested to me that he was not getting enough information, and that he, therefore, proposed to send two Lieutenant Colonels from his Headquarters to the Front Formations to get the latest news. I challenged him that if he did that, I would put those Officers under arrest. He could get all the information he needed from my Headquarters, besides which, of course, he was free to go anywhere in the front, himself. I am sure, my Headquarters were sending Situation Reports to his Headquarters regularly. His problem was his huge ego. He considered himself a world authority on Armour, and I used to argue with him that though I could not claim to be an authority on Armour, I knew what it could do and what it could not do; and that was enough from my point of view.

It may be reiterated that despite my regular pleas that any reserve forces to be committed against Sialkot must be launched from the area of Gurdaspur, so that initially they would be available to me as a reserve on the Punjab front, in case something went wrong there, General Chowdhary raised these reserve forces as I Corps, under Pat Dunn, and decided to launch them against Sialkot from Samba area, leaving me without any reserves on the Punjab front. And, as I have mentioned somewhere earlier, I was not told anything about these plans, nor even invited to the co-ordinating conference at which these plans were made. And yet, before their launching, I Corps was handed over to me for the conduct of the operations!

Since he had nothing else to do, General Chowdhary, as Chief of the Army Staff, without consulting me, started writing citations for senior officers - Army and Corps Commanders - with a view to giving them the award of Padma Bhushan. He had arranged with the Defence Minister, Mr Chavan, that he himself would be awarded the Padma Vibhushan. One day, he rang me up to say that he was recommending senior officers - that is Army and Corps Commanders – for the award of Padma Bhushan, but in the list he had left out Kashmir Katoch whom he had originally been very fond of. You may remember that Kashmir Katoch, General Officer Commanding, XV Corps, would ring him up directly, for instructions, at the early stages of the Operations, by-passing me, his Army Commander, until I put my foot down. During the operations, he had somehow fallen out of favour with General Chowdhary, who did not wish to recommend him for the award. I made it quite clear to him that if he was recommending Pat Dunn's name for the award, then he could not leave out Kashmir Katoch, because, according to my assessment, Kashmir Katoch had done better than Pat Dunn. Since I refused to budge on the matter, he relented, and finally included Kashmir Katoch's name also for the award.

I was intensely worked up over the whole affair of the awards, and sought an interview with the Defence Minister, Mr Chavan, to discuss the matter. I made it quite clear to him that General Chowdhary had hardly taken any part in the fighting and did not deserve to be awarded a Padma Vibhushan. He told me that in his case the award was only of symbolic value; and tried to mollify me by saying that the Government of India was considering me for a special award, and, had besides, decided to give me the rank of a full General. Mr Lal Bahadur Shastri, the then Prime Minister, died in Tashkent, soon thereafter, as did Mr Chavan, so nothing came of the special awards that I had been promised though I was given the Padma Vibhushan after retirement. This is what they call the luck of the draw!

The main reason why such large numbers of armed intruders were able to infiltrate, almost unnoticed, so far behind into the interior of Jammu and Kashmir and achieve a certain amount of success in destroying bridges and ambushing vehicle-convoys, was due to the fact that the various agencies responsible for dealing with such contingencies such as the Army Intelligence, the State Militia battalions, the Armed Police battalions, the Jammu and Kashmir Police, and so on, were not under one unified command. They had their respective 'Empires', and many of them were not willing to accept any help, guidance or direction from the Army. Even those, who were deployed for the defence of the cease-fire line, did not fall fully within the purview of the regional military commanders. The result was that the channel of command, military decisions, and more particularly, the acquisition and dissemination of information, was actually tenuous, circuitous and generally too long to fructify. Besides, there were the inevitable professional jealousies among these agencies which detracted from the smooth and harmonious functioning of defence arrangements in the State of Jammu and Kashmir.

Through the inter-cession of the United Nations Organisation, the 1965 War with Pakistan, came to an end at midnight, 22nd September, 1965. After dark on the 22nd of September, with the advent of the cease-fire, the Pakistani side fired off all the ammunition left over with them, and there was a tremendous din. What is more, the Pakistani Forces occupied all the areas in the no-man's land adjacent to the Front. I had warned the Corps Commanders concerned about this, but, it seems, they did nothing to prevent it. This is where we always lose out; while we play 'fair', Pakistan's attitude is entirely different.

42
PEACE TALKS & VISIT TO LAHORE

Within days, a representative from the United Nations Organisation, Brigadier General Marambio of Chile arrived in Delhi. General Chowdhary rang me up and asked me to come over to Delhi and meet General Marambio. Soon I was closeted with him and, naturally, asked him if he had been briefed at the United Nations as to how to proceed. He pulled a blue paper out of his pocket, which had Amritsar and Lahore shown as squares with a line drawn between them. At an equidistance from both squares he had drawn a dotted square, which donated the position of the neutral camp where discussions between both countries were to be held. I pointed out to him that the area where he desired to set up a neutral camp was barren and inhospitable. There was no electricity, no water and no shade. He then asked me what I would suggest. I said that I would go to Lahore first, and the next time round my Pakistani counterpart could come to Amritsar. He was surprised at my suggestion, and asked me if I had my Government's permission to go to Lahore first. I replied that I did not have to ask my Government's permission for this, and he could take it as final. He was very pleased with my suggestion, as it solved much of his problem.

Once the preliminaries were settled, my delegation for talks with Pakistan consisted of my ADC Captain Amarinder Singh, Lt Col Pade, General Staff Class I of Headquarters Western Command and I. The three of us arrived at Amritsar in early February 1966, ready to fly to Lahore, with General Marambio, in his United Nations aircraft. General Marambio, according to United Nations instructions, had directed the pilot to fly a circuitous route to the Lahore Airfield. I was able to spot this as I knew the route between Amritsar and Lahore like the back of my hand, having traversed it several times during my college days in Lahore. When we arrived at the Lahore Airfield, the Pakistani authorities had a Guard of Honour waiting there for my inspection. Having inspected the Guard, I sat with General Marambio in the rear seat of his car, which had an inter-com system, and it seemed that all measures had been taken for my safety. Glancing back, through the rear window of the car, to see if my ADC, Captain Amarinder Singh, scion of the Maharaja of Patiala, was following me, I saw to my surprise that he was embracing the young Captain commanding the Guard of Honour. When he joined me later, I asked him about this and he told me that the young man was the son of Colonel Majeed, the erstwhile Military Secretary of his father, the Maharaja of Patiala. Both of them had played together as kids in the palace grounds at Patiala!

The United Nations team was accommodated in hutments meant for the Horse Show, near the old bridge (of mughal vintage) over the canal. When I got down from General Marambio's car, in order to warm myself, since this was winter and it was pretty cold, I decided to stand in a sunny patch amongst the shade of the tall trees in the area. General Marambio was keen to lead me to the waiting room prepared for the Indian delegation while I preferred to stand in the sun and meet the Pakistan delegation there. I could see heads popping up occasionally over the balustrade of the old bridge, obviously Pakistan's Military Police had been assigned the responsible of my safety. Looking around, I saw a gentleman standing about 25 yards away from me, wearing a suit. He would look at me when I looked away, and look away when I looked at him. So I decided to walk up to him, and recognised him as Rizvi, my room mate during my first year at College in 1929. I asked him what he was doing there and learnt that he was Deputy Inspector General of the Civil Intelligence

The Author walking with Lt Gen Bukhtiar Rana as UN Peacemakers look on, at Lahore.

The Author with the Pakistani delegation & U.N. Officials at the Harmandir Sahib, Golden Temple, Amritsar.

The Head of the UN delegation meets with Sant Fateh Singh at the Golden Temple. The Author is standing in the middle.

Service of Pakistan, assigned for my protection. After this, I certainly felt in safe hands! I mentioned to him that as far as I was concerned, they could take me on a 'conducted' tour of Lahore, but since my ADC had come to Lahore for the first time, I wanted him to be taken to Anarkali or any other place that he might wish to go. Rizvi promised to do this.

Soon the Pakistani delegation arrived, headed by Lt Gen Bukhtiar Rana (whom I knew well, as we had been in the Indian Military Academy, Dehradun, together, he being a term behind me) with about seven officers. These included the Director of Military Operations Brigadier Gul Hassan, who was later to became Commander-in-Chief of the Pakistan Army, under Mr Bhutto, the Director of Intelligence, and so on. Before going to the Conference Room, for any discussion (for which nobody was keen, as parleys, between India and Pakistan were already in progress at Tashkent) we sat in the Refreshment Room, where there was plenty available in the way of eats and drinks. The Pakistani officers, however, refused to touch anything, as it was their 'Fasting Month'. I had asked to meet my old friends, Dara and Gulam Bheek, who had both been in Government College with me. They arrived one by one and had changed little. Dara said, he did not believe in fasting, and would eat anything by blowing on it and saying a 'Kalma'. Gulam Bheek, a Nawab's son from Karnal, who used to keep a bottle of whisky under his pillow during our college days, said he was now a 'half a bottle a day' man, and had no compunction in eating during the 'Roza'. After the reunion with old friends was over, we all went to the Conference Room as organised by the United Nations. The two delegations were seated across a table while General Marambio, with other United Nations representatives, sat at the head of a higher table. Having observed our interaction, General Marambio's first words were "Gentlemen, I feel that there is really no need for me to be here, as both sides are so friendly. I am sure that you can settle everything without me!"

When we dispersed, Bukhtiar Rana took me on a tour of Lahore in his car. He was keen to show me their 'Gulbargha' colony, along the canal, where most retired officers had built their houses. Beyond it, Pakistan had built a new Sports Stadium, which he also wished to show me. He pointed out the house of Hajji Iftikhar who had been with me in the Indian Military Academy but when I expressed a desire to meet him, Rana said Iftikhar was ill and bed-ridden and not fit to receive visitors. So, I gave up the idea. En route, I saw big buntings across the road, written in Urdu, which read: 'Dhoti Prasad ke Jonge ki Swari - 8, 8 annas'. I objected to this banner, and urged him to turn back as I did not wish to see more. He ordered the car to turn, but mentioned that they had already made more than Rs. 10,000/- giving rides in the Jonga jeep captured from Major General Niranjan Prasad. I completely denied that we had lost a Jonga jeep and warned him that if he did not desist from such trickery, when he visited Amritsar I would produce ten jongas, for his inspection, complete with Pakistani flags and other markings. Earlier, he had promised to show me photographs of our guns, worth a whole regiment, captured by them in the Akhnoor area, but I said I had no interest in seeing these pictures, as we had lost no guns in the Akhnoor area. I later learnt that they had circulated these pictures all over the world.

Bukhtiar Rana, then took me in his car on the Mall road of Lahore, past Lawrence Gardens, the Nedus Hotel, the Mall, and 'Bhangion-ki-top' to Government College. I noticed that the green hedge on the road-side of the Oval hockey ground, had been replaced by an ugly 8-foot brick-wall. The explanation given to me by Bukhtiar was that this had been erected to prevent student agitations. I did not think that this was a very valid explanation. I had expressed a desire to enter the gate of the College building, but Bukhtiar passed it off by saying that the College, like other similar institutions, was closed at the time. My information was that it was the threat of our invasion of Lahore that had caused the evacuation of Lahore and the closure of educational institutions there. I told Bukhtiar that I was not happy with the conducted tour, but that I could understand the reason for it in a controlled State like theirs. The next time they came to India, I would show them what a democracy was like. I would take them wherever they pointed a finger!

When the Pakistani delegation came to Amritsar, they expressed a preference to go to Harmandir Sahib in the Golden Temple where Sant Fateh Singh had ensconced himself, preparatory to self-immolation. I sent a military jeep ahead, with some military police personnel, to announce the imminent arrival of the Pakistani delegation, and the United Nations officers, in the streets leading up to Harmandir Sahib so that they could be given a fitting reception by the local populace, and similarly informed the Shiromani Gurudwara Prabandhak Committee. I put Bukhtiar in my jeep, followed by other jeeps carrying the rest of the delegation from Pakistan and the United Nations officers. The reception given to us was tremendous. The shopkeepers of Amritsar were all standing in front of their shops and showered us with flowers. On arrival at Harmandir Sahib's gate, we were received by the whole Prabandhak Committee which had lined up with garlands of flowers, to be presented to every member of the delegation, and the United Nations officers. We were all taken round the 'Parikrama' and then to the inside of the Holy Place, while the Secretary of the Shiromani Gurudwara Prabandhak Committee, Sardar Pritam Singh, described the artistry of all the fine work inside the temple. Eventually, he took us all to the common kitchen and around the Akal Takhat. Towards the end of the trip, Bukhtiar mentioned that according to his information, Sant Fateh Singh was ensconced somewhere in the temple and asked whether it was possible to meet him. I, naturally, turned to Pritam Singh, who asked us to follow him up narrow steps that led to Sant Fateh Singh's room. Sant Fateh Singh had, obviously, been warned, for when we arrived, he had a white-sheet spread over a cotton-quilt on the floor of his room and was sitting on it. We greeted him and sat down on the floor around him. I must say, that he made a very sensible opening statement, in Punjabi, of course, to the effect that: "We are brethren – the people of India and Pakistan - with the same blood flowing in our veins, why must we then continue to fight with each other?" He then followed this with a discourse on the qualities of the Sikh religion. In the end, he presented a set of Punjabi religious books to the leaders of the Pakistani and United Nations delegations. Before we departed, I asked both Bukhtiar and Marambio to ask any question they wanted from the Sant. But they seemed to have none. Thereafter, we returned to our Headquarters in the Amritsar Cantonment. And soon, the Pakistani and United Nations delegations left for Lahore, by air.

I paid another visit to Lahore, under the auspices of the United Nations, and this time I asked my ADC to take along a case of Dimple Scotch wrapped up in red cloth, with 'gota' and all that, as I wished to present it to my friend, Gulam Bheek. So on arrival at the United Nations Headquarters in Lahore, I sent for Ghulam Bheek, and presented him with a case of whisky. Despite the wrapping, he discerned what it was at once, and offered to take me to town so that he could buy me anything I desired. I declined his offer as I explained that this little gift from me was for old-times sake; to commemorate the time we had spent together as students in Government College, Lahore.

Before Shastri jee, our Prime Minister, left for Tashkent, he was invited over by the Sikh Community in Delhi who wished to honour him. The Chief of the Army Staff, General Chowdhary, and I were also invited to the function. Shastri jee had always been very kind to me, and made me sit next to him on the dais. After the normal speeches were over, Shastri jee was presented a 'saropa' and a sword. On receiving the latter, Shastri jee pulled me up by my hand and presented this sword to me, saying that it was of no use to him; but might come in handy for me! This sword is my prized possession till today. The inscription on it reads: 'Presented to Shastri jee, the Prime Minister of India, by the Sikh Community of Delhi; who in turn presented it to Lt Gen Harbakhsh Singh'. A picture of Shastri jee handing this sword to me adorns a wall in my study, and I value both the sword and the kind words he said about me on the occasion.

An Agreement was signed between India and Pakistan, sponsored by Russia, but it cost us the life of our beloved Prime Minister, Shastri jee. And with him disappeared the aspirations and expectations of many a man.

As the War ended, there was great jubilation in Punjab, as indeed in the whole of India. I received numerous congratulatory letters, for the part I played in the War, from leading dignitaries in the country. Out of these, the ones I value the most are two letters of appreciation from my GOC XI Corps, on the Punjab Front, who bore the brunt of the fight against Pakistan. In his letter, dated 22nd September, 1965, he wrote:

"On the eve of the cease-fire, may I offer you my congratulations and salutations from XI Corps for what you have achieved for India and the Indian Army.

The Author being presented a sword by Prime Minister Lal Bahadur Shastri in appreciation of services rendered to the Nation at a function at the Bangla Sahib Gurudwara in Delhi in the wake of the 1965 Indo-Pak War.

As I have stated before, there is no soldier in our Army who is more competent to commit troops to battle than yourself and in the two months you have proved it in what you have done for India at a critical juncture which will be remembered by generations to come. We are proud to serve you."

In his letter, dated 5th October 1965, he wrote:

"We are overwhelmed with both happiness and pride to read the statement of Shri Lal Bahadur Shastri at Gurudwara Bangla Sahib in the Tribune, dated 4th October 1965. I send you the warmest of congratulations on my behalf and that of my command.

It has been a wonderful experience to fight this War with Pakistan under your inspiring skippership. You have my assurance that we will not be found wanting in any sphere in the event of a fresh outbreak of hostilities."

After the war, rallies and receptions were held in the prominent towns of Punjab. At one such reception, held by the citizens of Amritsar and Ferozepore, I was presented a shield which bore a metal plaque of Harmandir Sahib and the temple of Durgiana, along with the formation insignia of formations under my command during the war. This shield, along with a replica of the Sarangarhi Memorial at Ferozepore, are also among my prized possessions. At a rally held at Karnal, to which both Air Chief Marshal Arjan Singh and I were invited, we were presented swords by the then Defence Minister, Mr. Chavan. I particularly remember this rally because it was here that I met my science teacher, Bhagwan Das, who taught me at Ranbir High School, Sangrur, after a gap of almost 45 years! I had no difficulty in recognising him, as he had a big scar on his forehead, sustained, so we were told in school, as a result of a mishap he had suffered in one of his science experiments. It was a great pleasure to meet him after so many years.

Soon after the 1965 War with Pakistan, General Kumaramangalam took over from General Chowdhary as Chief of the Army Staff, and the latter was posted as our High Commissioner to Canada. General Kumaramangalam kept on assuring me that he had recommended my name as the next Chief of the Army Staff, and I do believe that he did so. As is the practice, my name was considered by the Cabinet and passed and I was informed of it on telephone by Mr Malik of Intelligence, almost immediately. However, I believe, that Mrs Indira Gandhi, the then Prime Minister, was not at all happy to have me as the Chief of Army Staff. She had at the time, a 'Kitchen Cabinet', with Raja Dinesh Singh (Foreign Minister at the time) a prominent member. I am told that he advised her that as Prime Minister her desire should prevail. Accordingly, she had it announced in the next day's daily papers that the next Chief of the Army Staff was going to be her choice, and that she had selected General Manekshaw.

Just before my retirement, the then Defence Minister, Sardar Swaran Singh, sent for me in his office and offered me the Chairmanship of Hindustan Aeronautics Limited (HAL) but I replied: "Not before I am made a full General, as was promised to me by the Government of India after the 1965 War." And that was the condition I laid down for accepting any post under the Government of the time; and I have stuck to it ever since.

At the time of my retirement, I desired to start another tradition in the Army; that is of holding Farewell Ceremonial Parades by Formations rather than the practice of lining the route with men, or officers of the Formation pulling the jeep of the retiring Commander. I particularly remember the Farewell Ceremonial Parade held by 1 Armoured Division at Ambala. While inspecting the Parade, as a Reviewing Officer, I noticed Brigadier Calif, of Asal Uttar fame from the 1965 War with Pakistan, and felt the need to meet him and shake-hands with him. Making an exception, I got down from my Ceremonial Jeep and walked up to him. I am sure that it must have been noticed by the ranks on parade as well as the audience watching the parade, and that was, indeed, my purpose - to do honour to the War-hero.

Immediately after my retirement from the Army, I presented to the then Defence Minister, Mr Jagjivan Ram, by hand, two volumes of a manuscript of *War Despatches* – pertaining to the Indo-Pak Conflict of 1965 - for publication as a restricted document (as is the practice in all other countries). I pointed out to him that the Despatches contained lessons for young officers. But the Ministry of Defence held on to the manuscript for about twenty five years, without publishing it. When Mr Pant, whom I knew, became Defence Minister, I brought up the matter with him and he promised to have them published soon. On the way back from this interview, I met the Joint Secretary of Defence and mentioned that the Defence Minister had promised to have the Despatches published soon, and that if they were not published, within a fortnight, I would have them published myself. I waited for a fortnight and then had the Despatches published myself. It was, perhaps, for the first time in the history of a nation that the Despatches of a national war were being published by an individual, and not by the Government concerned. But then the Ministry of Defence had shown scant interest.

Last year, as ex-Army Commander, Western Command, I was invited to Chandimandir, where the 50th Anniversary of the Headquarters was being celebrated. Before leaving I was given a souvenir of the last fifty years. On opening it, I found that there were no pictures in it before the time when Lt Gen Raina was the Army Commander. Upon enquiry, I was told that the records of the Headquarters before that period had been lost in a fire that occurred in the Officers' Mess, in Simla, many years ago. Since the fire, there had been about six Army Commanders, yet none of them, it appeared, had tried to make up for the records lost, which included the record of the War of 1965 with Pakistan, the only worthwhile war fought by Headquarters Western Command. I was surprised how an Army organisation, especially Headquarters Western Command, was not concerned about maintaining links with its own history.

43

RETIREMENT

I retired from the Army at the end of September 1969. I had been General Officer Commanding-in-Chief Western Command, then based in Simla for nearly five years, from November 1964 onwards, the longest period any one had been Army Commander of this very active Command. Soon, the set-up of Commands in the country was converted from four to five, and Western Command was converted into two: Northern Command (which comprised mainly Jammu and Kashmir) and Western Command, whose responsibility was now the Punjab and the Rajasthan borders only.

I continued, however, as Colonel of the Sikh Regiment for another two years following my retirement, till the 27th of September 1971, when I handed over to Major General Satinder Singh. During this period we added a new golden coloured sash (dori), to be worn over the left shoulder, to the uniform of all officers and men of the Sikh Regiment. For 2 Sikh, which were a Royal Battalion, an exception was made on the recommendation of Major General Satinder Singh, who belonged to the battalion, and they were allowed to wear the golden sash over the right shoulder.

In March 1972, Satinder and Malhotra, both of the Sikh Regiment, came to visit me one evening to inform me of the government's decision to move the Centre of the Sikh Regiment from Meerut to Ramgarh, in Bihar. They wanted me to speak on their behalf with the Defence Minister, Sardar Swaran Singh, whom I knew, for they along with the entire regiment were very upset with this decision. So I rang up Sardar Swaran Singh at his house and he agreed to see me informally the next day, which was a Sunday. Satinder and I both went together to see him and learnt that he knew nothing of the matter. He felt that the move had perhaps been ordered by the then Chief of Army Staff, General Raina. Consequently, I rang up General Raina who very readily agreed to meet Satinder and me in his office the next morning. It appeared that the move had indeed been sanctioned by him and that he was adamant to stick to it as he argued that the built up area in Meerut was required for an active battalion. It was a sad day when the Sikh Centre was moved to Ramgarh, for not only did it have to leave the gurudwara that the jawans had so lovingly built behind, but it also cut it off from the Punjab which was its main recruiting area.

I was quite active on retirement, and in great demand as a speaker on the 1965 War with Pakistan as well as on matters concerning the country's defence. I was particularly happy to address an assembly of dignitaries from all walks of life (including Mr JRD Tata, Mr Minoo Masani and Mr AN Palkhiwala), who annually held a lecture in Bombay in memory of Dugee Sawhney, who had been a cadet with me at the Indian Military Academy at Dehradun, and had later married Mr JRD Tata's sister. He had, unfortunately, died soon after. The subject on which I spoke was 'Humanity in Adversity' and was based on my personal experiences as a prisoner-of-war of the Japanese during the Second World War.

As General Officer Commanding-in-Chief Western Command, I was made a member of the Board of Governors, Punjab Public School, Nabha, which had been started by Partap Singh Kairon, the then Chief Minister of Punjab. His idea was to offer free education, in the form of full scholarships, to children of retired and serving other ranks, who could not otherwise afford to send their children to a public school. For this purpose, he appointed a very high-powered Board of Governors for the School, which included the Chief Minister of Punjab and the

General Officer Commanding-in-Chief Western Command. The Governor of Punjab was the Chairman of the Board. The School was provided free accommodation by the Punjab Government, but I regret to say, that over the years, the School has deviated from its original objective and turned into an ordinary public school, catering to the children of the rich only.

The problem is that the money in the Rehabilitation and Reconstruction Fund, out of which it was planned to give the ex-servicemen's children scholarships to study, has been squandered and mismanaged by the financial bureaucrats of Punjab. This Fund had been originally created by the British for the scions and dependants of men who had lost their lives, or had become disabled, during the two World Wars. The financial bureaucrats merged it into a composite Fund, robbing it of its uniqueness and over time of its volume which dwindled to such an extent that it could no longer provide 100 per cent scholarships to ex-servicemen's children, as originally planned. I was told by the Headmaster of the School in 1998, that not a single ex-serviceman's son was studying in the School, as scholarships to them had been completely stopped. I have been fighting with the Board (as I am, perhaps, the oldest member on the Board of Governors, now, who knows the objective with which the School was started) for bringing the School on track again, but I doubt if I shall succeed.

44
KING'S COMMISSIONED INDIAN OFFICERS AND INDIAN COMMISSIONED OFFICERS

There is no doubt that the British were not at all keen to Indianise the Indian Army in India. It was only after the First World War, and due to pressure exerted by the Indian representatives in the Viceroy's Council, that the scions of some rich and important Indians were selected for training at the Military School at Indore which was set up under a British Major General. The next step the British took towards Indianisation was the setting up of the Royal Indian Military College at Dehradun. Here the scions of military Other Ranks killed in the War, and those of other dignitaries, who had helped them during the War, especially in the recruitment of personnel to the Indian Army, were given admission. They were imparted some academic and military training here prior to their going to the Officers' Training School at Sandhurst in England, for commissioning into the Indian Army. These officers, from Sandhurst, were known as King's Commissioned Indian Officers (KCIOs). They were few in number, and the British preferred to keep them as show-pieces, without giving them any worthwhile responsibility. They were considered to be 'poodle-fakers' in the units specially earmarked for them, for they were more concerned with wearing polished top-boots, tapping them with their 'swagger sticks' and pronouncing words such as 'Poona' and 'Polo' with the right British accent. Cariappa was one of them. By his seniority, he was selected to be the first Commander-in-Chief of the Indian Army, after Independence. As far as KCIOs were concerned, he was the most anglicised of them, and did not know a word of Hindi or Hindustani, and thus was unable to communicate with the men in the Indian Army.

In 1932, again due to pressure exerted by the Indians in the Viceroy's Council, the British decided to start the training of selected Indians as officers in India. From then on no Indian cadets were sent to Sandhurst, and instead a school was started at the Indian Military Academy at Dehradun, from where Indian Commissioned Officers (ICOs) were produced. They trained at the Academy for two and a half years, as compared to only one year at Sandhurst and yet, at the end of it, they were allowed to command only platoons in the units while their pay was also kept below that of the KCIOs who were on par with British officers from Sandhurst. What must be remembered is that even then the British were not serious about Indianising the Indian Army. This is clear from the composition of cadets at the Indian Military Academy, ten of whom came from the Army Other Ranks, mostly educated at Army schools, and thus considered to be loyal and submissive to the British, ten from the State Forces, again considered to be loyal British subjects, and only ten from the rest of India. The latter were admitted through an open competition, in which, again, the result depended on an interview which was conducted by a high-powered Selection Board, consisting of senior British officers. In my time, as I have already mentioned, there were 10,000 candidates from all over India competing for ten seats at the Indian Military Academy! So the British had a clear stranglehold over this category of selection also.

The funniest part is that when it came to joining the Indian National Army in Malaya as prisoners-of-war of the Japanese, this group of 'loyalists' (men, JCOs and officers from the Army) were the first to do so. In fact, the first Supreme Commander of the Indian National Army had been a cadet at the Indian Military Academy in the first term. The trouble with them all was that as they had been mostly educated at Army schools in India, they knew little about the outside world. It sickened us to hear them brag, in the prisoner-of-war camp at Bidadari in Malaya, about how under Japanese supervision they had thrown biscuits at hungry British prisoners-of-war who were incarcerated at Changi Jail.

When India gained its independence, on the 15th of August 1947, Indian officers, both KCIOs and ICOs, got promoted rather suddenly, often jumping a couple of ranks – from Major to Brigadier or from Colonel to Major General. There is no doubt that a few of these promotees found it difficult to adjust to the rank that had been thrust upon them. I would put officers like General Cariappa, General Kulwant Singh and Brigadier Sen in this category, though I am sure that there were others of the same ilk with whom I did not have a personal experience. KCIOs, by virtue of their seniority, held all the important key positions in the Army after independence, including that of Military Secretary. The latter position was a key post as it was the duty of the Military Secretary to deal with any grouses or complaints that an officer may have against a brother officer in a fair manner and ensure that harmony be maintained. I remember reading the plaque displayed outside the office of a KCIO who occupied this position which bore the following sentence in block letters: 'EVERY WORD SPOKEN IN THIS ROOM WILL BE REPORTED TO THE HIGHEST'. So, this avenue of complaint – the only one in the Army – was now effectively closed.

General Cariappa

I am constrained to pass an opinion on General Cariappa, the first Commander-in-Chief of the Indian Army.

There is no doubt that as its first Commander-in-Chief, he did a lot of good to the Army in the areas of 'spit and polish' (so necessary at the time) and barrack-discipline. He was punctilious about his personal appearance and always dressed immaculately. However, he was given to fads and even when alone at home would insist on wearing a dinner jacket for his meals. Another of his fads was to have a Gorkha boy at his residence, dressed in uniform, to receive guests - showing, perhaps, his liking for Gorkha troops. And as to his saluting a jawan's statue every morning - even after retirement – this was nothing but another example of his peculiar ways.

His anglicised manner, and the fact that he did not speak a word of Hindi, or Hindustani, made it difficult for him to build a rapport with the Indian jawans. There are many stories about his attempts to communicate with troops in Hindustani. I remember a time when, towards the end of 1947, he expressed a desire to address all officers and men in Srinagar. I was then commanding Sri Garrison, and had all officers and men, who were mostly administrative elements, collect in the cantonment in Srinagar (at Badami Bagh). The new Commander-in-Chief, General Cariappa, seemed to know the composition of his audience and had chosen his subject well – the need to guard against too large an administrative tail. However, his idiomatic expressions were too anglicised to be translated, let alone comprehended, by his audience. He talked about 'the heavy tail wagging the dog', and got into all kinds of difficulties trying to explain this in his broken and limited Hindustani. He even went to the extent of waving his hand behind his back to illustrate this! Not a very edifying sight of the new C-in-C!

His tiff with the first Defence Secretary of the country, Mr HM Patel, did the Army more harm than good. Army officers lost out on prestige and protocol. When it came to fixing the pay of officers, immediately after independence, he sided with the bureaucrats (mostly ICS), and gave the King's Commissioned Indian Officers (KCIOs) a higher pay packet than Indian Commissioned Officers (ICOs), who had passed from Indian institutions, although both categories did the same, if not similar jobs. This was nothing but discrimination, and it is a pity that our first Commander-in-Chief was party to it. It built resentment between the Indian Commissioned Officers (ICOs) and the KCIOs, who were nicknamed 'kasais'. The discrimination did not end here. I have already mentioned my personal case, when, for my conduct of the Tithwal Operations, my General Officer Commanding, General Thimayya, had recommended me for Mahavir Chakra (MVC) and not Vir Chakra (which is meant for personal bravery). But General Cariappa, as Chief of Army Staff, sitting in his office, decided for some reason or another, which I need not go into here, that it would be Vir Chakra (VrC). General Thimayya told me about this himself, and felt sorry for it, but there was nothing he could do. The trouble with General Cariappa was that he had never commanded troops in battle; nor even heard a shot 'fired in anger', so to speak.

45

POSTSCRIPT

I can claim to have lived a full life. It has been pleasant on the whole and I have no regrets. I bless the day when I, as a prisoner-of-war of the Japanese, sat with my back against a rubber tree and resolved the future course of my life. I have not deviated from it since. Of one thing I am certain, that it is adversity alone that brings out the best, or the worst, in a human being. Such has been my experience as described in this book.

I am friends with everyone, but have no special friends. Friendships that existed in the old days, such as between General Gurnam Singh and my father, are a thing of the past. One does not hear of 'Pagh Bat' brothers any more. This was friendship that involved self sacrifice. These days everyone is out to get what they can for themselves without thought of the other. They are prepared to use any means, be they dishonest, to attain this end.

My wife and I have had a happy married life and have two wonderful daughters. The elder of the two, Harmala, is active in providing support, comfort and information to people with cancer and their families. Lately, she has initiated a home care programme, called

The Author relaxing with his family at their summer residence in Kasauli, 1988.

'CanSupport at Home', for those who are too sick to visit the hospital any more. She is married to a brilliant professor of Social Anthropology, Dipankar Gupta, who teaches at Jawaharlal Nehru University, New Delhi. They have a 17 year old son, Dipayan, who is already 6 ft 5 ins tall! He is in his last year of school. Deepa, our younger daughter is a career woman, who after doing a course in interior design in Canada, is currently working with the Taj Group of Hotels. We enjoy a very close relationship with both our daughters.

I do not believe in the transmigration of souls or in an after life. When you die it is the end and darkness thereafter. We have no control over birth and death. The Sikh scriptures say, 'Nange auna, te nange jana' (you come into this world naked and leave it naked). Then why do we hanker after these worldly things? It is human nature, and as I have mentioned while describing my days as a prisoner-of-war, this remains with us right till the end.

I have highlighted the shortfalls in strategic thinking on the part of a few military commanders that caused us to lose the advantage, and later pay heavily to regain it, on many an occasion, during the J&K Operations in 1947, during the Sino-Indian conflict of 1962 and later during the Indo-Pak War in 1965. These lapses can perhaps be attributed to lack of experience, and we can learn lessons from them, but what I have found difficult to accept is the personal pettiness displayed by a few men in high position against those below them. I have not hesitated to cite these examples, for I believe that the personal attributes of a soldier are as important as his military capability.

Immediately after retirement I wrote articles, based on my experiences. I include some of them in this book as appendices.

APPENDIX A

THE VICTORIOUS WILL

"My Centre has broken, my right is collapsing,
The situation is excellent - I attack!"

FOCH (Battle of Morue)

General

It has been my experience that he who plays 'safe' lies low and awaits developments, usually comes off second best. The Commander who always tries to dominate a situation, is eager to seize the fleeting opportunities of war and is prepared to pounce upon the enemy with inspired 'audacity', usually carries the day, however adverse the circumstances of the battle. There are always more ways than one of fighting a battle successfully, but few of winning it cheaply. For while the rigid, slow plodder, the stickler for text book conventions, too, reaches the goal, his route of success is often littered with prohibitive cost in men and material. Quick, spectacular achievements, at comparatively low cost usually come to the audacious, the bold and the enterprising in battle.

The Cult of the Victorious Will

Military history is replete with examples of missed opportunities leading to disastrous set-backs in battle. There is the classic example of Napoleon himself, the foremost exponent of exploiting the opportune moment in battle. At Ligny, on the 16th of June 1915, with the Prussians disordered and retreating, after the trouncing he had given them, Napoleon, with an astounding lethargy, inexplicable in a man of his character, did not order the pursuit and destruction of ZIETEN; the opportunity of dispersing BLUCHER and isolating WELLINGTON, was allowed to slip away. Who knew, but for this the battle of Waterloo might have found a different place in the annals of military history!

Nearer home, during the 1965 War with Pakistan, there were a series of brilliant offensive actions but interspersed, far too frequently, with instances where we failed to take advantage of favourable situations through lack of enterprise. Often, we found the enemy reeling, but the knockout blow came too late, or not at all. I would commend you to study the early battles of Rommel and his Generals, in Eritrea, to appreciate the implications of audacity in action as practised by masters of the art. The uncanny instinct with which they spotted the passing chance in battle, and the alacrity with which they exploited these fleeting opportunities, makes inspiring reading. The instinct of the opportunity in action is often inborn - but it can also be cultivated through training and psychological development. It is a sad commentary on our training techniques, both during tactical exercise without troops and exercises with troops, that the rigid application of accepted tactical doctrines is often unimaginatively insisted upon - the unconventional is often frowned upon, whatever the justification of such action. The inevitable - 'well, it is not usually done' - dampens the spirit of the average officer during training, thus curbing his initiative in war.

While I am all for teaching correct procedures, drills and precepts of war, it must be appreciated that these are all means to an end - not the end in themselves; and once mastered, the average officer must retain an elasticity of mind to vary, deviate or depart from them to take advantage of a favourable situation. To do this, he must be encouraged to develop a mental attitude which, while respecting the established conventions of war, is, nevertheless, prepared to break away from them should the occasion so demand. There is therefore a definite requirement for a re-orientation in our attitude and methods of training. We should aim at cultivating in our Commanders a spirit and mental attitude which would welcome chances of bold action instead of indecisive wavering when faced with a situation.

Reorientation of Training Techniques

I give in the succeeding paragraphs a few general ideas and guidance for imparting the type of training I have in mind. I expect you to study them with care and implement them with imagination.

While in the initial stages, the correct application of established principles should be taught and practised once a sound foundation in this respect is laid, variations from accepted norms should be permitted and even encouraged, within reason. In exercises, situations should be created involving:

- the taking of calculated risks;
- the use of bold and audacious action, even at the risk of deviating from normal procedures and established principles of warfare.

The average officer should be impressed with the conviction that if a gamble is justified he must not hesitate to stake his all. The ideal, of course, would be achieved when an officer is so psychologically attuned to the offensive spirit that not only is he on the look out for the opportune moment in battle, but also eager to create for himself a favourable situation for bold action.

I have often noticed during tactical exercises, without troops/sand-model exercises, that even at lower levels most of the time is devoted to stereotyped and hypothetical problems, repeated with monotonous regularity; the 'action' required being pushed to the background and sometimes even ignored. It must be remembered that in battle it is more often the cumulative effect of a series of 'conduct actions' that carries the day and not the best laid plans on papers. While saying this, I do not deprecate the importance of planning but am against the disproportionate time devoted to what I call 'passive' training as opposed to 'active' problems associated with the conduct of the various individuals concerned on the battlefield. Problems requiring quick decision and involving aggressive action should be liberally introduced in tactical exercises without troops and in exercises with troops. It is more a question of laying the appropriate emphasis on a particular aspect of training.

Problems requiring syndicate solutions should be reduced to the minimum and generally interspersed with individual requirements. For, while 'committee' planning is inevitable on account of the complexity of modern warfare, the ability to make individual, on the spot, decisions is vital in the battlefield. An officer loses his capacity for independent thought and action if he is 'habituated' exclusively to syndicate work.

Nothing is more demoralising in war than inaction. The hesitant, the wary and cautious usually induce despair and despondency in their subordinates. This tendency must be ruthlessly stamped out during training. It must be impressed on all that any action, especially when the circumstances are grim and the situation confused, is better than listless waiting and hoping for the best. The type who is inclined to look over his shoulder for orders or requires prodding from the rear, must either change his attitude or quit a command appointment.

In exercises, some Commanders tend to take for granted the smooth functioning of supply lines, reliable communications, fault-less transmission of orders and flawless execution of plans, not realising that in war the malfunctioning of these agencies is the rule rather than the exception. During training, problems should be posed to depict the unexpected in war so that Commanders are mentally conditioned to take such situations in their stride rather than being paralysed into inaction. No 'imponderable' in war should be allowed to interfere with the tempo of action in battle.

The fog of war should be treated as a normal phenomenon in battle. The practice to base plans and actions on detailed information about the enemy glibly supplied by obliging umpires during exercises must be discouraged, as such an unrealistic training will habituate the average officer into expecting similar detailed information about the enemy during battle also. It is admitted that intelligence about the enemy is important but waiting for its complete fulfilment is fatal, especially where time favours the opponent. One must be trained to accept that in war more often than not, only scanty information about the enemy will be available and the gaps in the jigsaw puzzle will have to be filled-in by intelligent deduction, and even through sheer guess-work. The tendency to hold back action because adequate information is not readily forthcoming is the favourite refuge of the type who likes to play 'safe' - and 'safety' in the battlefield is synonymous with cowardice.

Conclusion

There comes a time in most battles when the opposing sides are evenly matched and vital issues hang in the balance. It is at this juncture, when the original plans and orders have gone hay-wire, that the Commander with greater stamina, grit and determination will rally his troops for one final, desperate effort and tip the scales in his favour. The will to outlast the opponent, the ability to draw on one last ounce of strength for this final, audacious fling at the enemy is the hallmark of a great field Commander. This must be emphasised in all training. For remember, as Napoleon said 'the fate of the battle is the result of a moment, of a thought! A mental flash decides and the last reserve accomplishes the object.'

It is a mistaken concept that the cult of the 'victorious will' finds expression only amongst Commanders engaged in offensive operations. This is not so. Even in defence, when there is a danger of armour over-running a locality, it is troops infused with audacity who will fire their anti-tank weapons to the last and then 'ducking down' let the enemy tanks pass overhead, but only to emerge again from their trenches to take the tanks from the rear. Bold and daring tank-hunting parties led by inspired Non-Commissioned Officers can play havoc with any intruding armour which may have escaped the fire of anti-tank weapons in the defensive localities.

The need for injecting a bold, daring and audacious attitude in our Commanders is vitally necessary, for in war the timing of an action and the speed of its mounting is all important. We must prefer the officer who acts and makes mistakes to the one who is never wrong, by playing 'safe'. I would, however, like to sound a word of warning here. A misplaced interpretation of the ideas I have given above may, if applied unimaginatively, produce the type who breaks conventions merely because he thinks it is fashionable to do so or who, under the mistaken guise of audacity, tries to play rashly with the lives of men. This must be guarded against. The aim of training I have in mind is to forge a Commander who blends a cool and calm mind with the swift and sure intuition of spotting and grasping the transitory chances in war and then acting on them with paralysing speed, delivers to the enemy the 'coupe de grace'. These, I think, are the symbols of the 'victorious will'. The ideas are high but they are worth striving for!

APPENDIX B

PORTRAITS OF COURAGE

There is no doubt that we have the finest human material in the jawans of our armed forces. I have always found them patriotic, loyal, obedient and imbued with the high traditions of valour and self-sacrifice. The same is true of our officers for they also come from the same stock.

Today I recall the feat of Havildar Abdul Hamid Khan who fought in the 1965 Indo-Pak War in Khem Karan Sector. He belonged to 4 Grenadiers and was commanding a 106 (recoil-less) anti-tank gun detachment. When Pakistani Patton tanks came rushing towards his post, he knocked out three of them before he was himself struck down by one of the tanks and died a gallant death. He was posthumously awarded the highest award for bravery - Param Vir Chakra.

In the same sector, a squadron of enemy armour came through Serjah enclave (between Khem Karan and Hussainiwala) and suddenly appeared behind the 18 Rajputana Rifles. The Commanding Officer of the Battalion, Lt Col Raghubir Singh (now a serving Brigadier), ordered his men to duck down in their open trenches whilst the enemy tanks passed directly over them and take on the tanks from the rear. As the enemy tanks arrived in the middle of the Battalion position, the enemy-tank Commander arrogantly asked our men to surrender. In reply, the tank force was instantly engaged by fire from all directions, killing the enemy Commander and knocking out two enemy tanks with the Battalion anti-tank weapon known as the bazooka. The remaining tanks took to their heels.

Another example that I remember is of gallantry and devotion to duty on the part of late Lieutenant Colonel NN Khanna, Officer Commanding 2 Sikh Battalion at that time. His Battalion had been ordered to capture one of the key heights known as Raja picket in the Poonch sector where they came up against very heavy opposition from mines, artillery and machine-gun fire causing very heavy casualties to our assaulting troops. When he discovered that personal leadership was the need of the hour, he rushed in front of the attacking troops and egged them on to the final objective with the war cries of "Bole So Nihal, Sat Siri Akal". As soon as he captured the objective, he was mortally wounded by a burst of .50 heavy machine gun fire from a neighbouring hill. He was so loved by his men that although exhausted and much reduced in number due to casualties, seeking revenge his men rushed to this hill feature (from where the fire had come) under the leadership of a Subedar and after hand to hand fighting snatched the deadly weapon, which had killed their Commanding Officer, from the hands of the enemy. This gun is now their proud possession as a war trophy and a living monument to the steadfast courage and the extreme sacrifice made by their Commander.

When after the war I visited Lt Col Khanna's family in Delhi, his wife showed me a letter that he had written to his 4-year old son mentioning that he was going into action the next morning and was confident of victory because the motto of his regiment (the Sikh Regiment) 'Nishchay Kar Apni Jeet Karun' (Victory will be Mine) was the vow which Guru Gobind Singh had taken when he took up the sword of righteousness against mughal oppression. This letter is the heritage of inspiration left by a brave father to his son!

There was Subedar Mal Singh of the 1st Battalion of the Sikh Regiment, which I was commanding in the Srinagar Valley during Pakistan's aggression into Kashmir. In April 1948, my battalion was deployed for the defence of the Valley in the area of Handwara. The battalion had a solitary picket, known as the Nagi picket, over-looking the enemy base in the village of Zechaldor where it rankled as a thorn in the enemy's flesh. It used to come in for a lot of plastering by the enemy, both by mortars and small arms fire. The picket was at the time commanded by Subedar Mal Singh, the bravest soldier I have ever known.

One day I received a challenge from the enemy through a local tonga driver who had been on his usual round to Zechaldor village that the men at Nagi picket were going to be butchered that night in spite of whatever I might try. On receiving this message, I got ready to go to the picket so as to convey the message to Subedar Mal Singh personally. Presently, General Thimayya, then my Divisional Commander, arrived at my Headquarters unannounced and when told of the message insisted on accompanying me to the picket. When we arrived at the picket towards the evening, it was under fire from snipers from a flank. The men were standing-to in our honour and Subedar Mal Singh came forward to meet us, with a neat little axe in his hand as a Khud-stick. The blade of the axe had been coloured red to represent, as Mal Singh explained, its having tasted blood. I conveyed to Mal Singh the challenge of the enemy and his reaction was to ask me to request General Thimayya to stay on for the night at the Battalion Headquarters and visit the picket again the next morning, so that he might see piles of enemy dead that would be strewn around the area. Such was his self-confidence and courage!

On the 28th of May 1948, it was Subedar Mal Singh's platoon that secured for us the height over-looking Richmar Gali in Tithwal area and it was in defence of this height on the 13th of October 1948, that he died a brave soldier's death when leading a counter-attack against the enemy who had managed to over-run a forward post of his Company. When his body lay shattered by a direct hit from a shell, his last words to his platoon were a request to shout the war cry of the Sikhs – 'Bole So Nihal, Sat Siri Akal' - because, he explained, a brave son of India was dying a death of his choosing. Subedar Mal Singh's name has become a by-word for bravery ever since!

I am also reminded of the brave conduct and aplomb on the part of Captain Sheikh of our 1 Armoured Division who was fatally wounded in the 1965 Indo-Pak War, in the Sialkot Sector. During the war, when I went to visit our Advanced Dressing stations to have a look at the casualties that had just come out of the battle, I recognised Sheikh's face (I had known him as a young officer when he was ADC to General JN Chowdhary). His head was swathed in bandages and he was lying on a stretcher with his eyes closed. As I advanced towards him the military surgeon who was accompanying me pulled me back by the arm and whispered that Sheikh was seriously wounded by shell splinters in his head and was not expected to live. I went upto him and called his name. He opened his eyes and recognising me stiffened his body as if to salute and said with a smiling face that he was perfectly alright and only slightly hurt. What an expression of a brave heart! I complimented him on his bravery and saluting him smartly, turned away, knowing in my heart that I would never see him again.

True bravery is witnessed only when you are in direct command of troops in battle. In Handwara Sector (Kashmir Valley) again, in the month of February 1948 when the area was under heavy snow and movement was possible only on foot over beaten paths, my battalion, 1 Sikh, was chasing an enemy force, having evicted them out of the village of Handwara, towards Dragumula and Magam. I was with my leading Company under the Command of Major Suri (who was later transferred to Artillery and met with a very serious vehicular accident that nearly crippled him. As far as I know, he is still serving in some administrative job in the Army). As the Company was struggling through deep and crusty snow in an open formation to capture a hillock near Wodhpur, heavy enemy fire opened up not only from this feature but also from the windows of a house only a 100 yards away from the beaten track in the snow. I ducked down behind the wall of snow on the side of the track. A light automatic gun was firing at the spot where I had taken shelter and the bullets were ricocheting through the snow over our heads.

Presently, I saw Subedar Ishar Singh, who was commanding the leading platoon of the Company, crawling towards me in the safety of the beaten track. I noticed that his right foot, still in a boot, was dangling behind him and he was leaving a heavy trail of blood behind. I tried to hold him up where I was so as to tie a torque on his leg but he waved me off saying that this was not the time to pause under fire. Notwithstanding, I quickly tied a tight bandage round his shin and noticed that both his shin bones had been shattered by a burst of a light machine gun from a very short range and his foot was joined to his leg only by flesh. In a jiffy, he was off on his crawl through the channel of snow that the track provided and refused to be picked up or helped by any one before he was out of the danger of fire. After the battle was over and we had dislodged the enemy, I went back to my Regimental Aid Post to see the wounded and arrange for their evacuation. There I met Subedar Ishar Singh again, lying on a stretcher. He greeted me with a cheerful "Sat Siri Akal". Such is the stuff our soldiers are made of! Subedar Ishar Singh was in hospital in Delhi for nearly 2 years after this incident and was then boarded out of the Service. I have met him a number of times since and like a valiant soldier, although he supports a stub foot, he always wears a cheerful smile on his face.

APPENDIX C

REVIEWING OFFICER'S ADDRESS ON THE SQUARE
TO
GENTLEMEN CADETS ON PARADE
OF
38 REGULAR AND 22 TECHNICAL GRADUATES COURSES
ON 24 DECEMBER 1966
BY
LIEUTENANT GENERAL HARBAKHSH SINGH VrC
GENERAL OFFICER COMMANDING-IN-CHIEF WESTERN COMMAND

The Commandant, the Staff and the Gentlemen Cadets of the Indian Military Academy.

Let me first of all congratulate you on the excellent show you have put up on parade this morning. Your smart turn-out, soldierly bearing and steadiness on parade reflect credit on your Institution.

Today is a great and memorable day for all of us. For the Commandant and the Staff because, after hard labour of a year and more, they have moulded raw material into an end product and presented it on parade for us to see. And they might well be proud of it! For the cadets, after hard training and imbibing of instruction, are ready to enter into a new phase of their life - a phase of honour and responsibility in the Officer Rank of the Army. And to me, - what could be greater than to be taking the salute at a Passing Out Parade of this great Institution, of which I am myself a product. I have drilled on this

Square, and stood in the ranks at a similar ceremonial parade held here nearly 34 years ago when this Institution was inaugurated, and I can remember hearing with my own ears, from the mouth of the author, the words that are inscribed in gold letters inside Chetwode Hall and which a moment ago you repeated after your Commandant. These words of advice are undoubtedly worth their weight in gold and truly the essence of leadership.

But this is an occasion for prospective officers on Parade this morning to take a personal vow of dedication and service to the Country, and I can do no better than quote the pledge taken by our great National and Military Leader Guru Govind Singh nearly 300 years ago when he took up the sword of righteousness against mughal oppression. Addressing the Almighty, he said:

दे शिवा वर मो ये है, शुभ कर्मन ते कबहुं न टरूँ
न डरूँ अरि सों जब जाय लरूँ, निश्चय कर अपनी जीत करूँ
अर सिख हूँ अपने ही मन को ए लालच हो गुन त्यों उचरूँ
जब आव की औध निधान बनें, अत ही रण में तब जूझ मरूँ।

"Grant me, O Lord, this boon that I may not falter in doing good. That I may entertain no fear of the enemy when engaged with him in battle. And that I may always be sure of my victory. May my mind be trained in the desire to dwell upon thy goodness. And, when the last moment of my life should arrive, may I die in the thick of battle."

This is a pledge which is applicable to any soldier, anywhere, at any time.

In the end I welcome you into the Brotherhood of Officers and wish you every success in your future lives.

JAI HIND

HARBAKHSH SINGH
DEHRA DUN Lieutenant General
24 December 1966 GOC-in-C Western Command

APPENDIX D

GENESIS OF YAHYA'S CRACK-DOWN ON BANGLADESH

I knew Yahya Khan personally and can quite believe that he was genuine in his desire to hand-over the administration of the State of Pakistan to a democratically elected civil Government. But what must have surprised him, no doubt, was the overwhelming success of the Awami League Party under the leadership of Sheikh Mujib-ur-Rehman. This was much against the estimate of the party's strength in East Pakistan as given to him by his political advisers. He would have been prepared perhaps to accept even that fact of life and, if necessary, make Mujib-ur-Rehman the Prime Minister of Pakistan in Islamabad and thus keep him away from his followers in East Pakistan. It might have been with this point of view that he proceeded to Dacca in early March, to induce Mujib-ur-Rehman to accept a compromise solution to his demand for complete autonomy for East Pakistan. It is now quite clear that there was a near agreement between Yahya and Mujib on this issue but for the bogey raised by the political leadership in West Pakistan, actively led by Bhutto, and the separatist demands by some

Provinces of West Pakistan and consequent disintegration of the country. Yahya was thus placed in a great predicament. However, before going to East Pakistan, Yahya had already ordered the move of a certain number of troops, by air to East Pakistan as a precaution, and to control the Civil Disobedience Movement there, started by Mujib and his followers. As a soldier, he must have known that a military crackdown on the whole population of the region was not only politically sterile, but also militarily inadvisable.

Political and Military Gamble

His final decision to take such an overwhelming risk of starting a war with India, I am sure, must have been based on the deep-rooted belief on the part of the Military Junta of Pakistan that the Indian people, nurtured as they have been, for the past so many centuries, on the Hindu philosophy of passivity and abhorrence of blood-shed and destruction, would not take up the cudgels of war against Pakistan. At the end of the 1965 War with them, when I went to Lahore and Rawalpindi, under the auspices of the United Nations, my counterparts in the Pakistani Army told me that they were completely surprised when we crossed the international border, for they never could imagine that the Indian Government under Mr Shastri's leadership, would take such a bold decision. This psychosis was prevalent not only amongst the military but also amongst the civil, and I have, no doubt, that it was that villian of peace, Mr Bhutto, who must have encouraged Yahya to take the plunge - a military gamble, with very heavy odds against it. For a well-trained military mind like Yahya to take a military decision of this nature is incomprehensible to me. It was hazardous, to say the least, to send practically all the reserve formations of his Army in West Pakistan, in penny-packets (plane-loads) with only personal weapons hidden under their civilian garments (because the authorities in Colombo - the only airport available to Pakistan for transhipment by air - did not allow military aircraft, or personnel, to touch down on their soil). The route they had to cover was also a circuitous one, round the coast of India, as over-land flying by Pakistan aircraft had been stopped by India due to the fact that a civilian passenger aircraft had been diverted by Pakistan to Lahore Airport, just a few days earlier.

Pakistan had, thus, not only diluted and weakened its Army in the West, but also the troops that arrived in Dacca in this manner, were militarily in no position to resist the Indian Army walk-in, if it was decided by India to do so. Besides, the Indian populace was at the time sympathetic to Mujib-ur-Rehman and his followers, who had expressed their will in an open election. This was well-known to the whole world. That the Indian Government showed restraint under these militarily favourable circumstances speaks volumes for its policy of peace and tranquillity and is quite unprecedented in the political annals of most nations in this world. That this restraint and the realities of the situation, should have failed to have any impact on the conscience of the world community is a sad augury of self-interest and misguided nationalism.

Military Assessment

By the last week of April, that is within a month of the military crackdown on Bangladesh, Pakistan had transported nearly three Divisions worth of troops into Dacca, but all of them had arrived with their personal weapons only - and thus with a limited capability to fight. Their heavy equipment and armament - such as tanks, guns, vehicles, ammunition, etc, - came by sea. These ships berthed in the port of Chittagong, but with no one to unload them, as the stevedores on the port, being sympathetic to Mujib, had gone on strike. The newly arrived troops in Dacca had to be despatched to Chittagong to unload the equipment from the ships.

Before the new troops arrived, East Pakistan had a force of about four Brigades, under 14 Division Headquarters, and about two Regiments of light armour (nearly 80 tanks) and two Squadrons (about 24 to 30 aircraft) of Saber Jets, in support. The whole of the paramilitary force, by way of EPR and Armed Police, had already deserted and joined the Mukti Bahini. This Force was woefully inadequate to maintain law and order in the whole country, secure its borders with India and, at the same time, be prepared to defend the country against the Mukti Bahini, supported, as they were, by the Indian Armed Forces. In the West also, the gaps that were left in the military plans, due to the sudden departure of troops to the East, could not be filled in a matter of years, let alone months, considering the long time it takes to train illiterate manpower in the use of modern technical equipment with which the Pakistani Army was equipped. Added to this was the great strategic handicap of there being no physical contact between the Eastern and Western wings of the Pakistani Army by land, air or sea. As against this, the Indian Army and Air Force on the two Fronts, were deployed on, what is known as 'Interior Lines', which allowed for flexibility of movement between the East and the West. While our Navy had freedom of movement in the Indian Ocean, this was denied to the Pakistani Navy due to lack of base-facilities outside Karachi harbour. Under these circumstances, the two wings of the Pakistani Army and Air Force had to fight as separate entities, without any hope of assistance or logistic support, from one another. This was a great strategic handicap. And it was to neutralise this handicap that Yahya had struck in the West. It might be likened to the last throw of a gambler!

His initiating hostilities in the West had, to my mind, a three fold objective. Firstly, to tie down to the ground our forces earmarked for the defence of the Western Border, particularly our reserves there, and thereby prevent us from moving a portion of them to the Eastern Front should we need them to hasten our advance in Bangladesh. Secondly, to provoke us to commit our reserves in the West, to prematurely attack the well-prepared and formidable defences in the Punjab Sector, and thereby wreak attrition on them. In this way, Pakistan hoped to nullify our advantage of superior strength in the West. And thirdly, to internationalise the Bangladesh problem and involve the good offices of the United Nations and other world powers to bring about a cease-fire before Pakistani forces could be evicted out of Bangladesh. For only then would there be any chance of retaining East Pakistan within the frame-work of the State of Pakistan.

Therefore, according to my assessment, leaving the political considerations aside (about which I do not claim to know anything), because of the foregoing, the most appropriate time to attack Bangladesh for us, was the month of April, 1972. And we should have gone straight for Dacca, the capital of the State, and carried out a coup-de-grace with one of the Para-Brigades, to capture the airfield there, followed by the landing of an Infantry Division by air. I say this with full knowledge and study of the situation at the time, as earlier I had been in command of 33 Corps at Bagdogra and the operations in Bangladesh were one of my responsibilities. As luck would have it, 19 Infantry Division was at the time in Calcutta, and could have been easily picked by air and landed in Dacca, in the wake of the Para-Brigade employed to carry out the coup-de-grace on the Dacca Airfield. It should be remembered, that in April the passes through the Himalayas from Tibet, would have been still closed due to snow and there would, therefore, have been no danger that the Chinese would interfere with the operations, on behalf of Pakistan. The passes open in the month of late May-June and failing any action in the month of April, the operations in Bangladesh would have had to be postponed for at least six months, till the passes closed again, for fear of Chinese interference. And this is what actually happened.

Now my information was (although I cannot vouch for it) that in actual fact, Army Headquarters had planned to capture the territory of Bangladesh only upto the confluence of the river Ganga and the river Brahmaputra, and not beyond. And it was at the initiative of the local Brigade Commander that we walked into Dacca and took the surrender of the Dacca Garrison. How far it is true is for historians to investigate.

APPENDIX E

THE SURRENDER OF DACCA- PAKISTAN'S FAULTY DEPLOYMENT OF FORCES

The inevitable has happened. In 12 days the Pakistani war machine has been brought to a standstill. That is what I predicted before General Yahya Khan's declaration of war. It was, I said at that time the last throw of a gambler, and it has been proved so. How strange that Yahya himself could not have realised this? Instead, he depended on false hopes held out by friendly powers and plunged the sub-continent into a holocaust which India had tried its best to avoid.

From the time Yahya launched his pre-emptive air attack on 3rd December, the war went against the Pakistani forces in every sector and in every sphere, land, air and sea. Pakistan hoped to be able to hold us on the Western Front against its well-prepared fixed defences- anti-tank canals, ditches, pill-holes, bunds and embankments. It had further strengthened these defences by extensive flooding of canals and ditches. Indeed, it wanted us to attack in the Punjab Sector where it was strong, so that it could wear down our marginal superiority of forces in the Western Front. It did not succeed in this. Our forces inflicted severe damage on the Pakistanis before withdrawing from enclaves across the rivers. In this way our defences became even stronger than before, for a water-line is always easier to defend than a line on the ground. In this category fall the battles of Hussainiwala, Ajnala and Chhamb. Likewise, we pushed the enemy from the enclave of Dera Baba Nanak, on our side of the river Ravi.

The Desert Offensive

The battle in the Rajasthan desert and the Rann of Kutch is another story. Here we surprised Pakistan by taking the offensive and captured nearly 8,000 square miles across the border. The idea was to forestall any Pakistani move and ensure the security of the lightly held and more or less open border between Rajasthan and Sind. It was this move that frustrated Pakistan's strong armour and infantry push towards Jaisalmer.

The Jammu and Kashmir Sector

In Jammu and Kashmir, we captured across the cease-fire line enemy posts which overlooked ours, as in Punch and Tithwal areas and dominated our vital communications, like the heights in Kargil. Wisely, we did not commit on the Western Front our reserve Corps, including the Armoured Division, which Pakistan had so earnestly hoped. It was to wear down such an offensive that Pakistan left its Armoured Divisions uncommitted. That is why there has been till two days ago no tank battle in this war like the one we fought in the Khem Karan or Sialkot areas in 1965, and there was comparatively less use of armour on either side during this war.

The Eastern Front

On the Eastern Front, I was for taking the initiative and liberating Bangladesh by our regular forces in one sweep, aimed at the capture of Dacca, rather than nibbling at the periphery in support of the Mukti Bahini. For there is nothing more disconcerting for regular troops than to play second fiddle to a para-military force. This is not to question the bravery, self-sacrifice and determination shown by the Mukti Bahini.

But in this case, time was of the greatest importance in view of the likely intervention by the United Nations, or other world powers. And the Mukti Bahini alone, even if the Indian Army was to stand in the background and give all help, could not have finished the job against the Pakistani regular Army so quickly.

It is now clear that the Pakistani senior military leadership in Bangladesh lacked the concept of defending themselves in a military situation as it prevailed there. They deployed their forces in penny pockets all over the country-side and along the periphery of Bangladesh and ordered them to hold on at all cost, failing to realise that the key to their stranglehold on Bangladesh lay in the capital city of Dacca. The defence of Dacca should have been their first priority; as the town, surrounded as it is by a network of river-sand distributories on its three sides, is easily defensible. It could have been converted into a fortress, difficult for the Indian Army to reduce in a hurry. On the contrary, Dacca was surrendered by General Niazi without a single shot having been fired in its defence.

We failed to take advantage of this faulty deployment on the part of Pakistan. Our first and foremost objective should have been Dacca, and we should have made for it in full strength and with the utmost speed. There is no reason why we could not have captured intact the Ashuganj bridge - the only bridge over the Meghna giving a direct route to Dacca - by a properly planned action, especially when the Pakistani forces would have been hesitant to destroy the bridge with a major portion of their forces still deployed on the wrong side of it. Similarly, we could have dashed for the Goalundo Ghat ferry from the other direction, by-passing the enemy's strong point at Jessore and crossed the Padma river using the engineering and local resources at our command. In this manner our objective could have been realised with comparatively little loss of life and material. This suggestion is purely from a military point of view. I am sure that there must have been political reasons for our armed forces to comb the whole area of Bangladesh.

Simultaneous Assault

Now to go over the operations as they took place. The Ganga and the Jamuna which join to form the Padma, divide Bangladesh into three distinct parts, that is, the eastern, northern and western areas. The eastern area consists of Mymensingh, Dacca and Comila Khulna districts; the northern of the western districts of Thakurgaon, Dinajpur, Rangpur, and Bogra. Rajashahi constitutes the third area, which lies in the fork formed by the Ganga and the Jamuna. Pakistan, it seems, had deployed a Division each for the defence of these three areas. We launched offensives in these areas, simultaneously using a Corps strength each. While the role of the Northern and Western Corps was to occupy rapidly the District Headquarters in their respective areas, the aim of the Eastern Corps, having entered its sector from the north and east, was to secure Jamalpur and Mymensingh on the one hand and Akhaura and Comila on the other, and then advance towards Dacca. These moves were dictated by the run of the rivers and their distributories.

The real advance from all directions started after the Pakistani attack on the Western Front, on the evening of 3rd December. Within ten days most of the District Headquarters, like Thakurgaon, Dinajpur, Rangpur, Rajashahi, Bogra, Kushtia, Jessore, Faridpur, Mymensingh, Sylhet and Comila were occupied.

The column from Akhaura, secured the ferry across the Meghnand Ashuganj on 12th December, but it failed to capture intact the railway bridge at Bhairab Bazar. This did delay the advance to some extent, but the forward elements of this column were soon on their way to Dacca along the railway line from Bhairab Bazar to Tungi. Simultaneously, the Northern thrust of the Corps, after capturing Mymensingh, made a dash towards Dacca via the Mymensingh-Tangail-Tungi road. As these two columns were nearing Tungi, a para drop was carried out north of Dacca on the night of 13th-14th December, presumably with a view to securing the bridges on the Lokhya distributory of the Meghnand and the Turag distributary of the Burhi Ganga.

Whether the para forces were able to carry out these roles successfully is not known, but they were certainly responsible for creating consternation and panic in Dacca and hastening the advance of the two columns. The capture of a Brigadier and five or six other officers north of Dacca, about this time, might well have been the work of the para force. And it could be that the Brigadier captured was in command of the covering force responsible for the defence of Dacca. By the evening of 14th December, our forces started knocking at the other defences of Dacca, and it was apparent that not much opposition was going to be encountered before entering the city.

While these two columns advanced from the north, other smaller columns converged along the rivers south of Dacca, from the southeast, south and south-west, and it appeared that a complete ring had been formed around this vital objective. The fall of Dacca now depended on the strength of the Garrison earmarked for the defence of the city, about which there were varying estimates, from a brigade to a Division, and the will of the Commander, Lt Gen Niazi. In spite of Gen Niazi's brash claim that he would hold on till the 'last man and the last round', his nerves are reported to have given way, and he sent an appeal for a cease-fire on the evening of 15th December, much too soon by military standards of perseverance and grit. Never before in military history has a capital city been surrendered without a single shot being fired in its defence, notwithstanding the handicaps of being cut off from the mainland of Pakistan and bereft of air support. Full marks to our Army for their courage, perseverance and tenacity.

Air Supremacy

Our Air Force also had done a wonderful job. We achieved complete supremacy in the Eastern theatre and near domination in the Western theatre. Unlike 1965, co-operation between the Army and the Air Force have also been of a high order, and many battles have been won through a combined effort.

As for our budding Navy, it has established its name and fame among the navies of the world. In spite of its small size, its daring action in the home waters of Pakistan, as, indeed, within the Karachi Naval base, is worthy of laurels of the highest order.

The contribution of these comparatively young services, that is the Air Force and Navy, in the defeat of the Pakistani forces in Bangladesh is no less than that of the Army. And they may justifiably claim full credit for the fine achievement. As an old soldier, I salute them all - the soldiers, the sailors and the airmen, and rejoice in their moment of glory.

APPENDIX F

MANPOWER VERSUS SOPHISTICATION

The 'arms race' is upon us again. It has become a recurring phenomenon repeated at the end of each decade since Independence: 1952, 1962, 1972 and now 1981. The reason as I see it, is that we have not planned our country's security on a realistic basis or from a long-term point of view. We have failed to realise, ever since the security of the country became our responsibility, that what was good for the goose, so far as the role of defence forces was concerned during the British days, need not be good for the gander, - independent India.

In fact, the requirements of security, and thus the role of the defence forces under the British were entirely different, thereby calling for a complete change in the composition, organisation and size of the armed forces. This did not happen and until today we have not got out of the military rut left behind by the British, not only in the way of organisation, staff tables, weapons and equipment, but also with regard to the concept of training, tactics, strategy and deployment of forces.

Military power is a combination of manpower and fire-power, aimed at attainment of optimum 'fire-effect' at a given time and place. After all, in the end it is the fire-effect (as different from fire-power) that wins a battle. Here, a distinction has to be made between fire-power and fire-effect. A machine-gun can fire so many rounds per minute in a fixed direction and achieve a certain fire-effect on a particular target. But if the same number of rounds, or even less, are fired by many riflemen from different directions on to the same target, the fire-effect would be many times more than that of the sophisticated machine gun. This means that the sophistication of a machine gun can be offset in its fire-effect by several men firing at the same target at the same time from different directions, albeit with a less sophisticated, single-action, rifle. The latter has the added advantage of allowing each shooter to use his own peculiar characteristic of accuracy, adaptability and initiative, while presenting, at the same time, a dispersed and ubiquitous target for counter action by the adversary. This corollary can be applied to any set of weapons or armaments designed for a particular fire-effect. This proves that sophisticated arms can be overcome by less sophisticated arms, provided the latter are in larger numbers.

We should draw a lesson from the current Iraq-Iran war. In spite of many handicaps, both military and political, the only advantage the Iranians have enjoyed in the recent fighting is their larger Army - 3,50,000 vs. 2,50,000 - with the result that a well-prepared Iraqi invasion has been thwarted and the war has practically come to a stalemate.

The Chinese People's Liberation Army, which is simply armed and indigenously self-sufficient, should be our model and not the western armies. The Chinese have now to modernise their Army to march with the Russians. We have no such compulsion as the Chinese modernised Army will be mostly deployed against the Russians in North China and not against us.

There is another aspect of sophistication which is high-lighted by the well-known cliché: 'It is not the gun that matters, but the man behind it', which means that the sophistication and the resultant technical complexity of a weapon must be related to the competence and genius of the man who has to handle it in the battlefield. With the illiterate, or semi-literate, manpower that we possess, the amount of sophistication and technology which can be effectively assimilated by our rank-and-file is naturally limited. It would be no use - perhaps a liability - to put an average Indian soldier behind the sophisticated missile, or the computerised gun. For one thing, not knowing its intricacy, he is unlikely to have faith in the effectiveness of the weapon. For another, it would take him much longer to learn to manipulate the armament, let alone master it.

I can cite two examples from the 1965 war with Pakistan: the Pakistani soldiers totally failed to handle the Patton tank and the 'Cobra anti-tank missile', because of the latter's mechanical and manipulative sophistication; whereas the much inferior and simpler Centurion tank and the Recoilless anti-tank gun (mounted on a jeep) were very much more effective in the hands of the 'rule-of-thumb' trained Indian troops.

In my opinion, the improved version of the Vijayanta tank and the anti-tank (RCL) gun, both of which we produce in the country, are more than a match for any sophisticated weapon in this line which Pakistan may acquire, provided we have them in large enough numbers.

But that does not mean that we should not improve upon our weapons and equipment. The Department of Research and Development must go on doing this all the time. But development should be compatible with the users' capabilities and the peculiar terrain over which our Army has to operate, viz, the mountainous and high-altitude regions of the Himalayas, the heavily cultivated plains of the Punjab and the sandy wastes of Rajasthan.

For instance, the anti-tank missile when indigenously produced should replace the RCL gun, but only in the desert area and not in the Punjab where its utility is limited. In the cultivated fields of the Punjab, intersected by high-bund irrigation channels and interspersed with tall maize and sugarcane crops, the RCL gun would be more manoeuvrable and effective until such time as we are capable of mounting the anti-tank missile on a helicopter of our own. Similarly, I should prefer a 'top-less' armoured personnel carrier rather than the modern imported version, for it is lighter, less costly and quicker to manufacture within the country.

The anti-tank (RCL) gun, in my opinion, is more effective in the hands of our rank-and-file than the imported anti-tank missile. It is inexpensive, fires a massive shell and provides a certain amount of protection to the crew from small-arms fire; and what is more, it is manufactured by us in its entirety. The imported anti-tank missile, on the other hand, costs a hundred times more (in foreign exchange) than the anti-tank shell of our own make. Further, it has little to show to our simple soldiers, being no larger than a 3-inch mortar bomb; and it has a mere 'thimble' for a mechanism to guide it on to its target, compared to the 12-foot, cold steel, barrel and the massive shell of the RCL gun. Besides, the launching-pad of the missile affords little protection against any kind of splinters or small-arms fire.

Pakistan seems to have realised the true worth of this weapon and has incorporated it in, what it calls, the Reconnaissance and Support Battalion, one each to a Corps. The battalion has a complement of 48 RCL guns and an equal number of medium machine guns, both mounted on four-wheel-drive jeeps, providing tremendous fire-power in the hands of only six to seven hundred men of the battalion. We should have this unit in our Army also, but at the increased scale of one per Division.

China, with a population of a 1000 million, has an Army of 4 million; Pakistan, with 80 million, has an Army of 0.45 million and we, a nation of over 680 million, have an Army of under one million. In keeping with the manpower to arms proportion of Pakistan, we could have an Army nearly five times its present size. But that is not immediately necessary for our defence needs. An addition of 1,00,000 personnel to the present strength of our infantry is recommended to begin with.

Another 4,00,000 men could be inducted into the Army, in subsequent phases, to raise additional units and formations, including supporting Arms and Services. The induction thus of 5,00,000 men into the Army should meet our requirement for the next 10 years. The situation could then be reviewed.

The increment of 1,00,000 men suggested above for the infantry in Phase I is only in the Sepoy rank, so that the number of units and formations remain, more or less, the same. It would only mean larger sections, larger platoons and larger Companies, which with increased manpower would be better able to carry out their defence role, especially in the mountainous terrain which constitutes a major portion of our international border.

I further recommend that the Army as a whole revert to the quadrangular pattern of organisation for sub-units and formations, up to the Divisional level, as opposed to the present pattern of a triangular set-up.

It may well be asked: how would you arrange for the training of so many Infantry recruits? Well, I have some revolutionary ideas on that subject also. But revolutionary only in our context, for we still follow the British legacy in India of Infantry training centres, each to a Regiment of Infantry. This system is peculiar to the Indian Army. No other Army in the world has any special training centres for the infantry except, of course, Pakistan. In other Armies, infantry recruits are trained by infantry battalions themselves.

In peace time, each infantry battalion is under-posted to the extent of a Company's worth of Sepoys, and the staff of this Company is detailed to impart training to an equal number of recruits inducted into the battalion. The period of training of these recruits is only three months, after which they are absorbed in the battalion as trained soldiers. Being a short-service Army, within this period as many men as they are newly trained soldiers are discharged from the service, and another lot of recruits are posted to the battalion. And the cycle goes on. In our case the period of the cycle of the recruits' training could be 4 to 6 months.

Most modern Armies in the Western world, so far as the rank-and-file are concerned, are short-service Armies, with only one and a half to two years colour service. However, taking the illiteracy and semi-literacy factor into consideration, there is no reason why, with simpler weapons and equipment, we should not be able to reduce the period of service of our sepoys to 3 to 4 years for the Infantry and 4 to 5 years for the mechanical and technical arms, such as Signals, Engineers and Electrical and Mechanical Engineers. This period is more than enough to teach the personnel the use of the simple and less sophisticated weapons and equipment proposed to be entrusted to them. Any proficient rifleman, mechanic or tradesman, with potential qualities of leadership, can within this period, pick up the rank of a Lance Naik and thereby be eligible to be retained in the Army for longer service.

I can say from experience that once a man is passed over for promotion to the Lance Naik's rank, he becomes a liability to the Service rather than an asset, and the sooner he is sent out of the Army the better.

I strongly believe that the manpower of the Army should be divided into two distinct categories.

The Professional Cadre. The professional cadre should consist of commissioned and non-commissioned officers selected to be retained in the Army on the basis of a permanent tenure. The personnel of this cadre would be responsible for the command, administration and training of the Army, both in peace and war. Accordingly, they would be entitled to emoluments specified for each rank, including family accommodation, children's education allowance and pension benefits on retirement. This cadre would constitute nearly 25 per cent of the strength of the Army.

The Service Cadre. The Service cadre should consist of men enrolled for a short service of 3 to 5 years (call it 'national service', if you like) in the Sepoy's rank. If not promoted to the Lance Naik's rank, they would be discharged from the service and receive only a nominal gratuity and not a pension. They would constitute the bulk of the Army and comprise nearly 75 per cent of its strength.

It will be seen that the service cadre of the Army would constitute nearly 75 per cent of its total strength. The turnover of this large manpower every 3 to 5 years will open a vast avenue for employment for the youth of the nation. If these men are enlisted at the age of 17 to 18 years, and discharged from the Service (except for those promoted to the rank of a Non-Commissioned Officer) at the age of 21 to 22 years and given only gratuity, there would be a great saving in the Defence budget. Besides, for such personnel no married accommodation, children's education allowance, or re-settlement by Government after discharge would be necessary, as they would be young enough, well-trained and disciplined enough to rehabilitate themselves in civil life.

Here I am reminded of another anomaly that exists in our Army since the British days - that is, the Junior Commissioned Officer (JCO), known as the Viceroy's Commissioned Officer (VCO) under the British. The VCO was created by the British to provide a link between the British officer and the Indian other rank because of the different cultures, customs and languages. It is a typical colonial legacy. When they introduced Indianisation in the Indian Army in the early thirties, the British themselves abolished this rank and replaced the VCOs with young Indian Commissioned Officers trained at the Indian Military Academy, Dehradun. This measure had to be shelved during the Second World War, as the output of officers from the newly established Indian Military Academy could not meet the requirement of the rapidly expanding Indian Army. With the introduction of short-service in the Army, as proposed, it is considered necessary that at the platoon level young Indian Commissioned Officers, instead of the JCOs should command troops. To meet this demand, we would have to increase our output from the Indian Military Academy.

The responsibility for the security of the international border cannot be separated as between peace and war. To this extent the role of the Border Security Force, a central organisation set up after the 1962 war with China, in so far as it is independently responsible for the security of a part of the international border in peace time, is anachronistic. This responsibility should devolve on the Army. It is suggested that the Headquarters of the Director General Border Security Forces alongwith its separate training and administrative establishment should be abolished. The personnel of the Border Security Force should be enlisted and maintained on a regional basis and put under the operational and administrative control of local Army formations. To break away from the past, the Force should be renamed 'Border Scouts'. Surplus elements of the Border Security Force could be absorbed in the Provincial Armed Police and Central Reserve Police Force, the role of both being essentially internal security. This would result in considerable saving to the national exchequer.

The Indo-Tibetan Border Police is another anachronism, passed down from the old days. Under the present conditions, its role on the Indo-Tibetan border is redundant and the organisation should be done away with.

On the face of it, it may seem that a larger Army would be more expensive than the present one. But we have to keep in view the economies that will ensue after implementing the proposals suggested above. These are the following:

- Army manpower would be divided into two distinct categories, viz, the professional cadre and the service cadre. The financial commitment towards accommodation, education allowance to children and pension benefits would be limited to the professional cadre only, which would be one fourth of the total strength of the Army. This would considerably reduce the expenditure incurred on the maintenance of Army personnel, largely off setting the cost commitment of the enlarged Army.
- The Infantry Training Centres, which are very expensive to run, would be done away with, resulting in a great saving to the defence budget.
- The ever-increasing outlay of foreign exchange set aside for the induction of sophisticated armaments would be reduced almost to nil. This saving could be utilised in research and development and for the increased production of defence armaments within the country.
- With a large 'service cadre' in the Army, there would be no need to have the Territorial Army, or the National Cadet Corps, resulting in saving on this account.
- The Headquarters of the Director General of the Border Security Force and attendant establishments would be abolished and the Force re-organised as Border Scouts, to be enlisted and maintained on a regional basis and placed under the operational command of local Army formations, a much cheaper arrangement.
- The Indo-Tibetan Border Police would be done away with - another substantial saving.

It is estimated that with the recommendations made above the financial commitment for the enlarged Army would not exceed the current defence budget, except for the addition of the annual inflation index. This is the crux of the proposal.

Manpower is the one commodity in which Pakistan cannot compete with us. Once we attain this unassailable position in the size of the Army vis-à-vis Pakistan, the latter would be in no position to pose a military threat to India. Besides, it would act as a deterrent to Pakistan from ever attempting a military adventure in Jammu and Kashmir.

We have to find a balance of military power with our likely adversary not through the 'arms race' but in some other way. And this other way is right at hand - that is our prolific manpower. This is something which cannot be matched by Pakistan.

Manpower is militarily our greatest asset. We should, therefore, capitalise on it and counter Pakistan's sophisticated armament with more numerous, although less sophisticated, weapons and equipment, the production of which is within our own capability thereby giving us self-sufficiency and self-reliance in defence matters and independence of decision at the political level.

If the highly expensive and mostly imported, sophisticated armaments are cut out and the larger Army, as suggested above, is equipped with hardware produced within the country, its cost should remain within limits of the present day defence budget.

Our defence production is sufficiently advanced to manufacture everything that our Army needs in its defence role. What would be needed is to increase production so as to meet the requirement of an enlarged Army. This is not to say that modernisation of armaments should not go on, but it must be compatible with the peculiar requirements of our Army and consonant with the capability of our manpower.

The Chinese Army should be our model and not the Western Armies.

APPENDIX G

SOME FAILINGS IN THE PRESENT DAY GAME OF INDIAN HOCKEY

General

In order to establish my bonafides to comment on the declining standard of our national hockey, I should like to mention that I played hockey as a student in Government College, Lahore, and at the Indian Military Academy, Dehradun, in the early thirties, when the standard of the game was at its highest. I was later concerned with selecting, training and captaining teams of the Sikh Regiment which participated in the Punjab Native Army Hockey Tournament, Jhelum, in 1937 and 1938. During this period, I had the opportunity to play with or against national players like Bukhari, Sardar Aslam, Jaffar, Dara, Dhian Chand, Rup Singh, and so on. My hockey-playing career was cut short by World War II, but I maintained my interest in the game by building up and coaching the Sikh Regimental Team which came up to be one of the premier teams in national hockey.

I have been witnessing the play of hockey teams, both Indian and foreign, in our national tournaments, as well as abroad. Therefore, my comments below are based on personal knowledge, experience, observation and study of the rise and fall of the standard of hockey in our country. My object is to point out some of the failings and shortcomings that have crept into the style and pattern of our game since the heydays of the pre-World War II era. It is interesting to note that Pakistan has kept up the traditional style and pattern and that is the key to their continued success.

Team-Work

Hockey is essentially a team-game. Victory can be assured only through a 'combination' of effort: combination within the *forward-line;* between the *wings,* and *insides* and the respective *half-backs;* between the *half-backs* and the *backs;* and an understanding to swap places and cover one another, when required.

Each player has a role, whether in attack or defence, even though it be only passive - as in the case of the *centre-forward* and the *wings* in defence. The ball is moved forward by long passes to the *wings* and criss-cross passing between the *forwards* and the respective *half-backs*. 'Dodging' an opponent should be an exception rather than the rule. Attempts should be made to by-pass a defender through judicious passing of the ball from *forward to forward,* or *forward to half-back,* and vice-versa. This is known as 'triangular' passing, and requires anticipation and finding a 'gap' to receive the pass.

I have noticed that almost universally, in all our modern teams, team-work is conspicuous by its absence. Individualistic play is the order of the day. Too much dribbling and dodging, mainly to attract the attention of the spectators, is acknowledged as the hallmark of good play. Judicious passing and the creation of a 'gap' are at a premium. The whole lot of players, from both sides, crowd round the ball wherever it might be, irrespective of their places on the field-of-play, resulting in jostling, pushing tripping and squabbling. In short, each player plays as an individual, rather than as a member of the team.

Place-Play

Each member of a team has a place for himself on the field-of-play, and in that 'place' he has a role to play as a member of the team. The movement of an individual player in the performance of his role must necessarily be confined to a particular area of the play-field. For example, the *wings* should move up and down the field within the side-lanes; the *centre-forward,* in the middle-lane; the *insides,* between the middle and the side-lanes, and so on. Interchange of players/places is permissible under certain circumstances only, and that also through mutual understanding. In this way, the ball can be pushed up and down and from side to side throughout the length and breadth of the play-field.

Defenders also have their area of responsibility, and while covering one another as necessary, in a sea-saw manner, they must try and manoeuvre within the limited area. I am glad to say that the place-play of our *defenders* today, is not lacking in this regard. There is orderliness, understanding and proper coverage and co-operation among the *backs* and the *half-backs,* except for occasional individualistic showmanship.

Pattern of Play

There is no doubt in my mind that the team-distribution of 5:3:2:1 on the play-field, is best suited to our basic physique and inherent aptitude for 'push-stroke' and 'short-passing' hockey - our traditional style. But this distribution will pay us dividends only if we stick to the old-vintage pattern of play, particularly of the *forward-line*. By this I mean, each *forward* moving up and down the field in his own lane; the *wings* staying well up, ready to receive a long clearance-pass from one of the *defenders;* in the meanwhile, the *insides,* who would have fallen back to thicken defence, should catch up with the *wings* and *centre-forward,* and move into the attack as a continuous, co-ordinated assault-line, closely followed and supported by the *half-backs*. It must be understood that it is only through the *wings* that the ball can move up fast, and by virtue of their placing on the field, it is the *wings* alone who can 'draw' the opponents' defence and keep it spread-out - thus making it easier for the attackers to secure a break-through and score a field-goal.

In the *forward-line*, the *insiders* have to work like beavers. They must not only join with the *forward-line* during the assault, but also rush back to thicken the defence against the opponents' attack. They are required to move up and down their respective lanes like a piston.

The *half-backs* also have a similar role, but within a shorter area of manoeuvrability.

Wing-Play

I feel it necessary to re-emphasise the importance of *wing-play* and the role in the *forward-line* of the two *wings* in a team. They are the key to the fast movement of the ball in the opponents' half during the assault phase. And during this move, on either flank, while the *insiders* are still in the process of catching up with the *forward-line* after having helped the *defence*, the *centre-forward* provides the link between the two *wings*. After the *insiders* join up, the whole *forward-line* moves forward, abreast, supported by the *half-backs*.

The *wings* and the *centre-forward* do not normally join in defence, but on the other hand wait on the *centre-line*, in their respective lanes, ready to receive a long clearance-pass from one of their *defenders* - thus gaining a head-start over the opponents' *defence*. Most *wings* do not realise that while seemingly 'idling' on the *centre-line* they are playing an important role of drawing the attention of, and tying down, one of the opponents' *backs*. In fact, while waiting for the long pass, the *wings* should keep as far forward as possible, by staying in line with the rear-most *back* of the opponents, but on the home-side, so as not to be 'off-side'.

The *wing* play, or the lack of it, is the greatest weakness in our teams today. Perhaps, because its importance is either not understood or is ignored. And this is why, I feel, we have not produced a *wing* worth the name for many years.

Penalty-Push, Penalty-Corner, Long-Corner Hit

These three provide the most hopeful opportunity of scoring a goal, in that order, and yet they are the most neglected facets of training. What is more, the whole attitude towards them on the part of the players seems casual. I have seen many a *penalty-push* thrown to the wind - and *penalty-corners* wasted one after the other - due to lack of subterfuge or alternative positioning. The *long-corner* is treated like just another kind of push from the *side-line*, unmindful of its potential for conversion into a goal. I clearly remember that the only goal scored by a West-European team against us in a test-match in Delhi a couple of years ago was through a long-corner.

Coaching

My impression is that our traditional pattern of play has been lost because of faulty coaching. I have met very few national coaches who understand the essentials of our traditional hockey. They might have been very good players themselves, but that is not the only requirement for a coach. The basic understanding of the pattern of play, and the role in it of each player is more important. In my opinion, it helps a coach to understand the game better if he is trained as an umpire as well.

Captaincy

Much of the indiscipline and individualistic play on the field is due to complete lack of exercise of control over players by the Captain of the team. It is difficult these days to tell on the field-of-play who the Captain is. The Captain should truly be the leader of his men. He should not hesitate to give instructions and guidance to the members of his team during play, in order to ensure that each of the players sticks to his place and plays the role assigned to him. He should be a source of inspiration to his players and see that they pull their weight together. It is because of this deficiency that our teams seem to lose heart when down by a goal, or fall back into defence, having scored an early goal.

Astro-Turf

Astro-Turf has been blamed by some for our debacle in the last Olympics and now in international hockey tournaments. In my opinion, astro-turf should, if anything, be a help to our style of hockey, if played properly. The even-surface of this type of play-field is ideal for our push-stroke, short-passing game, as against the hard-hitting and 'muscling-through' tactics of the Western teams. We in India are used to playing on varying types of field-surfaces, such as 'bajri', thin-turf, thick-turf, wet, dry, and so on, and it would not be difficult for our players to get used to astro-turf within a short time. There is no need for us to go in for this exorbitantly expensive play-field in India. A little practice on it before a tournament would be quite enough to get the hang of it.

Conclusion

If I were asked to name the greatest failing of our hockey today, I would say: *'wing-play'*. It just does not exist.

I have described above, briefly, my idea of *wing-play,* and how it should be integrated into the movement of the *forward-line.* And I should like to say here that the most essential requirement for an effective wing-player is *speed* of movement combined with absolute control of the ball - and for the *left-wing* particularly, mastery of the 'reverse stick'.

INDEX

A

Abdullah, Sheikh. 211 - 213, 219, 244, 333
Ace Armoured Division. 351, 355, 360
Adampur. 357
Adams, General. 320
Advanced Studies Institute. 329
Agya Singh. 26, 28, 30
Ahmedabad. 72
Airhitam. 136
Ajaib Singh, Lt. 51, 70, 119, 120
Akal Takht. 374
Akhnoor. 5, 210, 334, 335, 336, 362, 373
Alexandra Fort. 76
Alexandra Hospital. 99, 102, 144
Algeria. 133
All India Radio. 132
Allahabad, Captain. 51, 52, 70
Amar Singh, Lt Col. 280
Amarinder Singh, Captain. 325, 345, 350, 369
Ambala. 183, 189, 191, 294, 326, 345, 350, 357, 359, 378
Ameer Singh, Major. 119
Amritsar. 339, 344, 373, 377
AMX Tanks. 345, 363
Anant Singh. 47, 48
Anant Singh, Lt Colonel. 355
Angitha Sahib. 7
Anwar ul Haq, Sawar. 355
Argyll & Sutherland Highlanders. 41, 101
Arjan Singh, Air Chief Marshal. 191,
Armoured Corps. 300
Army Air Force Close Support Organisation. 326
Arora, Brigadier Jagjit Singh. 314
Asal Uttar. 348 - 351, 378
Atal Chania. 187
Atom Bomb. 172
Atomic Energy Commission. 355
Atta Mohd, Brigadier. 276
Attam Singh, Major General. 252
Attar Singh, Subedar. 77, 78
Auchinleck, Brigadier. 43
Aurangabad. 51, 67, 69, 72, 73
Avtar Singh. 318, 319
Axis Powers. 171

Ayub Khan, Field Marshal. 74, 304, 340, 345
Ayyappa, Captain AC. 112, 113
Azad Hind Fauj. 135, 137
Azad Kashmir Forces. 231, 239, 331

B

Badamibagh Cantonment. 216, 386
Badgaon. 201
Badrukhan. 7, 8, 12, 14, 297
Bagdogra. 314, 318
Baghel Singh, Lt. 51, 70, 72, 88
Bahadur Singh, Lt General. 329
Baldev Singh. 202
Baltistan. 226
Baluch Regiment. 189
Balwant Singh, Lt. 98, 99
Bamford, Captain. 70
Bandipur. 198, 251
Bangalore. 60
Banihal Pass. 192, 252
Baramula. 195, 209, 216, 228 - 230, 249, 267, 272
Barki, Battle of. 357
Barstow, Major General. 88
Basta Singh. 90
Bawa, Major. 263
BBC. 110, 132, 171, 172
Beacon. 308
Beas river 340, 351
Berlin. 27
Berripattan river. 210
Bhabha, Homi. 355
Bhagat Singh. 26,
Bharat Singh, Colonel. 362
Bhatgiran. 214, 216, 218, 228, 234, 243
Bhawani Singh, Lt Colonel. 362
Bhonsle, Major JKT. 112, 113, 134, 135, 140, 171
Bhupindra Singh. 18
Bhutan, King of. 317, 318

Bhutan, Prime Minister of. 318
Bhutan. 314, 315, 317, 320
Bhutto. 372
Bidadari Camp. 106, 108, 111, 114, 184, 385
Bihar Regiment. 304
Bikhiwind. 352, 356, 363
Binaguri. 317, 322
Bird, Colonel. 30, 33, 34
Bismark.1
Bomdila. 309
Bonaparte, Napoleon. 82
Bose, Netajee Subhash Chandra. 91, 133 - 135, 138, 140, 171, 184
Bose, Rash Behari. 138
Boy Scout, 6, 19
Brevet Lt. Colonel. 63, 64, 67, 68
Brevet Rank. 63
British Commonwealth. 24
British War Crimes Investigation Team. 3
Brown, Major. 90
Budh Singh. 145
Budwar. 106, 113
Burma. 130, 133, 175,
Buttalia, Brigadier KMS. 310

C

Calif, Brigadier. 353, 355, 378
Cargill, Captain. 67
Cariappa, General. 61, 301, 384, 385, 386
Cavalry Regiment. 106
Ceylon. 58, 174, 306
Chaiwalah. 41
Chandimandir. 379
Changi Jail. 105, 106, 113, 182, 385
Chatterjee, Lt Col. 142
Chavan, YB. 365, 366, 377
Chawla, Lt Col. GS. 149, 151, 153 - 155
Chenab river. 334, 335

Chetwode Hall. 6, 32 - 34, 291
Chhamb Sector. 334, 335
China. 108, 137
Chitral, Mehtar of. 227, 250
Chopra, Major General Bir. 4, 336, 337
Chowdhary, General. 320, 324 - 326, 336, 342, 343, 361, 364 - 366, 368, 375, 377
Chowdhry, Major Surita. 149, 151, 152
Chowdhry, Pritam Singh, Lt. 66
Collins, Brig. 30, 34, 40
Commonwealth War Graves Commission. 154
Commonwealth War-times Crimes Investigation Party. 172
Communist Resistance Groups. 152
Concentration Camp. 112, 113
Congress, Indian National. 24, 57
Conoly, Major. 53, 54, 66
Courtney. 81
Cowan, Major. 32
Cummings, Lt Col. 98

D

D'Mello, Lt. Melvile. 56
D'Souza. 90
Dal Lake. 213
Dalai Lama, His Holiness the. 329
Dalip Singh, Captain. 356
Dalip Singh, Kanwar. 329, 339
Daljit Singh. 190
Dalvi, Brigadier. 306, 309
Dara, Lt Col. 145, 146, 155, 185, 372
Dargalkar. 106, 113
Daroch, Captain. 57
Daulat Beg Oldi. 307
Daulat Singh, Lt General. 305, 306, 307
Daulatabad Fort. 69, 72,
DAV College. 25

Deepa. 389
Dehradun. 18, 28, 51, 74, 93, 150, 372, 383, 384
Delhi, Lt. Governor of. 18
Delhi. 189, 190
Dera Baba Nanak. 339, 345, 362, 363
Dhar, DP. 196, 229, 230, 233
Dhillon, Captain Gurdeep Singh. 74
Dhillon, Lt General Joginder Singh. 4, 308, 339, 343, 349
Dhillon, Major Mahabir Singh. 105, 106, 108, 112, 138
Dibipura. 353, 355
Dilbagh Singh, Brigade Major. 195, 196
Dinesh Singh, Raja. 378
Dominion Status. 24
Dragumula. 235, 236, 238, 239
Drang Zong. 308 - 310, 318, 319
Dras. 226, 250, 292
Dube, Major General Uday. 300
Duncliff. 25
Dunn, Lt General Patrick N. 338, 365, 366
Dupleix, General. 58
Dutta, Lt Col. 149

E

Edinburgh Festival. 295,
Engineer, Air Marshal. 313
Engineers. 60

F

Faqir Singh, Brigadier. 227, 250, 300
Fateh Singh, Sant. 373, 374
Ferozepore. 338, 377
Field Service Regulations. 194
Field, Major. 52, 70
First World War. 10, 30, 85, 383
Ford, Lt Col. 70, 71, 74, 77
Fort St. George. 57
Fujiwara. Major. 108

G

Gajjan Singh, 14
Ganderbal. 196
Gandhi, Indira. 212, 378,
Gandhi, Mahatma. 111, 125, 142
Gangtok. 315, 316, 320
Garial. 47
Garret, HLO. 21, 25
Gaza Strip. 295
Geisha. 128
Geneva Convention. 166
Gentlemen Cadets. 30, 31, 36, 290
Ghansara Singh, Brigadier. 226
Ghanshyam Singh, Major. 158
Ghellanai. 41, 43, 46
Gian Chand, Major. 112, 113
Gilgit Scouts. 226
Gilgit. 226, 227
Gill, Major Niranjan Singh. 138
Golden Cup Hockey Tournament. 27
Gopal Singh, Captain. 268, 270, 271
Gorkha Battalion. 344, 345
Gorkha. 385
Government College Lahore. 21, 24, 25, 109, 155, 177, 373, 375
Graham, Lt. F. 47
Grenadiers. 251
Grewal, Brigadier Prakash Singh. 340, 341
Grover, Captain. 344
Guides Battalion 44
Gulam Bheek. 23, 24, 372, 375
Gulmarg. 249
Gupta, Dipankar. 389
Gurbakhsh Singh, Major General. 320
Gurbaksh Singh. 21
Gurbakhsh Singh, Lt Col. 3, 105, 117 - 120, 132, 136, 138, 172, 173, 179, 180, 295
Gurcharan Singh, Captain. 119
Gurcharan Singh, Superintendent of Police. 143, 144
Gurdaspur. 365
Gurkha Battalion. 81, 82
Gurkhas. 198, 237, 238
Gurnam Singh, General. 17,18, 387
Guru Gobind Singh. 2
Guru Granth Sahib. 10, 110, 179
Gwalior. 27

H

Habib-ul-Rehman. 184
Hairbrush. 54
Hajipir Pass. 211, 213, 333, 334
Halwara. 357
Hamid, Havildar Abdul. 351
Handwara. 228, 230, 241, 242, 247, 248, 256
Hara Kiri. 125, 164
Harchand Singh, Jemadar. 277, 278
Hari Singh, Maharaja. 207, 211, 212
Hari Singh, Major. 149,
Harkeerat Singh, 2nd Lt. 60
Harmala. 387
Harmandir Sahib. 373, 377
Harnam Singh. 48
Hartley, Brigadier. 310
Harwant Singh, Jemadar. 114
Hassan, Brigadier Gul. 372
Henderson Brooks, Major General. 298
Hiroshima. 180,
Hitler, Adolf. 135,152,
Hong Kong & Singapore Artillery. 150
Huiliang. 311, 312
Humayun. 190
Hunza. 41
Hussain Mohammed, Lt. 51, 65, 70
Hussain, Dr Zakir. 295
Hussain, Lt. 70

I

Ichhogil Canal. 301, 326, 338, 339, 342, 360, 362 - 364
ICOs. 384, 385
Iftikhar, Haji. 372, 373
IMA – see Indian Military Academy.
Imperial Defence College. 303, 305,
Independence. 24,
Inder Kumar. 25
India Gate. 154
Indian Air Force. 80
Indian Independence League. 135, 136, 138, 143, 145
Indian Independence Movement. 136
Indian Military Academy (IMA). 2, 6, 27, 28, 30, 33, 36, 39, 40, 51, 56, 61, 74, 93, 133, 137, 138, 186, 289, 291, 372, 373, 381, 384
Indian National Army (INA). 91, 105, 106, 108, 110 - 115, 120, 133 - 140, 145, 146, 150, 152, 171, 177, 179, 183 - 186, 294, 303, 384
Indo Pakistan War of 1965. 329, 330, 367, 377 - 379, 381, 389
Indo-China. 94
Instrument of Accession. 330
Inter Services Scientific Team. 290, 292
International Commission for Korea. 297
International Red Cross. 182
Ipoh. 88, 89, 92, 105, 142 - 144

J

Jabar Jang Singh. 194
Jacobabad. 188
Jaggat Singh, Doctor. 145
JAI Division. 252
Jaipur, Maharaja of. 316, 362
JAK Forces. 204, 207, 210, 252
JAK Headquarters. 211, 214
Jalandhar. 300, 305
Jammu & Kashmir Militia. 257, 280, 284
Jammu & Kashmir Police. 366
Jammu & Kashmir State Forces. 196 198, 209, 210, 220, 237, 238, 330
Jammu & Kashmir. 72, 252, 331 - 333, 335, 361
Jammu. 210 - 212, 227 - 230
Japan, King of. 172
Japanese Air Force. 97, 117, 122, 124, 125, 152, 159, 160, 170, 172, 179
Japanese Eastern High Command. 163
Japanese Government. 136
Japanese Military Police. 147
Japanese Navy. 94
Japanese Police. 152
Jaswant Singh, Captain. 119
Jat Battalion. 240
Jaurian. 5
Jelep La. 315
Jhang. 88, 110
Jhangar. 210
Jhansi Heroes. 27
Jhelum river. 215
Jigme Dorji. 318, 319
Jilani, Lt. 56,
Jind Infantry. 10, 14, 15, 102, 105, 106, 114 - 120,132,134, 138, 142, 160, 169, 177, 297
Jind State. 7, 10, 18, 20, 177
Jind State Forces. 28,
Jinnah. 125, 330,
Jirga. 46,
JOCKS. 41, 46,
Joginder Singh, Captain. 215, 271,
Joginder Singh, Major General. 325, 326, 346, 359,

K

Kalah, Lt Col. Sahib Singh. 182, 345
Kalimpong. 315
Kamikaze. 127, 161, 162, 163
Kamptai. 125, 128
Kandy. 58
Kang, Captain. 259
Kanwar Singh, Major. 284
Kanyakumari. 58
Karachi. 189, 190
Kargil. 226
Karnail Singh, Major. 241
Kasauli. 141
Kashmir, Maharaja of. 207, 211 - 213, 300, 330
Katoch. Janak, Brigadier. 192,
Katoch, Lt General Kashmir. 5, 48, 196, 198, 251, 253, 286, 336, 337, 361, 362, 365, 366
Kaul, Lt General Biji. 257, 258, 306 - 308, 312, 313, 319, 320, 324
KCIOs. 68, 383, 385
Khanna, Major General KC. 313
Khanolkar, Captain. 51, 68, 70, 71, 83 - 85, 170
Khattak, Lt General Habibullah Khan. 303
Khem Karan. 355, 360, 363
Kiani, Major General Mohd Zaman. 139
Kishan Singh, Lt Colonel. 301
Kishanganga river. 273, 274, 278, 285
Kitchener's Folly. 85
Kluang. 125, 126, 130, 134, 145, 150 - 152, 159, 166, 173, 176, 184
Kluang Airfield. 117, 118, 128, 130, 131, 158, 162, 170, 174, 179
Kochar. Lt. Kumar. 60
Kochhar, Colonel Bhalloo. 320, 322
Kotli. 210

Kralpura. 247, 248,
Krishen Singh, Brigadier. 207,
Kuala Kangsar. 145,
Kuala Lumpur. 145, 146, 172, 175,
Kuanton Airfield. 95, 96, 97,
Kuanton. 91, 93 - 97,136, 182,
Kulwant Singh, Lt General. 204, 206, 207, 211, 214, 252, 297, 299, 300 - 302, 385
Kuman Singh, Lt Col. 280
Kumar, Ashwani. 339, 340
Kumaramangalam, Lt General. 303, 335, 336, 377, 378
Kuomintang. 126
Kupwara. 234, 235, 238 - 242, 258, 259, 280
Kushalpal Singh, Lt. 56, 58, 65
Kut Almarah fort. 8
Kwai River. 117

L

Ladakh. 226, 251, 306, 307
Laharu, Nawab of. 65
Lahore. 24, 25, 28, 190, 335, 338, 343, 360, 368, 369, 373, 375
Lajpat Rai, Lala. 25
Lakhinder Singh, Brigadier. 251
Lall, Brigadier. 309
Lane, Miss. 100
Langhorn. 25
Latif, Major. 189
Le Fleming, Major. 32, 40
League of Nations. 83
Leh. 226, 250, 251, 292
Leyte. Gulf of. 130
Lhasa. 317
Lobo, Lt Col. 260
Loretto Convent. 359
Lunt, Lt Col. 105

M

Madras, Governor of. 183

Madras. 88, 183
Mahabub. 146
Mahadev Singh, Brigadier. 289
Mahavir Chakra. 301, 386
Majeed, Colonel. 369
Makhan Singh. 36 - 38
Malaya. 3, 86 - 95, 102, 110, 119, 125, 132, 135, 144, 154, 155, 172, 173, 177, 184, 185, 294, 297, 384, 385
Malwinder Singh, Major. 102, 103, 143, 144
Man Singh. 145
Manchanda, Lt Colonel. 294
Manchuria. 108, 137
Manekshaw, Lt General FHS. 322, 378
Marambio, Brigadier General. 368, 369, 372, 374
Marmagoa. 60
Masani, Minoo. 381
Mastana Sahib. 7
Matah-ul-Mulk, Colonel Prince. 227, 250
McArthur, General. 130
McLaren, Captain. 33, 34
Meerut. 294, 356, 381
Megh Singh, Major. 361, 362
Mehar (Mehar Baba) Singh, Wing Commander. 200, 201, 211
Mehra, Major. 151, 184
Mehta. Lt Colonel. 309, 311
Menon Krishna. 305, 322
Menon, Lt Col. 249
Metcalfe House. 27
Mhow. 70
Minhas, Captain Shamsher Singh. 356, 357, 363
Mir Kalsi Ridge. 274 - 281
Mirza, Sikander. 304
Misra, Captain. 192

Misra, Colonel. 192
Mit Singh, Captain. 297
Mohan Mukand Singh, Captain. 119, 132
Mohan Singh, General. 105, 106, 111, 113, 114, 133, 134, 137 - 142, 152, 177, 183, 185
More, Captain. 32
Mohmand Operations. 41, 44, 76
Muhammed. Bakshi Ghulam. 196, 197
Multan. 187
Murreê. 47
Mussa, General. 304
Mussolini. 152, 171, 180
Muzaffarabad. . 272, 282, 254
Muzzafar Khan. 65
Mysore. 61

N

Nabha, Maharaja of, 61
Nagasaki. 180,
Nagin Lake. 196,
Naidu, Miss Padmaji. 314, 322
Nair, Brigadier. 252, 253
Namkachu river. 306, 309
Nand Singh, Jamedar. 217, 218, 295
Narain Singh. 16
Nasthachur Pass. 263, 264, 267, 271
Nathu La Pass. 314, 315
National Conference of J&K. 212, 213, 229, 236, 237
National Defence Academy. 219
National Defence Council. 311
National Relief Fund. 311
Naushera. 69, 210
Nausherwan Khan, Lt Col. 65, 231, 236, 237
Nazir, Major General Mohd. 229, 230, 233, 243, 244, 276
Neesson Hospital. 152, 184
NEFA. 306, 308, 310, 312, 320, 342

Nehru, Pandit Jawaharlal. 24, 111, 142, 211 - 213, 297, 306, 314, 320, 322
New Zealand. 94
Normandy. 133
North West Frontier. 41, 46, 70, 74
Nuwra Eliya. 58

O
Occupation Forces. 3,
Olympics. 27,
Ootacamund. 61,
Operation Surya. 272, 276, 280,
Order of the British Empire (OBE). 184

P
Pade, Lt Colonel. 369
Padma Bhushan. 365
Padma Vibhushan. 365, 366
Painter, Brigadier. 98
Pakistan High Commissioner. 190
Pakistan Occupied Kashmir. 332
Pakistan Rangers. 340,
Pakistan, 1965 War with. 367, 377 - 379, 381, 389
Pakistan, Civil Intelligence Service of. 371, 372
Pakistan, President of. 340
Pakistani Mass Artillery. 338, 339
Palit, Brigadier Monty. 320
Palkhiwala, AN. 381
Panjiri. 255, 256, 271
Pant, Apa. 318
Pant, KC. 378
Param Vir Chakra. 351
Parkins, Lt Col. 93, 98
Patel, HM. 386
Patel, Mani Behn. 202
Patel, Sardar Vallabhai. 202, 203
Pathak Brigadier. 4, 342

Pathania, Major General Mohinder S. 310, 312
Pathankot. 357
Pathans. 41, 124, 150, 218
Patiala State Forces. 174, 175, 194
Patiala, Maharaja of. 18, 90, 295, 326, 369
Patiala. 10, 190, 194, 195
Pattan. 195, 196, 200, 203
Pearl Harbour. 130
Penang Island. 145, 146
Perak, Raja of. 92
Peshawar. 41, 46, 190
Phillora. 360
Pir Sahiba. 279, 281, 283
Piyara Singh. 99
Pondicherry. 58
Poona. 68, 384
Popham Panel. 80
Prasad, Major General Niranjan. 4, 308, 310, 339 - 341, 343, 373
Pritam Singh, Colonel. 138, 146, 192, 195, 204, 206, 362, 374
Prithipal Singh, Captain. 106, 112 - 115, 119, 154, 155
Project Jyoti. 305
Punch. 333, 210, 213, 214
Punjab Public School. 381
Puri, Captain Jawaharlal. 119, 121, 147, 169
Purna Swaraj. 24

Q
Quetta. 67, 86, 187, 188 - 191

R
Rabal Island. 116, 180
Radhakrishnan, Dr. S. 329
Radio Bangkok. 110
Rai, Lt. Col. Ranjit, 191, 195
Rai, Lt. Dewan Ranjit. 51, 70
Raina, General. 381

Raja Sahansi Airfield. 330, 364
Rajindra Singh, Major. 264
Rajouri. 300
Rajwade, 'Bhaiya' Brigadier. 336
Ram Singh, Captain. 119, 169
Ramgarh. 381
Rana, Lt General Bukhtiar. 372 - 374
Ranbir High School. 21, 377
Rani of Jhansi Regiment. 136
Rann of Kutch. 331, 332
Rattan Singh, Lt. 141
Ravi, river. 24
Rawalpindi. 41, 46, 187
Ray, Siddharth Shanker. 311
Razmak. 70, 74 - 77, 80, 81, 85
Red Fort. 184, 185, 294
Rehabilitation Centre. 149, 158
Repulse, HMS. 94
RIASC. 102
Rikhye, Major. 204
Ripdaman Singh. 61
Rizvi. 23, 369
Roberts, Captain Russel. 182
Rondu. 226, 227
Rosha, Bhagwan Singh. 23
Roy, Dr Niharanjan. 329
Royal Army Service Corps. 174
Royal Engineers. 32, 103
Royal Indian Military College (RIMC). 150, 383
Russel, Lt General. 192

S

Saed, Maulvi Mohd. 233
Safdarjang Aerodrome. 191, 192
Sahai, Bhagwan. 329
Sahibzada, Captain. 88, 106, 110,111, 152
Saint Paul's School. 316
Sampuran Bachan Singh, Major. 196, 204, 217, 250, 301
Sampuran Singh, Subedar. 114

Samurai. 163
Sandhurst. 68, 84, 383, 384
Sangrur. 7, 10, 15, 19, 28, 180, 187, 377
Sant Attar Singh. 7
Sant Rama Krishna. 170
Saraghi. 8
Sardar Khan, Lt Colonel. 283
Sargoda Airfield. 346
Sarin, Harish. 202, 306
Satguru. 26
Satinder Singh, Major General. 380
Sato, Captain. 170
Saunders, PWO. 26
Save the Children Fund. 329
Savory, General Sir Reginald. 30, 32, 40, 186, 295
Sawhney, Dugee. 381
Second World War. 78, 194, 197, 207, 231, 356
Sela Pass. 308 - 312
Sen, Lt General LP. 202, 203, 206 - 208, 213, 214, 220, 240, 241, 253, 319,
Seramban. 172
Shah Niwaz. 133, 134, 183
Shammi, Brigadier AR. 351
Sharma, Major. 200, 201
Sharma, N. 206
Shastri, Lal Bahadur. 311, 335, 366, 375, 377
Shelatang. 203, 207, 208
Sherpur. 8
Shiromani Gurudwara Prabandhak Committee. 374
Shivinder Singh, Lt Col. 189, 190
Short, Lt Colonel Billy. 202
Shrinagesh. 56,
Shulur. 228, 242, 245 - 249, 259 262, 280, 284, 285
Sialkot. 338, 360, 365

Sibal, Major General Kishan. 340
Sibi Desert. 188
Sidhu, Lt Colonel Karnail Singh. 356, 357, 363
Sikh Regiment. 30, 51, 55, 64, 70, 72, 187, 202, 294, 316, 331, 337, 350, 356, 363, 380, 381
Sikh Regimental Centre. 69, 218, 219, 294, 363, 381
Sikkim, Chogyal of. 315, 316
Sikkim. 313, 316, 320, 322
Simla. 18, 189, 305, 313, 324, 325, 329, 336, 359 - 362, 379, 380
Singapore Broadcasting Centre. 152
Singapore Intelligence Section. 100
Singapore, Fortress Headquarters. 104
Singapore. 88, 92, 94, 95, 99, 100, 102 - 104, 113, 116, 126, 130, 131, 134, 137, 139 - 141, 148 - 150, 153 - 155, 159, 163 - 165, 173, 176, 179, 182, 184
Sitang river. 144
Skardu. 226, 227, 250, 300
Snake Temple. 146
Sobha Singh, Sir. 5
Sohan Lal. 6
Sonamarg. 251
Soofi. 229
Sopor. 228, 229
South Eastern Allied Command. 174
South Korea. 298
Spitfire Aircraft. 200
SRI Division. 252
Srinagar Airfield. 192, 201, 203, 204, 211, 212, 331
Srinagar Defence Scheme. 209,
Srinagar, 48, 192, 195, 212, 214, 219, 227 - 230, 243, 249 - 252, 292, 334, 386
Srinagesh, Lt General. 293, 297

Staff College, 67, 187, 188
Sucha Singh, Subedar Major. 114, 155, 175
Sukhdev. 26
Sumatra. 163, 182
Suri, Major. 234
Swaran Singh. 378, 381
Switzerland. 318

T

Tagore, Rabindra Nath. 315
Taj Mohammad, Major Khanzada. 65, 184
Tamashitta, General. 113
Tani, Major. 162, 163
Tashkent. 372, 37
Tata, JRD. 381
Teesta river. 322
Tejinder Singh.18
Tezpur. 308, 309, 310
Thailand. 94
Thapa, Major. 227, 250
Thapar, General. 307, 312, 313, 319, 320
Thimayya, Major General. 56, 249, 252, 260, 264, 272, 297, 306, 386
Thorat, Captain. 74
Tibet. 317
Tirah Campaign. 8
Tithwal. 254, 255, 263 - 269, 272 - 277, 280, 284 - 286, 300
Tojo. 152
Tokyo. 3
Trahgam. 236 - 238, 242, 246, 247, 256, 258, 260, 279
Tra-Uchi, Count. 172
Trichinapally. 57
Trivandrum. 58, 59
Tugnait, Lt Colonel. 344
Tuticorin. 58,
Tyrsal Park. 104 - 106, 114

U

Uberoi, Lt Col. 271, 272
United Nations Organisation. 297, 367 - 369, 374, 375
University of Benaras. 69
Uri. 207, 208, 210 - 217, 220, 230, 240, 241 - 243, 264, 276, 280, 333

V

Vande Mataram. 120
Vedanta. 69
Viceregal Lodge. 329
Viceroy's Council. 383
Victoria Cross. 44, 98, 295
Victoria, Queen.15
Vir Chakra. 301, 386
Vir Singh, Captain. 74
Vivekananda, Swami. 170

W

Walong. 310 - 312
Wapiti aircraft. 80, 81
War Despatches. 378
Wilcocks, Captain. 70
Wilkinson. 25
Wodhpur. 232 - 234, 238, 239
World War I. 10, 30, 85, 383
World War II. 55, 78, 194, 197, 207, 231, 356

X

XI Corps Tactical HQ. 340, 342
XI Corps. 339, 346, 348 - 351, 375

Y

Yadavendra Singh, Lt General. 295, 345
Yadavendra Singh. 18, 90
Yeti. 316

Z

Z - Brigade. 251
Zafarwal. 360

Zaman, Lance Corporal Mohammed. 30
Zojila Pass. 227
Zutshi sisters. 25, 26
Zutshi, PS to PM. 212

1 Armoured Division. 360, 378
1 Bihar. 251
1 Corps. 358, 360, 361, 365
1 Horse. 362
1 Jat. 338
1 Kumaon. 195, 208, 210, 214
1 Madras. 249, 253, 256, 257, 261, 262, 263, 264, 265, 278, 279
1 Patiala. 251
1 Sikh. 191, 192, 195, 196, 200, 203, 204, 206, 208, 214 - 218, 240, 242, 243, 246 - 250, 253, 261 - 265, 271, 273 - 277, 280 - 283, 295, 310, 311
10 Division. 336, 337
11 Corps. 339, 346, 348 - 351, 375
11 Sikh. 231
13 Punjab. 276
14 Infantry Division. 360
14 Punjab Regiment. 74
15 Infantry Division. 339 - 341, 343, 344
15 Infantry Division. 362
15 Punjab. 283
161 Artillery Regiment. 337
161 Infantry Brigade. 192, 202, 208, 216 - 218, 241, 243, 249, 253, 254, 286
17 Sikh. 350, 351
18 Rajputana Rifles. 347
19 Infantry Brigade. 298
1st Armoured Division. 338
1st Azad Kashmir Battalion. 236
2 Dogra. 216
2 Kumaon. 200, 201, 206

2 Punjab. 195, 197, 202, 209, 210
2 Sikh. 88, 380
2/12 Frontier Force. 97, 98
2/17 Dogra. 208, 210
2/8 Punjab. 283
25 Infantry Division. 300, 342
26 Infantry Division. 305, 292
3 Royal Garhwal Rifles. 94, 97, 253, 256 - 258, 260, 272, 273, 279 - 285
3 Sikh Light Infantry. 309
3/12 Frontier Force. 115, 134, 276, 283
33 Corps. 313 - 315, 317, 319, 320, 331, 334, 340, 351, 377, 385
39 Medium Battery. 337
3rd Sikh. 43
4 Cavalry. 351
4 Corps. 307, 308, 310, 313, 319, 320, 324
4 Grenadiers. 347, 351
4 Horse. 355
4 Infantry Division. 306, 308, 310, 311

4 Kumaon. 195, 200, 201, 203, 204, 206, 209, 214, 216
4 Mountain Division. 340, 346 – 351, 355, 356
4 Sikh. 8, 310, 312, 355 - 357, 363
4/12 Frontier Force Rifles. 276, 283
4/19 Hyderabad Battalion. 56
4/8 Gorkhas. 280
41 Mountain Brigade. 336, 337
43 Lorried Infantry. 360
5 Infantry Division. 305
5 Sikh. 67, 97, 106, 115, 119, 134, 154
5/11 Sikh. 56, 80, 81, 142, 182, 237, 294
5/12 Frontier Force Rifles. 276, 283
50 Para. 210
6 Rajputana Rifles. 209, 216, 217
7 Grenadiers. 347
7 Infantry Division. 340, 355
7 Sikh. 239 - 242, 245, 246, 251, 253
77 Para. 252, 264
7th Cavalry. 229, 247
9 J&K Rifles. 347